Lecture Notes in Computer Science

Edited by G. Goos, J. Hartmanis and J. van Leeu

T0250567

Advisory Board: W. Brauer   D. Gries   J. Stoer

Springer
Berlin
Heidelberg
New York
Barcelona
Budapest
Hong Kong
London
Milan
Paris
Santa Clara
Singapore
Tokyo

Jan Vitek   Christian Tschudin (Eds.)

Mobile Object Systems

Towards the Programmable Internet

Second International Workshop, MOS'96
Linz, Austria, July 8-9, 1996
Selected Presentations and Invited Papers

 Springer

Series Editors

Gerhard Goos, Karlsruhe University, Germany

Juris Hartmanis, Cornell University, NY, USA

Jan van Leeuwen, Utrecht University, The Netherlands

Volume Editors

Jan Vitek
University of Geneva, Computer Science Department, Object Systems Group
CH-1211 Geneva 4, Switzerland
E-mail: jvitek@cui.unige.ch

Christian Tschudin
University of Zurich, Computer Science Department
CH-8057 Zurich, Switzerland
E-mail: tschudin@ifi.unizh.ch

Cataloging-in-Publication data applied for

Die Deutsche Bibliothek - CIP-Einheitsaufnahme

Mobile object systems : towards the programmable Internet ; second
international workshop ; selected presentations and invited papers /
MOS '96, Linz, Austria, July 8 - 9, 1996. Jan Vitek ; Christian
Tschudin (ed.). - Berlin ; Heidelberg ; New York ; Barcelona ;
Budapest ; Hong Kong ; London ; Milan ; Paris ; Santa Clara ;
Singapore ; Tokyo : Springer, 1997
  (Lecture notes in computer science ; Vol. 1222)
  ISBN 3-540-62852-5 kart.

CR Subject Classification (1991): C.2, D.1.3, D.1.5, D.2.4, H.4.3, I.2

ISSN 0302-9743
ISBN 3-540-62852-5 Springer-Verlag Berlin Heidelberg New York

This work is subject to copyright. All rights are reserved, whether the whole or part of the material is
concerned, specifically the rights of translation, reprinting, re-use of illustrations, recitation, broadcasting,
reproduction on microfilms or in any other way, and storage in data banks. Duplication of this publication
or parts thereof is permitted only under the provisions of the German Copyright Law of September 9, 1965,
in its current version, and permission for use must always be obtained from Springer - Verlag. Violations are
liable for prosecution under the German Copyright Law.

© Springer-Verlag Berlin Heidelberg 1997
Printed in Germany

Typesetting: Camera-ready by author
SPIN 10549577   06/3142 – 5 4 3 2 1 0   Printed on acid-free paper

Preface

This book is a collection of papers on mobile agents and mobile object systems. The papers touch on many issues, both conceptual and implementation oriented, related to this new programming paradigm. Before we dwell on the details it is always fair to ask: If mobile objects are the solutions, what is the problem?

Computer science history, albeit relatively short, often repeats itself. We are now facing a situation similar to that of the 1960s. At the time we had a new hardware/software architecture (multiprocessing/multiprogramming/virtual memory) and we were trying to offer a utility to customers (time sharing systems). It took some time for the programming-language and operating-system specialists to come up with the proper programming paradigms. Since then we have seen many novel architectures (parallel computers, neural networks) but none have had the impact of what we are facing now. The Internet is the new architecture. Based on the Internet an immense utility is evolving for information, communication, and media services. So if the Internet *is* the machine, what is the proper programming paradigm to make it easier to develop the novel applications that this utility must offer?

We need a quantum jump in our conceptual framework. The interest of practitioners is so great that any new proposal for a tool or an environment, e.g., Telescript or Java, gets immediate attention. Eventually this attention is diluted by the specific details, and the discussion becomes influenced by commercial interests. The problem remains, what is the proper programming paradigm to program Internet applications? Needless to say, I do not believe that we have the answer yet. Not in this book and not in general. There are attempts, proposals, ideas, and tools but nothing that everybody would agree on.

It will not be so easy to find the right paradigm and model. Both in parallel computers and in neural networks we have had limited success with new programming paradigms and new tools. The Internet combines all the problems we have faced so far. Its parallelism is mind-boggling. It has the connectivity of neural networks. It is asymmetric with respect to connectivity bandwidths. It is dynamic in all its aspects. Last but not least, it is practically uncontrollable. For such an environment we need a paradigm which is highly robust and can deal with uncontrolled and even chaotic situations.

It is my opinion that mobile agents will offer such an environment, provided we can agree on what mobile agents are and what facilities they offer. It will take both discussion and experimentation. This book should be considered as a forum for discussion of mobile agents. In a few years we will be in a situation where defining terms like mobile agents is no longer needed, just as now nobody needs to define what is meant by "procedure" or "process". When this point is reached, then we can say that we have a new programming paradigm.

February 1997   D. Tsichritzis

Table of Contents

Appendix

Introduction

This book presents a collection of papers dealing with different aspects of *mobile computations*. Mobile computations are computations that are not bound to single locations, but may move at will to best use the computer network's resources. In this view, the network becomes a single, vast, *programmable* environment. Among computer scientists, many feel that this approach will have a profound effect on the way we design and implement distributed applications, and they agree that we are witnessing a paradigm change. However, this new and exciting paradigm requires advances, both theoretical and applied, in fields such as programming languages (where we need a sound semantic foundation and efficient implementations), operating systems and software safety and security. Some of the first steps towards a programmable Internet are documented here.

This book follows a particular approach to mobile computation. It emphasizes the synergy between mobility and object-oriented programming, hence the title *Mobile Object Systems*. Mobile object systems, in our view, are self-contained and autonomous groups of objects. They carry out a computation for an end-user in some initial computational environment and may dynamically change their environment for one that is on a remote computer. There is a close relationship between mobile object systems and research on so-called *mobile software agents*. In both cases, the focus is software mobility, but we prefer the terms *mobile computation* and *mobile object systems* as they are more accurate descriptions of the technology, while *mobile agents* has a fuzzy meaning that overlaps with artificial intelligence research. The papers in this book are more concerned with problems of software mobility per se. Nevertheless, the terms are quite close and are often used interchangeably even within the present work.

The starting point of this book was a number of discussions and presentations given at the second International Workshop on Mobile Object Systems[1] (MOS'96) held in 1996 in conjunction with the European Object Oriented Programming Conference (ECOOP'96) in Linz. The core of the book is made up of reworked versions of the submitted papers. However, we wanted to broaden the scope of this volume and survey a large portion of the research in this rapidly expanding field. We invited a number of researchers to contribute reprints of important papers or to write entirely new pieces. This book is the result.

Overview

The book is organized in three parts: (I) Foundations, (II) Concepts, and (III) Implementation, followed by an appendix. We detail the content of each part next.

Part I of the book contains chapters giving background and motivation for the research on mobile computations. The chapter by Cardelli is a brief introduction to the issues and challenges of mobile computation. It is followed by a reprint of a paper by Tsichritzis, written twelve years ago, which describes many of the features we are looking for in mobile object systems using the animal world as a metaphor for mo-

---

[1] The workshop home page is `http://cuiwww.unige.ch/~ecoopws`.

X

bile computations. The chapter by Waldo et al. was written in 1994 and convincingly argues against transparency in distributed computing. To some extent it motivates the work on mobile computations, as mobile computations naturally suggest making mobility and location visible to the programmer. The chapter by Chess et al. investigates advantages and disadvantages of mobile computations by looking at their application. The last chapter, by Tschudin, contains a philosophical and philological discussion of messages and instructions.

Part II contains descriptions of systems and concepts for mobile computations. The chapter by Cugola et al. analyzes languages that support some form of code mobility, trying to compare them and get at some of the basic principles of those languages. The chapter by Acharya et al. presents Sumatra, a Java based environment for mobile applications. The chapter by Bharat and Cardelli presents Visual Obliq, an implementation of mobile computation based on Obliq. The chapter by Tschudin presents a messenger environment. The chapter by Mira da Silva discusses the relationship between persistence and mobility. The chapter by Vitek et al. considers security for communication between object systems. The chapter by Kato looks further into security issues. The chapter by Ciancarini and Rossi presents an architecture for coordination and communication on wide area networks that can be used between mobile computations or plain Java programs.

Part III contains papers detailing implementation considerations and techniques. The chapter by Knabe looks at the trade-offs between different representations of agents and efficiency. In the second chapter, Franz presents a particular representation called Slim Binaries which is particularly well suited to mobile code, as well as a more general dynamic code optimization technique. The chapter by Dugan describes the implementation of mobility of polymorphic data in a strongly typed programming language. Finally, the paper by Dömel discusses the implementation of a system that allows Java programs to interact with Telescript agents.

Acknowledgments

We would like to thank the program committee of the MOS'96 workshop, Joachim Baumann, Luca Cardelli, Paolo Ciancarini, and Doug Lea, for their help and excellent reviewing.

February 1997

J. Vitek and C. Tschudin
Geneva and Zurich

Part I
Foundations

Mobile Computation

Luca Cardelli

Moving code, off-line and on-line

Looking back a few years, we may notice that we finally abandoned assembly language programming in almost every domain. How did that happen? In part, improvements in compiler technology and hardware speed made high-level languages competitive. But the main reason is that assembly code is inherently not portable: one cannot recompile it for a new architecture. Since recompilation is an off-line process, let us say that assembly code is *not off-line portable*. The main problems this causes are:

- *It is difficult to automatically translate assembly code to new architectures (with reasonable performance).*
- *New architectures have been emerging faster than any feasible rate of manual recoding for legacy software.*

New techniques can handle legacy assembly code, such as emulation and emulation-backed translation. But the combination of the two problems above has overwhelmed any consideration based on absolute coding efficiency. As a result, new programs are now written in off-line portable languages: they are routinely recompiled for different architectures.

We can now draw an interesting analogy. Until very recently no major language was *on-line portable*. That is, one could not take a running program and port it to a different architecture while the program was running. This, however, is precisely what must happen with network computations, because:

- *It is difficult to recompile source code on the fly for a new architecture (with reasonable performance).*
- *Connections to computers based on unknown architectures are established faster than the time it takes to recompile source code.*

Techniques have emerged to get some of the advantages of both off-line and on-line portability, such as just-in-time compilation and run-time linking. But the emphasis is now on mobility and quick compilation, not on optimized code generation.

Mobility poses a new basic question: what is the effect of taking a running computation and moving it to another network site? In most current languages, this makes little sense; the mechanisms for doing so are usually unavailable, and the effect would likely be unpredictable. In order to move computations we need languages and models where mobility makes sense; that is, where its effects are well defined.

Traditional languages and traditional compiler technology are not well suited for the world of network computing. Languages that are not off-line portable have already been abandoned (effectively, except for legacy and specialized tasks). In a similar way, languages that are not on-line portable will be abandoned because they do not provide what is increasingly perceived as basic functionality: mobility.

Moving computation, not just code

The framework we are interested in is that of *mobile computation*; that is, the notion that a computation starting at some network node may continue execution at some other network node. This framework involves much more than just moving code. Pure code mobility is useful, and has been used to great advantage in the form of Java applets, but it is also limiting. Fortunately, the other necessary components of mobile computation have already been widely studied and used.

The popular Remote Procedure Call (RPC) model is based on the notion of *control mobility*: a thread of control originating at some network node continues execution at some other network node, and then comes back. No code is moved in this process, just control, so the question of on-line code mobility does not arise.

The RPC model implements also *data mobility*: data is exchanged over the network in the form of parameters and results of RPC calls. This data must be on-line portable: data structures are *marshaled* (converted to portable form) at the originating side, sent over the network, and *unmarshaled* at the receiving site into corresponding data structures, possibly within a different computer architecture.

Some RPC systems also provide *link mobility*: the endpoint of a network connection can be sent over another network connection. The receiving party is then connected to the other endpoint.

Unlike RPC, mobile computation is based on the movement of code, not just the running of code that already exists in network nodes. The other components of RPC, however, are all very important. In mobile computation, control must move as well: the code that is transferred must be run. Data must also move, in order to preserve the state of mobile computations across moves. Network links must also move, since they are part of the state of the computation (at least, in models of mobility that support remote connections).

If code is represented as data (e.g. as the instruction stream of an interpreted virtual machine), then data mobility immediately implies code mobility. Therefore, mobile computation can be implemented rather easily over the RPC model by representing mobile code as mobile data, and taking advantage of the other facilities already provided by RPC. In fact, mobile computation can be implemented on top of various transport mechanisms, although in each case it may acquire some peculiarities of the transport. RPC is currently the most convenient substrate on which to implement mobile computation. HTTP can also be used, resulting in a more Web-oriented semantics of mobility. Thread and address space transport has been provided in the past by some operating systems and programming languages, but usually only within a single computer architecture.

How computation moves

I wish to compare three relatively well-defined and distinct models of mobile computation. Other models certainly already exist, and more will be developed in the future. These three models differ in what kind of entities can be transmitted over the network.

The most basic form of mobility consists in just moving code; this model is represented by Tcl [3] and Java [2] (pre- Remote Method Invocation). In these languages, an architecture-independent representation of program code (source text, or bytecodes) is shipped over the network and interpreted remotely. When code moves, the current state of the computation (if any) is lost, and connections that the computation had at the originating site vanish. State and connectivity must be reestablished at the receiving site. Control is reestablished by dynamic binding or dynamic linking.

A *computation*, however, is more than just code: it is code plus the context of its execution. A computation, in this sense, can be represented as a *closure*, which is the run-time description of a running procedure. Obliq [1] takes the approach of moving closures: the code and the necessary context in which the code operates are transmitted. The context may include data, active network connections which are preserved on transmission, and new connections that are created to keep the closure in touch with the site it leaves behind. In this approach live, active, computations can move, and their meaning is preserved upon transmission. Control is reestablished by running the closure at the receiving site, possibly supplying arguments that provide local information.

Telescript [4] takes the approach of moving *agents*. Agents are similar to closures in that they carry their context with them as they move from location to location, and are reanimated at each location. Agents, however, are meant to be completely self-contained. They do not communicate remotely with other agents; rather they move to some location and communicate locally when they get there.

Obliq is in a sense the most general of these three models: a closure with no data is just code; a closure with no connections is an agent. On a local area network this level of generality is very convenient. However, the Obliq model is also the most fragile when used in full generality over the Web: the rich set of connections created by Obliq computation may be easily upset by network unreliability. In contrast, the pure code and pure agent models can at least survive intermittent connectivity failures. Even those models, though, are supplemented in practice with forms of remote connectivity, making them partially vulnerable to network instability. It is not clear yet how this tension between generality and reliability can be solved.

Fundamental issues

The very notion of mobile computation is evolving rapidly. We should expect to see the emergence of new forms of mobile computation, and of new way of using existing mechanisms. I conclude by listing some basic questions that should be asked of any present or future mobile computation scheme.

- What does a mobile computation do? This is the simple issue of meaning. It has been common to extend existing implementation models to network programming with little regard for clean and consistent semantics. What are the meaningful models for mobile computation?
- Where does computation happen? In any model of mobility one must take the notion of multiple locations as fundamental. It should be possible to determine, in principle, where each piece of the computation happens. Location has an observable influence on behavior, on resource usage, and on the relative costs of

computation versus communication. Knowing where computation happens is necessary in order to program mobile computations effectively.

- What is the programmer's view of mobility? There are many ready answers: distributed objects, closures, threads, continuations, agents, actors, etc. In fact, a programmer's model should be tested against the unusual realities of network programming (especially on the Web). In the long term, the prevalent models are unlikely to be exactly any of the above.

- How is security handled? The main obstacle to the acceptance of mobile computation for commercial applications is the issue of security, which is peculiar to code mobility. The basic technology of security is well understood, but it is not yet clear how to deploy that knowledge into languages and implementations, and how to check that security is truly respected. What is the syntax, static checking, semantics, and logic of security?

References

[1] Cardelli, L., **A language with distributed scope.** *Computing Systems,* **8**(1), 27-59. MIT Press. 1995.

[2] Gosling, J., B. Joy, and G. Steele, **The Java language specification.** Addison-Wesley. 1996.

[3] Ousterhout, J.K., **Tcl and the Tk toolkit.** Addison-Wesley. 1994.

[4] White, J.E., **Telescript technology: the foundation for the electronic marketplace.** White Paper. General Magic, Inc. 1994.

Objectworld

D. Tsichritzis[1]

Abstract. An environment is outlined in which programming objects collect and disseminate information, using analogies from the animal world. Objects have their own rules of behaviour. They coordinate their activities by participating in events. Objects get born, move around, communicate and receive information and, eventually, die.

1 Introduction

The purpose of Office Information Systems is hard to define. Offices usually deal with everything which has any significance in an organization. It is easier to define what offices are not. They are not plants producing goods. Any other centre of activity can potentially be called an office. We can also generally accept that offices deal with information. Information is a resource for the organization like money, personnel, etc. It is critical for decision support within the organization. Like other resources, information has to be mobilized in order to achieve certain results, e.g., arriving at a proper decision. We can, therefore, assume that one of the primary goals of offices is the mobilization of information. That is, to concentrate the "right" information at the "right" time at the "right" place, in order to help office workers in their functions. There are two aspects of mobilization, give and take. It follows that, in order to mobilize information, offices should be able to collect and disseminate information effectively. Office Information Systems should therefore provide the appropriate tools for collecting and disseminating information. In this paper we mainly discuss the concepts which, in our opinion, are needed for the implementation of such tools.

One way of viewing the information present in an organization is as part of a global Knowledge Base from which office workers draw the proper subset when they need it. It is implied that when office workers have relevant information they voluntarily introduce it into the Knowledge Base. In this way the Knowledge Base is kept current and it accurately reflects the cumulative knowledge of all the people using it. Such a model of the world is very appropriate when we deal with a relatively closed domain of discourse. It is also helpful if people accessing the Knowledge Base usually draw rather than add information. For example, an expert can create a Knowledge Base by distilling his expertise into facts, data and rules, and encoding it into a Knowledge Base. From then on other experts can draw on this knowledge, occasionally adding to it. We claim that this situation is far removed from what happens in most offices.

There are several difficulties to viewing information in an office environment as being part of one logically integrated Knowledge Base. First, the domain of discourse is not adequately focused, hence it will be difficult to view all knowledge in an Office System within a general and consistent framework. Second, Office Systems are distrib-

---

1. This paper originally appeared in *Office Automation,* Springer-Verlag, 1985.

uted. It will be too much to expect that all persons will voluntarily place their knowledge in one system. Third, the knowledge in the office is continuously updated in a distributed fashion. There is a significant danger that the centralized, integrated Knowledge Base is not kept current of the latest activities and its usefulness will greatly diminish. It is a common practice, for instance, for people to keep their own databases on their personal machines without voluntarily notifying a central database about all their latest changes. Fourth, knowledge in the office is not monolithic. There are many inconsistencies among the Knowledge Bases of different persons, departments, etc. These inconsistencies are not unwelcome since they represent different opinions on common subjects. To integrate all these opinions in one Knowledge Base will be rather difficult. Many contexts will have to be defined which will create problems for inference. It is better to leave them in independent Knowledge Bases and collect them only when there is a need for consensus. If, however, we view the Knowledge Base as consisting of a set of independent yet cooperating Knowledge Bases then there is a need for tools for such cooperation. Probably the most important tool is a *knowledge collector and disseminator*, that is, an object that goes into different Knowledge Bases and obtains and leaves information on a specific topic. This knowledge carrier is fairly independent and able to have an existence of its own. We need, therefore, to view it as an object in an object-oriented environment with its own data, rules and behaviour.

We will define a KNOwledge collection and dissemination object (in short *kno*, pronounced *no*) as an object whose main purpose is to carry information around.

As an object, a *kno* consists of:

id: an identifier identifying it uniquely systemwide

r_i: rules, each rule consisting of preconditions and actions

v_i: variables providing storage and data structures for the object.

We do not elaborate on the exact definition of kno's as objects. We can assume without loss of generality that it follows the Oz definitions given in the companion paper by O.M. Nierstrasz [6], or any other reasonable definition of objects [1]. Kno's as objects have *acquaintances*, i.e., other objects with which they are supposed to coordinate their behaviour. They participate in *events*. When an event occurs all participating objects execute their corresponding rules and change state.

We will now elaborate on how such objects can help achieve the primary goal of Office Information Systems, i.e., the mobilization of information through collection and dissemination. In the scenario we will use analogies from the animal world. We hope to illustrate the points better and more easily in this manner. The reader is, therefore, advised to visualize kno's as funny animals (figure 1) in a funny imaginary world (for example, the world of *OZ*). Worms as in [3][8] are such animals and we will see that there are others.

2 Kno Environment

Like animals, kno's have to live in a certain environment created by computers, telecommunications and their software systems. To begin, we need a notion of *god*. In conventional systems god corresponds to the end user. All actions emanate from him and

A Kno

Figure 1

he absolutely controls his environment. This is not the case in the world of kno's. In order to achieve any degree of automation we prefer that kno's are freed from the bondage of the users. In this way, users are not bothered with detailed control of kno's (being god creates overhead). As far as kno's are concerned the *object manager* is god (figure 2). It controls their actions according to their scripts. In a distributed environment there are many object managers. As in Olympian times having many gods creates trouble. We will assume that a kno is within only one god's jurisdiction at any point in time. Problems between gods are handled by a superior god, i.e., we propose a hierarchy of object managers.

A kno environment and its object manager

Figure 2

Kno's mating to give life to a new kno

Figure 3

The reader may argue that object managers are not gods because people (system programmers) can go around changing them. We have to accept that situation. System programmers are high priests who define god and interpret its actions. However, as far as the kno's are concerned there is only one god, the object manager to which they currently belong.

We will assume that for each user there is a special anthropomorphic kno. It is not god, but it has special capabilities. This user kno (see example in O.M. Nierstrasz's paper) is capable of independent and unpredictable behaviour. It is capable of inspiration. Users interact from one object manager to another at their own request. Such a request is triggered by events and can be initiated by users through their special kno's.

Kno's, like animals can be *alive* or *dead*. An alive kno is one which can potentially participate in events. A dead kno cannot participate in events and the object manager does not worry about it. Alive kno's are *active* when they participate in an event. Most of the time they are *asleep* waiting for an event. During that time the object manager worries about the event's preconditions and wakes up all the appropriate kno's when the event occurs.

Kno's are born by having the object manager blow life into them. They have to have a proper body which can be created from data structures copied from other kno's. More than one kno can be involved in creating a new kno through a coordination event. We depart here slightly from the animal world by allowing one, two, or more parents for the newborn kno (figure 3). The usual case is for kno's to die and be resurrected intact, or to clone themselves by producing another similar kno.

Kno's die by committing suicide. They participate in an event which makes them go to their terminating condition. They immediately become permanently inactive. Since the killing event can be triggered by another kno we can say that kno's can get killed, or more accurately they can be induced to commit suicide. However, it is important to note that a kno gets killed only because it has an a priori weakness, a tendency to die. It is also killed by an acquaintance which triggers the event, not by any old kno. Kno's can also die from malnutrition, age and natural disasters. Malnutrition corresponds to the absence of events. Kno's can be programmed to become totally inactive (dead) if there are no events in which they participate over a long time. Age corresponds to timer intervals after which the object becomes inactive. Finally, a natural disaster implies that the system and the object manager go berserk and wipe out a kno population. All kno's die because god (the object manager) declares them dead and takes their souls. Any kno can ask to die, but the object manager is the one who decides when.

It is tempting in an object world to avoid the distinction between alive and dead objects. We could treat all objects as sleeping or active but never dead. The implication is that a memory manager underneath deals with their needs. We claim that the issue is more than addressing space. If all objects are alive the object managers will have to worry about them. This will create overhead which may limit the number of objects which we can effectively have. We believe that, especially in office systems, many objects, e.g., letters and memos have a definite lifespan. After a certain time they are literally dead and we should not be bothered with them. Their information content may still be needed but they are inactive until further notice.

Dead kno's are very important because they include the facts which they had when they were alive. We will assume that there are cemeteries of dead kno's, which are called *databases*. If we assume that any input into the system involves a transaction which creates an object, this is a reasonable analogy. Cemeteries of dead kno's, very much like databases, are nicely arranged so that we can stack dead kno's very effectively. For instance, kno's of the same kno class are stripped of their rules when they get buried. The class stores the rules only once. After all, we only need to find dead kno's; we do not need to keep all their acquaintance relationships for firing events. Since everything in the system is an alive or dead kno we can stretch things a little and look at databases not only as cemeteries but as mother earth. All kno's end up as part of mother earth and most of them emanate from mother earth.

3   Kno Behaviour

Kno's like animals move, eat, produce and mate. Before we can explain such behaviour, we need to elaborate more on the nature of kno's. We have already indicated that a kno at any point in time is under the jurisdiction of one object manager. This does not necessarily imply that a kno cannot span more than one object manager. The limitation is that all its parts are ultimately controlled by one object manager. We can think of kno's as having a brain (the master object) and legs (copies of the object). The legs can be with separate object managers, possibly different from the brain's object manager. However, the brain is only in one object manager at any point in time. This type of kno resembles the imessages as they appear in J. Hogg's companion paper [4]. A distributed imessage can have many copies but only one master copy. The coordination among the copies is achieved through metamessages between the object managers. A kno can generate legs at will. It can also lose some of its legs without any serious problem. It only becomes

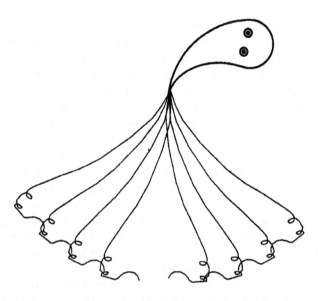

A complex kno

Figure 4

inactive if the brain is killed. We also make the restriction that legs cannot generate other legs. Only the brain can generate legs. We can visualize such a kno as an octopus with an unlimited number of legs (figure 4). The legs can be generated or cut off dynamically. We do not allow animals whose legs can be cloned to generate many more legs (the metamessage overhead would probably get very large).

We are ready now to discuss how kno's move. The simplest way they move is by hopping around (figure 5). Consider, for example, a simple kno with one copy (brain, legs and all). The kno can move from object manager to object manager at its request by doing a hop. No trace is left in the previous object manager and the kno is taken over by the next object manager. The kno's complete body moves as a message between then? Such hopping can be *predefined*, *dynamic*, or *random*. In the predefined case the kno's script has the exact series of locations that a kno has to pass through. In the dynamic case the environment of the object manager in each hop determines the subsequent destination(s). For example, imessages in J. Hogg's paper [4] could be routed dynamically. Finally, in the random case the kno's follow-up destination(s) is determined at random or according to a probability distribution. This case is not as funny as it seems. It can be useful for sampling information in an office environment. A randomly moving kno can also do other useful things like cleaning, reducing populations, etc. This may remind the reader of a commercial swimming pool cleaning device, which is thrown into a pool and moves around randomly eating up dirt. The result is that the swimming pool is continuously being cleaned.

Hopping around can also be visualized for complex kno's. In their cas, the legs and/ or brain hop around independently. This type of movement can get very confusing (and it will probably generate much overhead since the brain has to know where the legs are).

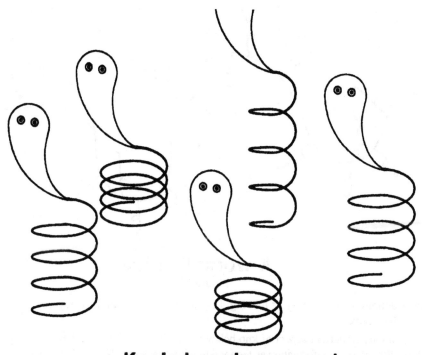

Kno's hopping around
Figure 5

It is therefore, better to move the legs and the brain in a much more organized way. A simple solution is to keep the brain static and to move only the legs. This is again the case of the centralized messages in J. Hogg's companion paper [4]. However, when "distances" between the legs and brain become large there is difficulty in providing the necessary coordination between them. We need, therefore, to move the brain. The safest operation is to move the brain to where a leg has already been. In this case the kno has already tried the environment by venturing a leg (which is, after all, dispensable and can grow back). When the leg becomes secure, control can pass over to the leg object, making it the brain. In this way, the kno can crawl all over by venturing out with legs then moving its brain then again venturing out, etc. The order and the rhythm with which the legs and brain move give us many kinds of kno's. For instance, a *worm* type kno has a sequence of legs with the brain somewhere in the middle (figure 6). It moves forward by moving a leg up front, then moving the rest of its legs and its brain, in sequence. The size (number of legs) of the worm and the position of the brain give us many types of worms.

A *spider* type of kno has many legs moving independently. The decision about when to move the brain can become complicated, depending on where the legs are and how securely they are fastened (figure 7). We hope that the reader is persuaded that kno's can move around in many complicated ways. One important aspect, therefore, of

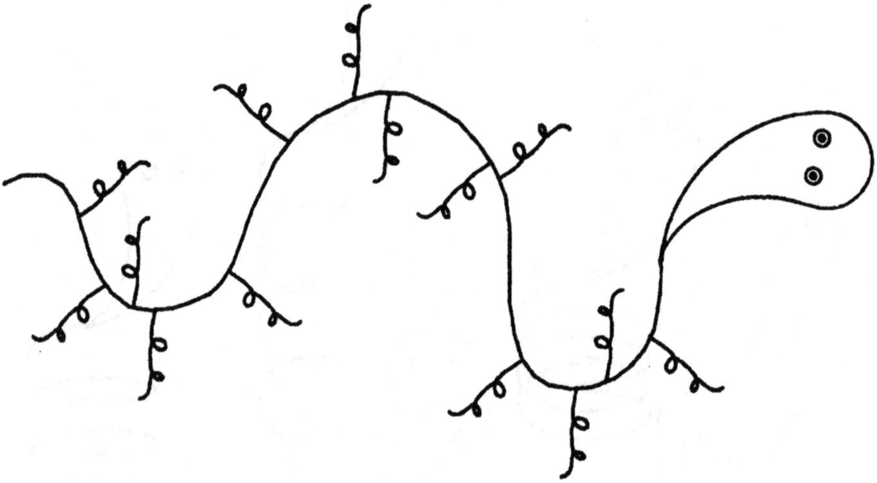

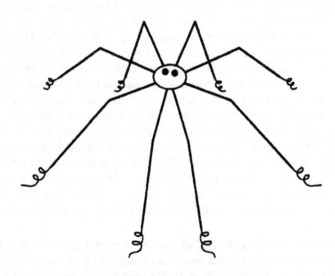

A worm like kno
Figure 6

their definition is their way of moving. Like animals, kno's can be categorized by the way they move.

Another important aspect of kno behaviour is the way in which they eat and produce. We visualize information as the food that kno's eat and also as what they can produce. This information can be both data and rules. Kno's can obtain (eat) information from mother earth (databases) and from other kno's. Since information can be copied,

A spider like kno

Figure 7

food is not strictly consumable (here is a case of eating your cake and having it too!). Kno's can also produce information which they have assembled during their lifespan while visiting places. Like animals kno's do not eat indiscriminately nor do they produce indiscriminately. They have rules which regulate what they eat, how they will digest it and how they will combine the information they eat in their product. We will call these rules *eating*, *digestion* and *producing* rules. Eating rules are filters, like database queries, which specify what kind of information a kno wants to get. Digestion rules take account of what the kno knows in its own variables to break down the information into what it keeps and what it discards. Producing rules indicate how a kno transforms the information into a form ready to be given out. For example, a kno (like an imessage) can ask questions and obtain answers (it eats answers). It then can discard some answers (digestion rules). It keeps and produces only statistics about the answers (producing rules). Such a kno can be sent out on a random walk to poll people's opinions on a subject. Like a cow, what a kno eats (grass) can be very different in format from what it produces (milk). The digestion rules can be arbitrarily complicated (data translation and text manipulation techniques apply here).

Finally, kno's mate (figure 8). Mating corresponds to coordination among objects as acquaintances to fire events and execute their rules together. Mating is under the strict supervision and initiation of the object manager. The case of complex kno's with many legs is interesting. In this case, the coordination can be among legs and/or among brains. It is reasonable to expect that complex objects will first coordinate among their legs and then move to coordinate among their brains. In this way, they can withdraw from the courtship by cutting a leg (no big loss) while preserving the purity of their brains. Complex objects can participate in many coordination activities through their legs r (even concurrently), before they decide on the proper coordination for 3 their brain.

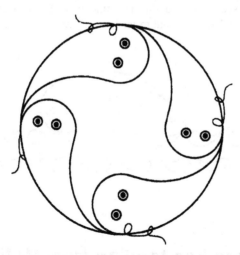

Kno's mating through a coordination event
Figure 8

As a result of coordination, two kno's can start moving together. This mating-turned-into-marriage allows kno's to coordinate moves and actions over the long term. We hope that the reader is persuaded that there are many ways for kno's to mate depending on courtship patterns, mating behaviour and after-the-fact behaviour. It should also be apparent that some very weird kno's can be defined. In the next section, however, we will concentrate on some well behaved species.

4   Kno Species

It will take a very long time to sort out useful from useless or even harmful kno's. We do not expect end users to be able to create nice kno's easily. We would expect that kno's are predefined by, experts, and are mainly taken over and used by end-users. Giving people in the office object-oriented programming environments may create more problems than it solves. What people in offices need is useful objects. In the rest of this section we will outline some examples of, what we consider to be useful objects. Most of these objects can be r readily defined within an object-oriented programming environment.

A useful type of kno is a *carrier* kno (horse, camel). A carrier kno moves around on a prespecified, or dynamic path. It has storage in its variables to store one or more records, documents, etc. It takes information and moves it around intact, without complex digestion and producing rules. Carrier kno's can be used not only to transmit information, e.g., messages, but also to request information. A request is indicated by sending out an empty carrier kno which waits patiently, obtains its load and brings it back to the sender.

Another type of useful kno is a *herbivore* kno (figure 9). Its purpose is to peruse databases and obtain and reduce information from them. It can have arbitrarily complex eating, digestion and producing rules. It can either be static or it can move around. We can keep a herbivore static and feed it data continuously. Alternatively, we can have a free roaming herbivore that is sent out to feed on data and reduce information from it.

A herbivore kno feeding from Mother Earth

Figure 9

A parasite kno
Figure 10

A kno can also copy information from another kno which it meets through a coordination event. An interesting case is a *parasite* kno which continuously follows another kno, drawing information from it (Figure 10).

Another useful type of kno is a *hunter* kno (figure 11). A hunter kno moves around and assembles other kno's that may have gone astray, e.g., randomly-moving kno's. The hunter kno coordinates with each hunted kno, taking over their path specification and bringing it back to a particular place. In this way we can send out kno's not caring where they go and later on we can collect them. The hunter kno can move on a prespecified path, dynamically, or randomly. It can collect all or a fixed number of hunted kno's.

Another useful kno is the *killer* kno. Its purpose is population control. It kills certain types of kno's by inducing their suicide when it coordinates with them within a particular object manager. Killer kno's only kill certain types of kno's, and only when they

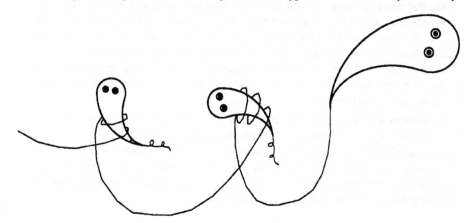

A hunter kno collecting other knos
Figure 11

A predator kno eating up another kno

Figure 12

catch them. Killer kno's allow us to issue kno's which never die from old age. At some later time we may decide to kill all or some of these kno's, or thin them out by sending out killer kno's. The killer kno's can themselves be killed or can die. For instance, they can be programmed to die after a certain time (old age), or if they cannot find kno's to kill (malnutrition). Killer kno's can be simple *killers* or *predators*. In the first case they kill and move on. In the second case they feed on the victims by retaining certain information (figure 12). For example, a predator may retain how many, or the id's of the kno's it has killed, for future reference.

This description may sound like a jungle book. It certainly resembles it. It is a tough world out there for the kno's. It has to be, or they will overburden the systems. We also expect that user's workstations will be farms where only nice, well behaved, kno's are allowed to exist. Crazy kno's may be defined and turned loose on the networks but users can strictly control the kno's coming into their farms. They can keep out harmful kno's. This can be done by issuing guardian kno's which kill all unwelcome kno's on sight. The object manager can also change an incoming kno's behaviour by altering its rules before it takes over the kno. In this way even a weird or ferocious kno can be killed or made docile just before it enters a nice farm of friendly kno's.

Kno farms will be either like family farms or like big commercial farms. The first case is a user workstation where the user has many different useful kno's for local use. A commercial farm corresponds to a large application system where a large population of kno's are bred, fed and sold. A user can get a newborn kno for his farm (predefined object) from a commercial place. He can also get a ready-to-consume kno (database query or other transaction) from a commercial place.

5 Kno Intelligence

In our discussion so far, we have had objects being born, dying, mating, killing, etc. All of these actions were according to the fixed predefined rules of the objects. Objects could change behaviour, but they always had to conform to their scripts. This brings out an important issue, i.e., can objects change their scripts? A kno whose rules can change dynamically is a superior kno capable of "learning". We will discuss in this section such a notion of "learning" and its different manifestations.

A simple way for a kno to change behaviour is through its offspring. The kno gives birth to a new kno with new rules. The parent kno may instantly die which means that the new kno takes its place. This situation is not exactly self "learning". However, it can be fairly powerful. The limitation is that the new kno will have a different id, hence it will not inherit all its parents history and actions. We can anticipate, however, a kno gathering rules in its history, and encoding them as data. it then gives rise to a new "smarter" kno by using the rules (experience) it has accumulated.

A second way for kno's to change behaviour is through their acquaintances. We do not allow a kno to change its own rules, but we allow a kno to export some rules to an acquaintance kno. Since users are represented by special kno's this capability allows users to indirectly change rules in kno's. It allows transfer of "intelligence" between kno's. The users can also inspire kno's to actions different from those with which they have been programmed. Notice, however, that apart from this user inspiration there are no new rules, no new form of "intelligence", no originality.

A third way for kno's to change behaviour is by godly command, i.e., by the intervention of the object manager. So far, the object manager has only coordinated kno events. We could, however, visualize a more sophisticated object manager which fixes kno's, especially when they are overstepping their boundaries. This may sound arbitrary but it is less arbitrary than allowing an object manager, or a user to kill a difficult-to-deal-with kno. The object manager can enforce global constraints in a kno population by arbitrarily refusing to allow their events and actions. It is probably better to tame them by introducing special temporary rules while the objects are within its jurisdiction. The object manager's intervention is not restricted to negative actions. It can also introduce rules which are helpful to a kno. For example, it can provide local structures of data, endow kno's with access privileges, etc. Finally, the object manager can introduce rules to kno's uniformly, or selectively. These additional rules may form the precondition for an object manager to take over an incoming kno.

The fourth way and probably the most intriguing is to allow for kno's to change behaviour by changing their own rules. Since rules are encoded as programs, there is no magic in that; it is simply programs changing other programs. This capability is very powerful, but it is also extremely dangerous. A self-changing kno can do many tricky things. It can masquerade as a benevolent kno while being a malicious kno. It can go absolutely crazy, so that we need to burn the forest and bring the system down to get it under control. It provides, however, the most intriguing examples of kno species. For instance, we can visualize a kno with no fixed rules a priori. It goes around borrowing rules from all over the place. It can grow up into almost anything, including a kno which nobody has ever thought of before. As much as we are intrigued by such potential, we will probably be better off without this capability. Not only because it will be hard to implement, but because it will probably be too dangerous to have around.

Finally, a philosophical note on kno intelligence. Most work on Knowledge Bases and Expert Systems concentrates on inference from a large set of facts, data and rules. This is similar to a guru in the Himalayan Mountains providing deep reasoning on a large but fixed amount of knowledge. Kno's do not provide exactly such intelligence. They do not know too much. Neither do they have complicated inference; but they can travel. They can travel far and wide collecting and giving information. Their intelligence is like Sinbad the sailor's. It comes not from reasoning and inference but from experience through travels. We feel that such intelligence is very useful, especially in an, office environment. We leave the deep reasoning to humans, so long as kno's can gather the appropriate knowledge. To end with a pun: kno intelligence is a form of intelligence.

6   Concluding Remarks

A kno environment is not very difficult to prototype but it will be hard to implement well. Some of the issues have already been discussed in the companion papers, "Object Oriented Systems" (O.M. Nierstrasz) [6] and "Intelligent Mail Systems" (J. Hogg) [4].

Simple kno's within one object manager are straightforward objects, e.g., *OZ* objects. We need, however, to expand their capabilities in many significant ways. First, they should be able to issue queries on a database and deal with the replies. Some of the problems of tying programming variables to databases have already been dealt with in other systems, e.g., PASCAL R [7]. The same approach can be followed. Second, we need to expand their rules to manipulate the data they receive (digestion and producing rules). We will inevitably have to deal with data translation and text manipulation issues for reformatting the information [5][2]. Third, we need to have a birth capability. Most object-oriented systems deal with new objects as instances of a well-known class from which they inherit their rules. To define an arbitrary object or a new class, the user reverts to a complex programming language. We need to provide tools for the definition of new objects. We also need to allow objects to issue a request to the object manager for the creation of a new object. This problem is similar to spawning processes in an Operating System. The main difference is that the new object does not inherit resources from its parent, nor is it tied up for life to its parent. Processes in Operating Systems are strictly structured. Objects float around in the system in an independent fashion. They certainly do not obey their parents, nor do their parents care about them. Objects only inherit properties from their parents.

Killer and hunter objects do not present many problems. Killing is easily done through a coordinating event that fires the victim's rule leading it to termination. For hunter objects we need to develop the notion of a leader object in a group. The implication is that the group moves together to the place where the leader object points. The leader object has the precondition in its rule of deciding where to move. The rest of the group has rules without preconditions which coordinate with the leader object. All this can be done easily if we allow the splicing of a rule in an object by a "superior" object.

Such capability is also needed for exporting rules as was discussed in the kno intelligence section.

Care should be taken, however, in exporting rules so that we do not end up with conflicting rules. We will have to assume that in the case of a discrepancy either the new or the old rules take precedence.

Complex objects present many more problems. We need to establish communication between object managers. Since the object managers are fairly independent and sometimes live incommunicado, we may have problems. We need to accept that the legs of the complex kno's can live for quite some time without proper direction from the brain. If they are fairly independent and start moving around we may end up with the brain losing track of its own legs! One solution is to restrict the legs to be fairly unsophisticated, e.g., they stay put unless they are told by the brain to move. Another solution is to allow complex kno's to disintegrate and lose their limbs. Finally, we can force object managers to cooperate by supervising their actions through other object managers. There is a complex trade-off here which is influenced by the properties of the communication network connecting the object managers. Clearly, in an environment of many personal computers occasionally talking to each other we can not expect their object managers to cooperate fully and continuously. On the other hand, perhaps this is not the proper environment for the survival of complex kno's.

When complex kno's move around we may need to pass control from the brain to one of the legs. This is different from doing a hopping operation of the brain. We feel that such change of control is smoother and more useful. It brings us back to the notion of a pack of objects with a clear leader. In this case the pack is distributed in different object managers and the leadership may change. We can encode leadership by placing a token among the set of grouped objects which can move around. Notice that a group of objects is different than a set of coordinating objects. Coordination is only temporary, while grouping is longer-range. We still have the problem of cooperation between different object managers. This problem looks similar to cooperation for firing events in a distributed fashion, which we do not allow. It has, however, the important difference that coordination allows interference and competition between objects for fitting events. Grouping does not allow objects to be in different and conflicting groups. The cooperation between object managers to keep the group together is therefore minimal.

Finally, if people are going to use kno's we need a nice user model. Our discussion can hopefully point to such a user model. We can illustrate kno behaviour with animation to explain their properties to users. Figures 1 to 12 are sketches which can be useful for visualizing kno's. The reader is asked to use his imagination to fantasize how all this kno behaviour will look in animation. Computers are used for animation. Kno animation can be useful for documentation of object-oriented systems for user interfaces and for tracing kno movements.

In conclusion, we should ask ourselves what the difference is between kno's and known concepts in Computer Science, such as objects, abstract data types, processes, actors, etc. Theoretically there is not much difference. In practice there are two important differences in emphasis. First, kno's are great in number, relatively stupid, and travel around. Second, kno's are not supposed to be a programming language. They are a user's tool, like spreadsheets or Query-By-Example. Everything we can do with kno's can be done in a programming environment. This is immaterial. Everything we can do with spreadsheets can be done within a programming language. Try, though, to substitute for a user MULTIPLAN or Lotus 1-2-3 with FORTRAN.

References

[1]   M. Ahlsen, A. Bjornerstedt, S. Britts, C. Hulten and L. Soderlund, "An Architecture for Object Management in OIS", *ACM Transactions on Office Information Systems,* 2(3), pp. 173-196, July 1984.

[2]   A.V. Aho, B. Kernighan and P. Weinberger, "Awk - A Pattern Scanning and Processing Language", *Report, Bell labs,* September 1978.

[3]   J. Brunner, *The Shockwave rider,* Ballantine, New York, 1975.

[4]   J. Hogg, Intelligent Message Systems. In [9].

[5]   A. Klug, *Theory of Database Mappings,* Ph. D. Thesis, Department of Computer Science, University of Toronto, 1978.

[6]   O. M. Nierstrasz, An Object-Oriented System. In [9],

[7]   J. W. Schmidt, "Some High-Level Language Constructs for Data of Type Relation", *ACM TODS,* 2(3), pp. 247-261, 1977.

[8]   J. Schoch and J. Hupp, :The Worm Programs - Early Experience with a Distributed Comptuation", *Communications of the ACM,* 25(3), pp. 172-180, March 1982.

[9]   D. C. Tsichritzis (ed.), *Office Automation - Concepts and Tools.* Springer-Verlag, 1985.

Commentary on "Objectworld"

D. Tsichritzis

Reading a paper written more than 12 years ago (it was published in 1985) needs a proper context. Without such a context both its strengths and its shortcomings will never be understood.

The early 80's saw a group of people who were fascinated by the possibilities of the then new PC's and were experimenting with tools for office systems. Although the area of Office Information Systems or Office Automation was never considered as a serious academic or research activity, many ideas which were promoted at the time were later extremely successful. As an example, Mike Hammer was formulating at the time his ideas about office processes and organization reengineering which became famous later on. We had a group at the University of Toronto, working on both models and tools for office systems. The results were personal database systems, intelligent e-mail systems, automatic form systems, etc. Many of these ideas were later introduced in commercial systems and were explained in the book on Office Automation in which also the "Objectworld" paper appeared [1]. We were frustrated in our research activity by our UNIX/C programming environment and its shortcomings as an effective prototyping environment. At the time Lisp was considered inefficient and Smalltalk was not considered as a serious alternative. Hence our interest to adopt a better programming environment, at least better suited for fast prototyping. This is the way we became interested in Object Oriented Systems and our ideas were later on further developed by some of the Toronto people (O. Nierstrasz, S. Gibbs) in our Geneva group [5].

The "Objectworld" paper was written in 1984 totally independent from our day-to-day implementation problems. If we were to adopt or build an object-oriented environment what would be the dream environment? What were the capabilities we would like to see? What were the problems we had to handle? The paper is not based (fortunately) on any existing technology. It was and is a think piece.

Later on in Geneva working with E. Casais we implemented many features as proposed by the "Objectworld" paper in a Lisp environment [2][3]. Our interest then turned to the more down to earth problems of Object Oriented Software development [4] and multimedia programming [5]. Lately, the work on Mobile Objects has again been restarted due to the interest of J. Vitek.

It is fair to ask after more than 12 years whether some of the capabilities we were introducing in "Objectworld" are common practice. It is also fair to ask whether we were completely wrong in terms of the environment. The answers to these questions are partially explored by the papers of this book. If nothing else this shows that our technology and its applications are evolving at a much faster pace than our conceptual framework.

References

[1]   Office Automation: Tools and Concepts, ed. D. Tsichritzis, Springer-Verlag, Berlin, 1985.

[2]   D. Tsichritzis, E. Fiume, S. Gibbs, and O. Nierstrasz, "KNOs: Knowledge Acquisition, Dissemination and Manipulation Objects," ACM Trans. Office Information Syst., vol. 5, no. 1, pp. 96-112, 1987.

[3]   E. Casais, "An Object-Oriented System Implementing KNOs," Proc. of the Conf. on Office Information Systems (COIS), Palo Alto, March 1988, pp. 284-290.

[4]   Object-Oriented Software Composition, ed. O. Nierstrasz, D. Tsichritzis, Prentice-Hall, 1995.

[5]   Multimedia Programming: Objects, Environments and Frameworks, S. Gibbs and D. Tsichritzis, Addison-Wesley/ACM Press 1994.

Mobile Agents: Are They a Good Idea?*

David Chess, Colin Harrison, Aaron Kershenbaum

Abstract. Mobile agents are programs, typically written in a script language, which may be dispatched from a client computer and transported to a remote server computer for execution. Several authors have suggested that mobile agents offer an important new method of performing transactions and information retrieval in networks. Other writers have pointed out, however, that mobile agents introduce severe concerns for security. We consider the advantages offered by mobile agents and assess them against alternate methods of achieving the same function. We conclude that, while the individual advantages of agents do not represent an overwhelming motivation for their adoption, the creation of a pervasive agent framework facilitates a very large number of network services and applications.

1 Introduction

The idea of performing client-server computing by the transmission of executable programs between clients and servers has been popularized in recent years by researchers and developers interested in intelligent network services, most notably by White & Miller at General Magic, Inc. [19], but also by the developers of TCL [14]. Mobile agent-based computing may be viewed as an extension of well-known methods of remote dispatch of script programs [7], or remote submission of batch jobs [3]. The most significant of the extensions lie in the area of security, since an important goal of this work is to enable spontaneous electronic commerce; that is commerce which does not require the prior conclusion of a trading contract between the two parties. Security is in fact a significant concern with mobile agent-based computing, as a server receiving a mobile agent for execution may require strong assurances about the agent's intentions.

These security concerns have led us to a critical examination of the use of mobile agents in network services, to determine whether the benefits they offer compensate for the concerns that they raise. In this paper we examine various arguments that have been adduced in favor of mobile agents, comparing the individual benefits they claim with alternative methods of achieving the same result, and also considering the overall benefit of a mobile agent framework for network services. This assessment considers both technical and commercial factors.

We begin with a description of the attributes of mobile agents and then proceed to analyze the pros and cons of the individual claims (trees) and the aggregate merit of an agent framework (forest).

---

* The original version of this paper was completed in 1994, but its main conclusions remain valid today; see the following article in this volume for a brief update.

2   Mobile agent based computing

The mobile agent concept is illustrated in figure 1. A client computer consists of an application environment, for example, OS/2 or Microsoft Windows, which contains one or more applications for interaction with a remote server. These applications may include information searching and retrieval, transaction front-ends, or mail clients. These applications are bound to an execution environment for mobile agents. Via the APIs, the application can pass parameters to various classes (not necessarily object-oriented classes) of agent programs, and likewise the agent programs can return parameters to the application programs. These classes may be part of the basic agent execution environment, agents distributed with the OS/2 or Windows applications, or agents received by the client from a server or other peer on the network. In principle there may be no application program; the agent programs can themselves perform presentation on the client device's user interface and collect information directly from a keyboard or other input device; in this case the agent programs - or the agent execution environment - must bind to the user interface libraries of the client device. The agent execution environment will also need to bind to various operating system functions, such as the memory manager, the timer, the file system and so forth. In particular the agent execution environment needs to bind to the message transport service in order to send and receive mobile agents via the communication infrastructure.

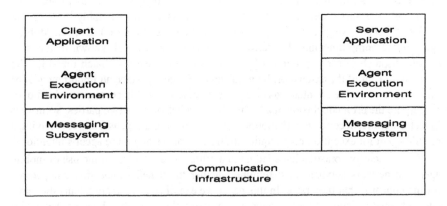

Fig. 1. Conceptual model for mobile agent computing

When an application needs to send mail or perform a transaction, it will assemble the required information and then pass this via the API into the agent execution environment. This will initiate the execution of an instance of a particular class of agent as a process within the agent execution environment. This may correspond to an operating system process or an operating system thread or it may be managed by a threads package within the agent execution environment. The agent execution environment will have access to many different agent programs, which provide different services to the client applications. For example, one may act as a delivery agent for electronic mail, another may deliver a database retrieval request to a server, submit the request and return the result to the client application. Yet another may navigate its way among multiple servers, asking each in turn for updates on a particular topic.

The agent program may be built from procedural components or from classes of objects. In either case, the agent has bindings to functions within the agent execution environment, including functions imported from the operating system, the application or other sub-systems, as well as other agent programs.

The program may be executed in either machine language or an interpreted (virtual machine). language. In order to support heterogeneity, it is often preferable to express the agent in an interpreted language. There is a performance penalty for this, but since most of the agent processing is done not in the agent itself, but rather in the functions to which it binds, this may be acceptable. Interpreted languages are also easier to render secure than machine language, since the language developer explicitly controls what system resources are accessible. (Provided that gaping loopholes such as PEEK and POKE are rigorously excluded.)

The information assembled by the application is accepted by the agent as part of its initialization and at a certain point in its execution, the agent will execute an instruction which has the following effects:

- Either the current agent process is suspended in the agent execution environment, or a new agent daughter process is created.
- The suspended process or the new process, including its process state, stack, heap and all external references is collected and processed into a message expressed in a machine-independent form, for example Abstract Syntax Notation 1 [13]. This step is facilitated if the agent is built from object classes and in an interpreted language. In particular, if it is known that the identical classes are resident at the destination, the agent may be reduced to object references, instance data and process state data. If the agent is expressed in an interpreted language, the state data is captured on the stack and there is no need to save registers.
- The message may be addressed explicitly to a final destination, or it may be directed initially to a post office function which can perform address resolution, or to inter-mediate destinations, which route the agent on the basis of its content (Semantic Routing).
- The message is handed to the message sub-system and routed directly or indirectly to the destination server, where it is delivered by the server's message sub-system to the agent execution environment.
- In the agent execution environment the received message is reconstituted into the executable and the process or thread is dispatched.
- Execution continues at the next instruction in the agent program.

This is effectively a process migration, but one that is performed for the purpose of moving the agent from a client which has a request - for information, for a transaction, for mail delivery - to a server which is capable of satisfying the request.

During execution at the server, the agent passes the information it received from the client application to server application functions and perhaps receives other information in return. At the completion of this stage, it might perform one or more of several functions:

- It might terminate its execution.
- It might simply suspend at the server, waiting for some event to be delivered from a server application. We would say that is has become a 'resident' agent at the server. Resident agents may become permanently resident if there is some repeated service desired by the user.
- It might repeat the migration progress, either by forking a new daughter process or by suspending and migrating itself. This second migration might return the agent to its originating client or it might continue to another server or another client.

In particular, the agent may be able to perform a recovery action and visit another server if the required service is not available or is otherwise unsatisfactory or (equivalently) the agent may be able to determine that it should also visit another server based on data it has received from the current server.

2.1 Security

There are several security issues to be considered in mobile agent-based computing:

- Authentication of the user, that is, the sender of the mobile agent, by the server, and authentication of the server or agent execution environment, by the agent. (It is not at all clear how this latter function can be implemented, given that the agent is passive during the authentication process.) The server may wish to be able to authenticate the sending user uniquely or it may be satisfied to know simply that the user belongs to a group of authorized users. Some servers may not require any authentication all, if they have no protected information or functions. The authentication information may be conveyed by the agent itself or it might be transmitted separately, for example between authentication servers at the client and server. The outcome of the authentication processes is that the user/agent knows the identity of the server/agent execution environment and the server/agent execution environment knows the identity of the user/agent. This authentication is based only on header information transmitted with the agent; the server still has no idea what the agent wants to do.
- Determination of whether the user has authorization to execute agents at the server and which functions may be used, and determination of whether the agent will attempt to infect the server, deny service to other agents or otherwise attempt to do harm to the server or other agents. The server's agent execution environment will re-constitute the agent into an executable. However, before the server dispatches the executable, it may wish to examine the agent code to see what resources it proposes to access. This may be part of a general access-control function or it may be part of a virus immune system function. If the agent language supports self-modification (as does Telescript), this may be an insufficient test, since the as-received agent may during execution be able to transform itself from a benign to a malignant entity.

Following successful completion of this test, the agent execution environment will permit the agent access to server resources, depending on the privileges of the user.

- Determination of the agent's ability or willingness to pay for services provided by the server (unless these are free). During execution the agent acts autonomously on behalf of the user. Since the agent is consuming at least computational resources at the server, and may in fact be performing transactions for goods, the user also requires considerable assurance that his or her liability is limited. In the case of General Magic's agents, the Telescript [2] language provides a method of authentication transmitted with the agent and also a method whereby the agent carries with it a quantity of an electronic currency (Teleclicks). During execution of the agent by the server, the server is entitled to transfer currency units from the agent to the agent execution environment as a form of payment. The user's liability is limited to the quantity of currency which the agent was issued by the client. In Telescript execution environments, an agent which exhausts its currency is killed. However, the user also requires assurance that the agent execution environment cannot fake the quantity of currency transferred and that the server is indeed providing the contracted services.

2.2 Virus detection

Analysis of the agent itself, to determine whether it is likely to exhibit virus-like behavior is a difficult problem. It is difficult to define necessary and sufficient tests that the agent must pass in order to determine whether its intentions are benign or whether it intends to infect or otherwise corrupt the host system.

Some informal discussions of computer viruses in agent settings have focused on the question of whether or not the agent language is Turing-complete (roughly, able to express any program expressible by a standard general-purpose programming language). But this is not in fact the key issue. It is not the case that virus detection is undecidable in (and only in) Turing-complete programming languages. Nor is it the case that it is possible to write a virus in any Turing-complete language. Turing completeness is really rather a red herring when thinking about viruses, because:

- It is easy to design a non-Turing-complete language in which a virus can be written (just include an "infect" verb somewhere in the set of primitives).
- It is easy to design a Turing-complete language in which no virus can be written (and in which, therefore, the virus-detection problem is easy; the answer is always: "No, that is not a virus"). Consider, for instance, a language with the full programming power of REXX, but able to do input only from the keyboard, output only to the screen, and with no access to any underlying operating system commands or functions. We could write arbitrarily-complex games or Eliza programs in it, but since programs written in it cannot read or write other programs, they cannot be viral. (In theory, we could write an entire virtual operating system, including a file system, in this language, and there could be virtual viruses within that system, but that is not of practical relevance.)

---

[2] Telescript and Teleclicks are trademarks of General Magic, Inc.

Turing completeness only comes in very slightly: if we have a language that includes the ability to implement the "spread" operation, and the language is Turing-complete, then Cohen [4] has shown that perfect virus detection is impossible. But his result does not say anything one way or the other about systems that are not Turing-complete, or that do not make the "spread" operation possible.

This is important for the mobile-agent question in at least one very large way: it means that one could design a mobile-agent system in which agents are written in a Turing-complete language, and as long as the "spread" operation cannot be implemented (as long, that is, as agents cannot alter other programs), we can still avoid having viruses.

A simple example of this would be an agent language with the basic syntax of REXX (say), but with only a very limited set of powers:

− To alter its own internal state variables,
− To make database queries in the current server,
− To move to another server,
− To send text messages back to its owner.

Despite being Turing-complete, there is no way to write a virus in this system. We can even allow such agents to add and update database entries (under proper access controls, of course), and as long as nothing ever interprets the contents of a database entry as an agent, we still do not have virus problems.

Mobile agents are not the only method by which viruses might be propagated in network services, although the use of mobile agents may greatly facilitate their propagation. Nor are viruses the only epidemic threat to network services; other effects such as mail broadcast storms are at least as likely and equally hard to deal with. J. Kephart [12] has been studying the propagation of viruses in networks, and creating an initial architecture for the detection and confinement of these and other abberant behaviors of network-based services.

2.3 Issues

The use of mobile agents appears to offer certain advantages for client-server computing, but as we have noted above, it also raises some difficult issues:

− Efficiency: Does the agent execution environment require significant computational resources? Does the transmission of a transaction or other request via a mobile agent result in more or less network traffic than alternate methods?
− Flexibility: Can the use of mobile agents provide a more flexible and robust method of communication than alternate methods? Is it likely that agent execution environments would be rapidly deployed on network servers?
− Security: Is there a useful compromise between the desire to isolate the agent execution environment from the system and application functions and the need to provide access in order to accomplish the users' tasks? Is is possible to define a language such that it provides sufficient expression for client-server interaction, while being sufficiently restricted that the server and other agents cannot be compromised?

3 Alternatives to mobile agents

For completeness, we mention here briefly the alternatives to mobile agents for client-server interactions. The dominant methods are messaging [6], simple datagrams [17], sockets [15], remote procedure calls [2], and conversations [5]. The primary distinction among these is between asynchronous protocols, for example, messaging, and synchronous protocols, for example, RPC. Mobile agents employ messaging frameworks for transport, and hence are asynchronous. In the rest of this assessment, we will use the term *messaging* to characterize asynchronous client-server interactions and *RPC* for everything else. In both cases, the client and server exchange data which is to be processed by specific procedures at the remote CPU. Neither party specifies how the data are to be processed; each has implicit knowledge of the capabilities of the remote procedures. This contrasts with mobile agents, which communicate both data and their own procedures and which exploit procedures resident at the client or server.

The *Remote Procedure Call (RPC)* extends the traditional procedure call mechanism of pushing parameters, registers and a return address onto the stack and then performing a jump to the procedure's entry point. In the RPC case, the client and server open a communications channel between the client application and the server process. The RPC parameters are passed to an interface routine, which marshals them into a form suitable for transmission and sends them explicitly to the server process. The RPC packets are received by a corresponding interface routine, unpacked and passed to the server procedure. The procedure processes the parameters and (generally) produces a return RPC, which is transmitted back to the client process. Both parties must use a common interface definition (although heterogeneity of hardware and operating system software is possible). While a local procedure call can be executed in at most a few microseconds (not including the execution time of the procedure itself), the RPC introduces overhead due to marshalling, transmission, and unpacking and has a typical latency of a few milliseconds Like the local procedure call, the RPC is synchronous; the client process suspends, maintaining the entire process state, until it receives the return RPC from the server. Secure RPCs add authentication and encryption facilities to the client-server communication, but introduce significant overhead [18].

Messaging is emerging as a popular alternative to RPC for client-server communication. It is an outgrowth of both electronic mail systems and earlier distributed computing schemes in which applications communicated via files or pipes. The client application composes a message, typically composed of tagged or structured text, which is to be delivered to an appropriate software processor for the type of message. Messaging systems may employ a message transport service provided by an electronic mail service or any similar service. The required processor type is indicated in the message header. The message is generally addressed indirectly, that is, the client may not know the explicit network address or even the identity of the destination server. The resolution of addresses is performed by intermediate steps of processing, such as post offices.

Messaging is inherently asynchronous; once the client has handed off the message contents to the messaging sub-system, it continues execution. If in the future, the client receives a response message from the server, it must restore the application state in order to process the response. For example, if the user is engaged in a dialogue with a reservation service, several iterations may be required between the client travel planning application and the Computerized Reservation Service (CRS), before the user has identified a suitable flight and seat; during these iterations, the client and the CRS must both maintain transaction state until it is committed.

Because the communication is asynchronous, the latency in messaging is both higher and less predictable than in the RPC case. As a result messaging may be less effective for one-to-one communication than RPC, but for one-to-many communication, which is typical of servers in network services, the throughput may be higher, since the client process does not need to suspend while waiting for the response. As in the RPC case, secure messaging can offer authentication and encryption; there is an equivalent overhead, but because the process is asynchronous, the overhead is less burdensome.

The strength of RPC lies in its high efficiency and low latency. The strength of messaging lies in its robustness, particularly over wide-area networks.

4 Assessment of individual advantages (Trees)

In this section we examine various individual claims related to mobile agents and consider arguments for and against their use. As a general statement, we have not discovered any client-server functions which are important for network services and which are uniquely enabled by the use of mobile agents. For almost every agent-based function proposed, we can propose an alternative based on existing protocols; this will become apparent in the discussions below. We believe therefore that the individual advantages of mobile agents are relative rather than absolute; the goal of our analysis is to determine whether these relative advantages are individually or cumulatively sufficient to warrant employing mobile agents as the basis for client-server applications and services.

4.1 Agents can provide better support for mobile clients

Mobile devices such as laptop and notebook computers, as well as emerging classes such personal communicators, have three characteristics relevant to this discussion:

- *They are only intermittently connected to a network, hence have only intermittent access to a server.* This is certainly true today, when most mobile access to networks is via circuit-switched lines, but may be less true in the future when wireless access to packet-switched networks will be prevalent. The advantage here lies in the mobile client's ability to develop an agent request while disconnected, launch the agent during a brief connection session, and then immediately disconnnect. The response, if any, is collected during a subsequent connection session.
- *Even when connected, they have only relatively low-bandwidth connections.* This is likely to remain true for some time to come. Retail modems now provide 28.8 kbps links on dial-up lines, but wireless links to public networks are unlikely to exceed 12 kbps per client this century. The advantage here lies in the ability of an agent to perform both information retrieval and filtering at a server, and to return to the client only the relevant information. Thus the information transmitted over the network is minimized, which has strong cost implications for devices connected by public wireless networks.

– *They have limited storage and processing capacity.* While there are laptop computers today with gigabyte disks and Pentium-class engines, there will always be a class of devices that tries to make do with 'minimal' resources; for example, Hewlett Packard's successful HP95/100/200 series, which natively offers only 2 MB of storage. The advantage here lies in the ability of an agent to perform both information retrieval and filtering at a server, and to return to the client only the relevant information. Thus the information transmitted to the device is minimized and the device does not itself need to perform filtering.

There are thus two technical features of agents at play here:

– *Reduction of network traffic.* In the case of RPC-based communication, there are typically several flows between the client and server in order to perform even a simple transaction. In the case of secure RPC, there may be several tens of flows for a complex transaction. It is expected that these flows could be reduced to a single mobile agent with a corresponding reduction in network traffic, most importantly on the low-bandwidth access network.
– *Asynchronous interaction.* However, we have seen that this is a property of any message-based system, and does not require in itself programmable agents. Message buffering on the client device (inbound) and on the communication server (outbound) are well known features.
– *Remote searching and filtering.* If all information were stored in structured databases, it would suffice to send a message to the server containing SQL statements and perhaps perform backend filtering on the search results. Given that most of the world's data is in fact in flat, free text files, remote searching and filtering does require the ability to open files, read, filter and possibly develop an index. Agent programs are certainly a plausible method of performing this service. We wonder, however, if they are are the only way to perform this service. It would seem that a search engine installed at the server could achieve the same results, without requiring the dangerous generality of a programming language and execution environment.

Assessment: There is a real problem to be solved for mobile clients, and mobile agents do have advantages for attaching mobile clients to networks. It is less clear that the entire network's servers need to be adapted to meet this need. Architecturally one might prefer to solve this problem at the edge of the network and make mobile clients as robust as non-mobile clients by providing proxy services at the edge of the network [9].

4.2 Agents facilitate semantic information retrieval

We should look at remote searching and filtering further, since it is one of the central issues in agent programming. Consider a more sophisticated information retrieval system based on Semantic Retrieval. The user enters a query at his or her client device. The system interprets this query semantically, possibly asking the user questions and getting clarification. This reformulated query is then transmitted via an agent to one or more servers, which retrieve information and present it to the agent, possibly getting additional feedback on the query and quality of the information retrieved.

In order to do this well, the system needs to be able to interact with both the user and the sources of information. Interaction with the user is easy, because he or she does not enter much information. Interaction with the multiple servers is not nearly so easy. First, the sources are likely to be distributed over many locations. Second, the amount of information involved (including most of the information which is in fact not relevant to the query, and hence should be filtered out) is huge.

The ideal system will possess knowledge specific to the domain in which it operates and specific to the user's interests, as well as the ability to filter data based on this knowledge. This knowledge will be based on exposure to a lot of current data in its area of expertise. It is far more efficient for the program extracting this knowledge to go to the source of the data instead of sending the data to the program, especially since the program is primarily filtering and summarizing the data. Thus an agent can do automatic indexing of documents, which will include identifying a small number of interesting documents from among a large number of uninteresting ones. It might also identify documents potentially interesting to other agents and inform them of this fact. Distributed indexes could be built up hierarchically, geographically, and by subject.

The difference between real semantic retrieval and simple keyword searches (which will differentiate offerings which people will pay for, from those currently available for free) is the amount of information which can be passed through the system to allow to it become a real expert in its field and to have high quality, current information at its disposal. Distributed intelligent agents, which are co-resident with the data sources and persist of their own accord (performing incremental indexing) have a real advantage in this respect over centralized, more static systems. To the extent that mobility allows the agents to get closer to the actual data source (e.g., real-time vehicular traffic data, weather data), mobility becomes a real advantage here too.

The counter argument to this is that it still appears possible to define standard retrieval and filtering programs, which could be installed at information repositories, and to send with the query a user context of previous searches that the user has found relevant. The information must be in any case be propagated among the various servers addressed by a query. This seems more efficient than propagating both the user context data and the search engine itself. It is true that it will be difficult to get agreement on a standard search engine, but then it will also be difficult to get agreement on a standard agent environment.

There is a second argument that in the future, bandwidth will be plentiful and cheap, and network carriers will be trying to earn money by selling computation services. In this case performing the searching locally on the user's own client device may save money, provided the client is strong enough to perform this task. It can also be argued that mobile agents would allow the user to choose between free local computation and for-fee vendor computation.

Assessment: This is an interesting new approach to information foraging in large networks. If mobile agent execution environments can be made prevalent throughout the network, this would offer a good support for this need. Equally however, the provision of intelligent search capabilities at all network servers using non-agent-based communication would seem to accomplish the same result.

4.3 Agents facilitate real-time interaction with server

Another reason for visiting a server is that it has an interface to a unique piece of external equipment, for example a machine tool. If the latency in network transmission is high compared to real-time constraints imposed by the external equipment, then it is desirable to send the controlling program to execute remotely on the server. An extreme case of this is the control software for space probes exploring the distant solar system. A program executing locally, even if interpreted, has a relatively low and certainly bounded latency and can provide more opportunities for error recovery.

Assessment: This seems very valid, although not in the mainstream of network services and hence not a major driver for this assessment.

4.4 Script languages provide better support for heterogeneous environments

Current networks are heterogeneous and will continue to be so. While developing, operating and maintaining heterogeneous network services is more difficult than the homogeneous case, it is less difficult than achieving or maintaining homogeneity in real-world environments. Passing data and commands among heterogeneous computers is more complex, but working solutions do exist and the actual number of useful permutations is not very high; heterogeneity among hardware and software in the same family is roughly as big a problem.

The use of a script language for program and data exchange enables the program and data representation to be independent of the platform, once the script environment has been ported to all necessary platforms. While this is a useful characteristic of script-based programming, it has little to do with mobile agents *per se*. The same advantages can be achieved by text representations of data or queries.

Assessment: This is an argument for a platform-independent means of representing queries, but again that does not require the full programmability of a mobile agent.

4.5 Agent-based queries/transactions can be more robust

In current implementations, RPC communication is relatively fragile. RPC client-server computing was developed for LAN-based systems, where the application developers could make strong assumptions about the integrity of the LAN communication and of the availability of the server. Experience shows that when these client-server applications are extended over wide-area networks, they become less reliable. It seems likely that this problem was responsible in part for GMI's introduction of mobile agents [20]. Mobile agents offer two areas of advantage here:

- The messaging aspect, which provides reliable transport between client and server, without requiring reliable communication. While in principle unreliable communication layers can support RPC, the synchronous nature of this method means that re-transmission delays eventually become unacceptable.
- The recovery aspect, in which the dispatched agent is capable of dealing with the required server being unavailable, or unable to provide the required service. This supposes that the mobile agent program carries with it or knows how to access

knowledge about alternate sources. To avoid this information becoming stale with time, it should either be provided to the agent by the dispatching client, which places a burden on the client to maintain this knowledge or otherwise access such a knowledge base itself, or the agent should itself know where to go and look for the knowledge.

While this appears plausible for simple cases, say duplicate servers, it seems to encumber the mobile agent unless the recovery mechanisms can be made sufficiently general that they are supported by the base classes of the agent framework. In less simple cases, the alternate server may have more or less the same information or transaction service, but require the request to be expressed in a different form. Techniques to permit this kind of transformation are being developed using the Knowledge and Query Manipulation Language (KQML) [8].

If this aspect of robustness is important, and it probably is, then RPC-based client (or server) applications can be made more robust in exactly the same way. If a given RPC request fails, the client can invoke exactly the same knowledge base to look for alternates and has the advantage that it can verify the alteration with the user,

Assessment: While this is a strong claim, it can equally be viewed as a motivation to make alternate communication protocols more robust for WAN-based network services.

4.6 Agent-based transactions & queries can be expressed more flexibly

One of the implicit hopes for intelligent agents is that they will enable (non-specialist) users to enter queries or transactions in natural language without knowing how or where the request can be satisfied. The agents will reformulate the concepts of the query into more precise terms and will identify one or more servers likely to be able to satisfy the request. A mobile agent will then be dispatched with the query and will presumably at some future time return the result to the delighted user.

This again has relatively little to do with mobile agents. The natural language support could be provided for any user interface. The matching of request to server could also be used to set up an RPC-based query. The transport of the request by the mobile agent has nothing to do with enabling the query to be expressed more flexibly.

Assessment: This has nothing to do with mobile agents *per se*.

4.7 Agent-based transactions avoid the need to preserve process state

The need to preserve the entire process state at a client and a server during each flow of a complex operation adds considerably to the burden of client-server computing. Unless the client and server applications provide methods for making the RPC state persistent, which adds a significant performance overhead, failure of either client or server results in the loss of at least one and possibly many operations and recovery mechanisms at either end may generate useless network traffic. The ability of the mobile agent to carry its state around with it appears to relieve the sending computer of the need to preserve state. The state data are also simplified by performing the operation in an interpreted language rather than machine code.

However, the state must now be carried around the network with the mobile agent. This may on the one hand enrich the agent's interactions with servers, since it can express much more of the user's context, but it can also result in the needless transmission of data that the agent will never use. This requires considerable skill on the part of the agent program developer to ensure that the mobile agent carries with it only the necessary and sufficient information.

Assuming that in the future this agent will return to the sending application (or one of the servers that it has visited will send a reply), the sending client must be able to relate the returning agent or other response to the original request. In other words, the sending application must preserve at least the application protocol state. This would seem to be roughly the same as the state information transmitted with the agent, modulo some fine details of the (interpreter) process state, so the saving may not be very great in terms of quantity of storage. However the mobile agent-based operation may be more recoverable than an RPC-based operation, because the operation is asynchronous, hence it can be re-started without strong time constraints and the saved state is at the application protocol, rather than the process level. The client application should, for example be able to re-create a 'lost' agent, which raises the question of how to detect that an agent has been lost [11]. The usual sorts of protocols for distributed transaction processing seem relevant [16].

Assessment: There is an advantage here in the use of mobile agents in terms of the robustness of client-server operations, but it raises also an overhead question and also challenges for the efficient design of mobile agents *per se*. It is likely that similar robustness could also be achieved with alternative client-server methods.

4.8 Agents enable electronic commerce

Mobile agents here offer a number of useful possibilities:

- The agent can express the application-level protocol required to perform a transaction. This includes dialogues on choices and options, configurations, availability, delivery methods, and opportunities for selling up as well as the complete and accurate capture of the information required by the vendor in a particular format. Mobile agents are a plausible method for vendors to distribute the client end of a transaction protocol in a device independent way.
- Alternatively, the mobile agent may be able to present the consumer's desire as a query to a number of potential vendors to determine degree of match, price, availability, and so forth.
- The agent may also be able to consult a 'consumer guide' or other advisor before making a purchase.
- The agent can provide a secure vehicle for the transaction, providing bilateral authentication and privacy.
- The agent can provide a transaction currency for settlement; the agent's account is presumably reconciled periodically against 'real' money.

Of these, the last two are certainly readily replaceable by secure RPC or secure message-based client-server interactions. The first offers a much better facility for software distribution than exists today, although again its functions can be equally well performed by RPC or messaging. Today's methods for distributing application protocols include:

- Application clients preloaded by PC manufacturers.
- Application clients distributed in conjunction with other products, for example modems.
- Application clients downloaded from network sources such as CompuServe (tm.).

The ability of the vendor to distribute clients via a network, preferably to targeted consumers, offers significant reductions in the cost of capturing new customers (on the order of $50 per new customer for application preload). It also exposes the 'dark side' of mobile agents: junk clients, virus clients, dishonest clients.

The second provides a new opportunity, not readily implementable by conventional methods, which is to the advantage of the consumer, in that he or she is not locked into dealing with a particular vendor. In today's model, vendors wishing to support electronic transactions have been forced to integrate their servers with monolithic network services such as Prodigy or America On Line. The user can access only those vendors supported by the service. The vendor can reach only those users subscribed to the service. This 'closed' market place is giving way quite rapidly to an 'open' market place in which users and vendors engage in direct (spontaneous) commerce. Obstacles to the more rapid evolution of this open market place are:

- The difficulties of finding the vendors (lack of a good, global service directory).
- Lack of a common application transaction protocol or the ability of the user to easily acquire the vendor's proprietary application protocol (see obstacle no. 1).
- Lack of privacy and security, although vendors appear willing to perform experiments without solving these problems.

We may expect see numerous experiments in this area in the near future, particularly in the area of extensions to World-Wide Web servers [10].

The third possibility further extends the world of electronic commerce and its analogy with the 'real' world of commerce. We may anticipate a wide range of secondary commercial or quasi-legal services in support of electronic consumerism. As with the second possibility, the degree to which these can be established will depend on the degree to which the service providers wish to establish 'free markets'.

Assessment: Although mobile agents do not offer any technical advantage here, they do offer interesting convenience for vendors and service providers wishing to enable spontaneous electronic commerce, and could offer advantages to consumers.

4.9 Agent-based transactions scale better than RPC-based transactions

This is basically the RPC versus messaging argument described above. The asynchronous nature of mobile agents appears likely to enable higher transaction rates between servers, but a similar result could be achieved by messaging alone. On the other hand, the need to execute the agents and to support rigorous security around the agent execution environment could become significant computational loads in themselves.

How many resident agents would, say, Dow Jones wish to support on its stock price servers? Is it really plausible that hundreds of thousands of agents sit there monitoring the ticker feed? Dow Jones may wish to sell the computational capacity to support this load, or alternatively, third-party servers, which receive the ticker feed from Dow Jones, may offer this as a valued-added service. Of course if Dow Jones can charge for the service of hosting a resident agent, this may be an interesting service business in itself.

Assessment: As a method of supporting simple queries and transactions, mobile agents benefit from the scalability inherent in messaging. Whether agent-based computing itself is efficiently scalable will depend on the extent to which service providers permit generalized computing by resident agents.

4.10 Secure agent-based transactions have lower overhead than secure RPC

The argument here is rooted in the fact that in general several RPCs are required to execute a given transaction, whereas the same transaction could be accomplished by a single mobile agent (presumably of roughly the same size as the total RPC traffic). The overhead of securing a single RPC is presumably similar to the overhead of a single secure agent, so the agent would appear to offer a technical advantage. In practice, secure RPCs are not used for every step of a secure transaction (because of the overhead), unless privacy is the main concern. If authentication is the main concern, practical RPC-based transactions will use a secure RPC only for the final commitment.

Whether the secure agent is more efficient than the secure RPC will also depend on the nature of the transaction; the use of agents may offer better scalability, but introduces much higher latencies.

Assessment: This does not seem very plausible.

4.11 Agents enable users to personalize server behavior

The view here is that servers should offer basic APIs and export them via the bindings of the agent execution environment for exploitation by mobile agent programs. The user (or other agent author) then has the freedom to use the server as he or she sees fit. Thus in the electronic commerce example, if the user wishes to browse the catalogues of several vendors rather than simply using the client application provided by the vendor, he or she has the freedom to dispatch a mobile agent to forage the vendors' servers for information relevant to a purchase. The dark side of this capability is the possibility that viruses and so forth could be introduced to servers as well.

Alternatively, the client could itself periodically execute a (script) program that would fetch information from servers using RPCs or messaging and perform the analysis locally. The arguments against this approach have been reviewed above; they relate to the efficiency of remote versus local filtering and the special problems of mobile computers.

Assessment: On technical grounds, setting the security problems aside, this is a very valuable new capability. We wonder, however, whether service providers will really encourage this form of interaction, which dramatically reduces the control they have over their customers and reduces the server interface to that of information transactor. Security concerns remain significant.

4.12 Agents enable semantic routing

Today's client-server interactions require detailed knowledge at both client and server of each other's application functions and communications protocols and addresses. One of the expectations expressed for mobile agents is to relieve the client and the user of much of these burdens. A user requiring specific information or any other service would express his or her needs in (something like) natural language and the query would be transmitted to a consultant agent. The consultant agent would reformulate the natural language query into the vocabulary and syntax of the Agent Communication Language. It would then consult its own index and possibly the indices of other consultants to identify one or more servers likely to be able to satisfy the query. The consultant would forward the query to these servers and the results would be returned directly to the requesting client. Alternatively, the results might be returned to the consultant which might then engage in a dialogue with the user to refine the search results. Thus the initial query submitted by the user is routed based on its semantic content. This example relates to information retrieval, but the same methods can be used for handling mail, transactions or indeed any of the documents handled by workflow systems.

Although mobile agents certainly facilitate several aspects of this process, there is again nothing here that can be performed exclusively by agents or indeed significantly better than by other means. The query reformulation process is purely a natural language activity that could equally well be applied to messages and could in principle be performed directly at the client rather than by a separate consultant. The indexing of server content is certainly facilitated by mobile agents, but can be accomplished in other ways. The submission of a reformulated query to multiple servers is well known in the absence of agents. The refinement of query results is certainly a good application for intelligent agents, but again is not specific to mobile agents.

Assessment: Although mobile agents offer no exclusive advantage for this application, nonetheless it is a very plausible application for mobile agents, because the same mechanism can be used to integrate clients, consultants and servers. While this case is not convincing alone, it illustrates nicely the flexibility of the approach.

4.13 Mobile agents enable intelligent mail handling

Intelligent mail handling is the ability to determine the method and timing of mail delivery based on the semantic content of the mail item, under the control of rules established by the recipient of the mail [9]. This is effectively a form of semantic routing. In the AT&T Personalink service [1], mail was transported by courier agents programmed in Telescript. Since the courier agent object class will be present at every agent execution environment, the courier agent actually needs only to identify itself as an instance of this class; there is no need to actually transport any method code in this case. The Personalink (or MagicMail) framework provides agent execution environments which can be visited by the courier agent and where the courier agent can engage in a dialogue with the host which routes the agent to the recipient's outpost (mailbox) in the current domain or directly to the recipient's domain (client device), if this is connected. The recipient's outpost may contain an intelligent agent which extracts key attributes from the courier agent and uses its rule set to determine how the courier item should be handled. The value of using a courier agent for mail transport rather than a simple mail transport protocol could lie in the general value of object encapsulation, in security services (authentication, non-repudiation, privacy, anonymity, payment), or in the ability to take part in translation services, although as usual, it is by no means clear that courier agents offer unique advantages for these purposes.

As with the semantic routing discussion above, there is nothing in this function which is intrinsic to mobile agents. The courier agent serves as the transport mechanism; the intelligent handling comes from the actions resulting at the intelligent agent from the mail arrival event.

Assessment: Intelligent mail services depend on the processing of mail attributes by an intelligent program. Mobile agents are a convenient transport mechanism for mail, but have no essential role in the rule-based attribute processing.

4.14 Agents can be prototypes for RPC applications

As was mentioned above, most applications which can be realized via mobile agents can also, often better, be realized via RPC. In order for this to happen, however, the application actually has to be implemented, standardized, and widely installed. This is, at best, a difficult and lengthy process. At worst, the application may be implemented poorly as standards constrain it before real experience with the application is obtained. In some cases, the application may never get off the ground at all, because it cannot gain wide enough acceptance without people actually seeing it work.

An agent-based interim implementation, on the other hand, can be done without a lengthy standards process. The agent is self-contained and flexible. It is thus capable of functioning with relatively little coordination with existing software. Even though it may function less efficiently than an RPC implementation which is more tightly coupled to the resident software and even though it may be functionally constrained to preserve the security of the host system, it can still be used as the basis for a prototype implementation of the application which can be used as a proof of concept and a vehicle to evaluate features and tradeoffs in the application. On the basis of experience gained with this prototype, a more informed decision can be made as to whether it ultimately is best to embark on a standardized RPC-based implementation, retain the agent-based implementation, or abandon the application entirely.

Assessment: Agent-based implementations offer the opportunity to rapidly prototype and refine an application more quickly and inexpensively than via RPC. The constraints which need to be imposed on the agents for security reasons and the inefficiencies imposed by relatively loose coupling with resident applications may lead to a pessimistic evaluation. Overall, however, it may be better to evaluate an application this way rather than simply by architectural discussions.

5 Assessment of Aggregate Advantages (Forest)

We have seen above that while there are many individual areas where mobile agents offer advantages, no single advantage is overwhelming alone. In almost every case, an equivalent solution can be found that does not require mobile agents. However, if we stand back and look at the sum of these advantages, that is all the functions that a mobile agent framework enables, then a much stronger case emerges. Benjamin Grosof has referred to this as the "software engineering" argument: *whereas each individual case can be addressed in some (ad hoc) manner without mobile agents, a mobile agent framework addresses all of them at once.*

Many of the counter arguments advanced above are of the form: "instead of using agents to do the work remotely at the server, you could just as well do it at the client". It may not matter in theory how we split up function between the client and the server, but it may be critical in practice, because clients and servers are controlled by different people, and work under different sets of constraints.

Consider PostScript (tm.), for instance (as GMI clearly did): it involves having a standard interpreter that runs on print servers. A user who wants something printed sends a program to the server, which executes it and produces the output. How valid would it be to argue that this is not really necessary, and the print servers themselves could be in charge of accepting and formatting passive input text, since if someone comes up with a new format for a document, one could just update all the printers in the world to know about the new format? It is true in theory, but absurd in practice.

The statement "It is true that it will be difficult to get agreement on a standard search engine, but then it will also be difficult to get agreement on a standard agent environment" misses this point in a similar way: we only have to get agreement on a standard agent environment once, and after that everyone can write whatever clever search and foraging agents they want to. If the function is implemented in the server code, on the other hand, any new kind of operation (a cleverer search, a personalized foraging style, etc.) will have to wait for server updates before it can be used.

We have seen in the last few years what can be achieved by providing and disseminating a standard information server (WWW server) and clients. The HTTP protocol has been so successful that further progress in making information available via the Internet is only discussed in terms of extensions to Web servers and clients. Various experiments to provide mobile agent extensions to Web servers are underway, and more will continue to appear. Eventually one of these will be successful and will be deployed very quickly on thousands of servers.

The argument is thus: once we have reached agreement on how to provide a generalized, machine-independent execution environment which can bind to and enable the secure exploitation of server-specific capabilities, we will have created a completely general framework for network-based services, including:

- Information foraging,
- Semantic routing,
- Electronic commerce,
- Targeted dissemination of information, and
- Dissemination of the client side of application protocols.

That is, the framework is almost arbitrarily extensible to support network-based services, provided that the infrastructure is essentially ubiquitous.

In practice, the success of a particular infrastructure for mobile agents depends upon:

- Doing the job well, and
- Getting it widely adopted.

The latter challenge seems to be at least as difficult as the former; at present, all attempts at frameworks built upon proprietary networks have either failed or, as in the case of Telescript, redirected themselves toward TCP/IP-based internets and intranets. On the other hand, the rapid spread of standards (and proto-standards) on the Internet suggests that an infrastructure for fully-mobile agents *could* become widespread quickly if it was perceived as valuable.

In summary, the lack of overwhelming strengths among the individual trees should not blind us to the overwhelming value of the forest as a whole.

6 Conclusions

- With one rather narrow exception, there is nothing that can be done with mobile agents that cannot also be done with other means. The exception is remote real-time control where the network latency prevents real-time constraints being met by remote command sequences.
- The individual advantages of mobile agents therefore rest on relative technical and commercial factors compared to alternative methods. The technical advantages of mobile agents identified in this assessment are:
  - High bandwidth remote interaction
  - Support for disconnected operation
  - Support for weak clients
  - Ease of distributing individual service clients
  - Semantic routing
  - Scalability
  - Lower overhead for secure transactions
  - Robust remote interaction
- While none of the individual advantages of mobile agents given above is over-whelmingly strong, we believe that the aggregate advantage of mobile agents is overwhelmingly strong, because:
  - They can provide a pervasive, open, generalized framework for the development and personalization of network services.
  - While alternatives to mobile agents can be advanced for each of the individual advantages, there is no single alternative to all of the functionality supported by a mobile agent framework.
  - In addition to providing an efficient support for existing services, a mobile agent framework also enables new, derivative network services and hence new businesses.
  - Mobile agents are expected to appeal strongly to the Internet community, since they can provide an effective means for dealing with the problems of finding services and information and since they empower the individual user.
- The individual technical disadvantages of mobile agents identified in this assessment are:
  - Need for highly secure agent execution environments.

- Performance and functional limitations resulting from security.
- Virus scanning and epidemic control mechanisms.
- Transmission efficiency, for example a courier agent compared to a simple SMTP mail object.

The security and virus problems in particular require very close study and considerable technical innovation.

- Commercial issues raised by mobile agents include:
  - Difficulty of propagating agent execution environments onto large numbers of third-party servers.
  - Balance to be struck between open and closed electronic commerce.
  - Trust on the part of third-party server providers in the face of security concerns.
  - Willingness of the third-party server providers to permit users the ability to customize server behavior.
  - Willingness of the third-party server providers to support the computational load of mobile agents.
  - Perceived value among users.
  - Enthusiasm for this approach among the Internet community.
- This assessment suggests further studies:
  - What degree of expressiveness can be safely accepted in an agent scripting language? Is it possible to devise languages that permit the expression of useful, quasi-general procedures, but which permit the non-existence of viruses to be proven?
  - How strong are the qualitative arguments for performance advantages? How do existing services compare with hypothetical mobile agent-based services?
  - Alternatively, what could be done to enable RPC-based client-server interactions to match the advantages of mobile agents?

The mobile agent approach continues to intrigue and shows signs of offering important qualitative advantages for network services. Assuming that solutions to the security problems can be found - and efforts are underway - the signs are sufficiently positive that we cannot rule out the possibility that mobile agents will be a successful new method of client-server interaction in network services. We are now engaged in developing plans to prudently explore this opportunity.

7 Acknowledgements

The need for this assessment emerged from many discussions of various topics related to intelligent and mobile agents. Many ideas expressed herein originated among members of the following group: Stephen Brady, Benjamin Grosof, Jeff Kephart, David Levine, the OREXX team, Colin Parris, Abhay Parekh, Phil Rosenfeld, Ted Selker, Steve White, Robin Williamson, and, of course, the Magicians.

References

1. Paula Bernier. Telescript's agents do the job. *Telephony,* 226(3):16, January 1994.

2. A. Birrell and B. J. Nelson. Implementing Remote Procedure Calls. *ACM Transactions on Computer Systems* 2:39-59, February 1984.

3. J. K. Boggs. IBM Remote Job Entry Facility: Generalized Subsystem Remote Job Entry Facility. *IBM Technical Disclosure Bulletin,* 752, August 1973.

4. F. Cohen. Computer Viruses: Theory and Experiment. *Computers and Security* 6:22-35, 1987.

5. R. J. Cypser. Communications for cooperating systems, pages 232-241. Addison Wesley, 1991.

6. R. J. Cypser. Communications for cooperating systems, pages 244-245. Addison Wesley, 1991.

7. M. Crowley-Milling et al. The Nodal System for the SPS. CERN, 78-87, 1978.

8. T. Finin, R. Fritzson, D. McKay, and R. McEntire. KQML as an Agent Communication Language. In *The Proceedings of the Third International Conference on Information and Knowledge Management (CIKM '94),* ACM Press, November 1994.

9. C. G. Harrison. Smart Networks and Intelligent Agents. *Proceedings of MediaCom '95,* April 1995.

10. T. Berners Lee, R. Cailliau, A. Luotonen, H. Frystyk Nielsen, and A. Secret. The World Wide Web. *Communications of the ACM,* 37(8):76-82, August 1994.

11. Y.-N. Lien and C-W. R. Leng. On the search of mobile agents. In *Proceedings of the 7th IEEE Symposium on Personal, Indoor, and Radio Communications,* October 1996.

12. Patty Maes and R. Brooks, editors. *A Biologically Inspired Immune System for Computers.* MIT Press, 1994.

13. Gerald Neufeld and Son Vuong. Overview of ASN.1. *Computer Networks and ISDN Systems* 23(5):393-415, February 1992.

14. J. K. Ousterhout. *TcL and the Tk toolkit.* Addison-Wesley Publication Commpany, 1994.

15. D. L. Presotto and D. M. Ritchie. Interprocessor Communication in the Eighth Edition UNIX System. Proceedings of the 1992 USENIX conference, June 1985.

16. M. Sherman. Architecture of the Encina distributed transaction processing family. *ACM SIGMOD, International Conference on Management of Data,* May 1993.

17. A. Tannenbaum. *Computer Networks, 2nd ed.* Prentice-Hall Publishing, 1988.

18. Chii Ren Tsai and V. D. Gligor. Distributed Systems and Security Management with Centralized Control. *Proceedings of the Spring 1992 EurOpen/USENIX Workshop,* April 1992.

19. J. E. White. Telescript Technology: The Foundation for the Electronic Marketplace. General Magic Inc., Mountain View, CA, 1994.

20. James White. *RPC over WANs.* General Magic, Inc., private communication, August 1992.

Mobile Agents: Are They a Good Idea? – Update

David Chess, Colin Harrison, Aaron Kershenbaum

1 Update

The original version of this assessment was carried out in 1994, but all the major issues that it identified are still true today, and some of its predictions are coming to pass.

Web-based technologies, and in particular Java and ActiveX, have taken the limelight away from the Telescript model, at least in the short term. Whatever intrinsic merits these new technologies have, from the point of view of mobile agent systems they are degenerate cases. In their current forms, neither Java nor ActiveX allows an executing agent to be packaged and transmitted to a new server; the only "mobility" an agent has in these systems is a single transmission, with no state information, from an http server to a Web client, where it is executed and where it ultimately terminates.

Even in this reduced form, security has proven to be a difficult problem. Java addresses security concerns by executing agents in an interpreted environment, and strictly limiting what agents loaded from remote servers ("applets") are permitted to do. ActiveX, on the other hand, provides digitally signed agents to allow a user to verify the identity of the agent's creator, but once the agent (or "ActiveX control") is allowed to execute, it has access to all the facilities of the system, with no further security applied. In both cases, the current security solutions are known to be less than optimal, and research on improving them is ongoing.

The main attraction currently driving the popularity of Java and ActiveX is the ability to easily (even trivially) distribute code to end users. The paper anticipates this, citing mobile agents as "a plausible method for vendors to distribute the client end of a transaction protocol in a device independant way". This motivation has turned out to be stronger than we anticipated, but it remains to be seen whether it can by itself cause true mobile agent technology to become widespread.

As of this writing, the primary use of mobile agent technologies in the World Wide Web is to add attractive graphics and other effects to Web pages. This is an application that we anticipated only very indirectly, under "real-time interaction with servers". In the present case, the server is in fact the end-user's workstation, and the "external equipment" is the user! By having the agent (Java or Javascript program or ActiveX control) run on the user's workstation, real-time graphics and interaction can occur without the latency of constant interaction with the http server.

Systems have appeared to allow resident agents to "camp" on a database or server and perform filtering and notification actions on a user's behalf, as we anticipated. (Companies such as Lotus and Verity provide languages and toolkits for creating such agents; as with so much other nascent network technology, these developments are advertised on the respective companies' Web sites, and not described in easily-citable publications.) These systems are just beginning to be used in real applications.

While these limited-mobility systems have taken most of the public's attention, work on truly mobile agent systems continues, as the other papers in this volume demonstrate.

Some of the authors of this assessment have gone on to explore possible architectures for heterogenous mobile agents [3], security considerations in agent systems [2], and the agent field as a whole [1]. While the jury is still out on just how large the niche for these systems will ultimately be, the arguments in the original assessment still stand, and we believe that time will show that overall mobile agents, whatever we eventually choose to call them, are in fact a good idea in many contexts.

References

1. A. K. Caglayan and C. G. Harrison. *The Agent Sourcebook*. John Wiley & Sons, Inc., May 1997.
2. D. Chess. Security considerations in agent-based systems. In *Conference on Emerging Technologies and Applications in Communications (etaCOM '96)*, Portland, 1996.
3. D. M. Chess, B. Grosof, C. Harrison, D. Levine, C. Parris, and G. Tsudik. Itinerant agents for mobile computing. *IEEE Personal Communications Magazine*, October 1995.

A Note on Distributed Computing

Jim Waldo, Geoff Wyant, Ann Wollrath, and Sam Kendall

1 Introduction[1]

Much of the current work in distributed, object-oriented systems is based on the assumption that objects form a single ontological class. This class consists of all entities that can be fully described by the specification of the set of interfaces supported by the object and the semantics of the operations in those interfaces. The class includes objects that share a single address space, objects that are in separate address spaces on the same machine, and objects that are in separate address spaces on different machines (with, perhaps, different architectures). On the view that all objects are essentially the same kind of entity, these differences in relative location are merely an aspect of the implementation of the object. Indeed, the location of an object may change over time, as an object migrates from one machine to another or the implementation of the object changes.

It is the thesis of this note that this unified view of objects is mistaken. There are fundamental differences between the interactions of distributed objects and the interactions of non-distributed objects. Further, work in distributed object-oriented systems that is based on a model that ignores or denies these differences is doomed to failure, and could easily lead to an industry-wide rejection of the notion of distributed object-based systems.

1.1 Terminology

In what follows, we will talk about local and distributed computing. By *local computing* (local object invocation, etc.), we mean programs that are confined to a single address space. In contrast, we will use the term *distributed computing* (remote object invocation, etc.) to refer to programs that make calls to other address spaces, possibly on another machine. In the case of distributed computing, nothing is known about the recipient of the call (other than that it supports a particular interface). For example, the client of such a distributed object does not know the hardware architecture on which the recipient of the call is running, or the language in which the recipient was implemented.

Given the above characterizations of "local" and "distributed" computing, the categories are not exhaustive. There is a middle ground, in which calls are made from one address space to another but in which some characteristics of the called object are known. An important class of this sort consists of calls from one address space to another on the same machine; we will discuss these later in the paper.

---

1. This paper (with the exception of the Afterword) was first published as Sun Microsystems Technical Report SML 94-29, 1994. Copyright Sun Microsystems. This version is dedicated tothe memory of Geoff Wyant.

2 The Vision of Unified Objects

There is an overall vision of distributed object-oriented computing in which, from the programmer's point of view, there is no essential distinction between objects that share an address space and objects that are on two machines with different architectures located on different continents. While this view can most recently be seen in such works as the Object Management Group's Common Object Request Broker Architecture (CORBA) [1], it has a history that includes such research systems as Arjuna [2], Emerald [3], and Clouds [4].

In such systems, an object, whether local or remote, is defined in terms of a set of interfaces declared in an interface definition language. The implementation of the object is independent of the interface and hidden from other objects. While the underlying mechanisms used to make a method call may differ depending on the location of the object, those mechanisms are hidden from the programmer who writes exactly the same code for either type of call, and the system takes care of delivery.

This vision can be seen as an extension of the goal of remote procedure call (RPC) systems to the object-oriented paradigm. RPC systems attempt to make cross-address space function calls look (to the client programmer) like local function calls. Extending this to the object-oriented programming paradigm allows papering over not just the marshalling of parameters and the unmarshalling of results (as is done in RPC systems) but also the locating and connecting to the target objects. Given the isolation of an object's implementation from clients of the object, the use of objects for distributed computing seems natural. Whether a given object invocation is local or remote is a function of the implementation of the objects being used, and could possibly change from one method invocation to another on any given object.

Implicit in this vision is that the system will be "objects all the way down"; that is, that all current invocations or calls for system services will be eventually converted into calls that might be to an object residing on some other machine. There is a single paradigm of object use and communication used no matter what the location of the object might be.

In actual practice, of course, a local member function call and a cross-continent object invocation are not the same thing. The vision is that developers write their applications so that the objects within the application are joined using the same programmatic glue as objects between applications, but it does not require that the two kinds of glue be implemented the same way. What is needed is a variety of implementation techniques, ranging from same-address-space implementations like Microsoft's Object Linking and Embedding [5] to typical network RPC; different needs for speed, security, reliability, and object co-location can be met by using the right "glue" implementation.

Writing a distributed application in this model proceeds in three phases. The first phase is to write the application without worrying about where objects are located and how their communication is implemented. The developer will simply strive for the natural and correct interface between objects. The system will choose reasonable defaults for object location, and depending on how performance-critical the application is, it may be possible to alpha test it with no further work. Such an approach will enforce a desirable separation between the abstract architecture of the application and any needed performance tuning.

The second phase is to tune performance by "concretizing" object locations and communication methods. At this stage, it may be necessary to use as yet unavailable tools to allow analysis of the communication patterns between objects, but it is certainly conceivable that such tools could be produced. Also during the second phase, the right set of interfaces to export to various clients—such as other applications—can be chosen. There is obviously tremendous flexibility here for the application developer. This seems to be the sort of development scenario that is being advocated in systems like Fresco [6], which claim that the decision to make an object local or remote can be put off until after initial system implementation.

The final phase is to test with "real bullets" (e.g., networks being partitioned, machines going down). Interfaces between carefully selected objects can be beefed up as necessary to deal with these sorts of partial failures introduced by distribution by adding replication, transactions, or whatever else is needed. The exact set of these services can be determined only by experience that will be gained during the development of the system and the first applications that will work on the system.

A central part of the vision is that if an application is built using objects all the way down, in a proper object-oriented fashion, the right "fault points" at which to insert process or machine boundaries will emerge naturally. But if you initially make the wrong choices, they are very easy to change.

One conceptual justification for this vision is that whether a call is local or remote has no impact on the correctness of a program. If an object supports a particular interface, and the support of that interface is semantically correct, it makes no difference to the correctness of the program whether the operation is carried out within the same address space, on some other machine, or off-line by some other piece of equipment. Indeed, seeing location as a part of the implementation of an object and therefore as part of the state that an object hides from the outside world appears to be a natural extension of the object-oriented paradigm.

Such a system would enjoy many advantages. It would allow the task of software maintenance to be changed in a fundamental way. The granularity of change, and therefore of upgrade, could be changed from the level of the entire system (the current model) to the level of the individual object. As long as the interfaces between objects remain constant, the implementations of those objects can be altered at will. Remote services can be moved into an address space, and objects that share an address space can be split and moved to different machines, as local requirements and needs dictate. An object can be repaired and the repair installed without worry that the change will impact the other objects that make up the system. Indeed, this model appears to be the best way to get away from the "Big Wad of Software" model that currently is causing so much trouble.

This vision is centered around the following principles that may, at first, appear plausible:

- there is a single natural object-oriented design for a given application, regardless of the context in which that application will be deployed;

- failure and performance issues are tied to the implementation of the components of an application, and consideration of these issues should be left out of an initial design; and
- the interface of an object is independent of the context in which that object is used.

Unfortunately, all of these principles are false. In what follows, we will show why these principles are mistaken, and why it is important to recognize the fundamental differences between distributed computing and local computing.

3 Déjà Vu All Over Again

For those of us either old enough to have experienced it or interested enough in the history of computing to have learned about it, the vision of unified objects is quite familiar. The desire to merge the programming and computational models of local and remote computing is not new.

Communications protocol development has tended to follow two paths. One path has emphasized integration with the current language model. The other path has emphasized solving the problems inherent in distributed computing. Both are necessary, and successful advances in distributed computing synthesize elements from both camps.

Historically, the language approach has been the less influential of the two camps. Every ten years (approximately), members of the language camp notice that the number of distributed applications is relatively small. They look at the programming interfaces and decide that the problem is that the programming model is not close enough to whatever programming model is currently in vogue (messages in the 1970s [7], [8], procedure calls in the 1980s [9], [10], [11], and objects in the 1990s [1], [2]). A furious bout of language and protocol design takes place and a new distributed computing paradigm is announced that is compliant with the latest programming model. After several years, the percentage of distributed applications is discovered not to have increased significantly, and the cycle begins anew.

A possible explanation for this cycle is that each round is an evolutionary stage for both the local and the distributed programming paradigm. The repetition of the pattern is a result of neither model being sufficient to encompass both activities at any previous stage. However, (this explanation continues) each iteration has brought us closer to a unification of the local and distributed computing models. The current iteration, based on the object-oriented approach to both local and distributed programming, will be the one that produces a single computational model that will suffice for both.

A less optimistic explanation of the failure of each attempt at unification holds that any such attempt will fail for the simple reason that programming distributed applications is not the same as programming non-distributed applications. Just making the communications paradigm the same as the language paradigm is insufficient to make programming distributed programs easier, because communicating between the parts of a distributed application is not the difficult part of that application.

The hard problems in distributed computing are not the problems of how to get things on and off the wire. The hard problems in distributed computing concern dealing with partial failure and the lack of a central resource manager. The hard problems in distributed computing concern insuring adequate performance and dealing with problems of concurrency. The hard problems have to do with differences in memory access paradigms between local and distributed entities. People attempting to write distributed applications quickly discover that they are spending all of their efforts in these areas and not on the communications protocol programming interface.

This is not to argue against pleasant programming interfaces. However, the law of diminishing returns comes into play rather quickly. Even with a perfect programming model of complete transparency between "fine-grained," language-level objects and "larger-grained" distributed objects, the number of distributed applications would not be noticeably larger if these other problems have not been addressed.

All of this suggests that there is interesting and profitable work to be done in distributed computing, but it needs to be done at a much higher-level than that of "fine-grained" object integration. Providing developers with tools that help manage the complexity of handling the problems of distributed application development as opposed to the generic application development is an area that has been poorly addressed.

4 Local and Distributed Computing

The major differences between local and distributed computing concern the areas of latency, memory access, partial failure, and concurrency.[1] The difference in latency is the most obvious, but in many ways is the least fundamental. The often overlooked differences concerning memory access, partial failure, and concurrency are far more difficult to explain away, and the differences concerning partial failure and concurrency make unifying the local and remote computing models impossible without making unacceptable compromises.

4.1 Latency

The most obvious difference between a local object invocation and the invocation of an operation on a remote (or possibly remote) object has to do with the latency of the two calls. The difference between the two is currently between four and five orders of magnitude, and given the relative rates at which processor speed and network latency speeds are changing, the difference in the future promises to be at best no better, and will likely be worse. It is this disparity in efficiency that is often seen as the essential difference between local and distributed computing.

Ignoring the difference between the performance of local and remote invocations can lead to designs whose implementations are virtually assured of having performance problems because the design requires a large amount of communication between components that are in different address spaces and on different machines. Ignoring the difference in the time it takes to make a remote object invocation and the time it takes to make a local object invocation is to ignore one of the major design areas of an application. A properly designed application will require determining, by understanding the

---

1. We are not the first to notice these differences; indeed, they are clearly stated in [12].

application being designed, what objects can be made remote and what objects must be clustered together.

The vision outlined earlier, however, has an answer to this objection. The answer is two-pronged. The first prong is to rely on the steadily increasing speed of the underlying hardware to make the difference in latency irrelevant. This, it is often argued, is what has happened to efficiency concerns having to do with everything from high level languages to virtual memory. Designing at the cutting edge has always required that the hardware catch up before the design is efficient enough for the real world. Arguments from efficiency seem to have gone out of style in software engineering, since in the past such concerns have always been answered by speed increases in the underlying hardware.

The second prong of the reply is to admit to the need for tools that will allow one to see what the pattern of communication is between the objects that make up an application. Once such tools are available, it will be a matter of tuning to bring objects that are in constant contact to the same address space, while moving those that are in relatively infrequent contact to wherever is most convenient. Since the vision allows all objects to communicate using the same underlying mechanism, such tuning will be possible by simply altering the implementation details (such as object location) of the relevant objects. However, it is important to get the application correct first, and after that one can worry about efficiency.

Whether or not it will ever become possible to mask the efficiency difference between a local object invocation and a distributed object invocation is not answerable *a priori*. Fully masking the distinction would require not only advances in the technology underlying remote object invocation, but would also require changes to the general programming model used by developers.

If the only difference between local and distributed object invocations was the difference in the amount of time it took to make the call, one could strive for a future in which the two kinds of calls would be conceptually indistinguishable. Whether the technology of distributed computing has moved far enough along to allow one to plan products based on such technology would be a matter of judgement, and rational people could disagree as to the wisdom of such an approach.

However, the difference in latency between the two kinds of calls is only the most obvious difference. Indeed, this difference is not really the fundamental difference between the two kinds of calls, and that even if it were possible to develop the technology of distributed calls to an extent that the difference in latency between the two sorts of calls was minimal, it would be unwise to construct a programming paradigm that treated the two calls as essentially similar. In fact, the difference in latency between local and remote calls, because it is so obvious, has been the only difference most see between the two, and has tended to mask the more irreconcilable differences.

4.2 Memory access

A more fundamental (but still obvious) difference between local and remote computing concerns the access to memory in the two cases—specifically in the use of pointers. Simply put, pointers in a local address space are not valid in another (remote) address space. The system can paper over this difference, but for such an approach to be successful, the transparency must be complete. Two choices exist: either all memory access must be controlled by the underlying system, or the programmer must be aware of the different types of access—local and remote. There is no in-between.

If the desire is to completely unify the programming model—to make remote accesses behave as if they were in fact local—the underlying mechanism must totally control all memory access. Providing distributed shared memory is one way of completely relieving the programmer from worrying about remote memory access (or the difference between local and remote). Using the object-oriented paradigm to the fullest, and requiring the programmer to build an application with "objects all the way down," (that is, only object references or values are passed as method arguments) is another way to eliminate the boundary between local and remote computing. The layer underneath can exploit this approach by marshalling and unmarshalling method arguments and return values for intra-address space transmission.

But adding a layer that allows the replacement of all pointers to objects with object references only *permits* the developer to adopt a unified model of object interaction. Such a unified model cannot be *enforced* unless one also removes the ability to get address-space-relative pointers from the language used by the developer. Such an approach erects a barrier to programmers who want to start writing distributed applications, in that it requires that those programmers learn a new style of programming which does not use address-space-relative pointers. In requiring that programmers learn such a language, moreover, one gives up the complete transparency between local and distributed computing.

Even if one were to provide a language that did not allow obtaining address-space-relative pointers to objects (or returned an object reference whenever such a pointer was requested), one would need to provide an equivalent way of making cross-address space reference to entities other than objects. Most programmers use pointers as references for many different kinds of entities. These pointers must either be replaced with something that can be used in cross-address space calls or the programmer will need to be aware of the difference between such calls (which will either not allow pointers to such entities, or do something special with those pointers) and local calls. Again, while this could be done, it does violate the doctrine of complete unity between local and remote calls. Because of memory access constraints, the two *have* to differ.

The danger lies in promoting the myth that "remote access and local access are exactly the same" and not enforcing the myth. An underlying mechanism that does not unify all memory accesses while still promoting this myth is both misleading and prone to error. Programmers buying into the myth may believe that they do not have to change the way they think about programming. The programmer is therefore quite likely to make the mistake of using a pointer in the wrong context, producing incorrect results. "Remote is just like local," such programmers think, "so we have just one unified programming model." Seemingly, programmers need not change their style of programming. In an incomplete implementation of the underlying mechanism, or one that allows an implementation language that in turn allows direct access to local memory, the system does not take care of all memory accesses, and errors are bound to occur.

These errors occur because the programmer is not aware of the difference between local and remote access and what is actually happening "under the covers."

The alternative is to explain the difference between local and remote access, making the programmer aware that remote address space access is very different from local access. Even if some of the pain is taken away by using an interface definition language like that specified in [1] and having it generate an intelligent language mapping for operation invocation on distributed objects, the programmer aware of the difference will not make the mistake of using pointers for cross-address space access. The programmer will know it is incorrect. By not masking the difference, the programmer is able to learn when to use one method of access and when to use the other.

Just as with latency, it is logically possible that the difference between local and remote memory access could be completely papered over and a single model of both presented to the programmer. When we turn to the problems introduced to distributed computing by partial failure and concurrency, however, it is not clear that such a unification is even conceptually possible.

4.3   Partial failure and concurrency

While unlikely, it is at least logically possible that the differences in latency and memory access between local computing and distributed computing could be masked. It is not clear that such a masking could be done in such a way that the local computing paradigm could be used to produce distributed applications, but it might still be possible to allow some new programming technique to be used for both activities. Such a masking does not even seem to be logically possible, however, in the case of partial failure and concurrency. These aspects appear to be different in kind in the case of distributed and local computing.[1]

Partial failure is a central reality of distributed computing. Both the local and the distributed world contain components that are subject to periodic failure. In the case of local computing, such failures are either total, affecting all of the entities that are working together in an application, or detectable by some central resource allocator (such as the operating system on the local machine).

This is not the case in distributed computing, where one component (machine, network link) can fail while the others continue. Not only is the failure of the distributed components independent, but there is no common agent that is able to determine what component has failed and inform the other components of that failure, no global state that can be examined that allows determination of exactly what error has occurred. In a distributed system, the failure of a network link is indistinguishable from the failure of a processor on the other side of that link.

These sorts of failures are not the same as mere exception raising or the inability to complete a task, which can occur in the case of local computing. This type of failure is caused when a machine crashes during the execution of an object invocation or a network link goes down, occurrences that cause the target object to simply disappear rather

---

1. In fact, authors such as Schroeder [12] and Hadzilacos and Toueg [13] take partial failure and concurrency to be the defining problems of distributed computing.

than return control to the caller. A central problem in distributed computing is insuring that the state of the whole system is consistent after such a failure; this is a problem that simply does not occur in local computing.

The reality of partial failure has a profound effect on how one designs interfaces and on the semantics of the operations in an interface. Partial failure requires that programs deal with indeterminacy. When a local component fails, it is possible to know the state of the system that caused the failure and the state of the system after the failure. No such determination can be made in the case of a distributed system. Instead, the interfaces that are used for the communication must be designed in such a way that it is possible for the objects to react in a consistent way to possible partial failures.

Being robust in the face of partial failure requires some expression at the interface level. Merely improving the implementation of one component is not sufficient. The interfaces that connect the components must be able to state whenever possible the cause of failure, and there must be interfaces that allow reconstruction of a reasonable state when failure occurs and the cause cannot be determined.

If an object is coresident in an address space with its caller, partial failure is not possible. A function may not complete normally, but it always completes. There is no indeterminism about how much of the computation completed. Partial completion can occur only as a result of circumstances that will cause the other components to fail.

The addition of partial failure as a possibility in the case of distributed computing does not mean that a single object model cannot be used for both distributed computing and local computing. The question is not "can you make remote method invocation look like local method invocation?" but rather "what is the price of making remote method invocation identical to local method invocation?" One of two paths must be chosen if one is going to have a unified model.

The first path is to treat all objects as if they were local and design all interfaces as if the objects calling them, and being called by them, were local. The result of choosing this path is that the resulting model, when used to produce distributed systems, is essentially indeterministic in the face of partial failure and consequently fragile and non-robust. This path essentially requires ignoring the extra failure modes of distributed computing. Since one can't get rid of those failures, the price of adopting the model is to require that such failures are unhandled and catastrophic.

The other path is to design all interfaces as if they were remote. That is, the semantics and operations are all designed to be deterministic in the face of failure, both total and partial. However, this introduces unnecessary guarantees and semantics for objects that are never intended to be used remotely. Like the approach to memory access that attempts to require that all access is through system-defined references instead of pointers, this approach must also either rely on the discipline of the programmers using the system or change the implementation language so that all of the forms of distributed indeterminacy are forced to be dealt with on all object invocations.

This approach would also defeat the overall purpose of unifying the object models. The real reason for attempting such a unification is to make distributed computing more like local computing and thus make distributed computing easier. This second approach to unifying the models makes local computing as complex as distributed computing.

Rather than encouraging the production of distributed applications, such a model will discourage its own adoption by making all object-based computing more difficult.

Similar arguments hold for concurrency. Distributed objects by their nature must handle concurrent method invocations. The same dichotomy applies if one insists on a unified programming model. Either all objects must bear the weight of concurrency semantics, or all objects must ignore the problem and hope for the best when distributed. Again, this is an interface issue and not solely an implementation issue, since dealing with concurrency can take place only by passing information from one object to another through the agency of the interface. So either the overall programming model must ignore significant modes of failure, resulting in a fragile system; or the overall programming model must assume a worst-case complexity model for all objects within a program, making the production of any program, distributed or not, more difficult.

One might argue that a multi-threaded application needs to deal with these same issues. However, there is a subtle difference. In a multi-threaded application, there is no real source of indeterminacy of invocations of operations. The application programmer has complete control over invocation order when desired. A distributed system by its nature introduces truly asynchronous operation invocations. Further, a non-distributed system, even when multi-threaded, is layered on top of a single operating system that can aid the communication between objects and can be used to determine and aid in synchronization and in the recovery of failure. A distributed system, on the other hand, has no single point of resource allocation, synchronization, or failure recovery, and thus is conceptually very different.

5   The Myth of "Quality of Service"

One could take the position that the way an object deals with latency, memory access, partial failure, and concurrency control is really an aspect of the implementation of that object, and is best described as part of the "quality of service" provided by that implementation. Different implementations of an interface may provide different levels of reliability, scalability, or performance. If one wants to build a more reliable system, one merely needs to choose more reliable implementations of the interfaces making up the system.

On the surface, this seems quite reasonable. If I want a more robust system, I go to my catalog of component vendors. I quiz them about their test methods. I see if they have ISO9000 certification, and I buy my components from the one I trust the most. The components all comply with the defined interfaces, so I can plug them right in; my system is robust and reliable, and I'm happy.

Let us imagine that I build an application that uses the (mythical) queue interface to enqueue work for some component. My application dutifully enqueues records that represent work to be done. Another application dutifully dequeues them and performs the work. After a while, I notice that my application crashes due to time-outs. I find this extremely annoying, but realize that it's my fault. My application just isn't robust enough. It gives up too easily on a time-out. So I change my application to retry the operation until it succeeds. Now I'm happy. I almost never see a time-out. Unfortunately, I now have another problem. Some of the requests seem to get processed two, three, four, or more times. How can this be? The component I bought which implements the queue has allegedly been rigorously tested. It shouldn't be doing this. I'm angry. I call the vendor and yell at him. After much fingerpointing and research, the culprit is found. The problem turns out to be the way I'm using the queue. Because of my handling of partial failures (which in my naivete, I had thought to be total), I have been enqueuing work requests multiple times.

Well, I yell at the vendor that it is still their fault. Their queue should be detecting the duplicate entry and removing it. I'm not going to continue using this software unless this is fixed. But, since the entities being enqueued are just values, there is no way to do duplicate elimination. The only way to fix this is to change the protocol to add request IDs. But since this is a standardized interface, there is no way to do this.

The moral of this tale is that robustness is not simply a function of the implementations of the interfaces that make up the system. While robustness of the individual components has some effect on the robustness of the overall systems, it is not the sole factor determining system robustness. Many aspects of robustness can be reflected only at the protocol/interface level.

Similar situations can be found throughout the standard set of interfaces. Suppose I want to reliably remove a name from a context. I would be tempted to write code that looks like:

```
while (true) {
    try {
        context->remove(name);
        break;
    }
    catch (NotFoundInContext) {
        break;
    }
    catch (NetworkServerFaliure) {
        continue;
    }
}
```

That is, I keep trying the operation until it succeeds (or until I crash). The problem is that my connection to the name server may have gone down, but another client's may have stayed up. I may have, in fact, successfully removed the name but not discovered it because of a network disconnection. The other client then adds the same name, which I then remove. Unless the naming interface includes an operation to lock a naming context, there is no way that I can make this operation completely robust. Again, we see that robustness/reliability needs to be expressed at the interface level. In the design of any operation, the question has to be asked: what happens if the client chooses to repeat this operation with the exact same parameters as previously? What mechanisms are needed to ensure that they get the desired semantics? These are things that can be expressed only at the interface level. These are issues that can't be answered by supplying a "more robust implementation" because the lack of robustness is inherent in the interface and not something that can be changed by altering the implementation.

Similar arguments can be made about performance. Suppose an interface describes an object which maintains sets of other objects. A defining property of sets is that there are no duplicates. Thus, the implementation of this object needs to do duplicate elimination. If the interfaces in the system do not provide a way of testing equality of reference, the objects in the set must be queried to determine equality. Thus, duplicate elimination can be done only by interacting with the objects in the set. It doesn't matter how fast the objects in the set implement the equality operation. The overall performance of eliminating duplicates is going to be governed by the latency in communicating over the slowest communications link involved. There is no change in the set implementations that can overcome this. An interface design issue has put an upper bound on the performance of this operation.

6 Lessons from NFS

We do not need to look far to see the consequences of ignoring the distinction between local and distributed computing at the interface level. NFS®, Sun's distributed computing file system [14], [15] is an example of a non-distributed application programer interface (API) (open, read, write, close, etc.) re-implemented in a distributed way.

Before NFS and other network file systems, an error status returned from one of these calls indicated something rare: a full disk, or a catastrophe such as a disk crash. Most failures simply crashed the application along with the file system. Further, these errors generally reflected a situation that was either catastrophic for the program receiving the error or one that the user running the program could do something about.

NFS opened the door to partial failure within a file system. It has essentially two modes for dealing with an inaccessible file server: soft mounting and hard mounting. But since the designers of NFS were unwilling (for easily understandable reasons) to change the interface to the file system to reflect the new, distributed nature of file access, neither option is particularly robust.

Soft mounts expose network or server failure to the client program. Read and write operations return a failure status much more often than in the single-system case, and programs written with no allowance for these failures can easily corrupt the files used by the program. In the early days of NFS, system administrators tried to tune various parameters (time-out length, number of retries) to avoid these problems. These efforts failed. Today, soft mounts are seldom used, and when they are used, their use is generally restricted to read-only file systems or special applications.

Hard mounts mean that the application hangs until the server comes back up. This generally prevents a client program from seeing partial failure, but it leads to a malady familiar to users of workstation networks: one server crashes, and many workstations— even those apparently having nothing to do with that server—freeze. Figuring out the chain of causality is very difficult, and even when the cause of the failure can be determined, the individual user can rarely do anything about it but wait. This kind of brittleness can be reduced only with strong policies and network administration aimed at reducing interdependencies. Nonetheless, hard mounts are now almost universal.

Note that because the NFS protocol is stateless, it assumes clients contain no state of interest with respect to the protocol; in other words, the server doesn't care what happens to the client. NFS is also a "pure" client-server protocol, which means that failure can be limited to three parties: the client, the server, or the network.[1] This combination of features means that failure modes are simpler than in the more general case of peer-to-peer distributed object-oriented applications where no such limitation on shared state can be made and where servers are themselves clients of other servers. Such peer-to-peer distributed applications can and will fail in far more intricate ways than are currently possible with NFS.

The limitations on the reliability and robustness of NFS have nothing to do with the implementation of the parts of that system. There is no "quality of service" that can be improved to eliminate the need for hard mounting NFS volumes. The problem can be traced to the interface upon which NFS is built, an interface that was designed for non-distributed computing where partial failure was not possible. The reliability of NFS cannot be changed without a change to that interface, a change that will reflect the distributed nature of the application.

This is not to say that NFS has not been successful. In fact, NFS is arguably the most successful distributed application that has been produced. But the limitations on the robustness have set a limitation on the scalability of NFS. Because of the intrinsic unreliability of the NFS protocol, use of NFS is limited to fairly small numbers of machines, geographically co-located and centrally administered. The way NFS has dealt with partial failure has been to informally require a centralized resource manager (a system administrator) who can detect system failure, initiate resource reclamation and insure system consistency. But by introducing this central resource manager, one could argue that NFS is no longer a genuinely distributed application.

7   Taking the Difference Seriously

Differences in latency, memory access, partial failure, and concurrency make merging of the computational models of local and distributed computing both unwise to attempt and unable to succeed. Merging the models by making local computing follow the model of distributed computing would require major changes in implementation languages (or in how those languages are used) and make local computing far more complex than is otherwise necessary. Merging the models by attempting to make distributed computing follow the model of local computing requires ignoring the different failure modes and basic indeterminacy inherent in distributed computing, leading to systems that are unreliable and incapable of scaling beyond small groups of machines that are geographically co-located and centrally administered.

A better approach is to accept that there are irreconcilable differences between local and distributed computing, and to be conscious of those differences at all stages of the design and implementation of distributed applications. Rather than trying to merge local and remote objects, engineers need to be constantly reminded of the differences between the two, and know when it is appropriate to use each kind of object.

---

1. It should be noted that even in the fairly simple case of NFS, this is not precisely true. There are failure conditions that require state on the client, and can require manual intervention to restore consistency.

Accepting the fundamental difference between local and remote objects does not mean that either sort of object will require its interface to be defined differently. An interface definition language such as IDL can still be used to specify the set of interfaces that define objects. However, an additional part of the definition of a class of objects will be the specification of whether those objects are meant to be used locally or remotely. This decision will need to consider what the anticipated message frequency is for the object, and whether clients of the object can accept the indeterminacy implied by remote access. The decision will be reflected in the interface to the object indirectly, in that the interface for objects that are meant to be accessed remotely will contain operations that allow reliability in the face of partial failure.

It is entirely possible that a given object will often need to be accessed by some objects in ways that cannot allow indeterminacy, and by other objects relatively rarely and in a way that does allow indeterminacy. Such cases should be split into two objects (which might share an implementation) with one having an interface that is best for local access and the other having an interface that is best for remote access.

A compiler for the interface definition language used to specify classes of objects will need to alter its output based on whether the class definition being compiled is for a class to be used locally or a class being used remotely. For interfaces meant for distributed objects, the code produced might be very much like that generated by RPC stub compilers today. Code for a local interface, however, could be much simpler, probably requiring little more than a class definition in the target language.

While writing code, engineers will have to know whether they are sending messages to local or remote objects, and access those objects differently. While this might seem to add to the programming difficulty, it will in fact aid the programmer by providing a framework under which he or she can learn what to expect from the different kinds of calls. To program completely in the local environment, according to this model, will not require any changes from the programmer's point of view. The discipline of defining classes of objects using an interface definition language will insure the desired separation of interface from implementation, but the actual process of implementing an interface will be no different than what is done today in an object-oriented language.

Programming a distributed application will require the use of different techniques than those used for non-distributed applications. Programming a distributed application will require thinking about the problem in a different way than before it was thought about when the solution was a non-distributed application. But that is only to be expected. Distributed objects are different from local objects, and keeping that difference visible will keep the programmer from forgetting the difference and making mistakes. Knowing that an object is outside of the local address space, and perhaps on a different machine, will remind the programmer that he or she needs to program in a way that reflects the kinds of failures, indeterminacy, and concurrency constraints inherent in the use of such objects. Making the difference visible will aid in making the difference part of the design of the system.

Accepting that local and distributed computing are different in an irreconcilable way will also allow an organization to allocate its research and engineering resources more wisely. Rather than using those resources in attempts to paper over the differences between the two kinds of computing, resources can be directed at improving the performance and reliability of each.

One consequence of the view espoused here is that it is a mistake to attempt to construct a system that is "objects all the way down" if one understands the goal as a distributed system constructed of the *same kind* of objects all the way down. There will be a line where the object model changes; on one side of the line will be distributed objects, and on the other side of the line there will (perhaps) be local objects. On either side of the line, entities on the other side of the line will be opaque; thus one distributed object will not know (or care) if the implementation of another distributed object with which it communicates is made up of objects or is implemented in some other way. Objects on different sides of the line will differ in kind and not just in degree; in particular, the objects will differ in the kinds of failure modes with which they must deal.

8 A Middle Ground

As noted in Section 2, the distinction between local and distributed objects as we are using the terms is not exhaustive. In particular, there is a third category of objects made up of those that are in different address spaces but are guaranteed to be on the same machine. These are the sorts of objects, for example, that appear to be the basis of systems such as Spring [16] or Clouds [4]. These objects have some of the characteristics of distributed objects, such as increased latency in comparison to local objects and the need for a different model of memory access. However, these objects also share characteristics of local objects, including sharing underlying resource management and failure modes that are more nearly deterministic.

It is possible to make the programming model for such "local-remote" objects more similar to the programming model for local objects than can be done for the general case of distributed objects. Even though the objects are in different address spaces, they are managed by a single resource manager. Because of this, partial failure and the indeterminacy that it brings can be avoided. The programming model for such objects will still differ from that used for objects in the same address space with respect to latency, but the added latency can be reduced to generally acceptable levels. The programming models will still necessarily differ on methods of memory access and concurrency, but these do not have as great an effect on the construction of interfaces as additional failure modes.

The other reason for treating this class of objects separately from either local objects or generally distributed objects is that a compiler for an interface definition language can be significantly optimized for such cases. Parameter and result passing can be done via shared memory if it is known that the objects communicating are on the same machine. At the very least, marshalling of parameters and the unmarshalling of results can be avoided.

The class of locally distributed objects also forms a group that can lead to significant gains in software modularity. Applications made up of collections of such objects would have the advantage of forced and guaranteed separation between the interface to an object and the implementation of that object, and would allow the replacement of one implementation with another without affecting other parts of the system. Because of this, it might be advantageous to investigate the uses of such a system. However, this activity should not be confused with the unification of local objects with the kinds of distributed objects we have been discussing.

References

[1]   The Object Management Group. "Common Object Request Broker: Architecture and Specification." *OMG Document Number 91.12.1* (1991).

[2]   [Parrington, Graham D. "Reliable Distributed Programming in C++: The Arjuna Approach." *USENIX 1990 C++ Conference Proceedings* (1991).

[3]   Black, A., N. Hutchinson, E. Jul, H. Levy, and L. Carter. "Distribution and Abstract Types in Emerald." *IEEE Transactions on Software Engineering* SE-13, no. 1, (Jan. 1987).

[4]   Dasgupta, P., R. J. Leblanc, and E. Spafford. "The Clouds Project: Designing and Implementing a Fault Tolerant Distributed Operating System." *Georgia Institute of Technology Technical Report GIT-ICS-85/29.* (1985).

[5]   Microsoft Corporation. *Object Linking and Embedding Programmers Reference.* version 1. Microsoft Press, 1992.

[6]   Linton, Mark. "A Taste of Fresco." Tutorial given at the *8th Annual X Technical Conference* (January 1994).

[7]   Jaayeri, M., C. Ghezzi, D. Hoffman, D. Middleton, and M. Smotherman. "CSP/80: A Language for Communicating Sequential Processes." *Proceedings: Distributed Computing CompCon* (Fall 1980).

[8]   Cook, Robert. "MOD- A Language for Distributed Processing." *Proceedings of the 1st International Conference on Distributed Computing Systems* (October 1979).

[9]   Birrell, A. D. and B. J. Nelson. "Implementing Remote Procedure Calls." *ACM Transactions on Computer Systems* 2 (1978).

[10]   Hutchinson, N. C., L. L. Peterson, M. B. Abott, and S. O'Malley. "RPC in the x-Kernel: Evaluating New Design Techniques." *Proceedings of the Twelfth Symposium on Operating Systems Principles* 23, no. 5 (1989).

[11]   Zahn, L., T. Dineen, P. Leach, E. Martin, N. Mishkin, J. Pato, and G. Wyant. *Network Computing Architecture.* Prentice Hall, 1990.

[12]   Schroeder, Michael D. "A State-of-the-Art Distributed System: Computing with BOB." In *Distributed Systems*, 2nd ed., S. Mullender, ed., ACM Press, 1993.

[13]   Hadzilacos, Vassos and Sam Toueg. "Fault-Tolerant Broadcasts and Related Problems." In *Distributed Systems*, 2nd ed., S. Mullender, ed., ACM Press, 1993.

[14]   Walsh, D., B. Lyon, G. Sager, J. M. Chang, D. Goldberg, S. Kleiman, T. Lyon, R. Sandberg, and P. Weiss. "Overview of the SUN Network File System." *Proceedings of the Winter Usenix Conference* (1985).

[15]   Sandberg, R., D. Goldberg, S. Kleiman, D. Walsh, and B. Lyon. "Design and Implementation of the SUN Network File System." *Proceedings of the Summer Usenix Conference* (1985).

[16]   Khalidi, Yousef A. and Michael N. Nelson. "An Implementation of UNIX on an Object-Oriented Operating System." *Proceedings of the Winter USENIX Conference* (1993). Also *Sun Microsystems Laboratories, Inc. Technical Report SMLI TR-92-3* (December 1992).

Afterword

Jim Waldo, Ann Wollrath, and Sam Kendall

At the time that this paper was written, the view that programming a distributed system differed fundamentally from programming a non-distributed system was controversial. It was a time of great hope for approaches that treated such differences as "quality of service" issues. The more distributed computing could be made to look like non-distributed computing, the more likely it would be that programmers would be able to produce distributed applications.

The views expressed in this paper seem much less controvesial today. This is due, in part, to the failure of systems that attempted to make distribution transparent; most of the systems discussed in this paper now proport to take the inherent differences in distributed systems seriously.

More important, we believe, has been the emergence of the Internet as a computing platform. In a tightly controlled, centrally located and administered local area network it was possible to treat the network as a logical bus, and to deal with inconsistencies caused by partial failures and concurrency violations outside of the design of the distributed application. Failure recovery in such small-scale distributed systems could occur when the whole system was halted, by a system administrator who could restore the system to a consistent state by use of tools that were not part of the overall system design.

The internet has changed all of this. There is no centralized system administration on the internet, and no way to halt the system when an unexplained failure causes a system distributed over the internet to become inconsistent. Large scale distribution has made the problems discussed in this paper a fact of life for a much larger percentage of the programmers in the world.

The greater connectivity between machines has also lead to the re-invigoration of mobile computing as a field of study. The model of distributed computing discussed in this paper was a traditional one in which data is moved to the computation, and the computation is associated with some particular machine or set of machines. With the increased network scales brought on by the emergence of the internet, the alternate approach of moving the computation itself becomes an important design paradigm.

Both the traditional approach to distributed computing and the mobile computing approach need to address the problems of partial failure, and both require similar recovery strategies. Partial failure and the lack of global knowledge are both facts of life for the programmer attempting to deal with mobile code, just as they are for the programmer dealing with more traditional approaches to distributed systems.

In both fields, it is vital that the recovery from these peculiar (and, in an important way, endevor defining) failure modes be taken into account at the time of designing the protocols and interfaces that are used by the cooperating processes. Dealing with these problems is not something that can be added in after the main design has been done. They must be dealt with from the very beginning. In both cases, this makes the design of a system fundamentally different than the design of a system that does not have these failure characteristics. Mobile systems, like distributed systems, are not just like systems designed for non-mobile (or non-distibuted) environments. More than a special platform, they are a separate design center that requires separate techniques and approaches if we are to produce reliable, stable systems.

The other change which impacts both traditional approaches to distributed computing and mobile computing has been the advent of the JavaTM platform. Java, by providing a machine-independent binary format, blurs the distinction between the traditional approach to distributed computing and the approach taken by mobile computing. Indeed, the Java Remote Method Invocation system[1] allows the passing of objects, including the code that is used to implement the methods of those objects, in a framework much like that of traditional remote procedure call systems. These objects can then have methods invoked on them locally in the machine to which they have been sent.

The Java RMI system is not exactly a mobile computing system (since the objects that are moved are not closures and do not have their own thread of control) but it is not exactly a traditional RPC system in which data is moved to the site of computation. It does make essential use of the ability to move code around a network in a machine-independent and safe way. Such a system hints at new ways of doing distributed computing, combining techniques from both traditional distributed computing systems and mobile computing systems.

1. Wollrath, Riggs, and Waldo, "A Distributed Object Model for the Java System", Proceedings of the USENIX Conference on Object Oriented Technologies and Systems, 1996.

Instruction-Based Communications*

Christian Tschudin

Abstract. This papers explores a mode of communication that is based on instruction rather than interpretation. Starting from Shannon's (interpretative) communication model, I link instruction–based communications to mobile code (messengers), to "signs" as they are defined in semiotics, and to the virus theme commonly found in cell biology, computer science and literature. Virus–codes are conjectured to be more powerful that the equivalence codes studied by Shannon.

1   Introduction

Some of the reviews I got in 1992 for papers on instruction–based computer communications were strangely emotional and were harshly rejected. After that mobile code was introduced to a larger audience through JAVA, such comments have virtually disappeared, but there are still quite prominent voices that recommend "Just say no to mobile code" [23]. In fact, it seems very disturbing that communication in its entirety could be based on instructions because this implies loosing control. As humans we sympathize quite strongly with the concept of a reader or interpreter that can, at any moment, decide to break a communication. Thus, going for truly mobile code, which is just an euphemism for virus-based computer interaction, is rather discomforting. The goal of this paper is to take a closer and more philosophical look at instruction–based communications.

That a fully instructional communication model was not proposed earlier may have several reasons. First, the Shannon model was so successfully adapted to computer communications that there was no need to question it. And second, Shannon's model is still valid for mobile code although it is restricted to a very primitive message exchange layer. The third reason has already been mentioned: there is a strong psychological bias against another communication model – a bias that is strengthened by genuine technical questions about safe and secure operation of mobile code. However, computers evidently enable instruction-based communication, so we should examine other places where this communication model was discovered, construed or imagined.

In section 2 we first look at Shannon's communication model, examine how instruction–based communication fit in there and justify why we use the term /messenger/ for the basic unit of instructions. Section 3 gives a brief introduction to semiotics in order to discuss the concept of "signs" and the problems of communicating "meaning". Using this background, section 4 links instruction–based communications with the virus theme and discusses various fields where this relation is prominent. In the concluding section 5 we look at the resulting execution substrate that is the home of messengers, mobile agents and active documents.

---

* This chapter is an excerpt from my Ph.D. thesis that was slightly rearranged and updated for this book.

2 Messages and Messengers

Computer communication models are all based on *message exchange*: Each communication context has an information source that sends a message through a communication channel to the destination. This model is known as Shannon's communication model (see figure 1).

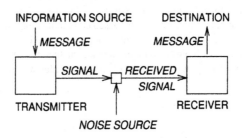

Fig. 1. Shannon's *"Schematic diagram of a general communication system"*.

While Shannon [21] examined the mapping of messages to signals (transmitter) and back (receiver), this configuration has been generalized and is now applied in a recursive manner that also includes the concept of a protocol: message transmission is mapped to the transmission of lower-level messages where a protocol defines their format and permissible exchange sequences. This defines a virtual channel (figure 2). The underlying lower-level channels do not need to be the final physical communication channels, thus can be virtual channels too. Eventually, having crossed multiple protocol layers, messages are mapped to physical signals.

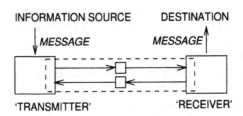

Fig. 2. Schematic diagram of a general communication system using a protocol.

Message exchange is a very general concept and metaphor e.g., showing up in object oriented programming ("sending a message to an object") where there is not necessarily a physical communication channel present. According to this metaphor it is up to the destination to analyze (interpret) a received message and to decide which communication effects it should have. We therefore call this the *interpretative mode* of communications.

2.1 Communications Messengers

The effect of receiving a signal or low-level message is – in Shannon's model and its generalization – fixed in advance by an agreement between source and destination (the necessity of such an agreement is the source of protocol standardization). In case we have (programmable) computers talking to each other, we could imagine that the effect at the destination side is not fixed by standards but would be communicated by the source as a sequence of instructions. Going one step further we can determine that source and destination solely exchange instructions such that messages are replaced at all levels by *instruction strings* or *communication messengers*[2]. This leads to a purely *instructional mode* of communication for which we give a reference model in five postulates.

I. Packet exchange: Communication messengers are delimited messages (packets) independently exchanged between computers. Nothing is assumed about the transmission reliability except that messengers shall be received unaltered (garbled messengers are simply dropped).

II. Mandatory execution of messenger instructions: The most distinct aspect of a messenger are its instructions. Messengers share a common syntactic structure (data format) that enables to locate inside the message one or more instruction sequences. A computer that receives a messenger has to blindly execute the found instruction sequence(s). Thus, messengers are programs exchanged and executed by the communicating hosts.

III. General purpose instruction set: The messenger's instructions are taken from a general purpose instruction set forming a (kind of) programming language. This set includes specific instructions that permit the submission of new messengers to other computers.

IV. Local state change: Messengers can query and modify (parts of) the local state of the computer they are executing on. For this, computers could provide a shared data space (memory cells, data base, file system) where messengers can deposit and fetch data values.

V. Symmetric, exclusive and explicit: In the messenger communication model, messengers are the only type of data exchanged. If the reception of a messenger should be acknowledged, this has to be explicitly requested by the arriving messenger by sending back another messenger. Thus, there is no implicit communication behavior (e.g., returning error codes) nor do means other than messengers exist in order to communicate with a neighboring computer.

Because there are (except for the instruction set and the 'mandatory execution' postulate) no agreements necessary between source and destination, we have a generic environment for any protocol whose effects can be described in terms of the instruction set. *Protocol genericity* is probably the most important characteristics of communication messengers. That an instruction set and messenger format have to be fixed in advance is a consequence of Shannon's model which applies to the lowest level of instruction–based communications. However, we refrain from structuring all communications along

---

[2] A justification for the term /messenger/ is given subsequently. An elder scientific contribution which already used this term is [26]: *"Active Message Processing: Messages as Messengers"*.

a message exchange hierarchy: messengers decide at run-time which communication behavior to implement and instruct the destination accordingly.

2.2 The Name of the Game

It is not by chance that I chose /messenger/[3] for denoting the basic unit of instructions exchanged between computers. The most important connotation of the term /messenger/ is *activity*: messengers are active messages just as messages are passive messengers. The other, equally important attribute is *autonomy*. A communication messenger, like a human 'courier', is assumed to make its decisions autonomously in order to fulfill its task. If necessary, a messenger (process) can solicit external help, for instance by synchronizing with other processes, but it keeps control of the actions to be performed. Based on the root term /message/, /messenger/ constitutes a very natural *extension* that retains a phonetic similarity with the original. At the same time it constitutes a *restriction*, because messengers are very specific messages (containing only instructions). To use the term /messenger/ thus, should represent no element of confusion. How /messenger/ is used in cell biology is briefly discussed in the following paragraphs. It is quite surprising

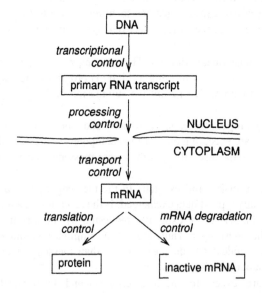

Fig. 3. Five different levels of gene expression control in eucaryotes (according to [1], page 437)

just how well the 'messenger interpretation' of the communication model can be applied to capture the protein synthesising process inside a cell. The term /messenger RNA/ in this context matches very well the meaning intented for /messenger/ in the context of computer communications.

---

[3] Like in [7] I use single slashes to denote a term or expression (in contrast to the *idea* for which it may stand for).

Messengers in Cell Biology The synthesis of *proteins* i.e., the working molecules of a cell, is at the heart of this discussion. Protein synthesis involves the cell's nucleus, where the genetic code is stored as DNA (deoxyribonucleic acids – the DNA contains the complete hereditary information), and the cytosol i.e., the cell compartment outside the nucleus. Inside the cytosol, specialized particles called *ribosomes* 'assemble' the proteins according to a 'recipe' presented in the form of *messenger* RNA (ribonucleic acids). The ribosomes are veritable fabrics where one amino acid after the other is glued together (according to the *m*RNA blueprint) to form a protein. Several ribosomes can work concurrently on one *m*RNA molecule. *m*RNA molecules are produced inside the nucleus compartment of a cell. The first step for their synthesis is the creation of an RNA molecule which is a cast of a part (called gene) of the DNA. The resulting RNA transcript is subject to several transformation steps ("splicing") before it is exported to the cytosol where ribosoms start their action. Figure 3 summarizes the different activities involved in the protein synthesis. The outlined protein synthesis shall now be discussed at the molecular level as a communication process between the nucleus and the cytosol.

mRNA: Message or Messenger? Because the protein synthesis is done at a place distant to and clearly separated from where the information for the synthesis is stored, one can conclude that some information transfer and communication occurs. A formulation in terms of Shannon's communication model is straightforward: the nucleus takes on the role of sender, the cytosol is the recipient. The encoding is materialized by the cast–making and the splicing process. A pore of the separating membrane represents the channel, and the *m*RNA relates to the information carrying message. Finally, the ribosomes are the receivers which interpret it.

A valid 'messenger' description can also be provided. Again, the nucleus represents the sender and the cytosol the recipient. A pore is used as channel. The nucleus seeks to change the behavior of the cytosol: it is to produce a specific protein. Instead of sending an order form that contains the protein's name (or another abbreviation etc.), a complete sequence of instructions is communicated. In strict accordance to the messenger paradigm each messenger RNA controls one (or more) execution threads: the messenger is duly executed by the cytosol's ribosomes.

3 Semiotics

Semiotics is a discipline that studies *signification phenomena*. It provides an interesting conceptual framework for discussing computer communications in a way that goes beyond the information theoretical approach of Shannon's communication model. This excursion lays the conceptual ground which will allow an examination of messengers from a – for computer science perhaps unusual – viewpoint.

This section provides a brief introduction to general semiotics, whereby I rely mainly on the work of Eco. The presentation must, of course, remain very superficial, but it should be sufficient to make the "common interests" visible which link computer communications and semiotics: in both cases a better understanding of communication phenomena, i.e. a theory of communication, is sought for.

The concept of 'sign' and 'unlimited semiosis' is introduced first. Then, clarifications of the meaning of 'code', 'signal' and 'stimulus' are given. This immediately leads to the question of 'how signs work' and to what "signs" in computer communications can be related to.

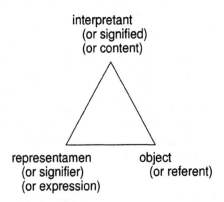

Fig. 4. A sign model.

3.1 Basics of Semiotics

The question at the base of semiotics is: how can *meaning*, and not just *information*, be communicated? How is it possible that gestures and both spoken and written words can be used to communicate intentions, views and believes about the world? The base for the modern theory of semiotics (or semiology) was laid in the second half of the previous century by Charles Sanders Peirce (logician, 1839–1914) and Ferdinand de Saussure (linguist, 1857–1913) (according to [20]), although first reflections on this topic can be traced back to greek philosophers.

The study object of semiotics is the concept of 'sign'. (General) semiotics is not interested in what in common parlance is the sign, i.e., a physical event or manifest. Instead, semiotics examines how such manifests can mediate meaning, the manifest being only a *sign-vehicle*. 'Sign', thus, is an abstract concept, and semiotics studies what signs are and how they work. However, /sign/ is, even in texts on semiotics, often used in both ways.

A first model for the sign concept was proposed by de Saussure when he distinguished between two elements: the *signifier* (or expression or representamen) and the *signified* (or content or interpretant or meaning). These two parts of a sign are linked through a *sign-function* – the sign function correlates an expression with a content. In Peirce's model of the sign concept, a third category is introduced (see figure 4): the *object* (or referent). The distinction between the interpretant and the object allows an examination of signification without having a metaphysical discussion about the reality of the sign's object. Our main interest is the correlation between representamen and interpretant, that is, the 'mental effect' of a sign-vehicle.

An important problem of the sign definition is to specify when 'something' becomes a sign i.e., why some manifest is a sign. A first and frequently used characterization is that 'a sign stands for something'. Eco proposes basing the 'signness' criterion on Morris' definition, saying that "something is a sign only because it is interpreted as a sign of something by some interpreter" (see [7], page 16). This interpretation process is called *semiosis*.

Fig. 5. The unlimited semiosis.

Semiosis is not a simple mapping between a representamen R and an interpretant I, although R 'stands for' the interpretant I. The relation between R and I can be understood as a *definition* of the representamen: *"R means I"*. However, Peirce has suggested that an interpretant I cannot be a final concept, because it too needs to be interpreted; each interpretant itself becomes a sign. That is, in order to define what I means, one has to refer to another I', and so on. The correlation between signifier and signified will have the form of an inference (and not an equivalence). Furthermore the semiosis or interpretation process will be an inference process 'with no end'. This is called the *unlimited semiosis*, where each interpretant becomes the representamen of another sign (see figure 5).

3.2 S–Codes and the Unlimited Semiosis

The requirement of an unlimited semiosis allows a differentiation between semiotics and the research done for instance by information theorists or cryptographers. Their concern is the mapping of messages onto other messages or signals (encoding) as well as the mapping in the opposite direction (decoding). This process, however, has nothing to do with signification: the examined mapping simply organizes (or structures) the possible signal values – they represent a syntactic *system*. Eco [7] calls this an *s-code*, where the *s* stands for *system*. Also an equivalence between two s-codes, for instance the mapping of a finite set of messages to a finite number of signals, is a system: what the messages 'mean' is unimportant. By definition the message to be encoded is considered void of its possible meaning. Only its *information* content, defined in a statistical way, is of concern. An algorithmic characterization of s-codes is that the encoding and decoding process of s-codes can be done by a deterministic algorithm (e.g. a lookup in a codebook, or a more complex cryptographic procedure) which terminates in finite time, regardless of the input given. No semiotic phenomena can be observed in this case.

How does this compare to a full semiosis process? While, in the case of s-codes, a deterministic procedure exists which leads from an expression A to its content B or vice-versa, a semiosis has a third, interpreting element C which we can call 'choice'. The relation between A and the interpretant B is then unpredictable in the sense that between A and B there may be a potentially infinite series of C's. Eco calls this the *C-space* and he leaves the question open of whether it will one day be possible to master this space in terms of algorithms ([9], page 9). He notes that this semantic space, as it is also called, has the structure of an encyclopedia ([8], chapter 2).

Code, Signals, Stimuli and Signs What has been introduced as 'mapping' during the semiosis process is, in common parlance, also called a **code** – signification is only possible because some code has been established by social convention. But the unlimited semiosis requires a type of 'code' which differs from the 'code' concept of information theory or cryptography. This is why one must speak of s-codes as against, as Eco calls them, *true codes* or *codes in the strong sense*. True codes require an inference of the form $R \supset I$ in order to elicit an interpretation, while *s-codes* work as equivalences of the form $R \equiv I$.

A problem with this subtle differentiation is that a true code never occurs in an isolated form: at the base of a signification phenomenon we always have some s-code. This coincidence often leads to confusion[4]. In the case of language, the s-code is the system of phonemes, for written expressions it is our alphabet. However, what is important, is the *usage* of s-code. An interesting characterization of (true) codes has been given by Eco, in saying that *"... semiotics is in principle the discipline studying everything which can be used in order to lie."* ([7], page 7). S-codes cannot lie, they only represent structure. Related to codes are the terms /signal/, /stimulus/ and /sign/. Based on the concepts developed so far, some subtle and important differences can be worked out.

/Signal/ stands for a physically observable pattern: signals reduce the arbitrariness of the real world. In Shannon's communication model the transmitter maps a *message* onto signals, while the receiver carries out the inverse operation. The problem domain of an efficient mapping between messages and signals belongs to the classical information theory. All arguments considered in this thesis disregard signals and examine the exchange of messages 'and beyond'.

One can ask how a signal or a message is 'processed' by a recipient. A message is considered to be a **stimulus** if there is a rule specifying the mandatory (but not necessarily visible) reaction of the recipient. An often cited example is the genetic code: a ribosome simply reads a messenger RNA and produces a protein according to the blueprint presented. Another example would be a protocol data unit exchanged between

---

[4] Within the context of computer science this becomes even more confusing: 'Code' designates the instruction part of a program, 'to code' then means to write a program. While I often use the word 'code' in this sense, I try to stick to the verb *encode* in case a representation activity inside a communication context is ment. However, it is one of the properties of the messenger paradigm that these two uses of 'coding' become indistinguishable.

two computers, where the arrival of the PDU triggers some well–defined actions. Since stimuli correlate an input to an unavoidable output on a one–to–one basis, they constitute an s-code.

Signs differ from stimuli in the way they have to be handled: "Signs always request an interpretation. Stimuli, on the contrary, produce or elicit a blind reaction." ([8], page 182) Although it seems that, with this definition, more clarity has been gained, it is now the term 'interpretation' that is not easy to grasp. This problem immediately boils down to the question of the *context* necessary for an interpretation: stimuli, then, rely on a very simple context, consisting only of a series of preconceived 'encoding/decoding' rules, while the interpretation of signs requires an encyclopedic context.

The Interpretation Context The previous paragraph compared signs with stimuli and pointed to the interpretation context. In which way does a 'simple' context differ from a 'complex' one? This is a major problem when one tries to make the concept of sign operational, e.g. by means of computers: a simplified argument would be that because computers are finite and deterministic machines, no really complex context can be created by them. No choice is possible, and consequently no semiotic phenomena can occur.

But, does the finiteness not also apply to molecular biology and human beings? Three things should be noted: first, although it is required that a sign be the *potential* source of an infinite semiosis, no recipient really carries out an infinite semiosis. Second, the context for a given sign does not necessarily reside in one subject or machine: The semiosis may be spread in time and space over multiple entities which, as a whole, constitute the context (scientific research works this way). Third, it is by no means unusual for a finitely describable algorithm to describe an infinite process: thus, the complexity of the context may be substituted by an algorithmic complexity. In the following paragraphs I try to relate the concept of semiosis with more operational or implementation specific considerations.

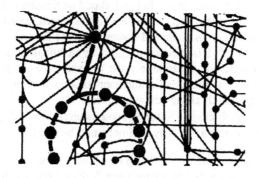

Fig. 6. A clipping from "*A maze illustrating the chemical reactions that interconvert small molecules and cells*" (in [1], page 42).

The protein synthesis in a cell can be considered a typical example of a stimu-

lus/reaction pattern. However, the synthesis process is not linear and deterministic –
many control paths influence (inhibit, amplify or modify) the gene expression. As an
illustration consider figure 6: it shows a small schematic excerpt of the control paths
existing inside a cell (which are currently only partially understood). Does such a non-
trivial interaction pattern constitute a complex context? For example, currently no one
can exclude the possibility that weather conditions and the way the owner of a cell feels
about them, influence this control path in some way. Or to word it differently: although
the genetic code is based on stimuli, the control paths allow for interferences from a context (see figure 3), which, as the weather example above shows, can be very complex.
The presence of stimuli does not exclude semiotic phenomena. In opposition to Prodi,
who in [18] proposes the comprehension of an enzyme as an interpretation engine and
the molecules (with which it collides) as signs, I consider the protein synthesis to be a
stimulus reaction. Only when control paths are in place that can influence the impact and
effect of a stimulus, and when the context (as the set of all possible configurations of the
control paths) is complex enough, can a semiosis be conjectured. Thus, the difference
between a stimulus and a sign seems to be a question of 'sufficient' complexity, as also
Prodi suggests ([18], page 63). Eco acknowledges in [8] ". . . that when studying both
bio–logic and conceptual logic we are in trouble when we try to distinguish correlation
from instruction, s-codes from codes." (page 184)

This topic is important when we consider messengers (consisting of instructions)
in terms of semiotics. The interesting aspect is the complexity required to 'interpret' a
messenger, i.e., to foretell its effects.

3.3   Semiotics and Protocols

It can be said that in semiotics the interaction aspect of two communicating parties is
often treated in a marginal way – often one simply refers to Shannon's communication
model[5]. This may be explained by the history of modern semiotics, which is largely
oriented towards linguistics: the focus is placed on an isolated sign-vehicle, be it a
written or spoken word, a sentence or a full text. Based on this static manifest, theories
are developed about the author and the reader. This approach, based on a communication one–way, takes a text as given and assumes it to be the only direct interaction
between author and reader[6]. It is of course a legitimate methodological choice to isolate
a prototypical communication situation in order to reduce the complexity. However,
this implicitly assumes that a communication configuration, in which the partners can
interact, does not significantly change the sign concept.

As I illustrated when discussing Shannon's communication model, protocols cannot
be expressed directly in such a one–way environment. The question is: is it permissible

---

[5] De Saussure proposed a circular model based on a speech circuit ("circuit de la parole")
(in [19], page 12 [page 28 in the standard pagination]) . However, I have the impression that
the consequences and possible implications of such a configuration are not often discussed in
modern books on semiotics.

[6] Indirectly, of course, there will be some interaction in the sense that the author will have a
model reader in mind, and that reactions from readers may influence the author's next œuvre,
and that author and reader may share some cultural 'codes' etc.

to make abstractions of protocols when discussing communication phenomena? The following argument shows that there are protocols, albeit representing a classical s-code, which allow a sender or a recipient to lie: protocol data units can become signs as a result of the protocol.

For illustrating this, I assume two message–exchanging computers. The point to be considered is that the simple *fact of receiving* a message from the peer 'signifies' something. Protocols usually exploit exactly this: the important aspect of a received acknowledgement is not the content of the received data packet but the fact that the peer has sent it, and therefore the peer has received and processed the host's previous message. One could pretend that in terms of semiotics the acknowledgement data packet is the representamen, that the object is the original packet sent to the peer, and that the interpretant is the certitude about the successful reception of the original data packet. However, this situation will probably not be considered as a signification process, because the ACK belongs to a simple s-code, the protocol, and requires virtually no interpretation effort: if during a fixed interval of time an acknowledgement is received, this means successful delivery. Otherwise a failure must be assumed. The 'meaning' of the ACK is fixed in advance – in other words, there is a simple interpretation context.

In a slightly more complicated scenario it shall be assumed that the previous protocol has been extended so that negative acknowledgements (NACK) are also used. The purpose of a NACK message, sent by the peer host, is to speed up the retransmission in case an obviously garbled data packet was received by the peer. The sender behaves as in the previous case, but the original data packet is automatically resent when a NACK message is received.

So far this extended protocol is still an s-code. However, as was said above, it is important to look at *how* this protocol is used. For instance, the sender can decide at any moment to examine (interpret) the time series of received ACKs and NACKs: a number of NACKs received in succession would signify that the quality of the transmission line is poor. A useful reaction could be to reduce the size of the data packets in order to increase the chance of an ungarbled transmission. The goal of such additional activity is to enhance the data throughput without changing the defined and mutually accepted protocol, simply in order to provide a 'clever' protocol implementation.

An interesting situation arrives if the remote peer knows about such efforts. The peer can, for instance, observe the length of received packets and correlate the decreased lengths with recent series of garbled messages. By deliberately inserting NACK messages, the peer can make the sending host believe that the transmission quality has degraded. In other words, the remote peer lies about the integrity of received messages and leads the sending host astray as to the quality of the transmission channel. This is the very same as a patient describing fictive symptoms which, for the doctor, are signs. Or to use Eco's terms: the peer lies *with* the rules (see his example *B* in [8], page 181).

Note that inserting NACKs does not violate the protocol: the generated sequence of exchanged messages still belongs to the language defined by the protocol. The protocol itself is and remains rigid (that is, a system), but the element of choice is the possibility of *extra* behavior, which from a purist's view (that is, by a 'strict' interpretation of the 'sense' of the protocol) are not necessary.

These examples bring the brief introduction to semiotics to an end. The intention was to present the basic concepts and to show that semiotics is an adequate 'philosophy' for discussing computer communications problems. The following section on viruses will make references to concepts from both sides by relating viruses with messengers as well as with signs.

4 The Virus Metaphor

"Language is a virus": this title of a Laurie Anderson pop song [2] – and attributed to the writer W. S. Burroughs – expresses metaphorically what seems to be the base of communication 'tout court'. I will try to make the link between viruses and communication more comprehensible by looking at viruses from three different disciplines: cell biology, computer science and literature. This descriptive excursion will provide a basis for examining viruses with a communication bias and will bring me back to communication messengers once again.

4.1 Viruses in Biology

While, historically, viruses (Latin for poison) were first defined by their *effects*, biological viruses are today designated by what they are thought to be: *mobile genes* ([1], page 232). In its 'external' form a virus is composed of a protein envelope that encapsulates the genetic information. I am primarily interested in the *mechanism* with which the genetic information of a virus modifies a cell's metabolism. All page numbers in this section refer to [1]; The technical terms used in the following paragraphs have already been presented in section 2.2.

Because a virus has no protein synthesising mechanism, it has to use the mechanism of a host cell. By attaching itself to the membrane of a cell, the virus' envelope enables the virus' content to invade the cytosol. Inside the cytosol the cell's ribosome molecules are ready to execute whatever blueprint of a protein they get in touch with. However, this blueprint (which is usually an *m*RNAmolecule) must be presented in the form of RNA. Either the virus' information is directly coded in RNA (a so called retro–virus), in which case the production of proteins can immediately start or the virus contains DNA, which must first be transcribed by a chemical process similar to the one found inside the cell's nucleus.

The scenario described so far is common to all viruses: the genetic information (the mobile gene) is embedded in a protein envelope. The virus' content, once inside the cytosol, triggers various chemical processes. I will call this scenario, which also encompasses the intrusion of the virus' RNA or DNA, *the* virus mechanism. The further actions which these mobile genes can trigger, are virus specific, and shall be discussed briefly.

The standard operation mode of a virus is to let the cell duplicate the virus' envelope protein as well as the mobile gene itself. However, for several reasons the sole transfer of RNA into the cytosol does not ensure a duplication of a virus. For instance, the cell's control paths could quickly lead to a degradation of the RNA, or the control paths could inhibit further protein synthesis based on the virus RNA (page 235). To cope with this, the virus' RNA may contain instructions to produce proteins which interact directly with the control paths. In its simplest form a negative feedback circuit is broken, leading the cell to produce as much envelope material and duplicates of the genetic information as possible until the cell bursts. In the case of a retro–virus the duplication of the virus gene is not straightforward. Normally, a cell does not know how to copy RNA material – the cell can only cast RNA *from* a DNA strand, but not the other way round. Therefore, the gene of a retro–virus contains instructions on how to produce a 'reverse transcriptase enzyme' which can generate the DNA needed for the procreation of the virus gene from the virus' RNA: this facility introduces into the cell the reverse path of DNA 'decoding'.

Immediate duplication is not the only scenario that has been observed. The virus code can, for example, instruct the cell to transport the virus DNA into the cell's nucleus and to splice it with the cell's hereditary information. With this, the virus has become part of the cell and is duplicated each time the cell divides (pp. 623). But the opposite process has also been observed: viruses are able to copy parts of the cell's DNA into their own gene, and then continue to duplicate, and in this way they export parts of a cell's genetic plan (page 628). Still another procedure observed is the delay of the malignant effects (latent viruses). Finally, 'defective' viruses represent a very interesting case: such viruses do not contain all instructions required for duplication. But, seen as a population of many distinct, possibly all defective viruses, this population contains all the genetic information necessary to enable their duplication: such a population forms a kind of 'virtual virus' and only works if all constituents gather by chance in a single cell (pp. 625).

What is important is the *mechanism* of mobile genes which enables to recode the functioning of a cell. This virus mechanism resurges in environments different from cell biology, but in an analogous form.

4.2 Viruses in Computer Science

The term /computer virus/, as it is used today, is attributed to Cohen, although the general idea and concrete experiments date back to the 60's. In his Ph.D. from 1983, Cohen describes experiments conducted with computer viruses on multi-user operating systems. For an updated and general presentation of Cohen's results see [6].

Cohen's basic idea exploits the fact that executable programs can be compressed before being stored on 'expensive resources' like mass storage devices. Where such a compressed program is to be executed, it has first to be uncompressed. Instead of rewriting all supporting programs (in order to add this compression functionality), Cohen proposed compressing the unchanged programs and attaching a small decompression routine to the compressed image. This routine would unfold the program on the fly whenever the program needed to be run.

The essential point is that this new piece of code can be extended to do more than just decompression. An automated version of this computer procedure, capable of compressing other programs, can scan the file system in order to select an uncompressed executable: the program, when found, is compressed, and a copy of the decompression routine is attached. Whenever this modified program is run, it will repeat this procedure, i.e., scan for uncompressed programs etc., and eventually execute the original decompressed code.

It is important to note why such a mechanism is technically conceivable. Todays operating systems treat instructions and (numerical) data in the same way, i.e. as a sequence of bits void of context. It is only by convention that an operating system recognizes which bits are instructions and which are not. On most operating systems the owner of a file can, at his own discretion, declare the data file to be a program[7]. This means that the 'signification' of bits (to be instructions or data) is based on conventions only. This allowed Cohen to treat a program file as if it were data and make programs the subject of data de/compression.

The link of Cohen's concept to biological viruses is evident: the described subroutine (computer virus) represents an element which is attachable in a generic way to program files. Thus, it corresponds directly with the 'mobile genes' of biology. The computer virus modifies the program's behavior – the program becomes infected and will help to diffuse the virus each time it is executed.

In order to spread a computer virus it is not necessary that the operating system have multi–user or multi–tasking capabilities. Imprudent users making copies of an infected program and physically transporting it from one computer to another, can also help achieve an epidemic effect. The other possibility is that several single–user computers share data via a network, which would eliminate the need of the physical transport of infected programs.

A variant of computer viruses are *worms*. Whereas computer viruses need some host *program* in order to become effective, worms are more autonomous. A 'worm' is a *complete* computer program which, once executed, can transfer itself to a remote host without external intervention. In this case one can say that it is not the *program* but the host computer (or the operating system) as a whole that becomes infected. Probably the most prominent case known and analyzed is the *Internet worm* that occurred in November 1988 [22]. I classify worms as a variant of computer viruses because, viewed at a coarse granularity from outside a computer, the effect is the same: parts of or complete programs can 'infect' a host by spreading duplicates of themselves, eventually resulting in an epidemic. Worms are also called 'networked viruses' and would also encompass what has more recently became known as 'mobile software agents'.

Worms and computer viruses are by no means special:

> "Computer viruses [...] are, in every sense of the word, normal user programs, using only the normal sorts of operations that every user of computers uses every day. It has been proven that in any system that allows information to be shared, interpreted [...], and retransmitted once received, a virus can spread throughout [...]." ([6], page 382)

They are here to stay and will not disappear unless computers cease to exist.

---

[7] The situation is slightly more complex: a program is more than just a sequence of instructions. In order to be recognized as a program, a file must often have a conforming inner (syntactic) structure and may require other attributes (e.g. filename extension) or the availability of external resources linked by implicit rules. It is the task of the operating system to take a file, recognize it as a program and to execute the instructions found.

4.3 Viruses in Burroughs' Œuvre

William S. Burroughs clearly is an important writer in English literature of this century. He is often cited in relation to the beatnik movement of the 60ties, although he has not always agreed with this classification (see e.g. [4], page 52). Burroughs has become famous and disputed mostly because of the prominent sex and drug topics of his work. With the novel *The Naked Lunch*, which appeared in 1959, he also introduced a new style of writing which he later developed as a technique called 'cut–up method' [8]. The cut–up technique (or its counterpart in computer science), applied to messengers, will be rediscussed in section 4.5: this section presents an isolated topic of Burroughs' work: the 'virus'.

A main theme underlying Burroughs' work (see e.g. [5, 4]) is *control*. Similar to Huxley (*Brave New World*) and Orwell (*1984*) he examines mechanisms used to control a society. In *Nova Express* there is a 'conspiracy' of extra-terrestrial 'Nova Criminals' for which junk drugs is a means to impose this control. Junk is just one form of the 'virus power' that can also be found in the form of love, images and words.

> "*Technical Deposition of the Virus Power*: "Gentlemen, it was first suggested that we take our own image and examine how it could be made more portable. We found that simple binary coding systems were enough to contain the entire image however they required a large amount of storage space until it was found that the binary information could be written at the molecular level, and our entire image could be contained within a grain of sand. However it was found that these information molecules were not dead matter but exhibited a capacity for life which is found elsewhere in the form of virus. Our virus infects the human and creates our image in him."

---

[8] I insert the following extended quote because the cut–up method has a very direct link to computer science, as Burroughs himself noted (from the same text as below): "Dr Neumann in his *Theory of Games and Economic Behavior* introduced the cut–up method of random action into game and military strategy". In computer science, cut–ups have been formalized and are being explored under the name of *genetic algorithms*: parts of solutions to a problem represented as a sequence of bits are 'crossed over' at random to produce another new solution, hopefully more fit that the preceding ones [13].

Burroughs explains his cut–up method as follows: "In the summer of 1959 Brion Gysin painter and writer cut newspaper articles into sections and rearranged the sections *at random*. "Minutes to Go" resulted from this initial cut–up experiment. "Minutes to Go" contains unedited unchanged cut–ups emerging as quite coherent and meaningful prose. [...] The method is simple. Here is one way to do it. Take a page. Like this page. Now cut down the middle and across the middle. You have four sections: 1 2 3 4 ... one two three four. Now rearrange the sections placing section four with section one and section two with section three. And you have a new page. Sometimes it says much the same thing. Sometimes something quite different – cutting up political speeches is an interesting exercise – in any case you will find that it says something and something quite definite. [...] Cut–ups are for everyone. Anybody can make cut–ups. It is experimental in the sense of being *something to do*. Right here write now. Not something to talk and argue about. Greek philosophers assumed logically that an object twice as heavy as another object would fall twice as fast. It did not occur to them to push the two objects off the table and see how they fall. Cut the words and see how they fall. [...] All writing is in fact cut–ups." (from *The Third Mind* in [5], pages 268–269)

Wrapped in a science fiction style it is explained that by 'stress deformation' using a cyclotron it is possible to burn images into mescaline. But apart from junk drugs the most prominent form of a virus for Burroughs is the *word*. "I advance the theory that in the electronic revolution a virus *is* a very small unit of word and image." ([4], page 14) In Burroughs view the written and spoken word as well as images hinder one from experiencing the real world. "[...] if you're absolutely bombarded with images from passing trucks and cars and televisions and newspapers, you become blunted and this makes a permanent haze in front of your eyes, you can't see anything" ([4], page 34). Mass media dump images and words on the world and by this means exert the control over the past and the future.

> "The mass media of newspapers, radio, television, magazines form a ceremonial calendar to which all citizen are subjected. The "priests" wisely conceal themselves behind masses of contradictory data and vociferously deny that they exist. Like the Mayan priests they can reconstruct the past and predict the future on a statistical basis through manipulation of media. It is the daily press preserved in newspaper morgues that makes detailed reconstruction of the past dates possible. How can the modern priests predict seemingly random future events? [...] It is precisely uncontrollable automatic reactions that make news. The controllers know what reactive commands they are going to restimulate and in consequence they know what will happen." ([4], pages 44–45)

History starts for Burroughs with the apparition of the word[9]. Since then the "word virus" is deeply buried in man. In *The Ticket that exploded* he details how this virus manifests itself:

OPERATION REWRITE

The "Other Half" is the word. The "Other Half" is an organism. Word is an organism. The presence of the "Other Half" a separate organism attached to your nervous system on an air line of words can now be demonstrated experimentally. One of the most common "hallucinations" of subjects during sense withdrawal is the feeling of another body sprawled through the subject's body at an angle ... yes quite an angle it is the "Other Half" worked quite some years on a symbiotic basis. From symbiosis to parasitism is a short step. The word is now a virus. [...] Modern man has lost the option of silence. Try halting your sub-vocal speech. Try to achieve even ten seconds of inner silence. You will encounter a resisting organism that *forces you to talk*. That organism is the word.

I have extensively quoted from Burroughs' work in a possibly very imprudent way and I have let the quotations speak, without discussing at all *who* is speaking, and if these characters may stand for Burroughs' viewpoints. Nevertheless the virus topic is clearly identifiable both in his novels and in his various interviews. He sees the virus topic as being closely related to the question of man's (limits of) perception and communication. It is exactly this topic I am interested in, although my motivation is different. It is not the *limiting* faculty of the 'word virus' that I want to examine, but the capacity of viruses to *enable* communication and signification.

---

[9] For a similar and more recent viewpoint see the song "Keep Talking" in [10]. Quote from the off voice (that sounds like the synthetic voice of astro–physicist Stephen W. Hawking): *"For millions of years mankind lived just like animals. Then something happened which unleashed the power of our imagination. We learned to talk. It doesn't have to be like this, all we need to do is make sure we keep talking."*

4.4 Viruses and Communication

So far I have presented three different areas (molecular biology, computer science and a literary œuvre) where the same term /virus/ is used. However, the correspondence goes beyond this textual level, and I claim that in all three cases /virus/ refers to a common 'virus concept' – the 'virus mechanism' being only the most obvious common (technical) aspect. Moreover, the virus concept seems to be intimately bound to communication and even signification phenomena. The relation between viruses and communication shall be discussed in this section. It should by now be clear that I equate messengers with viruses. In principle, messengers form a fourth area which is connected with the virus concept: in this case, of course, the communication aspect is intentionally present.

Viruses and Signs What is striking about the virus mechanism is that it was either discovered (cell biology), constructed (computer viruses) or postulated (Burroughs), but that in each case a communicative situation is involved or can be identified. What seems strange in this context is the fact that viruses are mere instructions, but according to common sense and semiotics, interpretation seems to play an important role in any 'true' communication. Thus, at the heart of this discussion is the dichotomy between a supposed instructional mode of communication and the usual interpretative mode. Again, I refer to Burroughs where he quotes the founder of the scientology sect:

> "Mr L. Ron Hubbard has given us an excellent definition of communication: cause, distance, effect, with intention, attention and duplication. More fully stated: 'Communication is the consideration and action of impelling an impulse or particle from source point across a distance to a receipt point with the intention of bringing into being at the receipt point a duplication of that which emanated from the source point.' Applying this definition it will be seen that the virus has achieved a precision of communication with particular reference a duplication of that which emanated from the source point far in advance of human speech. This precision depends on a rigid an unvarying order of programming at the cellular level." ([4], pages 206–207, typing errors as in the book)

This quote brings us back to the semiotic concept of 'sign': Hubbard's definition resembles a semiotic definition of the sign concept (the 'bringing into being' would be the process of semiosis, the 'what emanated from the source' is the interpretant). However, Burroughs identifies here in a simplistic way the duplication of the virus manifest with the 'duplication' of the content a sign stands for. A more established position of how to reconcile the instructional mode with the sign concept can be found in the classical work of the semiotician Morris (1901–1979): based on Peirce he has proposed a behavioristic approach to semiotics [15]. The central paradigm of behaviorism is to explain behavior (and how it is learned) by stimulus/reaction patterns. (Note by the way that if the sender knows some stimulus/reaction pair of the recipient, a stimulus becomes an instruction). The link between behavior and the concept of sign is documented in Morris' central quasi–definition of a sign (it is a quasi-definition because it does not say that all signs have to work this way: see the preface by Apel in [15], page 31, and Morris' original comment on page 354 of [14]):

> "If something, A, controls behavior towards a goal in a way similar to [. . .] the way something else, B, would control behavior with respect to that goal in a situation in which it were observed, then A is a sign." ([14], page 7)

What is most notable with this approach is that Morris bases his semiotic theory on the *reaction*. However, in contrast to the simplistic behavioristic approach which explains everything by stimulus/reaction patterns, he introduces further on in the same book a level of indirection in form of 'reaction dispositions'[10]. Thus Morris' sign, although being a stimulus, must not necessarily lead to an immediate reaction. The response to a sign depends on additional conditions – and signs are able to change such reaction disposition.

How does Morris' model of a sign, i.e. a preparatory–stimulus, relate to viruses? Consider biological viruses: clearly, a virus consists of stimuli – the RNA consists of mere instructions. However, as was stressed in the section on the interpretation context, these instructions are not as imperative as may appear: control paths inside a cell influence the protein synthesis, and make the execution of instructions dependent on a complex 'interpretation' context. It was also mentioned that viruses can influence these control paths in order to enable or speed up their own duplication (section 4.1): in other words, the virus changes the reaction disposition. It is now very tempting to say that a virus, therefore, conforms to Morris' definition of a sign, and in fact, more evidence will be given in support of this viewpoint.

Another argument for relating instructions to signs can be found in [3], where signs are identified with abstract automata (and thus with programs): Bogarin suggests that undecidable problems of formal logic are intimately bound to the quality of being a sign. As soon as expressions on natural numbers can be formulated within a sign, undecidable problems creep in because of Gödel's theorem. This property discriminates signs from other non-sign vehicles and matches the remark made in section 3.2 about 'sufficient complexity'.

An interesting point in this context is that 'interpretation' is not necessarily more powerful than 'instruction' and may even coincide with it. This is relevant because it is often assumed that interpretation is superior to 'blind' instruction execution. Consider for instance an alert messenger platform which wants to detect whether a received communication messenger incorporates some harmful routine (one could call this the virus-detection problem). It turns out that such a thorough check is, in general, not possible, due to undecidable questions of arithmetics (halting problem for Turing machines). This also applies to the analysis of messengers: i.e., in order to understand the effects of a messenger, a 'vigilant computer' – in general – cannot do better than to execute the messenger's instructions (instead of analyzing/interpreting them).

Viruses as Signs: the V–Code The reflections on Morris' sign definition have lead to the hypothesis that viruses can be signs. I propose to introduce the notion of a *v-code* (v for virus) and to speak about virus–based signs. In the following section I will try to relate v-codes to Eco's s-code and 'true code'.

By a v-code I mean a convention based on three elements: (1) a set of instructions, (2) a delimiting mechanism which allows the formation of finite sequences of instructions,

---

[10] The modified definition of Morris ([14], page 10): *"If anything, A, is a preparatory–stimulus which in the absence of stimulus–objects initiating response–sequences of a certain behavior-family causes a disposition in some organism to respond under certain conditions by response–sequences of this behavior family, then A is a sign."*

and (3) a basic 'interpretation rule' implying the execution of received instruction sequences. This definition simply restates what I have so far called the virus mechanism (aka messenger paradigm). The question is whether v-codes are just s-codes, or whether v-codes should be graded as Eco's 'true code', or, finally, whether v-codes remain limited to a position just beneath true codes.

Clearly, the v-code is based on some underlying s-code, present in the form of the instruction set. However, this also applies for true codes (see section 3.2). The important point here, as was the case with signs, is the *usage* of the underlying s-code. The virus–related arguments proposed so far required that a virus can express undecidable problems of arithmetics – it has been shown that under such circumstances an interpretation mode cannot do better than the instructional mode. Thus, an additional criteria for a v-code is that its underlying instruction set is sufficiently expressive to state computations with natural numbers. This guarantees that no (finite) equivalence relation can be established inside a v-code. By the way, it should be noted that the v-code also requires a recipient which has the computing capacity (and also the memory resources) to carry out arbitrary computations (otherwise we regress to a finite situation). This requirement has its equivalence in Eco's model of a true code in form of an encyclopedia: restricting an encyclopedia to a codebook yields simple s-codes.

Although the v-code does not appear to be isomorphic with true codes, one can try to understand the two codes as being dual concepts: on one side we have an inference mechanism relying on the complexity of an encyclopedia – on the other hand there is an instructional model which relies on the computational complexity. The (tentatively proposed) duality also means, that both concepts are equally powerful. Further examinations on relation between the two concepts are needed. One possible question is: can one type of code be used to realize all codes of the other type?

A simulation of true codes based on v-codes immediately bumps into the difficulty of having to make assumptions about the encyclopedia. Does it exist a priori, or is it constructed from scratch in every newborn mind? In order to avoid this difficulty, I propose another argument: how 'incompatible' is the view, that underlying our 'true code' there is a v-code?

Basing 'true codes' on v-codes means that every sign is at the base a virus. In fact, when applied to words, this is Burroughs thesis. Is not every book which enters the reader's mind and affects it for the rest of its life a virus? In fact, what Eco calls an 'inventive text', i.e., a text which creates or imposes a new code, is the perfect description of a virus. Nöth writes that an innovative text changes the code "... by determining the reader's future understanding of literature" ([16], page 195). In the same paragraph he also points to Lotman's view that the creation of new codes *constitutes* the act of reading, thus that there is no difference between a code and the understanding of a text. Inside the current simulation hypothesis, an interpretation of this situation is that the virus–mechanism is *the* minimal kernel enabling the creation of new codes. In other words: what we consider to be signs (and conventions) is only the effect of an underlying v-code. In the first place, viruses may specify inference modes as well as 'abbreviations', or in short, conventions. The more conventions are stacked, the more the instructional character is hidden. According to this model, even the recognition of a sign is 'learned', and, as Burroughs suggests, it hinders us in perceiving the world in an unbiased way.

The question of whether *all* signs (in Eco's sense) are based on some v-code (this question is the residue of Morris' quasi–definition of the sign concept), is impossible to answer formally. The reason lies in Church's well–known and unprovable hypothesis: it states that every 'effectively calculable' (i.e. intuitively calculable) function can be computed by a Turing machine. The proof of equivalence between signs and virus would demand that one make the working of a sign operational, so as to be able to compare the meaning transportation capability of a sign–based system and a virus-based one. Because every effectively calculable function, by which a sign's operation must be expressed, can be performed by a Turing machine, this results in a program for a Turing machine, or in other words in a virus. In other words: all formal comparison ends in coercing signs into viruses.

4.5 Viruses and Evolution

Following the repeated references to genetic code, it will not be considered unusual that this chapter contains some comments on evolution. What may surprise is that even in this area the instructional mode typical for the virus concept seems to occupy an important role. This section is based on theoretical work in computer science, and does not consider corresponding biological theories on evolution.

Genetic algorithms were proposed as a possible approach to find good (or optimal) solutions to problems which cannot be solved in an analytic way. The classical book in this domain was written by Holland [13] and appeared in 1975.

The approach of genetic algorithms consists in representing solutions for an adaptation problem as manipulable pieces of data, i.e., as strings of bits. Such a representation is repeatedly modified, yielding different variants of the original solution. Some selection criteria, e.g. picking up the 'fittest', are applied in order to select a new generation of solutions. Then, a new evolution cycle is started. There may be several strategies of how to modify the solutions and how to select the candidates which should enter into the next generation. Such a specific strategy is call an *adaptive plan*. One of the major results of Holland's work is that there are significantly better adaptive plans than a simple random trial and error process. The key to more qualified adaptive plans is the addition of structure to the representation so that *genetic operators* like cross-over or inversion do not occur at arbitrary places. Due to the phenomenon of *epistasis*, that is the fact that effects are not necessarily additive, selection and modification should respect co–adapted sets of alleles (*schemas*). Such adaptation plans are also called *genetic plans*.

In chapter 8 of [13], Holland asks if it is possible to relax the solutions' fixed representation which was chosen for a first theoretical treatment of genetic plans. The terms and concepts Holland proposes immediately make the relation to the currently discussed topic evident. The basic unit of manipulation is called a *broadcast unit*. Broadcast units are finite sequences of symbols, whereby the alphabet consists of ten symbols only. The symbols are used to code both data values *and* instructions: in fact, each broadcast unit is a small program which will be executed by the environment. A broadcast unit can indicate how other broadcast units are to be manipulated by the environment. That is: broadcast units are operator and operand at the same time. The resulting "broadcast language" allows everything except the ten basic symbols and the adaptive plan to be subject to adaptation.

Holland's execution model for broadcast units is blatantly identical to the messenger concept (or virus mechanism) which I have presented extensively by now: broadcast units contain explicit instructions which the environment has to execute. Surprising is the variety of fields where Holland demonstrates the use of broadcast units: simple programming tasks like string manipulation and arithmetics (!) are presented, but the possibility of self–reproduction and the modeling of the world of radiative signals (sound, light, etc) are also discussed. Based on this last point Holland would no doubt agree that communication phenomena in general can also be modeled by his environment, although he did not discuss this explicitly. In Holland's line of thought it would be interesting to examine a sign definition which is based on the power to express modifications of its own representation. This topic was already discussed when the problem of simulating 'true codes' with v-codes was examined. My assumption is that any code that can be used to extend and recode itself in a stronger way than an equivalence (that is, an s-code) is a *v-code* and provides a basis for forming signs.

4.6 Viruses and Teleology

Concerning the discussion of *v-code*–based signs, the reader may have shared my unease about the direct comparison of algorithmic complexity and the complexity of the encyclopedia. As a result of my own unease I have avoided to giving more precise information about the interpretant of a virus, i.e., a v-code based sign. Is the interpretant, as Peirce suggests, another sign, and therefore another virus? In order to circumvent this difficulty, I will embed this discussion in a more general context: this context is the philosophical debate which since long occupies researchers in the field of artificial intelligence (AI). One possible starting point to this debate is the question whether computer programs can 'understand', or whether they just mimic understanding. The following survey mainly follows [17].

One position, characterized as 'strong AI', claims that what is called 'spirit' or mind is the mere effect of executing algorithms (see e.g., Hofstadter [11, 12]). Not every algorithm has the attribute of showing intellectual qualities: only sufficient complexity (or higher order structures, self–referencing capability etc.) will display skills which are usually attributed to humans. The executing platform, the brain, is not essential for this task. In fact, any computing device suffices that operates reasonably fast and has enough memory resources to execute such algorithms. Devices are interchangeable, they only *show* spirit: it is the algorithms which represent meaning and spirit.

The other position argues that 'spirit' is more than just clever or fast computation. True intelligence requires consciousness. Consciousness, however, cannot be completely grasped by algorithms, as Penrose suggests: there must be a non–algorithmic ingredient. One argument proposed is that new mathematical theorems are often 'discovered' (but not constructed) *before* the mathematician can formally prove them i.e., humans have "a direct route to truth". This would also explain why mathematical discussions, despite the variety of internal images about an idea, can be led with such ease and despite the considerable imprecision of communication.

The previous example brings the discussion back to communication and significa-tion phenomena. The question is whether the instructional view of communication is compatible with the one or the other position. Clearly, the 'strong AI' viewpoint poses fewer difficulties: it even *requires* that meaning is exchanged on a algorithmic basis, and thus in the form of a virus. But Penrose' concept of consciousness is also consistent with the virus view. Because truth and signification exist, communication does not need to create it. The task of communication then is to *guide* the partner in his/her contacts with the platonic world[11]. This, of course, can best be represented in an instructional form, i.e., a virus.

In both positions the teleological question on the origin and purpose of the virus mechanism remains open. In the first case, an initial virus must have existed which set off this immense program we are all part of. In the second case one can ask whether the virus mechanism also belongs to the platonic world, and how it made the leap into our material world.

With an invitation to the reader to dive into this puzzling domain I want to bring to an end this lengthy exploration of the virus metaphor and its intrinsic communicative aspect.

5   Conclusions and Outlook

Deliberately I have refrained from discussing too much the implications of instruction–based communications on computer systems. This in fact is the topic of many research activities that have started by now. What I would like to discuss at this place is the perhaps even more puzzling question of where we are heading to. One observation is that our perception of computers and networks will change drastically. It will turn out that computers and networks are very poor media (thus, they are not the new (multi-) media we are looking for) and in fact are only the substrate for something else. Thus, we will realize that computers only provide the execution environment for the *true mediators* that is, the mobile software agents, active documents etc. which live in the networks. The power of this new media is its capability to carry and create meaning instead of just transporting data. We discussed in section 4.4 why communication messengers and the related V-code could be the basic sign mechanism on which true knowledge media can be built.

Another but related forecast is that research on artificial life will join instruction–based communications. It will turn out that it is not necessary to build special artificial biotopes for running related experiments: the networked execution environments for communication messengers will be the first "real" world for artificial life. At the begin-ning there will be only niches, but after having reached some critical mass and meshing, it will be virtually impossible to shut down this ecosystem (remember the quote in the footnote in section 9: "It doesn't have to be like this, all we need to do is make sure we keep talking."). That such a system can survive depends heavily on its ability to adapt

---

[11] The concept of encyclopedia should not be confounded with the platonic world mentioned by Penrose: the encyclopedia is just a characterization of how a 'true code' structures communi-cation. The encyclopedia is not a faithful image of the platonic world because it has to reflect the impossibility of perceiving this world undistorted.

to changing environments. My claim is that it is just a question of time before we will see evolving and self-adapting messengers.

As researchers and engineers we try to implement new computer systems based on mobile code because we believe them to have superior properties. In reality, however, we witness how computers are invaded by viruses. Or to put it in W. S. Burroughs wording once again: *"I advance the theory that in the electronic revolution a virus is a very small unit of word and image."* Our task is to make this become true.

References

1. Bruce Alberts et al. *Molecular Biology of the Cell.* Garsland Publishing, 1983.
2. Laurie Anderson. *Home of the Brave.* Compact Disc, Warner Bros. Records – Talk Normal Production, 1986.
3. Jorge Bogarin. *Semiotik der Automaten, Algorithmen und Formalen Sprachen.* PhD thesis, Universität Stuttgart, 1989.
4. William S. Burroughs. *The Job – Topical Writings and Interviews.* John Calder, 1984.
5. John Calder, editor. *A William Burroughs Reader.* Pan Books, 1982.
6. Fred Cohen. Implications of computer viruses and current methods of defense. In Peter J. Denning, editor, *Computers under Attack*, pages 381–406. Addison-Wesley, 1990.
7. Umberto Eco. *A Theory of Semiotics.* Indiana University Press, Bloomington, 1976.
8. Umberto Eco. *Semiotics and the Philosophy of Language.* Indiana University Press, Bloomington, 1984.
9. Umberto Eco. On semiotics and immunology. In *The Semiotics of Cellular Communication in the Immune System*, NATO ASI Series H, Cell Biology, pages 3–15. Springer, 1988.
10. Pink Floyd. *The Division Bell.* Compact Disc, EMI Records Ltd, 1994.
11. Douglas R. Hofstadter. *Gödel, Escher, Bach – ein Endlos Geflochtenes Band.* Deutscher Taschbuch Verlag, 2nd edition, 1992. Translated from *Gödel, Escher, Bach – un Eternal Golden Braid,* 1979.
12. Douglas R. Hofstadter and Danial C. Dennett. *Einsichten ins Ich.* Klett-Cotta, 1986. Translated from *The Mind's I,* 1981.
13. John H. Holland. *Adaptation in Natural and Artificial Systems.* University of Michigan Press, 1975.
14. Charles W. Morris. *Signs, Language and Behavior.* Prentice-Hall, New York, 1950. 4th printing.
15. Charles W. Morris. *Zeichen, Sprache und Verhalten.* Pädagogischer Verlag Schwann, Düsseldorf, 1973.
16. Winfried Nöth. *Handbuch der Semiotik.* Metzler, 1985.
17. Roger Penrose. *Computerdenken: die Debatte um künstliche Intelligenz, Bewusstsein und die Gesetze der Physik.* Spektrum der Wissenschaft, 1991. Translated from *The Emperor's New Mind: Concerning Computers, Minds, and the Laws of Physics,* 1989.
18. G. Prodi. Signs and codes in immunology. In *The Semiotics of Cellular Communication in the Immune System*, NATO ASI Series H, Cell Biology, pages 53–64. Springer, 1988.
19. Ferdinand de Saussure. *Course in general linguistics.* Duckworth, 1983. Translated and annotated by Roy Harris.
20. Thomas A. Sebeok (general editor). *Encyclopedic Dictionary of Semiotics*, volume 73 of *Approaches to Semiotics.* Mouton de Gruyter, 1986.
21. Claude E. Shannon and Warren Weaver. *The Mathematical Theory of Communication.* University of Illinois Press, 1949.

22. Eugene H. Spafford. The internet worm program: An analysis. *ACM SIGCOMM Computer Communication Review*, 19(1):17–59, January 1989.

23. Andrew S. Tanenbaum. Report on the seventh ACM SIGOPS European Workshop, systems support for worldwide applications, Sep 1996. Private copy, December 1996.

24. Christian F. Tschudin. Flexible protocol stacks. *ACM SIGCOMM Computer Communication Review*, pages 197–204, September 1991.

25. Christian F. Tschudin. *On the Structuring of Computer Communications*. PhD thesis, Université de Genève, 1993. Thèse No 2632, ftp://cui.unige.ch/pub/tschudin/phd-thesis{123}.ps.Z.

26. John Vittal. Active message processing: Messages as messengers. In *Computer Message Systems – Proceedings of the IFIP TC-6 International Symposium Ottawa*, pages 175–195, April 1981.

Part II
Concepts

Analyzing Mobile Code Languages

Gianpaolo Cugola, Carlo Ghezzi, Gian Pietro Picco, Giovanni Vigna

Abstract. The growing importance of telecommunication networks has stimulated research on a new generation of programming languages. Such languages view the network and its resources as a global environment in which computations take place. In particular, they support the notion of code mobility. To understand, discuss, evaluate, and compare such languages, it is necessary to develop a new set of programming language concepts and/or extend the concepts that are used to deal with conventional languages. The purpose of this paper is to provide such framework. This is done hand-in-hand with a survey of a number of existing new languages.

1 Introduction

Advances in telecommunication networks have given new impetus to research on distributed systems. This research is based on a long term vision where computers are no more viewed as mainly autonomous and self-contained computing devices accessing local resources which, occasionally, communicate with each other; rather, they are part of a global computing platform, built upon a synergy of local and remote resources, whose sharing is enabled by broadband communication networks.

According to this vision, a new generation of distributed applications is being envisioned, whose distinctive feature is the exploitation of some sort of "code mobility", These applications will be called *mobile code applications* (MCAs). By examining current scientific work, the approaches followed to build MCAs can be roughly classified as follows[1]:

- *The "Remote Evaluation" approach.* According to this approach, based on the work described in [15], any component of an MCA can invoke services provided by other components, that are distributed on the nodes of a network, by providing not only the input data needed to perform the service (like in a remote procedure call scheme) but also providing the code that describes how to perform the service.
- *The "Mobile Agent" approach.* The term "agent" is often abused and rarely defined precisely. In the context of this work, agents can be regarded as *executing units* (EUs). The term executing unit is used hereafter to denote the run-time representation, within a *computational environment* (CE), of a single flow of computation, such as a Unix process or a thread in a multi-threaded environment. The adjective "mobile" means that EUs running in a given CE can move to a different CE, where they resume execution seamlessly. MCAs based on this approach are composed of EUs that can move autonomously from CE to CE in order to accomplish some prescribed tasks. The definition of EU is similar to the definition of *mobile object*

---

[1] An evaluation and classification of mobile code design paradigms and mobile code applications is the subject of a parallel work, described in [5].

system given in [1], but our definition is not biased towards the object-oriented paradigm.

- *The "Code on Demand" approach.* According to this approach, the code that describes the behavior of a component of an MCA can change over time. A component running on a given CE can download and link on-the-fly the code to perform a particular task from a different (remote) component that acts as a "code server".

This paper does not discuss the pros and cons of these new approaches with respect to traditional ones, like the client-server paradigm, since this is out of the scope of this work (see [13, 5] for a preliminary contribution on this issue). Here it will suffice to say that, in principle, these new approaches can provide a more efficient use of the communication resources and a higher degree of service customization, but raise stronger requirements than traditional ones, for example in the area of security.

Moreover, the approaches that can be followed to build MCAs demand for dedicated mobile code technology. Traditional mechanisms, like RPC or sockets, are in fact either unsuitable or inefficient for the task. For example, the "Mobile Agent" approach demands for the capability of migrating EUs around a network. This has been investigated by many researchers in the OS [9] and small-scale distributed systems [2] areas, but they are far from being mainstream techniques in large-scale distributed systems.

The approaches described above can be exploited by using the mechanisms embodied in a new generation of programming languages, which are usually referred to as *mobile code languages* (MCLs). They can be regarded as languages for distributed systems, whose primary application domain is the creation of MCAs on large-scale distributed systems, like the Internet. These languages differ from other languages or middleware for distributed system programming (e.g., CORBA [12] and Emerald [2]) because they explicitly model the concept of separate execution environments and how code and computations move among these environments.

The goal of this paper is to propose an (initial) set of programming language concepts, abstractions, and mechanisms, that can be used to analyze, evaluate, and compare existing MCLs or to design new ones. Some are well-known concepts that have been routinely used for traditional programming languages, others are concepts that are shared with traditional languages, and yet become especially relevant or acquire new dimensions in the case of MCLs (e.g., scope rules and name resolution). Still others are typical of MCLs, e.g., the mechanisms to support dynamic linking, mobility, state distribution, and security. In this paper we concentrate on the characteristics that are typical of MCLs. The concepts we will develop are applied in the evaluation of a set of existing MCLs found in literature. In order to provide the reader with a minimum background, such languages are surveyed in Section 2. Section 3 describes in detail our analysis, while Section 4 describes further directions for the work presented in this paper.

2 A Survey of Mobile Code Languages

This section provides a sketchy overview of the languages that will be discussed in this paper. They are:

Java Developed by Sun Microsystems, Java [10, 21] is perhaps the language that raised most of the current debate on and expectations from mobile code. It turns out, however, that Java is perhaps the "less mobile" of the languages reviewed here. The original goal of the language designers was to provide a portable, clean, easy-to-learn, and general-purpose object-oriented language. Portability, security and safety features, a programmable mechanism for downloading application code from the network and, most important, a careful marketing that led to integration of a Java interpreter into the Netscape Navigator Web browser, are some of the keys of success of Java as "the Internet language".

Telescript Developed by General Magic, Telescript [25, 17] is a rich, object-oriented language conceived for the development of large distributed applications, oriented in particular to the electronic market. Security has been one of the driving factors in the language design, together with the capability of migrating EUs (Telescript threads) while executing. There are two kinds of Telescript EUs: *agents*, i.e., EUs that can migrate to a different *engine* by executing a go operation, and *places*, i.e., stationary EUs that can contain other EUs (agents or places). Besides the technical issues involved in EU migration, agents and places offer an intriguing and intuitive metaphor for building distributed systems.

Obliq Developed at DEC by Luca Cardelli, Obliq [4] is an untyped, object-based, lexically scoped, interpreted language. Obliq objects are local to interpreters but it is possible to move computations from one interpreter to another. Distributed lexical scoping is the glue of such roaming computations, allowing transparent access to objects distributed on a computer network.

Safe-Tcl Developed by the authors of the Internet MIME standard, Safe-Tcl [3] is an extension of Tcl [20] conceived to support active e-mail. In active e-mail, messages may include code to be executed when the recipient receives or reads the message. Since code is evaluated in the recipient's environment, care must be taken to protect the user from malicious or erroneous code. In the original implementation of the language, mobility was achieved by means of the MIME e-mail run-time support. Safe-Tcl does not provide support for active mail code mobility at the language level and therefore this kind of mobility will not be further analyzed. Instead, a kind of code mobility is achieved indirectly through a programmable dynamic code loading mechanism. Presently, most of the fundamental features of Safe-Tcl have been included in the latest release of Tcl/Tk.

Agent Tcl Developed at the University of Darthmouth, Agent Tcl [11] provides a Tcl interpreter extended with support for EU migration. An executing Tcl script can move from one host to another with a single jump instruction. A jump freezes the program execution context and transmits it to a different host which resumes the script execution from the instruction that follows the jump.

TACOMA In TACOMA [14] (Tromsø And COrnell Mobile Agents), the Tcl language is extended to include primitives that allow an EU running a Tcl script to request the execution of another Tcl script on a different host. The script code is sent, together with some initialization data, to the destination host where it is evaluated.

M0 Implemented at the University of Geneva, M0 [23] is a stack-based interpreted language that implements the concepts of *messengers*. Messengers, the M0 EUs, are sequences of instructions that are transmitted between *platforms* and unconditionally executed upon receipt. Each platform contains one or more EUs, together with an associative array (called *dictionary*) used to allow memory sharing among different EUs. Platforms are connected by channels which represent the communication path between different hosts.

Tycoon The overall objective of the Tycoon [19, 18] project, developed at the University of Hamburg, is to offer a persistent programming environment for the development of data-intensive applications in open environments. The Tycoon Language (later on, simply "Tycoon") is used as the application and system programming language in the Tycoon environment. Tycoon is a persistent, polymorphic, higher-order functional language extended with imperative features. All language entities in Tycoon (i.e., values, functions, modules, types, and also threads) have first class status and can be manipulated as standard data. Moreover, they are persistently managed by the Tycoon environment transparently to the programmer. Tycoon enables the programmer to use different programming paradigms: functional and imperative programming are supported directly. Moreover, using the higher-order language features, several variants of the object-oriented programming style are supported.

Facile Developed at ECRC in Münich, Facile [6] is a functional language that extends the Standard ML language with primitives for distribution, concurrency and communication. In [16] a further extension to support mobile code programming is described, which introduces advanced translation techniques and strongly typed resource linking. In the sequel, when talking about Facile, no distinction will be made between the language and its extension.

3 Relevant Issues in Mobile Code Languages

Mobility has a strong impact on programming language features. This section analyzes both the characteristics of conventional languages that must be extended to take into account mobility, and the completely new issues that must be considered. For each issue, a general discussion of the problem is presented, followed by an analysis of how such problems have been tackled in the MCLs surveyed in the previous section.

3.1 Type System

The decision about which type system to adopt is one of the most important design choices that have to be taken when defining a new programming language. The language can be defined to be *typeless*, i.e., all data belong to an untyped universe and can be interpreted as values of different types when manipulated by different operators. Typeless languages impose no restrictions on how data are manipulated. The resulting power and flexibility are counterbalanced by the impossibility of protecting data against nonsensical or erroneous manipulations.

At the other extreme, a language may adopt a *strong type system*. In such case, the language definition ensures that the absence of type errors can be guaranteed for a program statically. Languages of this class support the development of verifiable programs. To increase flexibility, however, languages may weaken the type system in such a way that full type checking may only be achieved dynamically, by verifying at run-time that typed data objects are manipulated only through legal operations. This design choice weakens program verifiability, since type errors can only be uncovered if particular input data are used during execution.

In MCLs, strong typing can be practically impossible to achieve for two main reasons. First, code can be downloaded from a remote site and linked dynamically to a running program. Second, resources may be bound to a program as it is executing (see Section 3.3). In both cases, type correctness of a program cannot be verified statically.

MCLs adopt different strategies to weaken their type system in order to allow code and resource dynamic linking.

A first strategy, exploited by several languages, is to complement compile-time type checking with several type checks performed at run-time. Java, Telescript, Facile, and Tycoon are all based on some form of dynamic linking. For instance, Java programs can dynamically download and link code from the network. Type checking is performed at run-time to ensure that this dynamically downloaded and linked code obeys the language type rules. Similarly, in Telescript, Facile, and Tycoon the run-time system performs type checking to evaluate the type correctness of remote resources accessed when EUs move.

Another strategy, adopted by Obliq and M0, is to perform all type checking at run-time only.

Yet another strategy would be to define a typeless language. Tcl derivatives, like Safe-Tcl, Agent Tcl, and TACOMA are examples of such languages. Tcl variables contain just strings. Tcl instructions elaborate these strings as appropriate. For example, arithmetic operators convert strings to the numeric values they represent, operate on such values and then translate the numeric results back to strings.

3.2 Scoping and Name Resolution

The scope of an identifier is the range of instructions over which the identifier is known. Name resolution rules determine which computational entity is bound to each identifier in any point of a given program.

All of the MCLs examined, with the exception of M0, use static scoping rules. This means that the scope of a variable name is determined by the lexical structure of the program. As will be explained later, in M0 the scope of a name can be modified at run time by the programmer.

Name resolution is critical in MCLs. In fact, during the execution of an MCA, the names that appear in the code may be bound to entities that may be located on remote computational environments. Name resolution can either be performed automatically by the run-time support or hooks in the language run-time support can be provided to allow programmers to define their own name resolution rules.

Most of the existing MCLs do not offer particular features to perform automatic name resolution for remote resources. Name resolution for local resources is often performed statically and remote resources have to be accessed explicitly. This means that the programmer is aware of the location of the various remote resources. For example, a Java program can download and link code from the network but the name resolution of dynamically downloaded classes has to be explicitly programmed. A Java programmer must write her own class loader that resolves the names of the classes that have to be downloaded from the network.

In Obliq, new objects created by an EU are stored in the local data space, that is, in the address space of the interpreer where the EU is actually running. The identifier for this object is bound to the storage area of the object. When the EU moves, references to objects in the origin data space are automatically transformed into *network references*. Further accesses to such objects will be transparently translated into callbacks to the interpreter that holds the variable value. Hence, the binding between the object identifier and the object storage area is established at run-time and cannot be changed. Moreover, name resolution rules hide the actual physical location of remote resources to the programmer.

Telescript has a sophisticated name resolution scheme too. As mentioned in Section 2, the migration unit in Telescript is the thread. Each thread, among its attributes, has a list (called *package*) that contains the code for some of the classes it uses. Moreover, the language formally defines the *ownership* relation between the threads and the objects they own. When an object Obj requests an operation that forces the engine to resolve the name of a class (e.g., a new operation), the class name is searched into the package of the thread that owns Obj. If the class name is not found there, it is searched in the package of the place containing the thread. If the class name is still missing, it is searched backwards in the enclosing places, until the root of the place hierarchy is reached. Hence, in principle, the name space of a Telescript engine can be enriched by sending "installer" agents that are able to put packages in the appropriate place at run-time, in a fully programmable way.

In M0, the name space of a messenger is defined by its *dictionary stack*. Each dictionary that composes the dictionary stack is an associative array that contains names and their definitions. Whenever an interpreter has to resolve a name in the messenger code, it looks up the dictionaries in the dictionary stack starting from the topmost, hence the first matching definition is used. The dictionary stack can be manipulated by the programmer. In addition to this run-time mechanism, M0 provides, at the language level, a mechanism to force the binding of procedure names in a particular name space. In fact, using the bind command, a messenger is able to substitute all operators and procedures names present in a procedure with their corresponding values, according to the messenger dictionary stack. This means that in M0 the scope of a variable can be explicitly programmed.

3.3 Dynamic Linking

Two kinds of dynamic linking are relevant for MCLs: *remote code dynamic linking* and *local resource dynamic linking*.

Code dynamic linking is not a new technique. For instance, many operating systems support dynamically linked libraries (DLLs). The idea underlying DLLs is that libraries do not need to be linked to the main program at compilation time, rather they can be linked at run-time, when they are accessed for the first time. Remote code dynamic linking in mobile code systems naturally extends the notion of deferred linking found in the above systems to network applications. Remote code dynamic linking, allows programmers to implement MCAs based on the "code on demand" approach, that is, applications that download their code dynamically from the network according to different strategies.

The second form of dynamic linking is *local resource dynamic linking*. When an EU moves from a computational environment to another, it must be able to access resources located on the destination environment. Therefore, resources must be linked to their EU's internal representation. Typical examples of such resources are files or libraries.

Java exploits remote code dynamic linking extensively to enable the implementation of scalable and dynamically configurable applications. As we will explain in Section 3.6, the Java compiler translates Java source programs into an intermediate, platform independent, language, called *Java Byte Code*. Java Byte Code is executed by an interpreter that realizes the *Java Virtual Machine* on different hardware and software architectures. The loading and linking of the different classes that compose a Java application are performed at run-time by the *class loader*, which is part of the Java Virtual Machine. Classes are loaded and linked only when required. The default class loader loads the required classes from the local host file system, but Java programmers can write their own class loader, implementing different policies. For example, taking advantage of the platform independence of the Java Byte Code, a network class loader that loads classes from a heterogeneous network can be easily implemented.

A similar behavior can be also implemented in TACOMA and Agent Tcl. When a Tcl interpreter does not find a command c, it invokes the command unknown. This command resembles the Java class loader. By default, it searches for c in local packages and libraries, and, if successful, loads and evaluates c. As in Java, the unknown command can be redefined in order to download a particular package from the network.

In Safe-Tcl the unknown command has been removed because it was considered to be unsafe. A different, secure, customizable primitive to dynamically load and link libraries is provided by the language.

The MCLs that exploit resource dynamic linking most are Facile and Tycoon.

In Facile, the programmer can specify interfaces for the resources that a function will access during its lifetime. The function will operate on these resources only through their interfaces. Each interface is composed of a set of function signatures which define the operations that can be performed on the resource. At run-time, any local resource that offers at least a set of operations matching those listed in the interface can be bound to the function. Hence, a function moving to a new computational environment can access any resource on that environment among those that match the resource interfaces contained in the function code.

In Tycoon, remote resources can be bound to a moving thread dynamically. Migrating threads can specify the type of the remote resources they will access on the destination *migration engine*. When a thread arrives, remote resources of the required type, if present, are bound to the thread and then the thread resumes execution. A special schema is used to allow type checking to be performed at departure-time, in order to prevent exceptions from being raised on the destination engine, due to the lack of suitable remote resources. Each thread, in fact, owns a type specification of the destination migration engine that includes the type specifications of the remote resources available. Mismatches between the types of the resources available remotely and the types used in thread scripts to denote such resources are detected at departure-time.

In Telescript, code dynamic linking is achieved by means of the package mechanism described in Section 3.2. Resource dynamic linking is achieved through the mechanism of places. Each resource is contained into a place that holds a reference to that resource. When an agent enters a place, it is given a reference to that place, that can be used to invoke methods or manipulate attributes of the place. In particular, the agent may access the resources contained into the place, provided that it has the appropriate access rights.

3.4 Mobility and State Distribution

A widely accepted definition for code mobility is still lacking in the research community. The term "mobile code" is often used with a different meaning by different languages (and by different researchers). The same holds for the related concept of state distribution.

Since our goal is to analyze and compare different MCLs with respect to mobility and state distribution, it is necessary to abstract away from the details of the various MCLs examined. It is necessary to identify a small set of abstractions that can be used to model the essential aspects of the various solutions provided by different languages.

The term "mobility" in the context of MCLs intuitively refers to mechanisms to move code, or execution flows (that is, code with state), among different hosts. In the previous sections the term "executing unit" was used to informally describe a running program with an associated state of execution. In the following section a more precise characterization of this term is given, together with the set of concepts needed to develop our model.

An Abstract Model for Mobile Code Languages This section provides a definition of the abstractions that can be used to provide a run-time model for mobile languages. The description will be precise, but still informal. A complete formal definition is the subject of our on-going research.

In a conventional sequential programming language, the run-time view of a program is an executing unit (see Section 1) which consists of a *code segment*, that provides the static description of the program's behavior, and a program *state* [8]. The state contains the local data of all active routines together with control information, such as the value of the instruction pointer and the value of return points for all active routines. Control information allows EUs to continue their execution from the current state supporting routine calls and returns.

To provide a conceptual run-time model for mobile languages, the above conventional framework must be extended and modified in the following ways:

1. A concept of *computational environment* (CE) must be introduced. A CE is a container of *components*. It is an abstraction which is not necessarily mapped onto a host; e.g., two interpreters running on the same host represent two different CEs. Components may be *resources* or *executing units*. Resources are passive entities representing data, such as an object in an object-oriented language or a file in a file system. EUs represent the computational elements of our model and may be modeled as the composition of a code segment and a state, as explained above.

2. The state of an EU can be decomposed into its constituents: the *execution state* and the *data space*. The execution state stores all the control information related to the EU state. The data space comprises all resources accessible from all active routines. For example, a Unix process P_X executing a program X written in C can be regarded as an EU whose code segment is the source code of X, whose execution state is the program counter and stack structure associated to P_X, and whose data space is the set of files opened by P_X and the set of memory locations P_X is able to access, either directly or through a reference. In other words, the data space for P_X contains all the data contained in the stack frames of the routines that were called so far and not yet returned, together with the heap data reachable through them.

3. It may be useful to identify a subset of the data space, called *data closure*. The data closure of an EU is the set of all local and nonlocal resources that are accessible by the currently executing routine and by any routine it may call. This data space constituent allows the computation to proceed, possibly calling other routines, but does not support the unwinding of the computation's frame stack upon termination of the current routine.

4. Similarly, it may be useful to identify a portion of the code segment of an EU by defining the *code closure*, which consists of all routines that are directly or indirectly visible from the current one.

Executing units may share part of their data space, that is, two or more EUs may be able to access the same resources. For example, Unix processes may share files, while threads may share memory, too. Moreover, the data space of an EU may include resources located on CEs other than the one containing the EU. When this happens, the EU is said to have a *distributed state*. Issues related to state distribution will be tackled further on.

Analysis, Classification, and Comparison In this section the MCLs presented in Section 2 are analyzed with respect to the model discussed so far.

In conventional languages, like C and Pascal, each EU is bound to a unique CE for its whole lifetime. Moreover, the binding between the EU and its code segment is generally static. Even in environments that support dynamic linking, the linked code is a resource of the current CE. This is not true for MCLs. Mobile code languages are characterized by the fact that the code segment, execution state, and data space of an EU are able to move from CE to CE. In principle, each of the constituents identified above (code segment, execution state, and data space) can move independently. Hereafter, we discuss the choices made by the languages surveyed in Section 2. Two classes of MCLs can be identified: MCLs supporting *strong mobility* and MCLs supporting *weak mobility*.

Strong mobility Strong mobility is the ability of an MCL (called *strong MCL*) to allow EUs to move their code and execution state to a different CE. Executing units are suspended, transmitted to the destination CE, and resumed there.

Weak mobility Weak mobility is the ability of an MCL (called *weak MCL*) to allow an EU in a CE to be bound dynamically to code coming from a different CE. There are two main cases for this. Either the EU links dynamically a code segment downloaded from the net (see Section 3.3) or the EU receives its code segment from another EU (that is, the code is explicitly sent from a source CE to a destination CE). In the latter case, two more options are possible. Either the EU in the destination CE is created from scratch to run the incoming code or a pre-existing EU links the incoming code dynamically and executes it.

In both strong and weak MCLs, when the code of an EU is moved, what happens if the names it contains are bound to resources in the source CE? In other words, what happens to the whole data space of the source EU (in the case of a strong MCLs) or to the data closure and code closure of the moved code (in the case of weak MCLs) upon migration? Two classes of strategies are possible: *replication strategies* and *sharing strategies*.

Replication strategies can be further divided in:
   Static replication strategy. Some resources, called *ubiquitous resources* [16, 18] can be statically replicated in all CEs. System variables and user interface libraries are good examples of such resources. The original bindings to such resources are deleted and new default bindings are established with the local instances on the destination CE.
   Dynamic replication strategies. A copy of the bound resources is made in the destination CE, the original bindings are deleted, and new bindings are established with the copied resources. Two further options exist:
   (i) remove the bound resources from the source CE (*dynamic replication by move*) or (ii) keep them (*dynamic replication by copy*).
Sharing strategy implies that the original binding is kept and therefore inter-CE references to remote resources must be generated.

Mobile code languages may exploit different strategies for different resources. Static replication can be used only for stateless resources or for resources whose state has not to be maintained consistent across CEs. Dynamic replication by copy is adopted to ensure resource *availability* both on the source and destination CE. Dynamic replication by move is adopted for resources that are neither to be shared nor to be available on both the origin and destination CE. Otherwise, when a resource vanishes, a dangling reference can arise. In addition, dynamic replication is adopted for simple values like integers or strings. Sharing is adopted for resources that have to be *shared* among EUs on different CEs. The sharing strategy leads to *state distribution*. In fact, when this strategy is adopted, the data space of the remote EU contains resources located in the source CE.

The languages surveyed in Section 2 differ in the way they support mobility and state distribution. With respect to mobility, TACOMA, M0, Facile, Obliq, Safe-Tcl, and Java are weak MCLs, while Telescript, Tycoon and Agent Tcl are strong MCLs. As for state distribution, only Obliq adopts a sharing strategy and supports distributed data spaces.

In TACOMA, EUs are implemented as Unix processes (the *agents*), while CE functionalities are implemented by the Unix operating system with some run-time support. In TACOMA, an agent A1 can require the execution of a new agent A2 on a remote CE. A1 provides A2's code and initialization data by copying them in a data structure (called *briefcase*) that is sent to the remote CE. Upon receipt, a new EU is created with the code provided. The new agent A2 is able to access the data in the briefcase provided by A1, that conceptually becomes part of the receiving CE. Since the code sent is not bound to any resource, the problem of data space handling does not arise.

M0 follows the same approach. *Messengers*, (the implementation of the EU abstraction) can *submit* the code of other messengers to remote *platforms* (representing CEs). Such code is executed as a new messenger on receipt. The submitting messenger may copy relevant data in the message containing the code submitted, making them available at the destination CE.

In Facile, *channels* can be used for synchronous communication between two Facile threads, that are run by different *nodes*, i.e., the Facile run-time support. In this context, threads are EUs and nodes are CEs. Channels can be used to communicate any legal value of the Facile language. In particular, functions may be transmitted through channels since they are first-class language elements. The programmer can specify whether the transmitted function is to be directly invoked by the receiver or a new Facile EU is to be spawned using the function code. Since Facile is statically scoped, both the data closure and the code closure of the function instance sent may be non-empty. These closures have to be attached to the migrating function. Therefore, dynamic replication by copy is adopted[2]. In addition, static replication is supported for *ubiquitous values* [16].

Obliq allows remote execution of procedures by means of *execution engines* which implement the CE concept. A thread, the Obliq EU, can request the execution of procedures on a remote execution engine. The code for such procedures is sent to the destination engine and executed there by newly created EUs. Obliq objects are bound to the CE in which they are created, and this binding cannot be broken. When an EU asks for the execution of a procedure on a remote CE, the references to the objects used by such procedure are automatically translated into network references. Accesses to these objects are translated into callbacks to the originating CE. This sharing strategy hides the actual location of the EU data space elements, but the use of network references may results in complex debugging and performance bottlenecks.

As mentioned in Section 3.3 Java provides mechanisms to dynamically load and link part of the code segment of an EU from a remote CE that acts as a code repository. If the downloaded code contains references to remote classes their code is automatically loaded when their names have to be resolved for the first time. In terms of the model previously given, this means that the code closure of the downloaded code is dynamically replicated. Since the loaded code is not bound to any resource in the code repository, the problem of data space handling does not arise.

As in Java, Safe-Tcl can load routine code dynamically from the network. As opposed to Java, this operation has to be explicitly performed both for the required routine and for the code of the routines called by this one.

In Telescript, the *engine* embodies the CE abstraction. Executing units are *agents* and *places*. Agents can move by using the go operation, whose effect is to discard the

---

[2] Facile adopts a sharing strategy only if the communication is established by threads on the same node, since they can share memory.

agent image at the source CE and to rebuild it at the destination CE[3]. Execution resumes from the instruction following the go. The ownership concept is used to determine which part of the data space has to be made available on the destination CE. During migration, the objects owned by a mobile agent are dynamically replicated by move to the destination CE together with the agent code and execution state. The remainder of the data space, composed of the objects referenced by the agent but owned by other EUs, are neither replicated nor shared.

In Tycoon, EUs are threads. Threads can be moved from a Tycoon virtual machine to another using the migrate primitive. The Tycoon virtual machine embodies the CE abstraction. As for the data space of the moving EU, Tycoon adopts dynamic replication by copy. The static replication strategy is also supported through *ubiquitous resources* [18].

In Agent Tcl, each EU is a Unix process running the language interpreter. The CE abstraction is implemented by the operating system extended with the language run-time support that manages the name space of agents and the interactions among different agents. Agent Tcl EUs can either *submit* a new agent to a remote CE or migrate to another CE. In the first case, the EU provides the code to be executed remotely by a newly created EU. In addition, the programmer can specify explicitly the resources that have to be dynamically replicated by copy on the destination CE. In the second case, the migrating EU moves its code, data space, and execution state, except for references to the local file system (i.e., a dynamically replication by move strategy is adopted).

3.5 Security

The computational environment of an MCL provides a general, distributed platform on which MCAs belonging to different users can be executed concurrently. CEs may host EUs that belong to different users and have different access rights to the hosting environment. In addition, the sites that compose the infrastructure may be managed by different authorities (e.g., a university or a company) and may communicate across untrusted communication infrastructures.

This scenario suggests two security domains: *interCE security* and *intraCE security*.

InterCE security encompasses mutual authentication between a moving EU and the destination CE, as well as integrity and privacy of the communication between two communicating CEs. Migrating EUs need to be authenticated by the destination CE in order to determine the identity of the sender. Moreover, moving EU should be able to authenticate the destination CE in order to be protected from spoofing of the destination site [7]. Once that EU and CEs have been mutually authenticated, the EU must be shipped from the source CE to the destination CE. Code travelling among CEs should be protected from tampering and unauthorized disclosure. Integrity mechanisms ensure that the EU representation transmitted over the lines is not modified, either by malicious intent or by errors in the transmission process. Privacy mechanisms ensure that third parties not involved in interCE communication cannot read the information transmitted over the network.

---

[3] Telescript provides also a send operation that can be used to transmit clones of the sending agent to one or more destination CEs.

IntraCE security, as noted in [24], encompasses security among different EUs, between EUs and the hosting CE, and between the CE and the supporting operating system. Most of these issues are addressed by access control techniques. Access control of EU to CE's resources is based on the identity of EUs, as determined by the authentication process. Each EU is given a set of access rights to local resources (including other EUs) that is determined by some policy. Typical policies ensure that EUs belonging to different users do not interfere and restrict access to the private data of other EUs. In addition, the ability given to EUs to dynamically link code coming from uncertain and possible malicious source requires strategies that allows *safe execution*, i.e., execution of code in an untrusted environment that protect from abuse of resources accessible under normal circumstances, e.g. sensitive files or EUs belonging to the same user. Safe execution can be ensured by controlling how incoming EUs access local resources and by limiting the number of operations that such EUs are allowed to perform.

One of the most difficult problem in intraCE security is represented by protection of EUs from the hosting CE. Since CEs must execute EUs, they must access their code and run-time representation. It is therefore very difficult, if not impossible, to protect EUs from malicious CEs. Attacks may include denial-of-service, service overcharging, private information disclosure, code and data modification. Usually, in MCLs CEs are considered trusted entities and the problem is not tackled.

As for the security mechanisms, they may be made available to the programmer or not. In the former case, security policies may be programmed. This choice results in greater flexibility, but may increase the language complexity, since concepts like object ownership or thread capabilities must be managed by the programmer. In the latter case, security policies are hardwired in the language run-time support.

Of all reviewed MCLs, Telescript provides the most powerful mechanisms to support security [22]. In Telescript, each thread object has attributes that can be used to determine its security-related characteristics. For example, attributes are provided to hold the *authority* of the thread, i.e., the real-world person or organization which it belongs to, and can be accounted for. A particular set of these attributes, called *permits*, grant the agent the right of performing a given set of operations (e.g., the go operation), or to use engine resources (e.g., the CPU time) in a specified amount. Permit violation is controlled by the programmer through the exception handling mechanism provided by Telescript.

The values of the security attributes are partly specified by the programmer and partly set by the Telescript engine where the trip originates, or by the engine where the trip ends. The mechanism by which the engine sets these values is fully programmable by the engine owner through the methods of the engine place, that is, the particular thread that represents the engine. Agent integrity is provided by packing and encrypting the agents before their trip.

In Safe-Tcl, security is based on a *twin interpreter* scheme which consists of a *trusted* interpreter, which is a full-fledged Tcl interpreter, and an *untrusted interpreter*, whose capabilities have been severely restricted, so that one can execute code of uncertain origin without being damaged. The owner of the interpreter may decide to export procedures which are ensured to be safe from the trusted interpreter to the untrusted one. For example, the trusted interpreter could provide procedures to access just a limited portion of the file system. When an e-mail message containing Safe-Tcl code is received, such code is passed to the untrusted interpreter for execution. The untrusted interpreter may require the loading of a Safe-Tcl library. As mentioned in Section 3.4, the loading mechanism can be programmed by the owner of the interpreter. The dynamically loaded code is evaluated by the trusted interpreter and therefore great care must be taken in order to avoid loading of code of unknown or uncertain source.

Java provides a somewhat similar scheme. Java Byte Code received from the network is not directly interpreted by the Java Virtual Machine. It is first scanned by a run-time module, the *Byte Code Verifier*, to check for the absence of potentially dangerous constructs and then it is controlled by a programmable *Security Manager*. Hence, security mechanisms are partly hard-wired into the language run-time support (i.e., the Byte Code Verifier) and partly programmable through the Security Manager.

The run-time support of Agent Tcl and TACOMA provides features to accept mobile EUs from selected hosts only. It provides no mechanisms to manage different EU owners and delegates access rights management and accounting to the underlying operating system. This solution seems to be inadequate for a complex mobile code application.

In M0, integrity of messengers transmitted over channels is supported via checksums included in the messenger message. While no mechanisms are provided for authentication, M0 provides the programmer with privacy and access control mechanisms. References to shared objects may have *attributes* that specify Unix-like access rights for a messenger with respect to the referenced object. In addition, messengers may use asymmetric encryption to create protected entries in shared memory, accessible by means of a public key, but modifiable only by means of a private key.

In Obliq there are no explicit security mechanisms. Lexical scope rules support an implicit form of safe execution. In fact, procedures evaluated by an Obliq engine, by default, may only access objects in their original scope. Therefore, access to objects and files residing at the engine CE must be granted explicitly by the remote engine passing a reference to a local component when invoking the procedure.

Facile lacks explicit security mechanisms, but research is on-going on the issue.

3.6 Translation Strategies

The choice of executing a programming language either through direct interpretation or through compilation is not distinctive of mobile code languages. Moreover, this has to do more with the language support environment than with the semantics of the language. Nonetheless, MCAs pose additional constraints and requirements that affect the criteria used traditionally to determine the choice. In fact, code exchanged in an MCA should be:

Portable The target platform is a computer network—be it a LAN or the Internet—and is to be thought of as a set of heterogeneous machines. The obvious goal is to write the mobile code once, and then be able to unleash it for execution on any machine of the target network, without being aware of the hardware and software requirements of each target machine. An interpreted approach can easily support the execution on such an heterogeneous environment, given that an interpreter is provided for each platform involved. A compiled approach, instead, would force the run-time support of the sender machine to be aware of the platform of the receiver machine in order to select the appropriate native executable code for transmission. If the destination platform is not known, the native code for each platform can be sent to the receiver.

Secure It is necessary to ensure that the code being executed on the target system does not damage system resources, as discussed in Section 3.5. Interpretation allows load-time or run-time checks on the source code in order to verify that only legal instructions are executed.

Mobility introduces additional options for compilation/interpretation. In fact, the code can be interpreted, or it can be compiled either on the sender machine or on the receiver machine. The resources that are actually linked to the code may be different when the code is compiled on one computational environment or on another because of different configurations (e.g., statically linked libraries).

A common strategy among MCLs is the adoption of a hybrid approach, consisting of compiling source programs into an *intermediate language* which is used for transmission and interpretation on the target machine. Using this approach, higher-level source code is compiled into a lower-level intermediate, portable code, designed to improve efficiency and safety of transmission and execution.

Facile supports all the patterns of compilation and interpretation described above. The source code can be transmitted as it is, translated into various intermediate representation with different abstraction levels, or the native code for the destination platform can be transmitted directly. In addition, to shorten compilation time on receipt in interactive applications, functions are compiled only when the application tries to invoke them, according to a lazy strategy [16].

Java uses a stack-based intermediate language, the *Java Byte Code*, which is interpreted by the *Java Virtual Machine*. The Byte Code is tested by a Byte Code verifier in order to watch for illegal instructions before interpretation. In addition, the Java Byte Code can also be compiled into native code on the fly (i.e., at run-time, when the code is run for the first time) through the *Just In Time* (JIT) compiler[4].

Low Telescript is the name of the stack-based language which constitutes the intermediate language for Telescript (more properly called High Telescript). In opposition to Java, the only purpose of this intermediate form is a more efficient transfer and execution. No security controls are performed, since security in Telescript is ensured at the language level. No compilation of Byte Code is allowed; Low Telescript is strictly interpreted.

Tacoma, M0, Agent Tcl, Safe-Tcl and Obliq are purely interpreted languages.

4 Conclusions and Further Work

Mobile code languages are a new trend in programming languages for distributed systems. They can enable brand new applications that can be expected to promote major technological breakthroughs. This work has analyzed a set of currently available mobile

---

[4] Different implementation of the Java Virtual Machine that perform JIT compilation are provided by several vendors and a JIT compiler was announced by Sun itself.

code languages, by proposing an initial set of concepts that can be used to assess and compare different languages and new features that might be added in new designs.

This initial work will be extended in three directions: first, we will extend our work to cover other languages that were not covered here. An example of such languages is Emerald [2]. Second, we will extend and refine our model to provide a formally defined abstract machine that can be used to specify the operational semantics of different MCLs. Work in this area is on-going. Third, we wish to understand what are the main design paradigms that can be followed to design MCAs and how different language features support or enforce such paradigms.

References

1. J. Baumann, C. Tschudin, and J. Vitek, editors. *Proceedings of the 2nd ECOOP Workshop on Mobile Object Systems*. Dpunkt, 1996.
2. A. Black, N. Hutchinson, E. Jul, and H. Levy. Fine-Grained Mobility in the Emerald System. *ACM Transactions on Computer Systems*, 6(1), February 1988.
3. N.S. Borenstein. EMail With A Mind of Its Own: The Safe-Tcl Language for Enabled Mail. Technical report, First Virtual Holdings, Inc, 1994.
4. L. Cardelli. Obliq: A language with distributed scope. Technical report, Digital Equipment Corporation, Systems Research Center, May 1995.
5. A. Carzaniga, G. P. Picco, and G. Vigna. Designing Distributed Applications using Mobile Code Paradigms. In *Proceedings of the 1997 International Conference on Software Engineering*, May 1997.
6. B. Thomsen et al. Facile Antigua Release Programming Guide. Technical Report ECRC-93-20, European Computer-Industry Research Centre, Munich, Germany, December 1993.
7. D. Chess et al. Itinerant Agents for Mobile Computing. Technical report, IBM Research Division - T.J. Watson Research Center, 1995.
8. C. Ghezzi and M. Jazayeri. *Programming Language Concepts*. John Wiley and Sons, second edition, 1989. Third ed. forthcoming.
9. A. Goscinski. *Distributed Operating Systems: The Logical Design*. Addison-Wesley, 1991.
10. J. Gosling and H. McGilton. The Java Language Environment: A White Paper. Technical report, Sun Microsystems, October 1995.
11. R.S. Gray. Agent Tcl: A Transportable Agent System. In *Proceedings of the CIKM'95 Workshop on Intelligent Information Agents*, 1995.
12. Object Management Group. Corba: Architecture and specification, August 1995.
13. C.G. Harrison, D.M. Chess, and A. Kershenbaum. Mobile Agents: Are They a Good Idea? Technical report, IBM Research Division - T.J. Watson Research Center, March 1995.
14. D. Johansen, R. van Renesse, and F.B. Schneider. An Introduction to the TACOMA Distributed System - Version 1.0. Technical Report 95-23, "University of Tromsø and Cornell University", June 1995.
15. J.W. Stamos and D.K. Gifford. Remote Evaluation. *ACM Transactions on Programming Languages and Systems*, 12(4):537–565, October 1990.
16. F.C. Knabe. Language Support for Mobile Agents. Technical Report ECRC-95-36, European Computer-Industry Research Centre, Münich, Germany, December 1995.
17. General Magic. *Telescript Language Reference*. General Magic, October 1995.
18. B. Mathiske, F. Matthes, and J. W. Schmidt. On Migrating Threads. Technical report, Fachbereich Informatik Universität Hamburg, 1994.

19. F. Matthes, S. Müssig, and J. W. Schmidt. Persistent Polymorphic Programming in Tycoon: An Introduction. Technical report, Fachbereich Informatik Universität Hamburg, 1993.

20. J.K. Ousterhout. *Tcl and the Tk Toolkit*. Addison-Wesley, 1994.

21. Sun Microsystems. *The Java Language Specification*, October 1995.

22. J. Tardo and L. Valente. Mobile Agents Security and Telescript. General Magic Technical Report, 1995.

23. C. F. Tschudin. *An Introduction to the* M0 *Messenger Language*. University of Geneva, Switzerland, 1994.

24. Jan Vitek. Secure object spaces. In *Proceedings of the 2nd ECOOP Workshop on Mobile Object Systems*, July 1996.

25. J.E. White. Mobile Agents. General Magic, 1995.

Sumatra:
A Language for Resource-Aware Mobile Programs*

Anurag Acharya, M. Ranganathan, Joel Saltz

Abstract. Programs that use mobility as a mechanism to adapt to resource changes have three requirements that are not shared with other mobile programs. First, they need to monitor the level and quality of resources in their operating environment. Second, they need to be able to react to changes in resource availability. Third, they need to be able to control the way in which resources are used on their behalf (by libraries and other support code). In this chapter, we describe the design and implementation of Sumatra, an extension of Java that supports resource-aware mobile programs. We also describe the design and implementation of a distributed resource monitor that provides the information required by Sumatra programs. changes.

1 Introduction

Mobile programs can move an active thread of control from one site to another during execution. This flexibility has many potential advantages. For example, a program that searches distributed data repositories can improve its performance by migrating to the repositories and performing the search on-site instead of fetching all the data to its current location. Similarly, an Internet video-conferencing application can minimize overall response time by positioning its server based on the location of its users. Applications running on mobile platforms can react to a drop in network bandwidth by moving network-intensive computations to a proxy host on the static network. The primary advantage of mobility in these scenarios is that it can be used as a tool to adapt to variations in the operating environment. Applications can use online information about their operating environment and knowledge of their own resource requirements to make judicious decisions about placement of computation and data.

Many systems provide some form of support for program mobility. The simplest form of support is the ability to download code and execute it to completion at a single site – as provided by systems like Omniware [3], Safe-TCL [6], Java [14]. Other systems like Avalon [11], NCL [13] REV [18] and Obliq [9] allow programs in execution to initiate computation on remote nodes and wait for their completion. The most sophisticated support is provided by systems like Agent TCL [15], Emerald [17], Mole [24], Aglets [20], TACOMA [16] and Telescript [26] which permit an executing program to move while it is in execution.

Programs that use mobility as a mechanism to adapt to resource changes have three requirements that are not shared with other mobile programs. First, they need to be aware of their execution environment. In particular, they need to monitor the level and

* This research was supported by ARPA under contract #F19628-94-C-0057, Syracuse subcontract #353-1427

quality of resources in their operating environment. We refer to this as the *awareness* requirement. Second, they need to be able to react to changes in resource availability. We refer to this as the *agility* requirement. Third, they need to be able to control the way in which resources are used on their behalf (by libraries and other support code). We refer to this as the *authority* requirement.

In this chapter, we describe the design and implementation of Sumatra, an extension of Java that supports resource-aware mobile programs. We also describe the design and implementation of a distributed resource monitor that provides the information required by Sumatra programs.

We first discuss the constraints that the requirements of awareness, agility and authority place on languages for mobile programs. We then describe Sumatra and discuss how its design decisions have been guided by these constraints. Next, we discuss the considerations that guide the design of resource monitors, in particular, fault-tolerance and the need to allow applications to control the use of resources on their behalf. We describe Komodo, a distributed resource monitor and discuss how well its design meets the requirements. Both Sumatra and Komodo have been implemented and are available to individuals and organizations with a Sun JDK license. We provide implementation details wherever appropriate.

In this chapter, we assume that the reader is familiar with mobile code languages (like Java, Obliq, Agent-Tcl). Several chapters in this book provide excellent introductions to this class of languages and the mechanisms used to implement mobility.

2 Design constraints

In this section, we discuss the language design constraints that arise from the desire to be resource-aware and the use of mobility as a mechanism to adapt to changes in resource availability. We discuss the requirements of awareness, agility and authority and the constraints each of them generates. In the next section, we describe Sumatra and discuss how its design has been guided by these constraints.

2.1 Awareness

Resource-aware programs need to be able to monitor the availability and quality of the resources in their environment. A resource can be monitored either on-demand or continuously. Both kinds of monitoring are useful. On-demand monitoring is useful in three kinds of situations. First, if the resource in question is used infrequently but is expensive to use – e.g. an application on a mobile host that uses a cell-modem to periodically scan incoming mail being held at a post-office machine. Second, if the availability of the resource in question changes infrequently – e.g. an application that chooses the location from which it monitors a process based on the amount of disk space available at that location. Third, if the resource is expensive to monitor and the cost of monitoring outweighs the potential gains – e.g. an application that accesses large volumes of data over a very slow link. Continuous monitoring is useful if the resource is frequently used or if the resource changes frequently or is cheap to monitor.

On-demand monitoring is, by necessity, synchronous. The request for information does not return till the information is available. Continuous monitoring can, on the other hand, support both synchronous and asynchronous interfaces. A synchronous request would return immediately with information about the current availability of the resource in question whereas an asynchronous request would monitor the resource and notify the application only when the resource availability no longer satisfies an application-specified predicate. A synchronous interface is suitable, for example, for an application that sends a sequence of large messages and checks the state of the network before sending each message. An asynchronous interface is useful, for example, for an application that uses a resource continuously (like receiving a video stream over the network) or an application that does not use the network itself but calls library routines which may do so. An asynchronous interface is also useful to inform applications about a qualitative change in the operating environment, for example if the platform is mobile and may need to switch between multiple wireless networks [19].

For continuous monitoring, an important decision is the granularity at which resource change is to be monitored. The simplest alternative is to report every change to the requesting application. This is often impractical as most resource levels have some jitter which usually has little impact on application performance. The next simplest alternative is to use a jitter threshold and track only those changes that larger than this threshold. Jitter-threshold-based schemes have been proposed by several researchers as a way of dealing with resource variability on mobile platforms [7, 8]. Jitter-threshold-based schemes work well if changes in the resource levels are usually stable. Transient changes (usually just spikes) in the resource levels can cause spurious responses. The alternative is to augment the jitter-based scheme with a filter that eliminates transients. This allows the applications to track only the stable changes. It is therefore important to allow applications to register application-specific (or resource-specific) filters that determine which changes in resource availability/quality should be reported to the requesting application.

To summarize, languages for resource-aware mobile programs should provide a resource-monitoring interface that allows on-demand monitoring as well as continuous monitoring. For continuous monitoring, the resource-monitoring interface should allow programs to register a application-specific filter which determines which resource changes should be reported.

2.2 Agility

To achieve agility, a mobile code language should provide mechanisms that allow programs to react quickly to asynchronous events like revocation of allocated bandwidth/memory or qualitative changes in network connectivity (e.g. on a mobile host). Two mechanisms are required. First, the ability to receive the event in an asynchronous manner (a la Unix signals) and second, the ability to take appropriate action in response to such events including moving program execution to a different site.

The requirement that programs be able to move within event handling code constrains the choice of mobility mechanisms. There are two major alternatives: (1) a go() (or a jump) primitive that freezes execution at current site and resumes execution at target site; and (2) a function-call-like mechanism which allows programs to execute a procedure at a specified site. Most mobile code languages have selected one of these two alternatives. Agent-Tcl [15], Telescript [26] and Aglets [20] use a go-based mechanism whereas Obliq [9], Avalon [11], NCL [13] REV [18] and TACOMA [16] use a function-call-based interface. To ensure a prompt response to asynchronous events, a function-call-based interface would require one of two things: (1) either the language automatically captures the continuation at the point at which an event occurs and makes it available for use within the corresponding event handler; or (2) the programmer emulates this functionality by writing a large number of functions that represent continuations at different points in the programs. In both cases, the language has to allow the use of a continuation-passing style. We believe a go()-based interface is simpler to use; the astute reader has probably already noted that the first option has exactly the same effect as a go().

2.3 Authority

The requirement of authority is, by far, the most demanding. It requires that language allow programs to control the way in which resources are used on their behalf by system support as well as by libraries. In effect, it requires that module boundaries not be completely opaque and that they allow resource-usage related restrictions to pass through and enforced as a part of execution.

There is a trade-off between the extent to which programs are allowed to control resource-use and ease of programming. At one extreme, a language can require that operations that use resources of interest be performed only after they have been explicitly authorized. This allows complete control over resource usage. Unauthorized accesses would raise an exception. A scheme similar to this is used by Java applets to control access to local resources (see Figure 1 for an example). This works well for Java applets as the level of access to local resources is not usually changed during the execution of a program and there is no advantage in retrying the operation.

On the other hand, it is entirely possible that the response to authorization failure for resource-usage can be (and in many cases, will be) to change the level of authorization. In such cases, retrying the operation would be desirable. This can be a problem if authorization failures occur deep in library code. It may or may not be possible to restart the operation if the failure is delivered as an exception. For example, consider the code in Figure 2. For this example, assume that the resource of interest is the number of sockets. If the first call to checkCreateSocket() succeeds and the second fails (say the program has already created as many sockets as it was permitted to), an exception will be raised. A common response to this situation would be to negotiate with the resource manager for a higher limit on the number of sockets and to restart the operation. However, a clean restart for createTwoSockets() is not possible as the first socket has already been created.

This situation can be dealt with by treating resource-use violation as an asynchronous event and allowing programs to associate a handler with every restriction on resource-use. The handler would be executed in the same context as the operation that caused the violation and would allow the operation to be restarted, if that is what is desired.

To summarize, both forms of control over resource use are desirable: (1) checking all operations that might use resources of interest for authorization and delivering an exception if the usage is not authorized; (2) considering resource-use violation as an asynchronous event and allowing programs to associate event handlers to resource-use restrictions which execute in the same context as the faulting operation.

```
public boolean mkdir() {
  SecurityManager security = System.getSecurityManager();
  if (security != null) {
    security.checkWrite(path);
  }
  return mkdir0();
}

public boolean renameTo(File dest) {
  SecurityManager security = System.getSecurityManager();
  if (security != null) {
    security.checkWrite(path);
    security.checkWrite(dest.path);
  }
  return renameTo0(dest);
}
```

Fig. 1. Excerpts from Java class libraries that illustrate how access to local resources is controlled. The actual operations of creating a directory and renaming a file are performed by mkdir0() and renameTo0().

3 Design and implementation of Sumatra

Sumatra is an extension of Java that supports resource-aware mobile programs. Platform-independence was the primary rationale for choosing Java as the base for our effort. In the design of Sumatra, we have not altered the Java language. Sumatra can run all legal Java programs without modification. All added functionality was provided by extending the Java class library and by modifying the Java interpreter, without affecting the virtual machine interface.

Sumatra adds four programming abstractions to Java: *object-groups, execution-engines, resource-monitoring* and *asynchronous events.* An object-group is a dynamically created group of objects. Objects can be dynamically added to or removed from object-groups. All objects within an object-group are treated as a unit for mobility-related operations. This allows the programmer to customize the granularity of movement and to amortize the cost of moving and tracking individual objects. Object-groups also allow the programmer to control the life-time of objects. Objects that are included in an object-group continue to live on a host even after the thread that created them completes

```
public boolean createSocket(String host, int port, boolean stream) {
  ResourceManager resource = System.getResourceManager();
  if (resource != null) {
    resource.checkCreateSocket(host,port,stream);
  }
  return Socket(host,port,stream);
}

private Socket socket1;
private Socket socket2;
....
public void createTwoSockets(String host1,String host2,int port,
    boolean stream) {
...
  socket1 = createSocket(host1,port,stream);
  socket2 = createSocket(host2,port,stream); // fails authorization check
}
```

Fig. 2. Sample Java code to illustrate the problem with restarting operations that fail authorization checks. This code assumes that Java is extended with a Resource Manager similar to its current Security Manager.

execution or migrates to some other host. Objects that do not belong to an object-group are subject to garbage-collection as usual.

An execution-engine corresponds to the notion of a "location" in a distributed environment. In concrete terms, it corresponds to an interpreter executing on a host. Multiple engines can exist on a single host. Sumatra allows object-groups to be moved between execution-engines. An execution-engine may also host active threads of control. Currently, multiple threads on the same engine are scheduled in a *run-to-completion* manner. We plan to implement other scheduling strategies in future. Threads can move between engines.

The resource-monitoring support in Sumatra allows programs to either query the level of resource availability or to control the extent to which various resources are used by the program itself as well as library code it is linked to. Both on-demand as well as continuous monitoring is supported. For continuous monitoring, the resource-monitoring interface allows programs to register jitter thresholds which determine which resource changes should be reported.

In Sumatra, asynchronous events are used to notify executing programs about urgent changes in their execution environment. These notifications can come either from the interpreter or from the external environment (the operating system or some other administrative process). We expect that the interpreter would use asynchronous events to notify the program about violations of resource-restrictions requested by the program itself; we expect that the external environment would use asynchronous events to inform the program about changes in the environment of the interpreter including resource revocation. Sumatra allows programs to register handlers for asynchronous events. The handlers for asynchronous events are able to inspect the current state of execution and can take appropriate action including moving away from the current execution site or changing the resource-restrictions in force.

In Sumatra, computation begins at a single site and spreads to other sites in three ways: (1) remote method instantiation, (2) remote thread creation, and (3) thread migration. Remote method instantiation corresponds to the familiar notion of RPC (remote-procedure-call) whereby the calling thread is suspended while an operation is performed, on its request, at a remote site. Remote thread creation differs from remote method instantiation in that the new thread is independent of the creating thread; the creating thread continues execution once the creation is complete. Finally, thread migration involves stopping the execution of the calling thread at the current site, transferring its state to another site and resuming execution at that site.

In the following subsections, we describe the design and implementation of Sumatra. The first three subsections describe the programming abstractions mentioned above. The final subsection discusses how the design decisions have been guided by the constraints described in the previous section.

3.1 Execution-engines

Execution-engines correspond to interpreters and are identified by a hostname and a port number that they listen on. They are created by specifying these parameters to the constructor. Several error conditions are possible – the remote host could be unreachable (due to a network partition), the remote host could be down, the remote host may not allow creation of interpreters, the desired port number could be in use. An exception is returned for each of these error conditions along with an error message that provides additional information. Other possible error conditions include authorization errors. Execution-engines support three operations: thread migration, remote thread creation and downloading code. Figure 3 presents the execution-engine interface.

Sumatra allows explicit thread migration using a go () method that bundles up the stack and the program counter and moves the thread to the specified execution-engine. Execution is resumed at the first instruction after the call to go. To automatically marshal the stack, the Sumatra interpreter maintains a type stack parallel to the value stack, which keeps track of the types of all values on the stack. When a thread migrates, Sumatra transports with it all local objects that are referenced by the stack but do not belong to any object-group. Objects that belong to an object-group move only when that object-group is moved. Stack references to the objects that are left behind (i.e were part of some object-group) are converted to proxy references. After the thread is moved to the target site, it is possible that its stack contains proxy references that point to objects that used to be remote but are now local. These references are converted back to local references before the call to go returns. Several error conditions can occur during the execution of go – the remote host could be unreachable, the remote host may be down, the interpreter implementing the execution-engine might have died, the remote site may not have all the local classes that this program might need while executing on that site. An exception is returned for each of these error conditions along with an error message that provides additional information.

A new thread can be created by *rexec*'ing the `main` method of a class existing on a remote engine. The arguments for the new thread are copied and moved to the remote site. Remote thread creation is non-blocking and the calling thread resumes immediately after the `main` method call is sent to the remote engine. Note that remote calls to the `main` method are blocking – the calling thread is suspended till the execution of `main` completes. Remote thread creation is different from thread migration as it creates a new thread at the remote site that runs concurrently with the original thread; thread migration moves the current thread to the remote site without creating a new thread. Concurrent threads communicate using calls to shared objects. The thread creating a new thread can share objects with the child by passing it references to these objects as arguments to `main`.

Sumatra does not automatically move code for either the `go` operation or the `rexec` operation. The `downloadClass` method can be used to download the class template for an object (and the associated bytecode) to an execution-engine. This allows programs to control their environment to some extent – for each class, a program can decide whether to use its own implementation or an implementation provided by the host on which it is executing. Downloaded class-templates are cached; the `ClassLoader` checks this cache before checking the local file system. The host, however, retains complete control over which classes can be downloaded and can reject `downloadClass` operations that attempt to replace critical classes.

Implementation. We use a mechanism similar to the familiar `inetd` daemon to manage the creation of execution-engines. A master daemon runs on all machines that allow creation of execution-engines and listens on a well-known socket. When a execution-engine creation request is received, it creates a new interpreter process which attempts to bind to specified socket. If either of these operations fail, an exception value is returned. The master daemon is also responsible for checking authorization. Currently, no authorization checks have been implemented. Execution-engine operations are currently implemented in C (as native methods). Figure 4 shows the interface for the Sumatra communication package which is used to implement these operations. Note that except `saveState()`, none of these *need* to be in C – `invokeRPC()` can be implemented using Java RMI [25] and the others can be layered on other Java classes. Java RMI was not used as it was not available when we were implementing Sumatra. Since Java does not provide a user-level primitive to serialize the stack, `saveState()` has to be implemented in C.

3.2 Object-groups

There are three primary properties of object-groups. First, they are aggregates. That is, they move only as a group. Second, they are sticky. That is, they can only be moved by an explicit move-object-group operation; they do not move with migrating threads. Third, they are persistent. That is, they are not garbage-collected. As long as an object is a member of some object-group, it is spared by the garbage-collector.

Figure 5 presents the Sumatra object-group interface. A string name can be associated, at creation time, with each object-group. The name can be used to identify different

```
public final class Engine {
   public String hostname;
   public int port;

   public Engine(String hname,int portno);
   public void downloadClass(String Classname);
   public void go();
   public native void rexec(String classname, String[] args);
}
```

Fig. 3. The Sumatra engine interface

```
public final class Comm {
   /* save state of current thread and transmit */
   public static native void saveState(String hostname,
          int portno);
   /* invoke an rpc call, walks stack to get arguments */
   public static native Object invokeRPC()
          throws ObjectMovedException;
   /* Download a class to an execution engine */
   public static native void downloadClass(String classname,
          Engine engine);
   /* Start an execution engine at a given machine */
   public static native void startEngine(String hostname,
          Engine engine);
   /* Find my current engine */
   public static native Engine myEngine();
}
```

Fig. 4. The Sumatra communication package

object-groups. Sumatra does not check for system-wide uniqueness of this name. It does, however, check for local uniqueness – attempts to create an object-group with a name that is in-use raises an exception.

Objects can be dynamically added to or removed from an object-group using the checkIn() and checkOut() methods respectively. The moveTo() method is used to move the object-group to a different execution-engine. Membership of object-groups is explicit, that is, every member of an object-group must be checked in explicitly. Also, moveTo() does a shallow move – only the objects that have explicitly been checked in are moved. This is in accordance with the *authority* requirement – no communication takes place without an explicit request.

Thread objects cannot be checked into an object-group. This restriction is imposed as including a thread object in object-group would require the thread to move along with the object-group. This causes two problems. First, this could cause migration of executing threads at arbitrary points. Restricting migration to syntactically marked program points has advantages (see [2] for one such advantage). Second, since moving a thread could cause other objects to be moved, it would violate the *authority* requirement.

During a moveTo() operation, objects in an object-group are automatically marshaled using type-information stored in their class templates. When an object-group is moved, all local references to objects in the group (stack references and references from other objects) are converted into *proxy references* which record the new location of the object. Some objects, such as I/O objects, are tightly bound to local resources and cannot be moved. References to such objects are reset and must be reinitialized at the new site. Several error conditions are possible – the remote host could be unreachable (due to a network partition), the remote host could be down, the remote execution-engine may not contain the classes corresponding to the objects being moved and the remote execution-engine may already contain an object-group with the same name. An exception is returned for each of these error condition along with an error message that provides additional information.

Method invocations on proxy objects are translated into calls at the remote site. Type information stored in class-templates is used to achieve remote-procedure-call functionality without a stub compiler. Exceptions generated at the called site are forwarded to the caller. In accordance with the *authority* requirement, Sumatra does not automatically track mobile objects. Requesting a remote method invocation on an object that is no longer at the called site results in an *object-moved* exception at the calling site. To facilitate application-level tracking, the exception carries with it a forwarding address. The caller can handle the exception as it deems fit (e.g., re-issue the request to the new location, migrate to the new location, raise a further exception and so on). This mechanism allows applications to locate mobile objects lazily, paying the cost of tracking only if they need to. It also allows applications to abort tracking if need be and pursue an alternative course of action.

It is also possible for an application to specify that an exception should be delivered on all methods invoked on proxy objects. This allows the application to avoid communication if it so desires. Furthermore, Sumatra does not support direct access to instance variables of remote objects. Such variables should be accessed through remote invocation of access methods that return the values of instance variables. This is in keeping with the *authority* requirement.

Implementation. Object-groups are implemented as lists of objects. Each execution-engine has a list of such lists. The object-group operations have been implemented in C (as native methods). The main reason for this is the interaction between object-groups and the garbage-collector. Objects that belong to an object-group are not garbage-collected. It is, however, possible to re-implement this feature portably using a keep-alive thread that lives forever and exists for the sole purpose of keeping these objects from being garbage-collected.

```
public final class ObjGroup {
  public String groupname;

  public ObjGroup (String name);
  public native void checkIn(Object object);
  public native void checkOut(Object object);
  public native void moveTo(Engine engine);
  public native Engine location();
  private native void internGroup();
}
```

Fig. 5. The Sumatra object-group interface

3.3 Resources and asynchronous events

Sumatra provides two resource-monitoring interfaces, one that allows the application to poll the state of a particular resource and the other that allows it to request asynchronous notification when the availability of a resource goes outside a specified threshold. Figure 6 presents the interface for on-demand monitoring. A program indicates its interest in a resource by creating a `Resource` object with appropriate arguments. If the resource to be monitored is associated with a single host (e.g. server load), the last argument is ignored. A request for continuous monitoring consists of a pair of values defining a range of resource availability (e.g. upper and lower bounds on bandwidth), an upper bound on frequency of polling and a function to be called when the resource availability is no longer within the range (this uses the interface for asynchronous events which will be presented shortly).

```
public final class Resource {
  public Resource(String type, String from, String to);
  public int read_value();
}
```

Fig. 6. The Sumatra on-demand monitoring interface.

Sumatra provides a single interface (shown in Figure 7) for handling all kinds of asynchronous events. To create an event handler, the user creates a new subclass of the `Callback` class, creates an object of that class and registers it using `System.registerCallback()`. The event handler function is specified by overriding the `callback()` method. Note that this method has been declared to be `abstract` and every subclass has to override it. After the `callback()` method completes, control returns to the point where the interruption happened. If a call to `go()` is embedded in a `callback()` method, execution resumes on the target host.

Three kind of asynchronous events are currently supported – asynchronous notification for continuous resource monitoring, violation of resource-restrictions and external events in the form of Unix signals. The first class of events require upper and lower bounds and a frequency bound which are specified using the `setLow()`, `setHigh()` and `setFreq()` methods. The second class of events requires only an upper bound. The third class of events, Unix signals, require only the signal number. Signals can be used by the external environment (the operating system or some other administrative process) to inform the application about urgent asynchronous events, in particular resource revocation. Using a handler, the application can take appropriate action including moving away from the current execution site.

Implementation. Sumatra assumes that a local resource monitor is available which can be queried for information about the environment. When an application makes a monitoring request, Sumatra forwards the request to the local resource monitor. If the monitor does not support the requested operation, or if no monitor is available, an exception is raised. The communication between Sumatra and the monitor is via a well-known shared memory segment. This allows Sumatra to cheaply acquire rapidly changing resource information. On-demand monitoring requests are implemented by directly reading this segment. For on-demand monitoring, default polling frequency of the resource monitor is used.

Event handlers need to be registered explicitly. Depending on the type of the event being registered, different structures are set up inside the interpreter. Asynchronous notification for continuous monitoring is implemented using Unix signals. The interpreter uses the same handler for all Unix signals - the identity of the signal is saved and an event is queued. The event queue is checked between every Java virtual machine instruction.

Resource-restrictions are implemented within the interpreter by activating counters that keep track of resource usage. These counters have been collected in a single module which is currently implemented in C. It is easy to re-implement this entirely within Java/Sumatra, much along the same lines as the Security Manager. Currently, only the "memory-use" restriction is implemented.

3.4 Discussion

In this section, we discuss the ways in which the design of Sumatra is influenced by the *agility* and *authority* requirements.

– **Calls to** `go()` **can occur anywhere:** In particular, they can be embedded inside callback methods. This allows Sumatra programs to react quickly to asynchronous events like revocation of allocated bandwidth/memory or qualitative changes in network connectivity (e.g. on a mobile host). The design alternative to using a `go()`-like interface was to allow migration only at function-call boundaries. To ensure a prompt response to asynchronous events, this would require one of two things: (1) either the language automatically captures the continuation at the point

```
public abstract class Callback {
    /* these callbacks are used for asynchronous notification */
    public Callback(Resource rsid);
    /* these callbacks are used for external event handlers */
    public Callback(int type);
    public void SetLow(int low);
    public void SetHigh(int high);
    public void SetFreq(int freq);
    public Resource get_resource();
    abstract public void callback();
}
```

Fig. 7. The Sumatra event handling interface.

at which an event occurs and makes it available for use within the corresponding callback method ; or (2) the programmer emulates this functionality by writing a large number of functions that represent continuations at different points in the programs. In both cases, the language has to allow the use of a continuation-passing style. We believe, the go() -based interface provided by Sumatra is both simpler to use and easier to implement.

— **All remote accesses can be trapped:** there are two parts to this. First, Sumatra does not allow programs to access instance variables of remote objects. Attempts to do result in an exception being raised. Second, programs can request that an exception be raised for all methods invoked on proxy objects. Using both these features, a program can turn off all communication if it so desires.

— **Objects moved and tracked in groups:** this allows application to control the granularity of both operations.

— **Object-groups are tracked lazily:** and under application-control. Requesting a remote method invocation on an object that is no longer at the called site results in an *object-moved* exception at the calling site. The exception carries with it a forwarding address which allows the application to continue tracking by re-issuing the request to the new location or to abort tracking if it so desires.

— **Membership of object-groups is explicit:** only those objects that have been explicitly added to an object-group belong to it. If an object with one or more component objects is added to an object-group, only the top-level object becomes a member of the object-group. To include the component objects in the object-group, each of them has to be explicitly added. This allows the application to precisely control which objects are moved and when.

— **No distributed garbage-collection:** Sumatra provides no distributed garbage-collection. It is the responsibility of the application to ensure that objects that are no longer needed are removed from object-groups. Note that Sumatra does provide local garbage-collection.

- **Object-groups are sticky:** Objects that belong to an object-group move only when that object-group is moved. When a thread migrates, Sumatra transports with it all local objects that are referenced by the stack but do not belong to any object-group.
- **Life-time of an object can be controlled:** Object-groups and their member objects are not subject to garbage-collection. This is implemented by adding the list of object groups to the set of roots used by the garbage-collector. This ensures that all objects that belong to object-groups (and their transitive closure) are spared by the garbage-collector. This allows applications to temporarily deposit data at intermediate execution sites as well as to extend existing servers by downloading objects that extend current functionality. It is legal for an object to belong to multiple object-groups. Membership of multiple object-groups can be useful in situations where there are multiple reasons to keep an object alive. This can, however, lead to unexpected communication if one of the object-groups moves and takes the object with it. It is, however, the programmer's responsibility to ensure that multiple membership does not lead to unwanted communication.
- **Location of an object can be queried:** Sumatra allows programs to query for the location of an object. This allows programs to selectively control communication – if desired, a program can allow critical remote operations while restricting all other remote operations.
- **Memory use can be bounded:** Sumatra programs can specify an upper bound on memory allocation. Attempts to allocate memory beyond this bound results in an asynchronous event which be handled if so desired.

3.5 Example

In this section, we provide a feel for the Sumatra programming model using a simple example. The task is to scan through a database of X-ray images stored at a remote site for images that show lung cancer. This task can be performed in two steps. In the first step, a computationally cheap pruning algorithm is used to quickly identify lungs that might have cancer. A compute-intensive cancer-detection algorithm is then used to identify images that actually show cancer.

One way to write a program for this task would be to download all lung images from the image server and do all the processing locally. If the absence of cancer in most lung images can be cheaply established, this scheme wastes network resources as it moves all lung images to the destination site. Another approach would be to send the selection procedure to the site of the image database and to send only the "interesting" images back to the main program. If the selection procedure is able to filter out most of the images, this approach would significantly reduce network requirements. A third, and even more flexible, approach would allow the shipped selection procedure to extract all the interesting images from the database but return only the *size* of the extracted images to the main program. This information can be be used, in conjunction with information about network bandwidth between the current location and the database site to estimate the transfer time for the selected images. If the estimated time is too large, the program may choose to move itself to the database site and perform the cancer-detection computation there rather than downloading all the data. This avoids downloading most images at the cost of (possibly) slower processing at the server. On the other hand if the transfer time is small enough, the data can be shipped over and processed locally. Figure 8 shows code for the third approach.

```
.....
filter_object = new Lung_filter();
cancer_object = new Lung_checker(filter_object);
myengine = System.comm.myEngine();

// Create a engine at the xray database site.
remote_engine = new Engine("xrays.gov");
// Indicate interest in monitoring bw to xrays.gov
bw = new Resource("bandwidth",myengine.hostname,"xrays.gov");
// Send the lung_filter class to the remote engine
remote_engine.downloadClass("Lung_filter");
// Create a new object group.
objgroup = new ObjGroup("lung_filter_group");
// Add the lung_filter_object to the object group
objgroup.checkIn(filter_object);
// Move the object group to the database site
objgroup.moveTo(remote_engine);

// a remote method call selects interesting xrays
size = filter_object.query(db, "DarkLungs");

// compute estimated time to transfer images
transfer_time = size * bw.read_value();
// Does it take too long?
if (transfer_time > threshold) {
  // Migrate thread, process images and return.
  remote_engine.go();
  result = cancer_object.detect_cancer();
  myengine.go();
}
else {
  // the estimated transfer time is small enough
  // Fetch them and process locally.
  objgroup.moveTo(myengine);
  result = cancer_object.detect_cancer();
}

// display result locally
System.display(result);
```

Fig. 8. Excerpt of a Sumatra program that migrates depending on the time required to transfer data.

Sumatra assumes that a local resource monitor is available which can be queried for information about the environment. In the next section, we describe Komodo, a distributed resource monitor which can provide information for Sumatra applications.

4 Komodo: a distributed resource monitor

For different applications, different resource constraints are likely to govern the decision to migrate - for example network latency, network bandwidth, server load (as in number of server connections available), CPU cycles etc. We have propose that a single monitor be used for all resources. Using a single monitor facilitates applications that might need information about multiple resources. It also reduces communication requirements for distributed monitoring as information about multiple resources can be sent in the same message.

In our design, each host runs a monitor daemon which communicates with peers on other hosts. The monitoring daemons are loosely-coupled and use UDP for communication as well as for monitoring the network. A simple timeout-based scheme is used to handle lost packets and re-transmissions.

Applications register monitoring requests with the local daemon. If the resource mentioned in the request can be monitored from the current host then the local daemon handles the request. Requests that cannot be handled locally, for example, network latency between two remote sites, are forwarded by the local daemon to the daemon on the appropriate host.

Applications can request the current availability of a resource (on-demand monitoring) or they can request periodic checks on resource availability (continuous monitoring). On-demand monitoring returns a single snapshot. Continuous monitoring applies a resource-specific filter to eliminate jitter in resource levels. Eliminating jitter helps reduce the reporting requirements (and therefore the communication needed) without impacting application performance. Data corresponding to remote requests for continuous monitoring is forwarded to the requesting sites as and when the filtered value of the resource changes. Requests for continuous monitoring may also specify a sampling frequency, subject to an upper bound. Komodo enforces an upper bound on this frequency to keep the monitoring cost at an acceptable level.

Each daemon supports a limited number of monitoring requests. This limit applies to both local and remote requests. Together with the limit on sampling frequency, this ensures the monitoring load on individual hosts is within acceptable limits.

Each request has an application-specified *time-to-live*. There is an upper bound on the *time-to-live* which allows the daemons to clean-up requests made by applications or hosts that have since crashed. Applications need to refresh requests within the *time-to-live*. Requests that are not refreshed are dropped. If a daemon runs out of entries in its monitoring table, the least recently requested entry is ejected.

Monitoring requests are passed from Sumatra to the local Komodo daemon using a well-known Unix domain socket. The resource information is made available by the daemon in a read-only shared memory segment. This allows applications to rapidly access the latest available monitoring information.

Implementation. The current implementation of *Komodo* monitors network latency. Each Komodo daemon pings a network link for which it has received monitoring requests, by sending a 32-byte UDP packet to the daemon on the other end of the link of interest. If an echo is not received within an expected interval, (the maximum of the ping period or five times the current round trip time estimate) the packet is retransmitted.

To eliminate short-term variation in latency measures, we developed a filter based of an extensive study of Internet latency [1]. This study revealed that: (1) there is a lot of short-term jitter in the latency measures but in most cases, the jitter is small; (2) there are occasional jumps in latency that appear only for a single observation; and (3) In most cases, a short window of values around the mode contains a large fraction of the observations (this indicates that the mode would be a good characteristic value for RTT distributions). Based on this, we have developed a filter for latency measures that returns a moving window mode if there is a well-defined mode, else it returns a moving window mean.

We plan to extend Komodo, in the near future, to monitor network bandwidth and server load (number of available server connections).

4.1 Discussion of the design of Komodo

In this section, we discuss the design of Komodo and how it has been influenced by the *awareness* and the *authority* requirements.

Komodo provides both on-demand and continuous monitoring. It allows applications to select the monitoring mode on a per-resource and a per-host basis (or host-pair basis for network latency and bandwidth). For resources that are monitored in a continuous mode, Komodo allows applications to control the frequency with which the resource is monitored. This allows the applications to control how much effort is spent in monitoring on their behalf and is in keeping with the *authority* requirement. To safeguard hosts from malicious or runaway applications, Komodo enforces an upper bound on the monitoring frequency.

Komodo provides both a synchronous interface and an asynchronous interface. In the current implementation, asynchronous notification is implemented using UNIX signals. For the asynchronous interface, Komodo allows resource-specific filters which pre-process the information about individual resources; individual applications do not have to replicate this functionality. They can, however, control its operation by providing their own values for the filters' parameters. This allows the applications to track only the stable changes.

For network-related resources, there is the choice of active versus passive monitoring. Komodo provides only active monitoring. It assumes that passive monitoring is the responsibility of the applications. For applications that do not coordinate their operations, this can lead to some loss of information. For example, if two applications independently access the same server, they could share information about the network connection to server but if they have not been designed to cooperate in this manner, they will not be able to utilize the information acquired by the other. Since Komodo is a user-level monitoring system, it can keep track of network performance for other programs in only two ways: (1) applications are required to measure performance for every network access and supply the information to the local Komodo daemon or (2) all messages are routed through Komodo. Neither of these are attractive options. We believe that cooperating applications should share such information instead of requiring all applications to acquire/provide it. Such an approach was been used by Mummert et al [22] in the *Coda* file system which is able to adapt to changes in network connectivity. Individual components of *Coda* cooperate in monitoring the bandwidth and maintain the information in a shared location.

5 Discussion

Currently, much of the core support for resource-awareness has been implemented in C. As has been discussed in individual sections, much of this can be re-implemented as Java/Sumatra libraries with relative ease. In particular, the resource-restrictions can be implemented using a Resource Manager similar to the current Security Manager module. It is, however, not possible to re-implement all of Sumatra in a portable manner. The primary limitation is the lack of a portable way to save and restore the stack. Another limitation is support for handling external events like Unix signals.

Process migration and remote execution have been proposed, and have been successfully used, as mechanisms for adapting to changes in host availability [10, 12, 21, 27]. Remote execution has also been proposed for efficient execution of computation that requires multiple remote accesses [11, 13, 18] and for efficient execution of graphical user interfaces which need to interact closely with the client [5]. Both these application scenarios use remote execution as a way to avoid using the network. Most proposed uses of Java [14] also use remote execution to avoid repeated client-server interaction. In these applications, decisions about the placement of computation are hard-coded. To the best of our knowledge, Sumatra (together with Komodo) is the first system that allows distributed applications to *monitor* the network state and *dynamically* place computation and data in response to changes in the network state.

Network-awareness is particularly important to applications running on mobile platforms which can see rapid changes in network quality. Various forms of network-awareness have been proposed for such applications. Application-transparent or system-level adaptation to variations in network bandwidth has been successfully used by the designers of the Coda file system [22] to improve the performance of applications. The Odyssey project on mobile information access plans to provide support for application-specific resource monitoring and adaptation. The primary adaptation mechanism under consideration is change in data fidelity [23]. Athan and Duchamp [4] propose the use of remote execution for reducing the communication between a mobile machine and the static network. In all these systems, location of the various computation modules is fixed; adaptation is achieved by changing the way in which the network is used.

Two other recent Java-based systems, Aglets [20] and Mole [24] provide some support for mobility. Both these systems have been implemented using Java and Java RMI and as such are unable to provide true thread migration. They provide only object mobility. A weak form of process migration can be achieved by programmers by explicitly unwinding the stack and copying whatever is needed into appropriate instance variables. Both systems provide an explicit restart method that is called to start the processing at the destination site. Sumatra provides true thread migration but requires C code to do so. This distinction can be eliminated if future versions of Java provide a portable way to pack the stack. Other major features of Sumatra that are not provided by Mole and Aglets are object-groups, support for application-level tracking of object-groups (or objects in their case), control over lifetime of objects (which is needed to implement distributed garbage-collection at the application-level). Neither system provides resource-monitoring facilities. Nor do they provide the capability to cleanly move within exception handlers (it is hard to unwind the stack in such a situation). Finally, Aglets proposes asynchronous mobility requests. Sumatra guarantees that threads will not be moved without an explicit request.

A point to note is that the constraints introduced by the *awareness* and *authority* requirement are common to all resource-aware programs, in particular programs that execute on resource-limited platforms like mobile computers. Noble, Price and Satyanarayanan [8] as well as Badrinath and Welling [7] propose notification-based schemes for tracking resource changes for mobile hosts. Both propose an interface that allows applications to specify a jitter threshold. The constraints introduced by the *agility* requirement, however, are specific to mobile programs.

Acknowledgments

We would like to thank Shamik Sharma for many thought-provoking discussions. We would like to thank Mustafa Uysal for being our resident skeptic.

References

1. A. Acharya and J. Saltz. A Study of Internet Round-Trip Delay. Technical Report CS-TR-3736, University of Maryland, December 1996.
2. A. Acharya and J. Saltz. *Dynamic Linking for Mobile Programs*, chapter unknown. Springer Verlag, 1997. Jan Vitek and Christian Tschudin (eds).
3. A. Adl-Tabatabai, G. Langdale, S. Lucco, and R. Wahbe. Efficient and Language-Independent Mobile Programs. In *Proceedings of the SIGPLAN'96 Conference on Programming Language Design and Implementation*, pages 127–36, May 1996.
4. A. Athan and D. Duchamp. Agent-mediated Message Passing for Constrained Environments. In *Proceedings of the USENIX Mobile and Location-independent Computing Symposium*, pages 103–7, Aug 1993.
5. K. Bharat and L. Cardelli. Migratory Applications. In *Proceedings of the Eighth ACM Symposium on User Interface Software and Technology*, pages 133–42, Nov 1995.
6. N. Borenstein. Email With a Mind of its Own: The Safe-TCL Language for Enabled Mail. In *Proceedings of IFIP Working Group 6.5 International Conference*, pages 389–402, Jun 1994.
7. B.R.Badrinath and Girish Welling. Event Delivery Abstractions for Mobile Computing. Technical Report LCSR-TR-242, Rutgers University, 1996.
8. Brian D. Noble and Morgan Price and M.Satyanarayanan. A Programming Interface for Application-Aware Adaptation in Mobile Computing. *Proceedings of the Second USENIX Symposium on Mobile and Location Independent Computing*, Feb. 1995.
9. L. Cardelli. A Language With Distributed Scope. In *Proceedings of the 22nd ACM Symposium on Principles of Programming Languages*, Jan. 1995.

10. J. Casas, D. Clark, R. Konuru, S. Otto, and R. Prouty. MPVM: A migration transparent version of PVM. *Computing Systems*, 8(2):171–216, Spring 1995.

11. S. Clamen, L. Leibengood, S. Nettles, and J. Wing. Reliable Distributed Computing with Avalon/Common Lisp. In *Proceedings of the International Conference on Computer Languages*, pages 169–79, 1990.

12. F. Douglis and J. Ousterhout. Transparent Process Migration: Design Alternatives and the Sprite Implementation. *Software - Practice and Experience*, 21(8):757–85, Aug 1991.

13. J. Falcone. A Programmable Interface Language for Heterogeneous Systems. *ACM Transactions on Computer Systems*, 5(4):330–51, Nov. 1987.

14. J. Gosling and H. McGilton. The Java Language Environment White Paper, 1995.

15. R. Gray. Agent TCL: A Flexible and Secure Mobile-agent System. In *Proceedings of the Fourth Annual Tcl/Tk Workshop (TCL 96)*, July 1996.

16. D. Johansen, R. van Renesse, and F. Schneider. An Introduction to the TACOMA Distributed System Version 1.0. Technical Report 95-23, University of Tromso, 1995.

17. E. Jul, H. Levy, N. Hutchinson, and A. Black. Fine-Grained Mobility in the Emerald System. *ACM Transactions on Computer Systems*, 6(2):109–33, Feb. 1988.

18. J.W. Stamos and D.K. Gifford. Implementing Remote Evaluation. *IEEE Transactions on Software Engineering*, 16(7):710–722, July 1990.

19. R. Katz. The Case for Wireless Overlay Networks. Invited talk at the ACM Federated Computer Science Research Conferences, Philadelphia, 1996.

20. D. Lange and M. Oshima. *Programming Mobile Agents in Java*. In progress, 1996. (ch 2,3).

21. M. Litzkow and M. Livny. Experiences with the Condor Distributed Batch System. In *Proceedings of the IEEE Workshop on Experimental Distributed Systems*, Huntsville, Al., 1990.

22. L. Mummert, M. Ebling, and M. Satyanarayanan. Exploiting Weak Connectivity for Mobile File Access. In *Proceedings of the Fifteenth ACM Symposium on Operating System Principles*, Dec. 1995.

23. M. Satyanarayanan, B. Noble, P. Kumar, and M. Price. Application-aware Adaptation for Mobile Computing. *Operating Systems Review*, 29(1):52–5, Jan 1995.

24. M. Straßer, J. Baumann, and F. Hohl. Mole - A Java Based Mobile Agent System. In *Proceedings of the ECOOP '96 workshop on Mobile Object Systems*, 1996.

25. Sun Microsystems. *Java Remote Method Invocation*. http://chatsubo.javasoft.com/current/rmi/index.html.

26. J. White. Telescript Technology: Mobile Agents, 1996. http://www.genmagic.com/Telescript/Whitepapers.

27. E. Zayas. Attacking the Process Migration Bottleneck. In *Proceedings of the Eleventh ACM Symposium on Operating System Principles*, pages 13–24, Nov. 1987.

Migratory Applications

Krishna Bharat, Luca Cardelli

Abstract. We present a new genre of user interface applications: applications that can migrate from one machine to another, taking their user interface and application contexts with them, and continue from where they left off. Such applications are not tied to one user or one machine, and can roam freely over the network, rendering service to a community of users, gathering human input and interacting with people. We envisage that this will support many new agent-based collaboration metaphors. The ability to migrate executing programs has applicability to mobile computing as well. Users can have their applications travel with them, as they move from one computing environment to another. We present an elegant programming model for creating migratory applications and describe an implementation. The biggest strength of our implementation is that the details of migration are completely hidden from the application programmer; arbitrary user interface applications can be migrated by a single "migration" command. We address system issues such as robustness, persistence and memory usage, and also human factors relating to the application design process, the interaction metaphor and safety.

1 Introduction

The goal of the human computer interaction community is to make powerful applications easy to use, while retaining their full potential. For this purpose metaphors have been devised; metaphors like overlapping windows, direct manipulation, and hypermedia. A successful metaphor hides complexity, and allows users to accomplish their tasks with little effort. Often, a metaphor requires advances in technology before it can be effectively implemented. Conversely, a new technology often needs the introduction of new metaphors to harness it.

As the infrastructure for ubiquitous computing comes into place, new demands will be placed on the way applications cope with the needs of mobile and distributed users. New metaphors will be necessary to cope with these demands.

We present a new genre of user interface applications: *migratory applications*, which can migrate from one host to another, maintaining intact the state of their user interface. After migration, a former host may shut down without affecting the application.

We discuss how an application migration facility can be implemented at the programming language/environment level. Our approach places some demands on the programming environment, but almost none on the application programmer. No restrictions are placed, in principle, on the type of the application being migrated. The migration operation is realized by the execution of a single command, which if successful transfers the application to a new machine, and upon failure returns control to the application. The same technique used for transmitting an application can be used to save the running application to file and transmit it over other channels to be resumed at a later time. In effect, this makes an executing application as portable and architecture independent as any other piece of data.

Application migration is useful in the context of many agent-based collaboration metaphors. For example:

1. Applications that follow a user across physical locations: the *ubiquitous computing* metaphor. For 'eager' behavior, some applications could use a location sensing device such as an 'active badge'[14], to automatically follow the user. This approach has been used to 'teleport' X applications [20].

2. Applications that serve a group of people by travelling to each person's site in turn (e.g., a meeting scheduler): the *electronic secretary* metaphor.

3. Applications that interact with people on a user's behalf and carry out an agenda: the *interactive agent* metaphor.

4. Communication over email that is interactive and intelligent: the *interactive message* metaphor. Unlike previous implementations of 'active mail' [6], the recipient is able to forward the interactive message after interacting with it.

In addition to self-induced migration as described thus far, it is equally easy to allow a program to be migrated under external control. This would allow the user to 'drag-and-drop' programs across machines in the same manner as files between folders, and windows between screens.

We are frequently seeing the use of light-weight, diskless, portable computers for personal computing (e.g., as organizers and notepads). In the future they will be used in collaborative work situations as well (e.g., at a meeting or conference). These portable network computers will run a compute server such as the Java Virtual Machine[13], and have a set of standard utilities hard-wired. They will rely on intermittent wireless connectivity to servers and peer computers for the rest of their computational needs. While launching applications from file-servers is straight-forward, they will often need to engage in data-exchange with peer (diskless) computers. This will often happen in situations in which the code needed to manage the data may not be available at the recipient. A good approach to supporting such 'active documents' across computers would be to migrate the document-viewer in its entirety to the peer. Writing re-entrant code by hand is likely to be tedious. Our approach provides a way to automate this process.

In this chapter we first describe our approach to programming agent-style applications. In the following section, we show how this paradigm was applied in the Visual Obliq development environment (described in [2, 3]) to support the migration of (arbitrary) user interface applications. Finally, we discuss some pragmatic issues raised by migration, and conclude with a discussion of related work.

2 Programming Model

Our programming model is based on the facilities available in the Obliq distributed scripting language [7].

2.1 Network Semantics

In Obliq, arbitrary data, including procedures, can be transmitted over the network. A piece of Obliq data can be viewed as a graph wherein some nodes are *mutable* (meaning

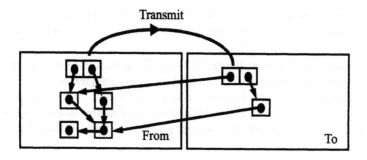

Transmit

From

To

Figure 1. Transmission of a data graph

that they have local state that can be modified by assignment) and other nodes are *immutable* (meaning that they cannot be modified). For example, the program text of a procedure is immutable and cannot be modified, while fields in an object are mutable because they can be assigned new values.

2.1.1 Network Transmission

When a data graph is passed to a remote procedure, or returned from a remote procedure, we say that it is transmitted over the network.

The meaning of transmitting a data graph is the following (see Figure 1):

Starting from a given root, the data graph is copied from the source site to the target site up to the point where mutable nodes or network references are found.

Mutable nodes (indicated by shaded boxes in the figure) are not copied; in their place, network references to those nodes are generated. Solid pointers represent either local or remote references. Existing network references are transmitted unchanged, without following the reference. Sharing and circularities are preserved.

For example, an Obliq *object* (one of the basic data structures) is never copied over the network on transmission, since objects have state. A network pointer to the object is transmitted in its place. The object can then be referenced remotely through that network pointer; for example, one of its methods may be remotely invoked. Arrays and updatable variables are similarly not copied on transmission, since they have state.

Obliq procedures are first-class data and, like other data, have a value that can be manipulated and transmitted. The value of a procedure is called a *closure*; it consists of the program text of the procedure, plus a table of values for the global variables of the procedure.

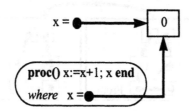

$x =$ 0

proc() x:=x+1; x **end**

where   x =

Figure 2. The closure of a procedure

Figure 2 shows the closure for a procedure incrementing a global variable x; the variable x denotes a mutable location containing 0. The closure table contains a single entry, indicated by "where x = …".

The transmission of a closure (Figure 3) follows the same rules as the transmission of any data graph. When a closure is transmitted, all the program text is copied, since it consists of immutable data. The associated collection of values for the free variables within it is copied as per the general rule. In particular, the locations of global updatable variables are not copied: network references are generated to their location, so that they can be remotely updated.

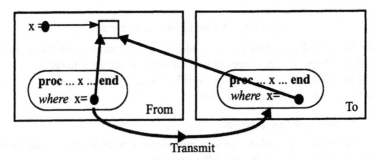

Figure 3. Transmission of a closure

2.1.2   Network Copy

In contrast to the default transmission mechanism, which stops at mutable nodes and network references, a special primitive is provided to perform a *network copy* of a data graph. This primitive makes a complete local copy of a possibly mutable and distributed graph.

Network copy is useful, for example, when moving a user interface along with a migrating application.

A user interface is normally closely bound to site-dependent resources, such as windows and threads. Since these resources cannot migrate, a stand-alone snapshot of the user interface is first assembled. The snapshot is typically a complex data structure, which includes a representation of the current state of all the live windows of the application. This data structure, resembling the graph in the picture above, can be copied over to the target site, and then converted back to a live interface.

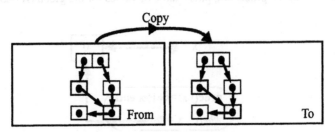

Figure 4. Network Copy

2.2 Agents

An agent is a computation that may *hop* from site to site over the network.(terminology borrowed from White's Telescript[22]). We review the concepts of agents, agent servers, suitcases, and briefings. In Section 2.3, we describe an Obliq implementation of agent hopping.

A *suitcase* is a piece of data that an agent carries with it as it moves from site to site. It contains the long-term memory of the agent. It may include a list of sites to visit, the tasks to perform at each site, and the results of performing those tasks.

A *briefing* is data that an agent receives at each site, as it enters the site. It may include advice for the agent (e.g., "too busy now, try this other site"), and any site-dependent data such as local file systems and databases.

An *agent server*, for a given site, is a program that accepts code over the network, executes the code, and provides it with a local briefing.

A *hop instruction* is used by agents to move from one site to the next. This instruction has as parameters an agent server, the code of an agent, and a suitcase. The agent and the suitcase are sent to the agent server for execution.

Finally, an *agent* is a user-defined piece of code parameterized by a suitcase and a briefing. All the data needs of the agents should be satisfied by what it finds in either the suitcase or the briefing parameters. At each site, the agent inspects the briefing and the suitcase to decide what to do. After performing some tasks, it typically executes a hop instruction to move to the next site.

If an agent has a user interface, it takes a snapshot of the interface, stores it in the suitcase during the hop, and rebuilds the interface from the snapshot at the destination.

2.3 Agent Migration

As we said previously, an agent is a procedure parameterized with a suitcase and a briefing; the suitcase travels with the agent from site to site, while a fresh briefing is provided at each site. We assume that the agent code is self-contained (that is, it has no free variables).

Agents move from site to site by executing a *hop instruction*:

```
(* definition of the recursive procedure agent *)
let rec agent =
            proc(suitcase, briefing)
                  (* work at the current site *)
                  (* decide where to go next *)
                  hop(nextSite, agent, suitcase);
                  (* run agent at nextSite with suitcase *)
            end;
```

In Obliq, agents, suitcases, briefings, and hop instructions are not primitive notions. They can be fully understood in terms of the network semantics of the Section 2.1.

Agents are just procedures of two parameters. Suitcases and briefings are arbitrary pieces of data, such as objects. Each agent is responsible for the contents of its suitcase, and each agent server is responsible for the contents of the briefing. Agent servers are simple compute servers whose main task is to run agents and supply them with appropriate briefings (and maybe check the agent's credentials).

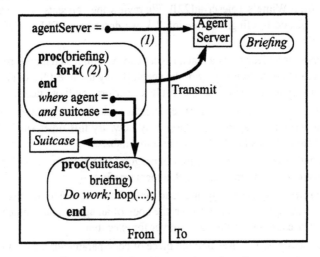

Figure 5. The hop instruction - Part I

The hop instruction can be programmed in Obliq as follows:

```
let hop =
                proc(agentServer, agent, suitcase)
                    agentServer(
(1)                     proc(briefing)
                            fork(
(2)                             proc()
(3)                                 agent(copy(suitcase), briefing);
                                end);
                        ok
                    end);
        end;
```

Suppose a call hop(agentServer, agent, suitcase) is executed at a source site. Here, agentServer is (a network reference to) a remote compute server at a target site.

The call agentServer(...) has the effect of shipping the procedure *(1)* to the remote agent server for execution. At the target site, the agent server executes the closure for procedure *(1)* by supplying it with a local briefing.

Next, at the target site, the execution of the body of *(1)* causes procedure *(2)* to be executed by a forked thread. Immediately after the fork instruction, procedure *(1)* returns a dummy value (ok), thereby completing the call to hop that originated at the source site.

The source site is now disengaged, while the agent computation carries on at the target site. The thread of computation at the target site is driven by the agent server. At the target site, the forked procedure *(2)* first executes copy(suitcase). The suitcase, at

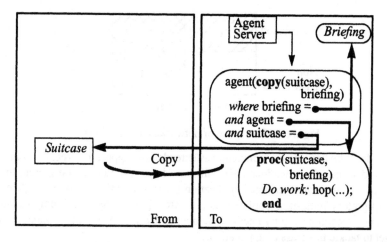

Figure 6. The hop instruction - Part II

this point of the computation, is usually a network pointer to the former suitcase that the agent had at the source site. The copy instruction (an Obliq primitive) makes a complete local copy of the suitcase, as described earlier. Therefore, the result of copy(suitcase) is a suitcase whose state is local to the target site, suitable for local use by the agent.

After the copying of the suitcase, the agent migration is complete. The source site could now terminate or crash without affecting the migrated agent.

Finally *(3)*, the agent is invoked with the local suitcase and the local briefing as parameters. The program text of the agent was copied over as part of the closure of procedure *(1)*. Since the agent has no free variables, it can execute completely locally, based on the suitcase and the briefing.

In the special case when the suitcase contains the entire application state, we have a migratory application.

3 Application Migration

We used the agent migration paradigm described in the previous section to implement migratory applications in Visual Obliq.

3.1 Visual Obliq

Visual Obliq is an environment for rapidly constructing user interface applications by direct manipulation [2]. It consists of:

- An interactive application builder that allows the user interface to be drawn and programmed. The builder generates code in Obliq.
- Runtime support, consisting of libraries and network services.

In previous work [2] we showed how the Visual Obliq environment supported the construction of distributed, multi-user applications (II, in Figure 7), in addition to traditional, non-distributed applications (I).

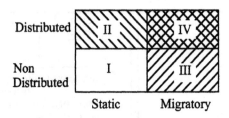

Figure 7. The space of networked applications

Here we describe how the environment was extended to support the creation of migratory, non-distributed applications (III). This was done in a manner transparent to the user, allowing any non-distributed application (in I) to be migrated by a single command. Migratory multi-user applications (IV) are significantly more complicated to implement, since connectivity needs to be maintained as the migration happens. We have yet to tackle this class of applications.

The support for distribution in II (described in [3]) has little in common with the support for migration. Hence we do not describe it here. However *Visobliq*, the GUI builder used to draw and program the interface has remained the same.

3.1.1 Visobliq

Figure 8 shows *Visobliq* in action. The window on the left (in the background) is called the *design window*, and the window on the right (in the foreground) is known as the *attribute sheet*. The design window has a palette of widgets at the top, and a drawing area below, where widgets may be pieced together to form application windows. The application windows thus designed are called *forms*. The figure shows a single form being designed, containing the following widgets: a video-player, a button, a browser, and a file-browser. Widget geometry and the hierarchical nesting of widgets within a form can be manipulated interactively. All other resources are specified via the attribute sheet.

Double-clicking on a widget causes the resources of the widget to be loaded into the attribute sheet, for modification by the programmer. This includes attributes that determine the appearance and interactive behavior of the widget, as well as any code that is attached to the widget. When the resources have been modified, the programmer presses the 'Apply' button to make the changes take effect.

Pressing the 'Run' button causes the application to execute within an internal interpreter for testing and debugging. The 'Code' menu option provides a facility to output code in Obliq, for stand-alone execution within a Visual Obliq interpreter. We talk more about the interpreter and its special features to support migration in Section 3.3.

3.1.2 Programming a single-user application

Each form defines a class of window objects, and can be multiply instantiated at run-time. Every instance of a form receives a unique index, and can be referenced through a global array that bears the form's name. For example, if the form being designed in Figure 8 were called MainWin, there would be an array called MainWin [...] , containing references to instances of MainWin created at run-time.Widgets are implemented as

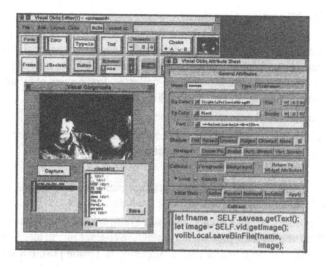

Figure 8. The *Visobliq* application builder

objects nested inside the form instance. Suppose the button labeled 'Capture' were named CaptureBtn, the programmer would refer to the button within instance n of MainWin as MainWin[n].CaptureBtn.

While building a single-user application in Visobliq, the programmer is asked to write four types of code in Obliq:

1. Callback code, which is attached to a widget
2. Form support code, which is associated with a form.
3. Global code. Any other code needed by the application can be placed here.
4. Initialization code, which gets executed when the program starts up and creates the initial form instances. After this the execution is fully input driven.

The above programming framework is general enough for the construction of most single-user UI applications.

3.2 Implementing Migration

The programmer makes the application migrate to a new site by executing the *migration command* within a callback.

Specifically, one of the following commands is executed:

- MigrateTo(Host)
- MigrateToServer(ServerName, Host)

The first command migrates the application to a default agent server called VOMigrate, on the machine named Host. VOMigrate continues the application from where it left off, and does not provide any briefing. This is sufficient for basic application migration.

The second command causes the application to migrate to a customized agent server called ServerName, on the machine named Host. In both cases the agent server is run by the user who receives the application after it migrates.

3.2.1 The Migration Command

The semantics of the migration command is that it returns true if the application is migrated successfully, and false upon failure. If it succeeds, the local instance of the application terminates the moment the callback finishes. The user interface is destroyed and the entire application state gets garbage-collected. In the event of failure, the application continues to execute locally as if nothing happened.

The migration command executes the following steps:

1. It first contacts the agent server at the destination to ensure that the migration can happen. Upon failure it returns immediately with a false value.

Otherwise...

2. It checkpoints the state of the user-interface into the Obliq objects that make up the widget hierarchy.

This step is necessary because widgets in Visual Obliq are high-level 'interface objects' in Obliq, which realize their presentation using lower-level interactors in the local UI toolkit. Currently, the only toolkit that is supported is Trestle [18], but if Obliq were ported to a different environment, the local toolkit would be used. Hence, Visual Obliq widgets do not maintain all of their state explicitly. In particular they do not maintain an up-to-date copy of attributes that can be changed interactively by the user (e.g., the geometry). These attributes are retrieved from the underlying toolkit whenever needed; either when the programmer's code requires them, or when the user interface state is being checkpointed.

3. The user interface is destroyed. This breaks links between the application's state and the running (user interface) thread.

4. Links to the local runtime are explicitly removed.

5. It prepares a suitcase containing links to relevant state, and executes the hop instruction discussed in the Section 2.3. Recall that a suitcase is a data structure that gets copied to the destination. In this case, the suitcase contains a reference to each of the form-instance arrays in the program.

If the hop instruction executes successfully, true is returned. Upon failure (if the network operation raises an exception), the command rebuilds the user interface from the saved state in the same way that the agent server at the destination would have, and returns false.

The hop instruction causes the agent server to perform a network copy of suitcase. Since the suitcase contains references to all form-instance arrays, this involves copying every piece of data that is reachable from a form-instance. It is easy to see that this will copy over every piece of the application state that is relevant to future execution. If a piece of data is not accessible from any form-instance, it will never be used, and so it is not copied.

At the source site, due to step 3, all links between the interpreter's UI threads and the application are destroyed. Once the existing callback exits, the application state becomes inaccessible to any thread in the system. The Obliq interpreter has automatic garbage-collection. Hence shortly after migration, the application state gets garbage collected.

Step 4 ensures that the application state has no references to the Visual Obliq runtime (also implemented in Obliq) when it is copied. This was done to prevent the runtime from being copied as well. At the new host, the local runtime is patched in, causing the local environment to take effect.

3.2.2 The Agent Server

The agent server is an extended Visual Obliq interpreter. In addition to an internal UIMS (User Interface Management System) thread which implements the user interface, the agent server has a 'migration' thread to assist incoming agents.

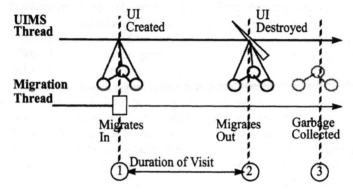

Figure 9. Operation of an Agent Server

When an application migrates in (at step 1 in Figure 9), the agent performs the following operations:

1. It performs a network copy of suitcase, causing the entire application state to be copied over.
2. References to the local Visual Obliq runtime are added.
3. For each form-instance in the application, it rebuilds its user interface based on its saved state. Callbacks are re-attached. This sets up links between the application and the local UIMS thread.

When an application migrates out (step 2), links from the UIMS are broken, and soon its state is garbage-collected (step 3). In this manner, the agent server allows applications to migrate in and out of the host repeatedly, without running out of memory. Multiple applications can co-exist within the interpreter, because they will not have links to each other.

User-defined agent servers are created by extending the default agent server to provide application-specific briefing and access control. To be useful, the agent server needs to have a user interface of its own to help the user monitor and regulate the activities of migratory applications. For example, the user might stipulate: "I will entertain only applications of type X"; "I will be back at time Y"; "If you get an agent from so-and-so, provide Z as input". This presupposes an underlying mechanism for authentication and encryption.

In practice, there are likely to be other locale-specific resources, such as file-handles and network connections, that need to be preserved during migration. The replication of such resources cannot be automated since it is highly application and situation dependent. For instance, it is not clear how open files should be treated. One option would be to have the system reopen all open files upon reaching the destination, but often the two sites may not share a common file-system.

Recently there has been interest in developing facilities to support the needs of mobile applications. Mobile-IP [17] allows network connections to be maintained as applications move around. It makes use of a forwarding service at the 'home base' of the application to relay network traffic. The Rover mobile application toolkit [15] provides dynamically relocatable objects and queued, asynchronous remote procedure calls. This non-blocking mode of operation allows both parties the flexibility to move or be disconnected while the procedure call is being handled. Xerox PARC's Bayou [10] is a replicated and weakly consistent storage system designed for collaborative mobile applications with intermittent connectivity. Novel aspects include support for application-specific detection and resolution of update conflicts, eventual replica convergence through a peer-wise anti-entropy process, and per-client consistency guarantees. Stanford's MosquitoNet project [8] addresses the problem of helping applications cope with connections with different bandwidth, latency and quality of service parameters, as a mobile user moves around wired and wireless networks with widely varying performance characteristics.

This was not a problem we set out to solve. Hence, in the current implementation of Migratory Applications in Visual Obliq, we let the application programmer deal with the checkpointing and reinstantiation of OS and network resources. The programmer is given the option of adding code to two system-defined routines: PreMigrate() and PostMigrate(), which are invoked before and after migration respectively.

3.3   The Visual Obliq Runtime

The 'Visual Obliq interpreter' is simply the Obliq interpreter with a set of support libraries (known as the *runtime*) preloaded. The original purpose of the runtime was to provide access to the local UI library and implement abstractions needed by distributed applications. Subsequently, the runtime was redesigned and extended to meet the needs of migratory applications.

First, since the runtime is closely tied to the local environment, it was decided that it would not be copied when the application migrates. Hence, all access to the runtime is through handles which are local to the interpreter in which the application is currently resident. The handles are removed before migration, and get patched in when the application arrives at a new host. Hence, all operations that involve local system resources such as the network, processor, file-system and the UI toolkit, are customized to the local environment.

In addition, the runtime provides the following facilities:

3.3.1   Migration Support

The runtime implements the migration commands described earlier. At the source it accesses the agent server using the remote-object access mechanism called 'Network

Objects' [5]. Then the local interface is checkpointed. At the target site, the agent server copies the application state over and uses the local runtime to rebuild the interface.

The two operations on the interface are implemented thus:

- **Checkpointing the user interface.** This is done by walking the Visual Obliq widget hierarchy for each form-instance in the application, and copying relevant state information from the UI toolkit into the Obliq object that manages the widget. Any attribute that cannot be modified by the user (and can only be modified under program control) need not be checkpointed, since the widget will already have the latest value.

- **Rebuilding the user interface.** The same mechanism used to create the original user interface is used to rebuild it at new sites. The routine walks the Visual Obliq widget hierarchy for each form-instance and creates for each widget therein, a corresponding interface using interactors in the local toolkit. In doing so it may adhere to the checkpointed geometrical attributes or decide to override them, e.g., if the application migrates to a portable computer with a substantially smaller screen, an alternate design may be used and dimensions might shrink. This provides the flexibility needed to cope with the differences between individual machines, while preserving the appearance of the interface as far as possible.

In our present implementation, we have another intervening layer, FormsVBT[[1]. FormsVBT allows Visual Obliq widgets to be described in terms of symbolic expressions representing the hierarchical arrangement of (smaller) UI components. The runtime generates the symbolic expression corresponding to each Visual Obliq widget by replacing tokens in a template with the attributes of the widget. Users can customize the appearance of the widgets displayed by their agent server by manipulating the template.

Once the user interface has been rebuilt, the runtime re-attaches callbacks so that interaction can resume.

3.3.2 Safety

The runtime is responsible for safety, and protects the user from attacks and privacy violations by the applications that migrate in. It does this by disabling all unsafe commands (namely commands that could be used to damage the user's environment and/or violate privacy), and instead provides safe alternatives that are subject to user-specified checks before execution.

In Obliq, all unsafe operations are readily identified by the fact that they require the use of 'access' handles to system resources. For instance a processor handle is needed by routines that create new processes and execute system calls. Similarly there are handles to provide various levels of access to the file-system. This allows for the creation of a security scheme based on the notion of capabilities.

The Visual Obliq runtime hides all system handles (by re-defining them to be nil) after having defined a "safe" version of each routine that uses a handle. The scope rules of the language ensure that the latest definition supersedes previous definitions. Safe-routines have access handles bound inside them by static scoping. An alien program can access a safe-routine but not the handles within it. These routines are considered safe because they compare their op-code and argument list with patterns in a user-

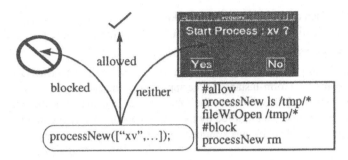

Figure 10. Safe Routines in Visual Obliq

specified configuration file (called .vorestrict), to decide which operations are to be allowed and which are to be blocked.

Operations that are allowed by the configuration file are executed in the regular manner. When a blocked operation is encountered, the runtime notifies the user that the program is attempting something illegal and aborts the application. When an unsafe operation falls in neither category (which is the default case when no preferences have been specified) the runtime rewrites the operation in a human intelligible form, and pops up a notice to ask the user if it should be allowed to go through.

Unlike in Safe-Tcl [6], where a special-purpose "safe" interpreter with a restricted command-set was required, we are able to implement safety entirely within the programming language, in a portable fashion. This makes it possible to provide strong arguments that the environment is indeed safe and allows the safety level to be relaxed flexibly. Most users would use a default .vorestrict file provided by the system administrator. The ability to customize the file and relax the restrictions is useful within workgroups, where there is a high level of trust.

3.4 Variants

An advantage of the language-level implementation of migration is that variants are easy to implement and prove correct using the language semantics.

- **Cloning** is one variant. An application is cloned by network copying it to the new site without destroying the instance at the original site. One possible application of cloning is in debugging. When a bug is encountered in an application, the user can send a clone of the application to the person responsible for debugging it, instead of a mere 'bug report'. Another application would be a divide-and-conquer agent mechanism, wherein an agent *splits* into multiple agents that interact independently with various users, and later *merge* or resynchronize.

- **Persistence.** Obliq provides a *pickle* operation, which is very similar to the network copy. Instead of replicating the data-graph, it serializes it to a buffer. The contents of the buffer can be saved to a file or transmitted over another transport, e.g., e-mail. At a later point in time, it can be converted back into the original data-graph, by the complementary *unpickle* operation. This allows Visual Obliq programs to check-point their state to file when necessary. If agents are expected to be persistent and endure machine crashes, they will need the ability to periodically save their state to stable storage, and resume from a saved configuration when the machine restarts.

4 Issues Raised By Migration

The ability to migrate applications can substantially change the way we view programs, and the way we interact with them.

- **Interaction Techniques.** The distinction between executing programs and data becomes blurry with the ability to migrate and checkpoint applications. Correspondingly, direct manipulation techniques such as drag-and-drop will now be applicable.

- **Privacy.** The ability to operate on an application from afar raises privacy and access-control issues. Does the person who started the application have 'yank' and 'kill' privileges? Most people would not like others to know what applications they have on their desktop; yet users would like to keep track of the agents they have sent out. It should be possible to restrict access to users within a group.

- **Secrecy.** Then there is the issue of privacy in the reverse direction. The user who receives an agent may violate the privacy of the sender by examining its hidden agenda. For instance a car dealership may wish to send an agent to a client, with a list of cars and a strategy to negotiate the price. It should not be possible for the client to learn what the strategy is, by examining the agent code or modifying the interpreter. It seems impossible to prevent this from happening in software. It could possibly be achieved by having a trusted third-party implement the interpreter in hardware, with encryption of the agent code.

- **Protocol.** In any agent-human interaction there is the issue of protocol. How long does an agent wait for a user to respond before deciding to move on? Does it leave a note? How does it know if the user is busy or away? The agent could look at the idle time. How does a user prevent unwanted agents from bothering him, while keeping the door open for acceptable agents? Do agents have a classification?

It is clear that some form of shared knowledge representation is need to express exapections and permissions in the interaction between agent and human. One such representation is provided by KQML. KQML (Knowledge Query and Manipulation Language [11, 16]) is a language and protocol for exchanging information and knowledge in agent-systems as part of an ARPA sponsored knowledge sharing effort. Their specification incorporates a message format and a message-handling protocol to support run-time knowledge sharing among agents. Intended uses are for an application program to interact with an intelligent system or for two or more intelligent agents to share knowledge in support of cooperative problem solving.

They define a set of 'performatives'; these are the permissible operations that agents may attempt on each other's knowledge and goal stores. This set comprises a substrate on which higher-level models of inter-agent interaction such as contract nets and negotiation may be developed. In addition, the KQML distribution provides a special class of agents called communication facilitators which coordinate the interactions of other agents

- **Heterogeneity.** If applications are to migrate between diverse architectures, the user interface needs to be designed with care so that it can rendered efficiently in all environments. When rebuilding an interface, the checkpointed state should be re-interpreted in the light of the available resources and local preferences. Fonts and labels should change to match the language used at the local site. We address this by transmitting the user interface using an abstract representation during migration, to be turned into a concrete user interface using local preferences expressed as FormsVBT templates.

5   Related Work

Application migration most closely resembles the work on process migration in Operating Systems [19,23], although the aim of process migration is to do load-balancing and improve parallelism. Process migration is usually implemented at a low level, making no assumptions about the application structure, or even about the programming language. The machine architecture and environment are assumed to be very similar, if not identical, at the two ends of the migration. Process migration is unable to cope directly with applications that keep part of their state externally, e.g., when much of the user interface state information is stored within a window system server (as in the X window system).

Our priorities are very different. We expect to cope with heterogeneity (interoperabilty with diverse machine architectures), support customization to the local environment (the user interface should be built using the local UI toolkit), and provide the flexibility that comes with implementing migration at the programming language level. In our system, the application programmer can implement new migration strategies by re-programming the migration mechanism. For instance migration could be limited to selected parts of an application by appropriately modifying the suitcase. Split and merge techniques could be used to deploy agents in parallel.

One of the strengths of our design is that migration is completely captured by the semantics of the programming language. This makes it easy to comprehend the program and troubleshoot it if it does not behave as expected. Also, heterogeneity is not a problem, since correct implementations of the language are guaranteed to interoperate.

Migratory applications may also be viewed as mobile, interactive agents. The term "agent" has been used with so many different connotations, that the word has been practically stripped of all meaning. An important characteristic of the use of agents is the ability to delegate tasks to the agent, as one would to a human helper.

There are agents in AI, in databases, and in application software; classification and search agents (robots and knowbots) in information retrieval [12, 21]; agents within adaptive applications and learning-by-demonstration systems [9]; and assistants in design automation and help systems [4]. Typically, these mobile agents are not interactive; for example, search agents operate silently on behalf of a client which interacts with the user. Conversely, interactive agents are usually not mobile across machines; they are usually 'symbiotic' and exist within some application context or workspace; for example, helpers in learning-by-demonstration systems such as Eager [9], and 'Balloon Help' on the Macintosh desktop.

Agents that support collaborative work on the other hand require to be mobile or at least distributed, and also need a user interface to interact with users. A major advantage of our design is that *any* single-user application in Visual Obliq can be turned into a mobile, interactive agent by invoking the migration command. When not in use, an agent can write its state to disk and be restarted when needed.

Obliq resembles Java [13], with its object oriented, multi-threaded features, but also has integrated support for distributed objects. Most web browsers supporting Java applets and Safe-Tcl [6] have taken steps to ensure safe execution of external code. A difference between the execution of external programs in these systems and the migratory applications in Visual Obliq is that in the former case the applications always begin executing from a default (start) state when they arrive at an interpreter, instead of continuing from where they left off as in our case. Hence it would not be possible to forward an arbitrary program to a new user after interacting with it, as one could with a piece of annotated electronic mail.

6   Summary

The ability to migrate applications has several applications. In a world of ubiquitous computing, users may like their applications follow them – from home to work and to a colleague's machine. A migratory, interactive application can act as an agent, moving from one user's machine to another, interacting with each user, and carrying out an agenda. Such agents may be short-lived, and could be deployed by a user or a group for a specific task. They could be long-lived as well and perform a role in a work-group as a human colleague would. All of this presupposes a mechanism to migrate arbitrary applications between machines.

In this chapter, we have presented a distributed language semantics that supports application migration, and an architecture for migratory applications. The architecture has been incorporated into the Visual Obliq application programming environment [3]. We have yet to explore the full potential of this paradigm in collaborative work, but we have successfully migrated a number of small to medium size applications. In these cases, the migration operation took between 5 and 45 seconds over a local area network, depending on the program size and network traffic.

References

[1]   Avrahami, G., Brooks, K.P., and Brown, M.H., "A Two-View Approach to Constructing User Interfaces." *Computer Graphics*, 23(3), pp. 137-146, 1989.

[2]   Bharat, K. and Brown, M.H., "Building Distributed Multi-User Applications By Direct Manipulation." *Proc. ACM Symposium on User Interfaces Software and Technology*, Marina Del Rey, 1994, pp. 71-82.

[3]   Bharat, Krishna, and Cardelli, Luca, "Migratory Applications." *Proceedings of ACM Symposium on User Interfaces Software and Technology '95*.

[4]   Bharat, K. and Sukaviriya, P., "Animating User Interfaces with Animation Servers." *Proc. ACM Symposium on User Interfaces Software and Technology '93*, pp. 69-79.

[5]   Birrell, A.D., Nelson, G., Owicki, S., and Wobber, E.P., "Network Objects." *Proceedings of the 14th ACM Symposium on Operating System Principles*, pp. 217–130, December 1993.

[6]   Borenstein, N. and M.T. Rose, "MIME Extensions for Mail-Enabled Applications: application/Safe-Tcl and multipart/enabled-mail", *Draft*, Bellcore, Dover Beach Consulting, September, 1993.

[7]   Cardelli, Luca, "A Language with Distributed Scope." *Computing Systems*, 8(1), pp. 27-59. MIT Press. 1995.

[8]   Cheshire, S. and Baker, M., "Experiences with a Wireless Network in MosquitoNet." *Proceedings of the IEEE Hot Interconnects Symposium '95*, August 1995.

[9]   Cypher, A. [Ed], "Watch What I Do - Programming by Demonstration", MIT Press, 1993.

[10]   Demers, A., Petersen, K., Spreitzer, M., Terry, D., Theimer, M., and Welch, B., "The Bayou Architecture: Support for Data Sharing among Mobile Users." *Proceedings of the Workshop on Mobile Computing Systems and Applications*, Santa Cruz, California, December 1994, pp. 2-7.

[11]   Finin, T., McKay, D., Fritzson, R., and McEntire, R., "KQML: An Information and Knowledge Exchange Protocol," in *Kazuhiro Fuchi and Toshio Yokoi (Ed.), Knowledge Building and Knowledge Sharing*, Ohmsha and IOS Press, 1994.Goldberg, D., Nichols, D., Oki, B. and Terry, D., "Using Collaborative Filtering to Weave an Information Tapestry", *Communications of the ACM*, 35(12), pp. 61-70, 1992.

[12]   Goldberg, D., Nichols, D., Oki, B. and Terry, D., "Using Collaborative Filtering to Weave an Information Tapestry", *Communications of the ACM*, 35(12), pp. 61-70, 1992.

[13]   Gosling, J., Joy, B., and Steele, B., "The Java Language Specification." *Addison-Wesley, The Java Series*, ISBN 0-201-63451-1, 864 pp., 1997.

[14]   Hopper, A., Harter, A., Blackie, T., "The Active Badge System." *Proceedings of ACM SIGCHI '93 (INTERCHI)* , Amsterdam, April 1993.

[15]   Joseph, A.D., DeLespinasse, A.F., Tauber, J.A., Gifford, D.K., and Kaashoek, M.F., "Rover: A Toolkit for Mobile Information Access." *Proceedings of the Fifteenth Symposium on Operating Systems Principles*, December 1995.

[16]   Labrou, Y. and Finin, T., "A Semantics Approach for KQML -- a General Purpose Communication Language for Software Agents." *Third International Conference on Information and Knowledge Management (CIKM'94)*, November 1994.

[17]   Maguire, G., Reichert, F., and Smith, M., "A Multiport Mobile Internet Router." *Proccedings of the 44th IEEE Vehicular Technology Conference*, Stockholm, Sweden, June 94.

[18]   Manasse, Mark S., and Nelson, Greg, "Trestle Reference Manual." *Digital Systems Research Center - Technical Report 68*, Palo Alto, CA, Dec 1991.

[19]   Powell, M., and Miller, B., "Process Migration in DEMOS/MP." *Proceedings of 9th ACM Symposium on Operating System Principles*, 1983, pp. 110-119.

[20]   Richardson, Tristan, "Teleporting - Mobile X Sessions.", *Proceedings of Ninth Annual X Technical Conference*, Boston MA, January 1995.

[21]   Sheth, B., and Maes, P., "Evolving Agents for Personalized Information Filtering." *Proceedings of IEEE Conference on AI for Applications*. 1993.

[22]   White, J.E., "Telescript Technology: The Foundation for the Electronic Marketplace." *White Paper. General Magic Inc.*, 1994.

[23]   Zayas, E., "Attacking the Process Migration Bottleneck." *Proc. of 11th ACM Symposium on Operating Systems Principles*, 1987, pp. 13-24.

The Messenger Environment MØ – A Condensed Description

Christian Tschudin

1 Introduction

Implementation techniques for distributed applications can be positioned in a spectrum that ranges from data–exchange to code–exchange. Date–exchange means that the logic (i.e., code) of a distributed application is statically installed and that coordination is done by exchanging messages with predefined meanings. Code–exchange, on the other hand, means that coordination is achieved by sending around code fragments which alter the data that is bound to the network's hosts. Actual systems usually pick and combine several techniques that are positioned at different places in this spectrum. Sun's JAVA and the corresponding code-on-demand approach, for example, would be closer to the data–exchange viewpoint, while Stamos' and Gifford's REMOTE EVALUATION is more in the line of mobile code because the initiator has more instructional capabilities. Mobile software agent systems are quite close to pure code–exchange, although they often mix-in classical data–exchange techniques (data streams between agents, or mailboxes). The aim of the mobile code environment MØ (m-zero) is to be as faithful as possible to the code–exchange point of view.

1.1 Messengers

Mobile computations are called *messengers* in MØ. Messengers are simple code fragments for which MØ provides the execution environment. They differ considerably from the usual "full blown mobile agents": messengers are cheap so they are launched en masse. Loosing several of them should not harm the application: this unreliability is just another facet of the unreliable character of networked systems (see the paper by Waldo et al. in this volume). With MØ we are interested in the "essential" elements of a code–exchange based system, where fore we try to keep the features for messengers as small as possible.

This paper briefly presents the main characteristics of MØ and documents at the same time some of the design principles that have been found useful in this context. The most important of them is the *locality* principle. It states that an execution environment should not provide services which require the coordination with other execution environments (beside the exchange of messengers, of course): network–wide services should be implemented by messengers. What we are looking for is a minimal and hopefully universal core that still enables the safe operation of a truly mobile code system.

2 The Messenger Environment MØ

MØ is at the same time: (i) a programming language for messengers, (ii) a format for representing messengers "on the wire", and (iii) the name of an execution environment that is able to interpret the language. In this section we give an overview of the concepts behind MØ and report on the corresponding software. The MØ language itself resembles very much POSTSCRIPT: It is an interpreted, stack-based and high-level (i.e., pointerfree) but not object-oriented language.

2.1 The Execution Platform

The execution platform is the core of MØ (figure 1). Its main role is to turn incoming messengers into concurrent threads i.e., to execute them. These threads are anonymous and can therefore not directly communicate with each other. Data exchange has to be done via a persistent *shared memory* area, synchronization is supported by simple *thread queues*. The submission and reception of mobile code is not restricted by security protocols as we follow an *open security model* for mobile code (see section 2.9).

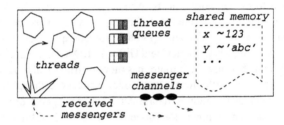

Fig. 1. The logical view of a messenger execution platform.

Platforms are linked by communication channels which offer a simple and unreliable datagram service (garbled messengers are silently dropped). Because most channels impose limits on the admissible datagram length, messengers must provide their own fragmentation and reassembly logic. In fact, messengers have full control over the external representation sent along the channels (they could send arbitrary byte strings).

2.2 External Messenger Format

The external messenger format is part of the basic message exchange layer and has a very simple structure (figure 2): The main code field is preceded by some header fields and may be followed by an optional data field[1].

The header contains a version number, the lengths of the following fields, a checksum over header and code (checking the integrity of the data field is left to the messenger programmer) and a 64-bit key that identifies the thread queue in which the messenger thread should be started. The code field must contain a MØ program that is to be interpreted by the platform.

---

[1] Having an (optional) data field violates in some sense the purist code-exchange-only approach. However, from a programmer's viewpoint it is a very convenient feature. Moreover does a platform not look at the data field's content, thus it remains the code field's responsibility to interpret it.

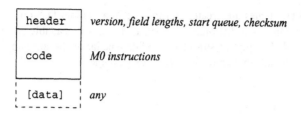

header	*version, field lengths, start queue, checksum*
code	*M0 instructions*
[data]	*any*

Fig. 2. The external messenger format.

2.3 Threads and Queues

Messengers are single-threaded and anonymous. There are no "handles" or thread identifiers that could be used to address or act on a thread. If the thread was not programmed to cooperate in some way, it remains invisible to other threads (except for its side effects, of course). A remote thread is created by sending a messenger (datagram) through a communication channel. It is also possible to create a new concurrent and coresident messenger thread which will be anonymous too.

Threads can decide to queue up in a thread queue. Queued threads which are not at the queue's head become blocked until they advance or a self-chosen timeout occurs. Thread queues are created on demand and can be put into a stopped state, allowing to control the progress of the queued threads.

2.4 Data model

In M∅ there are "simple" data instances and "composite" ones. Simple data objects (int, time, name etc.) fully fit into a slot of the so called element table while composite objects (array, dict etc.) are represented by references – the composite object's content is placed in a special heap area (called *virtual memory* in POSTSCRIPT). Simple and composite objects behave differently when a copy is made. After a dup, there will be two copies of the simple objects on the operand stack. For a composite object, only the reference is duplified such that changes applied to one reference are also visible through the other reference.

Keys are special names with a width of 64 bits. Keys are like "handles" and play a crucial role in M∅: they are used to select thread queues, they refer to communication channels and most of the time they are created randomly.

M∅ offers several conversion operators. The most important among them is the *convert–to–external* operator which – for almost every data instance – returns a code sequence that, when executed, creates a copy that is in conformance with the original instance. This functionality is usually called *serialization*, which in our case simply yields a M∅ program.

2.5 Memory model

The platform's shared memory area is accessible through several public "dictionaries". These dictionaries allow messengers to persistently store data under self-chosen names.

Most of the time these names are created at run-time in a random fashion in order to avoid name clashes. One such dictionary – g l o b a l d i c t – is readable and writable but cannot be browsed. This gives a simple form of data isolation, because an entry can only be accessed by threads that know the entry's exact name.

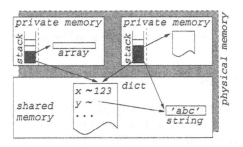

Fig. 3. Private and shared memory area.

The default mode of operation is that each messenger thread works within its own private memory area (figure 3). If data should be shared between threads, they have to reside in the shared memory area. The transfer from the private to the shared memory area is semi-transparent: adding an entry to one of the predefined shared dictionaries or arrays automatically creates a copy of the private variable. If the thread wishes to keep a handle on the now shareable copy, it has to explicitly fetch it from the shared data structure afterwards. The MØ interpreter keeps track of variables for being shared or private: putting a private value into a shared data structure automatically involves a copy, so that there are never references from the shared memory area back into some private memory area.

2.6 Native Code Support

An MØ interpreter can provide access to the underlying hardware or to several other execution environments (e.g., CPU emulations) in order let messengers circumvent the considerable interpretation overhead of MØ. Threads can query the set of supported CPUs, select a default CPU, assign values to registers and define the (virtual) address space in which a native computation should be performed. All these actions can be programmed in MØ. The _run command switches to native code execution for a single time-slice and returns either after a low-level error (e.g., access violation) or explicit request (e.g., supervisory call).

With native code support, messengers form a configuration and control plane e.g., for distributed operating systems (see the configuration in figure 5). Each MØ platform becomes a microkernel on top of which native processes are executed under the control of messengers. Messengers can decide to migrate the execution of a native process to other platforms as well as they mediate all communications between the processes.

2.7 Money model

The MØ platform provides a special data type called `account`. Accounts store a certain amount of money in units of fictitious "conchs". Each messenger thread has a default account to which consumption of platform resources is debited. Account variables can be shared by coresident messenger threads even as their default account. This enables division of labor: one thread concentrates on the distributed algorithm it implements while another or even several other messengers are responsible for "fund raising".

There are no operators for direct account–to–account operations: instead money has first to be withdrawn, resulting in a *check* (in form of a 64-bit key) that can be freely passed between threads and then be cashed on another account. Detecting double-spending is easy because checks have local validity only. Thus, each platform has its own local currency.

A platform acts like a national economy i.e., it controls the flow of money and fixes tax rates. All resource consumption (CPU time, memory and bandwidth) is accounted for and debited to the thread's default account. If there is no money left on that account, the thread goes bankrupt and is removed. The prices for specific resources are fixed by the platform according to the resource's current load. Incoming messengers receive some start money. This amount of money must be used by a messenger to either find other money sources or to send a messenger back telling that this platform is too expensive.

2.8 Resource Management

Money is used as the vehicle to allocate the platform's limited resources to requesting threads. The more money a messengers offers, the higher are its chances to obtain a specific resource.

CPU time is allocated in single timeslices and in a random fashion by running a lottery Messenger threads can influence the chance to obtain a timeslice by buying additional lottery tickets. Statistically, this results in a distribution that reflects the amount of money invested.

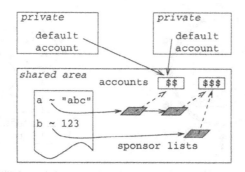

Fig. 4. The sponsoring of shared dictionary entries.

Memory for composite objects is implicitly allocated to the threads at the time additional memory is needed. This may fail because there is no (physical) memory left or because the thread has not sufficient money for extending its private memory area. Messengers can acquire (i.e., buy) memory resources "in advance" by specifying the amount of memory that should be put aside right now. The platform will make a reservation and implicitly satisfies subsequent memory requests from this pool: a messenger can thus avoid failures due to memory shortages (or learn about them at reservation time). Once this pool becomes empty, memory has to be acquired "at the spot market". Private memory that is freed during an operation is returned to the pool. Messengers can also adjust the pool size in the other direction: lowering it means that reserved memory is given back to the system and the messenger is reimbursed.

In the shared memory area we have no data owners because entries should persist even if the creating messenger terminates. Entries in composite shared objects (dictionaries and arrays) must be *sponsored* i.e., each entry needs an account to which some persistency tax is debited. Entries for which there is no sponsor money left are removed which means e.g., for shared dictionaries, that we undefined an entry, or for shared arrays that we replace an entry by a `null` value. Figure 4 shows the relation between accounts and entries in shared data structures.

2.9   Security Model

MØ does not impose any security protocol: it accepts arbitrary messengers from arbitrary origins. However, the platform provides a set of mechanisms which can be used by the messengers to implement themselves the safety and security they need. The idea is to avoid delegation of security issues to the mobile code system. Access restrictions for special resources like the file system, or communication channel, are subject to agreements between (human) users and the platform operator — such agreements are out of the scope of the messenger world and require no special language support. Figure 5 gives a pictorial description of the approach adopted by MØ.

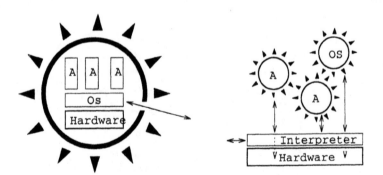

Fig. 5. Protection provided by the system vs. interacting messengers protecting themselves.

The mechanisms offered by the platform comprise encryption routines and cryptographic hash functions like DES and MD5. A special operator linked to asymmetric kryptosystems is called `elaunch`: its single argument is a messenger string that was encrypted with the platform's public key. Elaunch instructs the platform to decrypt the string and to execute its content as a new and independent messenger thread. Only the platform with the right private key is able to correctly decrypt the string, which gives a guarantee that the messenger is executed on the desired platform only.

2.10 Name Resolution and Syntax Rules

Name resolution in MØ is identical to the way it is done in POSTSCRIPT. Each messenger starts with a dictionary stack that includes a common system dictionary and an empty user dictionary. The `systemdict` is read-only and contains all basic operators of the MØ language. Each name that the MØ lexical scanner encounters is resolved by looking up the top dictionary and going down the dictionary stack if no entry with the given name is found. Entries in the user dictionary (or any other dictionary pushed on the stack) thus hide definitions in the lower dictionaries, which allows for an easy redefinition of operators or procedures.

A the syntactical level, however, MØ departs considerably from POSTSCRIPT. Having a compact coding of messengers in mind we assigned the most important MØ operators to the uppercase and punctuation characters. Each of these characters is defined to be a single token, which enables to concatenate them back to back without space characters between them. Multicharacter names are restricted to lowercase characters and the underscore. Digits, finally, form another character class where the token ends when the next character does not belong to the current character class anymore. The following three lines are equivalent MØ programs (a random key is generated, it is stored in a variable k, the thread enters and implicitly creates the queue k and sets it into the stopped state):

```
randomkey currentdict 'k 2 index put enter currentqueue 1 queuestate
;           .          'k 2 I    :   E      ,            1 Q
;.'k2I:E,1Q
```

These special syntactic rules lead to programs which resemble byte codes. However, this analogy is not quite true because the assignment from a single-byte token to an operator or procedure can be redefined in MØ at will. This also prevents a byte code verifier approach like the one found in JAVA.

2.11 An Implementation

A first implementation of MØ was published in the newsgroup `comp.sys.unix` in june 1994. Since then, MØ was further developed and also ported to bare ("OS-less") i386 machines for experimenting with native code execution under messenger control i.e., distributed LINUX. The UNIX version simulates thread switching in C while the i386 version has true preemptive scheduling. The latest version of MØ has the following performance figures on a Sun Sparc10/model 40:

#/sec	activity	msec	#/sec	activity	msec
58'800	empty MØ loop	0.02	2'800	local data exchange	0.36
11'600	shared dict read or write	0.09	740	local hop	1.35
5'300	inter-thread sync	0.19	245	complete UDP hop	4.08

The MØ source code has some 18'000 lines of ANSI-C code which also includes crypto-graphic routines, drivers for the datagram channels (UDP, ethernet and serial line) and miscellaneous utilities (MØ code preprocessor, messenger formatter, interactive command interpreter etc.).

3 Outlook

There is no optimal position on the spectrum we mentioned in the introduction. Data–exchange has the advantage that is can be very fast once the environment is static enough. Code–exchange is very flexible but is potentially slow because it has to adhere to a very late binding philosophy: first, functionality is not determined or known in advance, and second, the location at which some function should be executed is not known either. Hybrid approaches may in the future well be the answer, where mobile code is used as a configuration language helping to explore and parametrize all the resources that are distributed in the network. These resources, however, will probably operate according to the ordinary data–exchange approach.

MØ is in a first place an exploration tool for the basic principles of a pure code–exchange world. By refraining from looking at problems that are specific to object orientation or security, we hope to better understand and propose solutions to operational problems (e.g., resource control) and to find mobile code based implementation alternatives for distributed applications. At the same time should our minimalistic approach facilitate a more theoretical treatment of mobile code.

Although this seems like a fundamental research oriented approach, we think that the MØ software is stable enough to do real messenger programming. In several ways could MØ be compared to TEX: Plain TEX implements a basic type setting engine but has a rather cumbersome level of abstraction when it comes to debugging and type setting for larger documents. The aim and status of MØ is similar: to provide a common low-level basis on top of which manifold distributed applications can be run. What is currently missing for MØ is some kind of LATEX package that would provide a useful set of high-level routines for messenger programming.

http://cuiwww.unige.ch/tios/msgr/msgr.html

Mobility and Persistence*

Miguel Mira da Silva

Abstract. In the last three years we have been working with persistence and distribution, in particular migration of higher-level objects between autonomous persistent programs. In this chapter we introduce persistence and then present a few examples of *opportunities* and many more *challenges* that exist in the combination of persistence and mobility.

1 Introduction

Mobile objects are active objects that migrate between programs. These active objects are commonly implemented as procedures, instances of classes or abstract data types, or threads. A persistent program is a program written in a language that permits to create and manipulate objects independent of their life time (see section 2).

The main motivation for the research work described here is our perception that persistence has not been properly addressed by the research community studying mobile objects. Persistence is important because many of the examples for mobile object applications presented in the literature include local or remote database access. Free variables (e.g., objects carrying other data) are also of interest, and unavoidable in a persistent environment, because data and code are highly and strongly inter-connected in the persistent store.

For example, Java [AG96] has been recently proposed as "the network language" because it was designed for migrating code between heterogeneous machines on the Internet. However, Java suffers from at least three limitations: 1. examples of Java applets are confined to use the Java standard library; 2. since Java has no integrated persistent support, applets access databases in an *ad-hoc* manner; and 3. it is not possible to migrate complex data structures between Java programs in Java itself.

There are no answers yet concerning the first limitation. The second is partially solved by using a Java interface to access relational databases like JDBC [Sun96d]. In order to address the third limitation, Sun has proposed a CORBA-like RPC based on IDL [Sun96c] and an RMI (remote method invocation) system [Sun96b] on top of the Java system. Both are limited in the data types they can migrate and are not intended to transfer code (i.e., these systems are not intended to replace the functionality provided by applets).

The chapter is based on our experience with persistent systems and higher-level distributed computation, two research areas that combined address many of the same issues as those of mobile objects. One of our current research goals is to contribute for

---

* This chapter is an extended version of a joint paper with Malcolm Atkinson, "Combining Mobile Agents with Persistent Systems: Opportunities and Challenges" [MdSA96a] that was originally published in the Proceedings of the Second ECOOP Workshop on Mobile Object Systems [BTV96].

a mobile object system that offers the application programmer none of the limitations with Java described above. Thus we aim at building a programming environment with: general and flexible support for free variables; migration of code and data in an integrated manner between autonomous programs; and better access to local and remote databases.

In order to experiment with persistence and distribution we used Napier88, a research orthogonally persistent programming language briefly described in section 2. Napier88 and its extensive list of features have immensely helped our research. For example, we describe elsewhere how a type-safe persistent RPC was implemented in three months by the author alone [MdS95a]. This RPC has since then been continually extended and partially rebuilt, demonstrating how persistence and Napier88 are suitable for incremental program construction.

Recently we have started to address mobile objects in our research work, a natural consequence of trying to support (persistent) higher-order objects as arguments to (persistent) remote procedures. In the process we have encountered some *opportunities* in the combination between persistence and mobility that are described in section 3.

However, we have also encountered many difficulties and problems that are summarised as *challenges* in section 4. These are mostly a consequence of the rich type system provided by Napier88 and an orthogonally persistent system that maintains all relationships between data and code, safely and permanently.

Throughout the chapter we restrict the examples to the following systems: Java, Facile, Obliq, MOLE, Aglets, Tycoon, our own Napier88/RPC and PJava. This does not mean these systems are better or have more features than others, but simply that they are representative of both research areas. In addition, we had better access to their characteristics, for example, material about them has been published and/or we have made contact with their authors. However, any eventual mistakes and omissions are purely our fault.

2 Persistent Systems

The persistence of an object is the period of time for which the object exists and is usable [ABC+83]. A *persistent system* ensures that objects remain available as long as they are required for computation, thus eliminating the need for files or databases (see figure 1 below).

A conventional, as opposed to persistent, programming language manipulates only objects that are resident in memory. If these objects are to be used later by the same or another program, then the data has to be explicitly transfered from (volatile) program data structures to some sort of permanent (non-volatile) storage, generally utilising a different representation, naming scheme, access methods, etc.

A persistent language avoids the need for the programmer to worry about these two worlds and to write code to transfer data between them. All data are available for computation as long as they are required. This simplicity permits to use much more complex data structures because they do not have to be flattened to a file or relational database.

However, not all persistent languages offer this extreme simplicity because there are increasing levels of commitment to the persistence abstraction. *Orthogonal persistence*

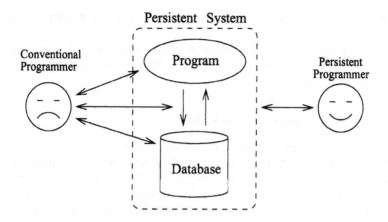

Fig. 1. Architecture of a Persistent System

[ABC+83, AM95] is the most exigent and can only be achieved by applying three principles: 1. *persistence independence* (i.e., programs look the same whether they manipulate short or long term data); 2. *data type orthogonality*(i.e., there are no special cases for certain types [ACC82]); and 3. *persistence identification* (i.e., persistence is not related to the type system, for example, by inheriting from a *Persistent* class like in ObjectStore [LLOW91]).

The benefits of orthogonally persistent systems, described extensively in the literature, have been summarised in a recent survey [AM95]. These are: increased programmer productivity; better data protection; long-term referential integrity; and incremental software construction. In short, orthogonally persistent systems are expected to provide better support for the design, development, operation and maintenance of complex database applications.

2.1 The Napier88 Persistent System

Napier88 [MBCD89, MBC+94] is a research persistent programming language that supports *orthogonal persistence*. Persistence of an object is defined by reachability from a single persistent root. Objects that cannot be reached are unusable and thus can be garbage collected.

The Napier88 rich type system is described by a set of base types and a set of constructors, and the recursive composition of these [Con91]. The language supports abstract data types [Cut93] and parametric types, including parametric procedures. The type of an object can be obtained at run-time, and type equivalence is structural. (Napier88 has currently no support for inheritance but it has been recently proposed [CBM96].)

Procedures are first-class objects in Napier88. This means procedures cannot only be declared at run-time, passed as parameters to other procedures, and executed, but also be assignable, the result of expressions or other procedures, elements of structures and vectors, and made persistent to survive program execution. First-class procedures can be used to implement abstract data types, modules, separate compilation, views and data protection [AM85].

Other features of Napier88 include dynamic binding and type-checking, memory and disk garbage collection, type-safe linguistic reflection, heterogeneous architecture, all with acceptable performance.

2.2 Why Combine Persistence and Mobility

In his thesis, Knabe gives several examples of applications for mobile objects [Kna95]. The main idea behind mobile objects is that an RPC is not flexible enough because the interface is fixed to the set of remote procedures available at the server. By permitting to send code to the server instead of mere data, a mobile object system—as opposed to an RPC system—can *program the server dynamically* by extending the set of remote procedures as needed. In the other way round, mobile objects can *reduce the load at the server* and also *reduce communication costs*, both achieved by downloading and executing part of the server program at the client.

However, it is interesting to note that many of the example applications given for mobile objects also include migrating data or accessing databases. The examples presented by Knabe himself in chapter 5 of his thesis are mostly applications remotely accessing databases (a map, a diary, etc). That is only natural; we have to accept that most programs downloaded to interact with the end-user need to carry some data to display, use local objects or access a remote database.

These examples suggest the need for addressing persistence in a mobile context. For example, if an object uses a local database, then migrates to another program, should the object carry the database with it ? Should it access the database remotely ? Should it use a local (equivalent) database ? Should it duplicate the database ? If yes, should there exist any replication protocol to keep the replicas consistent ?

Unfortunately, these questions are typically not addressed by the literature on mobile objects. But if persistence is a common requirement for mobility, then there can be advantages in addressing these two research areas together. As we will see in the next two sections, this integration creates a few opportunities but also poses a number of challenges to both the mobile objects and persistent systems research communities.

3 Opportunities

In this section we give examples of opportunities in the combination of persistent systems with mobile objects. These opportunities occur both ways: using persistence to build better mobile objects, and using mobile objects to built better distributed persistent applications.

3.1 Mobility as Persistence

The basic idea behind persistence is to exchange objects automatically between the database and the program as needed by the application. Initially, objects are created in the program but they move to the store before the execution terminates, so they will be available for the next program execution. In an orthogonally persistent system with a rich type system like Napier88, these objects include data (integers, reals, strings, structures, vectors and so on) and code (procedures, abstract data types, etc).

Many researchers have noted that mobility and persistence are intrinsically related because mobility is conceptually similar to persistence if the store is replaced by another program. The same can be observed the other way round: persistence is just mobility in which one program behaves as being the store. This argument can be found repeatedly in the literature [HL82, BJW87, DSP87, Cra93, Mun93, MMS96, Bau96].

Figure 2 illustrates how the same algorithms can be applied to both program-store and program-program communication. For example, the Napier88 standard library [KBC+94] offers some basic support for distribution implemented by modifying the procedures that already existed to implement persistence [Mun93]. Both Tycoon/RPC [MMS95, MMS96, Mat96] and the latest version of Napier88/RPC [MdS95b, MdSA96b] use the same approach.

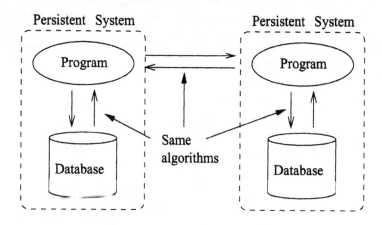

Fig. 2. Similarities of Persistence and Mobility

The opposite is also true. The same procedures for marshaling and un-marshaling arguments to remote procedures can be used to export objects to a file or import (previously exported) objects from a file. We give as an example the pickling procedures for Modula-3 — later incorporated into Network Objects [BNOW93] — that can also be used to implement a limited form of persistence. Another example can be found in JavaSpaces [Sun97], a persistence mechanism for Java that is being implemented based on *object serialization* [RWW96, Sun96a] originally developed for Java RMI [Sun96b].

Mobile object systems in a persistent environment can take advantage of these algorithms instead of (re-)implementing their own migrating procedures. For example, the implementors of MOLE [SBH96] have already demonstrated interest [Bau96] in a forthcoming persistent version of Java [AJDS96, ADJ+96].

However, this opportunity should be addressed with caution since *persistence is not exactly the same as mobility*. The store is guaranteed to contain all objects reachable from any other reachable object. This is not true between programs developed and executed independently. In a persistent system only the newly created or changed objects have to be put in the store. Without proper treatment of transitive closures, large parts of the program would always have to be transmitted to the other program (see section 4.1).

This opportunity may also suggest there could be advantages to work with mobility at the same level as persistence, namely within the run-time system itself. However, it may be difficult to work at such a low-level, especially since the facilities for mobility have to be translated into high-level language constructs to be of any use to application programmers. Another problem may occur if the implementation of the run-time system is continually changing, as happens with any experimental research language like Napier88.

3.2 Database Access Language

Relational database systems accept queries written in SQL, a declarative language. More recently, with the advent of client/server computing, it has become typical for a PC (the client) to send SQL requests to a UNIX machine (the server) so that the query can be executed where the database resides (see figure 3). Even if it sounds strange, at least in this sense SQL is a well-know, established *mobile object language* specifically developed for accessing databases.

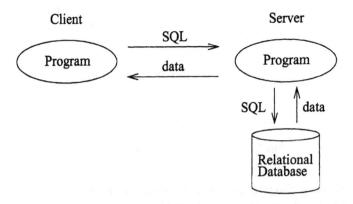

Fig. 3. Database Query using SQL

However, SQL is a proprietary language since each database vendor offers its own extensions to the standard SQL. This makes difficult for a client to be developed independently of the database or make requests against different databases. To solve this problem, Microsoft has proposed ODBC—for Open DataBase Connectivity—to offer an API for a well-defined, stable sub-set of SQL. ODBC is now supported by most database vendors and has become a standard *de facto*.

The only mobile object system to our knowledge with specific support for ODBC is the Aglets Workbench [IBM96]. Aglets are small Java programs that can be sent between stand-alone Java applications and—unlike applets—return to their originating site.

The workbench, a development tool to write distributed applications based on aglets, includes a database access library (called JoDax) that uses ODBC and thus supports most relational databases.

More interestingly, when aglets migrate they carry data and their state—not only code like Java applets. Although there is very little information publicly available on implementation details, we have learnt that aglets use the standard Java run-time system and Sun's Java libraries [Lan96]. For example, aglets are linearized for migration by the object serialization mechanism [RWW96, Sun96a] that will probably be part of the next major release of Java [Sun96a].

Recently, Sun has proposed a variation of ODBC for Java called JDBC [Sun96d]. With JDBC, an applet can have access to one or more relational databases, either local or remote (not taking into account security restrictions). In addition, JDBC is supported by a (increasing) number of database vendors. For all these reasons we expect JDBC to become a standard database access language for Java, and as a consequence, for mobile object systems based on Java.

3.3 Higher-order RPC

An RPC system permits to call a remote procedure in another program. Conventional RPC systems, especially commercial products, are usually very restrictive in the types they support as arguments to the remote procedures. For example, Sun/RPC [Sun93] only supports a few base types and simple constructors such as structures. Even modern "object-oriented" RPC implementations based on CORBA [OMG95] such as Java/IDL [Sun96c] do not extend this set significantly (most of all they add remote references).

We have discussed in section 2.2 how mobile objects have appeared as an answer to this limitation. However, there is a new brand of *higher-order RPC systems* that support much richer data types as arguments to remote procedures, namely procedures themselves. (Sometimes these RPC systems are embedded in a distributed programming language, although in this chapter we only consider systems that pass arguments explicitly by copy.) Examples of these higher-order RPC include *remote evaluation* [SG90] and more recently Obliq [Car95, BC95]. In the persistent community we find *remote execution* [DRV91], Tycoon/RPC and our own Napier88/RPC.

Although from a different starting point and with different objectives, many of these projects achieve the same results and share the same problems as systems like Facile [Kna95] and MOLE [SBH96]. (This is indeed the *raison d'être* of this chapter.) For example, remote execution was proposed but *never implemented* because of the difficulties we describe in section 4.

3.4 Java as the Unifying Concept

A final issue is the common ground for the integration between mobility and persistence provided by Java [AG96]. Apart from the qualities or limitations of Java, many persistent and mobile object systems are now being built based on Java. This creates a tremendous opportunity that we missed in the original paper [MdSA96a]. The two most representative examples are the PJava project at Glasgow and the Aglets Workbench from IBM.

PJava [AJDS96, ADJ$^+$96] is a persistent version of Java that maintains the same syntax. Like Java, PJava is also object-oriented, type-safe, and has garbage collection (now extended to the database). Like Napier88, PJava implements persistence by reachability so classes are stored in the database together with their objects (and vice-versa).

The first prototype of PJava (PJava0) is now working. PJava0 was built as a "proof of concept" only, and as a result it has a number of limitations such as: limited store size, simple garbage collection and no support for persistent threads. A second prototype (PJava1) is currently being implemented and will solve these limitations. As one of the Tycoon developers (Bernd Mathiske) is now part of the PJava team, we can also expect thread migration between PJava programs in the near future.

The Aglets Workbench was already described in section 3.2 because it includes support for persistence, both access to relational databases and mobile objects carrying data. The Aglets Workbench is also based on Java; not only programmers write their mobile objects in Java, but—unlike PJava—it generates code for the standard Java run-time system.

None of these systems, however, has all the facilities for implementing persistent mobile objects [MdSRdS97]: the Aglets Workbench needs more elaborate persistent support (e.g., to store code in the database) while PJava needs more mobility support (e.g., to migrate code between autonomous programs). Both systems will no doubt add functionality to overcome these limitations, but since they are both based on Java, it should be much easier to port solutions from one system to the other. Eventually, an attempt could be made to integrate the best features of each system into a single *persistent mobile object system.*

4 Challenges

Most challenges in this section are based on the fact that mobile objects should migrate by copy, and the complexity and size of their transitive closures. Migrating objects by reference, in which only a remote reference for the object is actually sent to the target program, creates availability and scalability problems [MdSAB96]. Migrating by reference is even less appropriate for mobile object systems where autonomy between programs is one of the main requirements.

4.1 Reducing the Transitive Closure

Migration by copy means that free variables that are bound to the object have also to be copied to the target program. The problem is what to do if these variables reach large parts of the program. For example, most procedures in Napier88 have very large transitive closures and frequently they reach the entire database ! Traditional (as opposed to persistent) but still type-safe programming languages have a similar (if reduced) problem: even if transitive closures are limited to the program address space, libraries and other local resources used by mobile objects—such as system calls, site-specific objects and so on—have to be dealt with properly or the object will fail remotely. (A good example is provided by Java applets, which are typically very restricted in their functionality to avoid these issues.)

A well-known approach to reduce the transitive closure of an object is to ask application programmers to make a distinction at compile-time between those objects that migrate by copy and those that migrate by reference only (i.e., that are not really mobile). For example, large objects or site-specific objects can be accessed remotely by defining an interface written in IDL as in CORBA [OMG95] or in a more flexible manner by specialising the arguments of the remote procedures to transmit only part of the object graph [Lop96].

On-demand, shallow, partial, or lazy object migration can also be used automatically by the system at run-time as in Emerald [BHJ+87, JLHB88], DPS-algol [Wai88], HiRPC [KOMM93, KKM94] and GUM [THM+96]—with or without *hints* by application programmers. However, all these solutions are just clever optimisations of migrating by reference and still maintain the basic potential to suffer from partial failures with unpredictable consequences.

Another approach to reduce the transitive closure which does not create remote references, proposed independently by several researchers, is simply not to migrate objects that already exist in the target program. For example, Facile proposes *ubiquitous values* for which equivalent implementations of the value exist in both the originating and destination sites. Tycoon/RPC lets programmers register modules as *ubiquitous resources*—such as parts of standard libraries. Step 4 of the migration command in Obliq says that "links to the local runtime are explicitly removed" [BC95]. Octopus [FD93, FD94] is another proposal to allow application programmers themselves to manipulate bindings in persistent objects.

As part of our work with Napier88 we have designed and implemented a mechanism called *migration by substitution* [MdSAB96, MdSA96b, MdS96] in which only a surrogate identifying the object migrates to the target program. In the implementation, the surrogate is just a name that has been previously agreed between the source and target programs (see next paragraph). On arrival at the target program, the name is replaced by an equivalent object of the same type. Standard utilities such as the Napier88 Standard Library [KBC+94] and Glasgow Libraries [WWP+95] always migrate by substitution in our experiments with mobile objects.

Migration by substitution is similar to other approaches, but has three important differences: 1. equivalent objects are defined *dynamically* (i.e., new objects can be added or existing ones removed at run-time); 2. defined by *name* (i.e., we do not require equivalent objects to have the same value); and 3. the mechanism is still *strongly type-safe* (i.e., equivalent objects are type-checked between the source and target programs). Other mechanisms fail to provide one or more of these characteristics.

4.2 Sharing Objects Between Stores

Although most mobile object applications will probably not require any remote connection to the originating program, some applications will require this facility. For example, an object sent to a server program to execute a computation remotely may need further data only if some assumption at the destination is true; the object may require more code (e.g., a word processor may require a spell checker); or the object may need to access some rapidly changing data such as a stock value.

But remote access is already a solution to a more general problem: How to share objects between other objects that reside in different programs ? There are basically two approaches to solve the sharing problem in a distributed system: one copy (by remote access, see previous paragraph) or many copies (using some sort of replication protocol) [DC93]. Below we describe each of these approaches in turn.

Figure 4 illustrates the *one-copy approach*. If both A and B refer to C, then if A migrates to another program, a remote reference to C can be created and the new object A' only carries this remote reference with it. (A and A' are two distinct objects because each has its own local OID.) Remote references are convenient because they provide a simple programming model, but remote access is *slow* (typically 4 to 5 orders of magnitude slower than a local reference) and *unreliable* (because it may not work due to failures/congestion at the server/network).

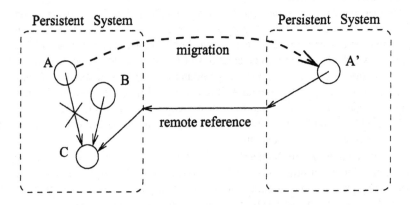

Fig. 4. Inter-store Object Sharing with One Copy

A better approach, especially for mobile objects in a persistent environment, is to duplicate the shared object remotely (see figure 5). In this approach, C also migrates to the destination program together with A. The problem now is to maintain the replicas consistent when they are updated. (We assume C is mutable; if C is constant, then duplication can be a good solution). Strict replication protocols that maintain the replicas always consistent can be used, but they require remote references and thus suffer from similar problems as the one-copy approach.

Obliq is a truly distributed language and permits to share objects remotely using the one-copy approach. A similar behaviour can be achieved in Tycoon/RPC by calling remote procedures. In Facile there are no high-level provisions for sharing at present, but a data type called *channel* can be used to access an object remotely (the application has to implement its own protocol, marshaling, etc). In addition, all these languages also permit to duplicate objects remotely, although no help is provided for maintaining replicas consistent.

In order to deal with distributed sharing we proposed and implemented a compromise between the one-copy and many-copies approaches called *persistent spaces* [MdSA96b, MdS96]. Using persistent spaces, a *publisher* releases objects that can be later fetched

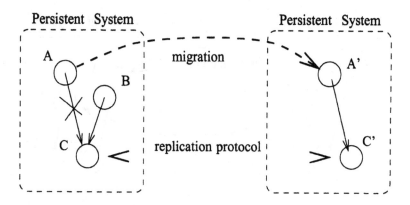

Fig. 5. Inter-store Object Sharing with Many Copies

by any number of *subscribers*.

By putting them in a persistent space, A and C can be updated at any time but the replicas A' and C' are synchronised explicitly by each subscriber. This synchronisation incurs the same costs as the many-copies approach but we allow the application programmer to choose when to pay the price, not every time A or C are updated.

In a persistent space *marshaling is made at publishing time*. This means persistent spaces have many other advantages: they permit to check locally if a group of objects can be exported; they amortise marshaling over a number of clients; they return the packet size (containing the marshaled objects) before the transmission; and packets can be transmitted at any convenient time (e.g., at 4am) and using a wide range of media (e.g., by e-mail or ftp).

4.3 Maintaining Sharing Semantics

Another problem with free variables occurs when two or more objects that locally share another object(s) migrate to the target program. (The same happens if the same object migrates more than once). Figure 6 shows what happens in a typical RPC system when A migrates, then B also migrates but in another remote call. The duplication of C in the target program produces: *semantic decay* because A' and B' do not offer the same behaviour as A and B; *transmission and space wastage* because C is transfered twice and stored twice; and *state ambiguity* if many updates or separate program executions occur between the call that sends A and the one that sends B. A combinatorial explosion occurs if C is large and/or shared by many other objects.

Persistent spaces can also be used as a first step towards solving this problem because *within persistent spaces the common sub-structure sharing is maintained.* Thus if A and B belong to the same persistent space, only one copy of C will be created in the target program. Persistent spaces also keep only one copy of C' if A and B migrate separately because *the common sub-structure in a persistent space is maintained between successive transmissions.* (However, separate spaces will have separate copies of sub-structures. The application programmer can then opt for maintaining or avoiding common sub-structures).

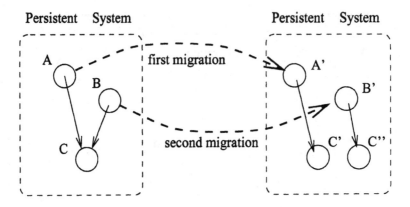

Persistent   System   Persistent   System

Fig. 6. Loss of Object Sharing in Successive Migrations

4.4 Efficient Marshalling and Unmarshalling

Even after applying migration by substitution and deciding to use persistent spaces, the number of migrating objects may still be very large. For example, in one of our experiments we migrated a map representing an index containing 3,389 entries. The total number of objects amounted to 10,486 and the packet size (containing the marshaled index) to approximately 500 KB. The index took 37 minutes to be transmitted and rebuilt at the destination program.

However, just sending a byte array with 500 KB from one program to another program across our departmental Ethernet takes only 3–4 seconds, including the time to open the socket connection. The conclusion we take is that *the time to pack and unpack is clearly dominant for large and/or complex objects.* More worryingly, migration time in Napier88/RPC increases *quadratically* to the number of objects being migrated as a result of the packing algorithm. Finally, because these operations are CPU intensive, significant performance improvements are also limited by the implementation of the language itself.

The problem is that, for each object, the marshaling algorithm has to check whether this object has already been packed to deal with shared and cyclic data structures [HL82]. In order to implement this check, a data structure is used to maintain a reference to all packed objects. Ideally, this data structure would permit fast access by reference, such as a b-tree or an hash table. However, in a *threaded persistent system with garbage collection* references may change at any time from a volatile representation (memory pointer) to a persistent representation (object identifier). (The reader is referred to [MdS96] for a better discussion and solutions to this problem).

Recently, the research work on Tycoon has produced efficient marshalling and unmarshalling of persistent objects [Mat96]. This was achieved by implementing the algorithms within the run-time system, that is, in C and having access to implementation details. This solution was facilitated because in this case the RPC implementor had helped to build the Tycoon run-time system itself. Even though, Tycoon/RPC still shows poor performance when compared with non-persistent RPC systems such as

Sun/RPC [MdS96]. (It may be argued, however, that Tycoon/RPC was not optimized because it is a research prototype. Further research is required to confirm if an efficient implementation of marshalling is possible in a persistent programming language.)

4.5 Mobility Orthogonal to Type

Until now we have assumed that certain objects can migrate whereas others cannot. But why should only special objects in the language be mobile ? Why is not possible to migrate objects of *any* type ? Does it make sense ? Can it be implemented ?

These questions are interesting because most mobile object systems identify a mobile object at compilation time, thus restricting the set of objects which can later migrate. For example, Facile identifies "possible transmissible functions" by relying on the programmer to annotate these before compilation; only these functions are potentially mobile. In Obliq, mobile objects are special procedures that contain a *suitcase* and no other free variables (except if belonging to the user interface, which do not truly migrate because the links to them are cut by the migration command). Finally, only applets can migrate in Java, not an arbitrary Java class.

On the other hand, one of the requirements for orthogonally persistent systems is that "all objects in the language have the right to persist". So at least for a persistent programmer it makes perfect sense that "all objects in the language have the right to migrate". Migration orthogonal to type is specially important because non-orthogonal migration will eventually suffer from the same problems of non-orthogonal persistence [ABC+83, AM95]. What if the application semantics requires to migrate non-migratable objects ? What if the programmer decides later to migrate an object that is non-migratable ? What if a migratable object refers to a non-migratable object ?

Migration orthogonal to type is also possible to implement—in principle at least, if we can solve the challenges described in this section—as there are no such restrictions on mobile types in both Tycoon/RPC and Napier88/RPC. (Instances of abstract data types pose special problems that we are still investigating. This is the reason why threads, implemented as instances of the abstract data type *Thread* in Napier88, cannot migrate in Napier88/RPC.)

We propose that any procedure in any program—or indeed any object which refers to an object that contains code—is potentially a mobile object. This generality is convenient but introduces new problems. For example, because the transitive closure of a persistent object is typically large, there may be cases in which the entire transitive closure cannot migrate. These include *semantic restrictions* (e.g., there is a single persistent root in each store so it is meaningless to migrate the root to another store) or *engineering limitations* (it may be difficult or simply take too much time).

According to Knabe, the reason for restricting the set of transmissible values is "performance, performance, performance" [Kna96]. In a mobile object system based on native (machine) code such as Facile, generating machine-independent byte-code can double the space needed for programs. However, as Knabe also notes, run-time (also called just-in-time) compilation can be used to generate machine code on demand. Byte-code can also be used directly, as in Java and Napier88.

Knabe's thesis [Kna95] has achieved some interesting results, but more research is needed to assert the trade-offs between different *code representations* (compilation on-demand, native code, byte-code, and their multiple combinations) when compared with *space requirements* and *transmission time*.

4.6 Failure Model for Migration

Unlike static analysis of code or compile-time rules to decide if an object can migrate, the decision to migrate or not can instead be delayed until migration time. When migration cannot be achieved, the attempt should raise an exception. The exception should ideally explain — in terms understandable to application programmers — why the migration could not succeed. For example, the program can pass information about the failure to the end user or may try to migrate another object (probably smaller or simpler).

A model based on a single exception as Facile [Kna96] is not enough because it does not convey enough information to enable the program to take decisions. Instead, a sophisticated failure model is needed that can explain why a migration did not succeed. Examples of these reasons are: references to the outside world that only make sense locally (e.g., descriptors to open files); values with types that do not exist remotely (so they cannot be used); values that create implementation problems for transmission (e.g., instances of abstract data types); and semantic problems (such as private data or attempting to transmit the persistent root).

Persistent systems have many years of experience with these kind of failures because migration is similar to putting an object in the store or fetching an object from the store. As a result, the Napier88 failure model is quite comprehensive [KBC+94]. Persistent spaces may also contribute to this failure model because marshaling — the tricky part of migrating an object — occurs *locally* in the publisher program. This simplifies the detection and treatment of some kind of errors, but a general approach to deal with all failures which may occur during migration is still needed.

4.7 Standard Mobile Object Language

Each mobile object system uses its own model, language and algorithms to migrate procedures and other objects between programs. This diversity resembles the first days of RPC, when each RPC system was designed for a particular language and marshaled arguments in a manner different from any other RPC system.

Eventually, CORBA [OMG95] was proposed to allow programs written in different languages to exchange data between them, and a number of CORBA implementations have since then been built. Now the latest CORBA specification even supports interoperability between different CORBA implementations via a standard transport protocol and data format. CORBA suggests that standards can succeed if properly backed by a significant number of companies offering commercial products.

The experience with persistent systems is also revealing. More than 20 years of research on persistence have failed to produce a standard persistent system, not even a standard set of features a persistent system should support. However, the commercial cousins of persistent systems, object-oriented database systems, have at least agreed on an "object query language" [ODM93] that is intended to avoid the problems that occurred with SQL. Again, the commercial world defined what is "standard".

Although probably not a major technical challenge, the following questions still make an interesting topic for the mobile object community. Does it make sense to propose, design and support a standard mobile object language ? Would this standard language be based on an existing language ? Can we dream of one day migrating mobile objects between different mobile object systems provided by different vendors ? The answer to all these questions is probably yes, so the main question becomes: will the research community or the commercial world design this standard ?

5 Summary

In the last 3 years we have been working with persistence and distribution. During this time we have built a higher-order RPC mechanism that permits to exchange procedures and other complex data structures between autonomous persistent programs. It was not by chance that we have achieved many of the same results—and encountered many of the same difficulties—as researchers working with mobile objects.

Our objective with this chapter is to bring into the mobile objects research community ideas from our own research work with distribution and persistence. In order to achieve this objective, the chapter has: 1. introduced persistence, Napier88, and our own research with Napier88/RPC; 2. presented the opportunities that exist in the combination between mobility and persistence; and 3. discussed a number of challenges that we have encountered in that same combination.

These challenges will become more important as mobile objects start to play an ever greater role in real-world distributed applications. This is because many of the practical uses for mobile objects access databases or carry other objects with them, including more code.

In order to deal with these problems, we have proposed migration by substitution and persistent spaces. Migration by substitution offers a flexible mechanism to reduce the transitive closure of an object by cutting links to objects that already exist in the target program. Persistent spaces help with sharing objects between programs and maintaining sharing semantics, even between transmissions.

Remaining challenges for which we have not found yet a satisfactory solution are: marshaling algorithms that scale for large data structures; efficient migration orthogonal to type; a simple but comprehensive failure model; and the model for a future standard mobile object language.

Acknowledgements

The author would like to acknowledge Malcolm Atkinson, his PhD supervisor, for the last three years in Glasgow where these ideas originated and were developed. Fritz Knabe and Bernd Mathiske read previous versions of this chapter and made innumerous comments. Many other people have contributed to this research work, specially Andrew Black, Joachim Baumann, Peter Dickman, Peter Larsson and the participants in the 2nd ECOOP Workshop on Mobile Object Systems.

172

References

[ABC⁺83] M.P. Atkinson, P.J. Bailey, K.J. Chisholm, W.P. Cockshott, and R. Morrison. An approach to persistent programming. *The Computer Journal*, 26(4):360–365, November 1983.

[ACC82] M.P. Atkinson, K.J. Chisholm, and W.P. Cockshott. PS-algol: An algol with a persistent heap. *ACM SIGPLAN Notices*, 17(7):24–31, July 1982.

[ADJ⁺96] M.P. Atkinson, L. Daynès, M. Jordan, T. Printezis, and S. Spence. An orthogonally persistent Java. *SIGMOD Record*, December 1996.

[AG96] K. Arnold and J. Gosling. *The Java Programming Language*. The Java Series. Addison Wesley, 1996. ISBN 0-201-63455-4.

[AJDS96] M.P. Atkinson, M. Jordan, L. Daynès, and S. Spence. Design issues for persistent Java: A type-safe, object-oriented, orthogonally persistent system. In Atkinson et al. [AMB96].

[AM85] M.P. Atkinson and R. Morrison. Procedures as persistent data objects. *ACM Transactions on Programming Languages and Systems*, 4(7):539–559, October 1985.

[AM95] M.P. Atkinson and R. Morrison. Orthogonal persistent object systems. *VLDB Journal*, 4(3):319–401, 1995.

[AMB96] M.P. Atkinson, D. Maier, and V. Benzaken, editors. *Proceedings of the Seventh International Workshop on Persistent Object Systems (Cape May, New Jersey, USA, May 29-31, 1996)*. Morgan Kaufmann Publishers, 1996.

[AT96] Paolo Atzeni and Val Tannen, editors. *Proceedings of the Fifth International Workshop on Database Programming Languages (Gubbio, Umbria, Italy, 6th-8th September 1995)*, Electronic Workshops in Computing. Springer-Verlag, 1996.

[Bau96] J. Baumann. Private communication, 1996.

[BC95] K. Bharat and L. Cardelli. Migratory applications. In *Proceedings of ACM Symposium on User Interface Software and Technology '95 (Pittsburgh, PA, Nov 1995)*, pages 133–142, 1995.

[BHJ⁺87] A. Black, N. Hutchinson, E. Jul, H. Levy, and L. Carter. Distribution and abstract types in Emerald. *IEEE Transactions on Software Engineering*, SE-13(1):65–76, January 1987.

[BJW87] A. Birrel, M. Jones, and E. Wobber. A simple and efficient implementation for small databases. In *Proceedings of the Eleventh ACM Symposium on Operating Systems Principles*, November 1987.

[BNOW93] A. Birrell, G. Nelson, S. Owicki, and E. Wobber. Network objects. In *Proceedings of the 14th ACM Symposium on Operating Systems Principles*, pages 217–230, December 1993.

[BTV96] J. Baumann, C. Tschudin, and J. Vitek, editors. *Proceedings of the 2nd ECOOP Workshop on Mobile Object Systems (Linz, Austria, July 8-9, 1996)*. dpunkt, 1996.

[Car95] L. Cardelli. A language with distributed scope. *Computing Systems*, 8(1):27–59, January 1995. A preliminary version appeared in Proceedings of the 22nd ACM Symposium on Principles of Programming Languages.

[CBM96] R.C.H. Connor, D. Balasubramaniam, and R. Morrison. Investigating extension polymorphism. In Atzeni and Tannen [AT96].

[Con91] R.C.H. Connor. *Types and Polymorphism in Persistent Programming Systems*. PhD thesis, University of St Andrews, 1991.

[Cra93] D.H. Craft. A study of pickling. *Journal of Object-Oriented Programming*, January 1993.

[Cut93] Q.I. Cutts. *Delivering the Benefits of Persistence to System Construction and Execution*. PhD thesis, University of St Andrews, 1993.

[DC93]   J. Daniels and S. Cook. Strategies for sharing objects in distributed systems. *Journal of Object-Oriented Programming*, January 1993.

[DRV91]   A. Dearle, J. Rosenberg, and F. Vaughan. A remote execution mechanism for distributed homogeneous stable stores. In P. Kanellakis and J.W. Schmidt, editors, *Database Programming Languages: Bulk Types and Persistent Data*. Morgan Kaufmann Publishers, 1991. Proceedings of the Third International Workshop on Database Programming Languages (Nafplion, Greece, 27th–30th August 1991).

[DSP87]   G.N. Dixon, S.K. Shrivastava, and G.D. Parrington. Managing persistent objects in Arjuna: A system for reliable distributed computing. In R. Carrick and R.L. Cooper, editors, *Proceedings of the Second International Workshop on Persistent Object Systems: Their Design, Implementation and Use*, pages 246–265. Universities of Glasgow and St Andrews, 1987.

[FD93]   A. Farkas and A. Dearle. Octopus: A reflective mechanism for object manipulation. In C. Beeri, A. Ohori, and D.E. Shasha, editors, *Proceedings of the Fourth International Workshop on Database Programming Languages: Object Models and Languages (Manhattan, New York City, USA, 30th August–1st September 1993)*. Springer-Verlag in collaboration with the British Computer Society, 1993.

[FD94]   A. Farkas and A. Dearle. The Octopus model and its implementation. *Australian Computer Science Communications*, 16(1), 1994.

[HL82]   M. Herlihy and B. Liskov. A value transmission method for abstract data types. *ACM Transactions on Programming Languages and Systems*, 4(4):527–551, October 1982.

[IBM96]   IBM Tokyo Research Lab. *Aglets Workbench: Programming Mobile Agents in Java*, 1996. http://www.trl.ibm.co.jp/aglets/.

[JLHB88]   E. Jul, H. Levy, N. Hutchinson, and A. Black. Fine-grained mobility in the Emerald system. *ACM Transactions on Computer Systems*, 6(1), February 1988.

[KBC+94]   G.N.C. Kirby, A.L. Brown, R.C.H. Connor, Q.I. Cutts, A. Dearle, V.S. Moore, R. Morrison, and D.S. Munro. The Napier88 standard library reference manual version 2.2. Technical Report FIDE/94/105, ESPRIT Basic Research Action, Project Number 6309—FIDE₂, 1994.

[KKM94]   K. Kono, K. Kato, and T. Masuda. Smart remote procedure calls: Transparent treatment of remote pointers. In *Proceedings of the 14th International Conference on Distributed Computing Systems (Poznan, Poland, June 21–24, 1994)*. IEEE Computer Society Press, 1994.

[Kna95]   F. Knabe. *Language Support for Mobile Agents*. PhD thesis, Carnegie Mellon University, Pittsburgh, PA 15213, USA, December 1995.

[Kna96]   F. Knabe. Private communication, 1996.

[KOMM93]   K. Kato, A. Ohori, T. Murakami, and T. Masuda. Distributed C language based on a higher-order RPC technique. *JSSST*, 5:119–143, 1993.

[Lan96]   D.B. Lange. Private communication, 1996.

[LLOW91]   C. Lamb, G. Landis, J. Orenstein, and D. Weinreb. ObjectStore. *Communications of the ACM*, 34(10):51–63, October 1991.

[Lop96]   C. Lopes. Adaptive parameter passing. In *Proceedings of the 2nd International Symposium on Object Technologies for Advanced Software (Kanazawa, Japan, Mar. 11-15, 1996)*, volume 1049 of *Lecture Notes in Computer Science*. Springer-Verlag, 1996.

[Mat96]   Bernd Mathiske. *Mobility in Persistent Object Systems*. PhD thesis, Computer Science Department, Hamburg University, Germany, May 1996. In German.

[MBC+94]   R. Morrison, A.L. Brown, R.C.H. Connor, Q.I. Cutts, A. Dearle, G.N.C. Kirby, and D.S. Munro. The Napier88 reference manual release 2.0. Technical Report

FIDE/94/104, ESPRIT Basic Research Action, Project Number 6309—FIDE₂, 1994.

[MBCD89]   R. Morrison, A.L. Brown, R.C.H. Connor, and A. Dearle. The Napier88 reference manual. Technical Report PPRR-77-89, Universities of Glasgow and St Andrews, 1989.

[MdS95a]   M. Mira da Silva. Automating type-safe RPC. In O.A. Bukhres, M.T. Özsu, and M.C. Shan, editors, *Proceedings of The Fifth International Workshop on Research Issues on Data Engineering: Distributed Object Management (Taipei, Taiwan, 6th– 7th March 1995)*, pages 100–107. IEEE Computer Society Press, 1995.

[MdS95b]   M. Mira da Silva. Programmer's manual to Napier88/RPC 2.2. Technical Report FIDE/95/133, ESPRIT Basic Research Action, Project Number 6309—FIDE₂, 1995.

[MdS96]   M. Mira da Silva. *Models of Higher-order, Type-safe, Distributed Computation over Autonomous Persistent Object Stores*. PhD thesis, Submitted to the University of Glasgow, 1996.

[MdSA96a]   M. Mira da Silva and M. Atkinson. Combining mobile agents with persistent systems: Opportunities and challenges. In Baumann et al. [BTV96].

[MdSA96b]   M. Mira da Silva and M.P. Atkinson. Higher-order distributed computation over autonomous persistent stores. In Atkinson et al. [AMB96].

[MdSAB96]   M. Mira da Silva, M.P. Atkinson, and A. Black. Semantics for parameter passing in a type-complete persistent RPC. In *Proceedings of the 16th International Conference on Distributed Computing Systems (Hong-Kong, May, 1996)*. IEEE Computer Society Press, 1996.

[MdSRdS97]   M. Mira da Silva and A. Rodrigues da Silva. Insisting on persistent mobile agent systems. In *Proceedings of the First International Workshop on Mobile Agents (Berlin, Germany, April 7-8, 1997)*, 1997. To be published.

[MMS95]   B. Mathiske, F. Matthes, and J.W. Schmidt. On migrating threads. In *Proceedings of the Second International Workshop on Next Generation Information Technologies and Systems (Naharia, Israel, June 1995)*, 1995.

[MMS96]   B. Mathiske, F. Matthes, and J.W. Schmidt. Scaling database languages to higher-order distributed programming. In Atzeni and Tannen [AT96].

[Mun93]   D.S. Munro. *On the Integration of Concurrency, Distribution and Persistence*. PhD thesis, University of St Andrews, 1993.

[ODM93]   ODMG—Object Database Management Group. *Object Database Standard*, 1993. http://www.odmg.org/odmg-93.html.

[OMG95]   OMG—Object Management Group. *The Common Object Request Broker: Architecture and Specification (CORBA)*, 1995.

[RWW96]   R. Riggs, J. Waldo, and A. Wollrath. Pickling state in the Java system. In *Proceedings of the 2nd Conference on Object-Oriented Technologies and Systems (June 17-21, 1996, Toronto, Ontario, Canada)*, 1996.

[SBH96]   M. Strasser, J. Baumann, and F. Hohl. MOLE: A Java based mobile agent system. In Baumann et al. [BTV96].

[SG90]   J. W. Stamos and D. K. Gifford. Remote evaluation. *ACM Transactions on Programming Languages and Systems*, 4(12):537–565, October 1990.

[Sun93]   Sun Microsystems. *RPC Programming Guide*, 1993.

[Sun96a]   Sun Microsystems. *Object Serialization*, 1996. http://chatsubo.javasoft.com/-current/serial/.

[Sun96b]   Sun Microsystems. *Remote Method Invocation*, 1996. http://chatsubo.javasoft.-com/current/rmi/.

[Sun96c]   Sun Microsystems Inc. *Java IDL*, 1996. http://splash.javasoft.com/JavaIDL/pages/.

[Sun96d]   Sun Microsystems Inc. *JDBC: A Java SQL API*, 1996. http://splash.javasoft.com/-jdbc/.

[Sun97]   Sun Microsystems. *JavaSpaces*, 1997. http://chatsubo.javasoft.com/javaspaces/.

[THM⁺96]   P. Trinder, K. Hammond, J. Mattson, A. Partridge, and S. Peyton Jones. GUM: A portable parallel implementation of Haskell. In *Proceedings of the 1996 Conference on Programming Language Design and Implementation (Philadelphia, USA, 1996)*, 1996.

[Wai88]   F. Wai. *Distributed Concurrent Persistent Programming Languages: An Experimental Design and Implementation*. PhD thesis, University of Glasgow, April 1988.

[WWP⁺95]   C.A. Waite, R.C. Welland, T. Printezis, A. Pirmohamed, P. Philbrow, G. Montgomery, M. Mira da Silva, S.D. Macneill, D. Lavery, C. Hertzig, A. Froggatt, R.L. Cooper, and M.P. Atkinson. Glasgow libraries for orthogonally persistent systems: Philosophy, organisation and contents. Technical Report FIDE/95/132, ESPRIT Basic Research Action, Project Number 6309—FIDE₂, 1995.

Security and Communication in Mobile Object Systems

Jan Vitek, Manuel Serrano and Dimitri Thanos

1 Introduction

The rapid growth of computer networks has created an opportunity for developing massively distributed computer systems. Such systems will likely consist of loose communities of heterogeneous machines running different operating systems with different security policies. The challenge is to design a reliable, and yet efficient, infrastructure trustworthy enough for electronic commerce and flexible enough to allow software upgrades as well as new functionality to propagate in a decentralized, inherently insecure, wide area network. *Mobile object systems* embody a paradigm where computations, *i.e.* running programs, may move across the network and carry out truly distributed computations. The vision is that computations structured as autonomous systems of objects will roam the network performing complex tasks on the behalf of their human owner. These mobile systems of objects carry their data as well as their code with them during their journey; thus allowing almost unlimited extendability. Such unfettered mobility raises justified security concerns. From the host's stand point first. Can an arbitrary code fragment be entrusted with local resources? To what degree is it possible to control the behaviour of downloaded code? How can secrecy and integrity be preserved? From the sender's stand point next. Is it possible to entrust the network with mobile computations that encode valuable knowledge and are empowered to carry out commercial transactions? Even though it is technically feasible to charge foreign computations for small service such as execution time or storage [39]. The key question whether there is a way to achieve a sufficient level of security for this approach to be viable? Currently, we must answer by the negative. None of the existing mobile computation systems meet the security requirements of electronic commerce. Lack of security fosters a *just say no* attitude towards mobile computations in portions of the scientific and business community [38]. The proverbial ball is now in the camp of mobile computations research. It is up to us to demonstrate that mobile objects may meet the stringent security criteria of real world applications.

The main contribution of this chapter is the study of security threats inherent to communication in mobile object systems. We will study how mobile object systems communicate. Describe the dangers of traditional communication mechanisms and outline two research directions currently being investigated. The structure of the chapter is the following. Section 2 describes security issues in mobile object systems. From this general overview we will focus on communication between object systems. Section 3 more precisely describes the threats that an object systems may be faced with. Section 4 is the heart of the chapter, it describes the shortcomings of existing communication mechanisms. In particular, we give examples that show the inadequacy of the security models of languages such as Java and Telescript (examples in Appendix). Finally, Section 5 sketches on going research.

2 Security and Mobile Object Systems

The term security has been subjected to much abuse lately. A secure programming system is not one that give the means to write secure application as argued by the likes of [17] and [40]. Instead a secure system is a programming system that prohibits insecure programs. While it is unrealistic to expect to present a comprehensive solution to the multiple security issues of real world applications, it is possible to study and solve subproblems. This is what we set out to do in this chapter. We provide examples that attest to the weaknesses of commercial environments such as Java and Telescript. We wish to emphasize before hand that even though some of these examples (but not all) may be avoided by changing coding style, the point is that it is possible, and even more, that it is easy to breach security in those environments.

A mobile object system architecture is composed of four components: (a) the host—a computer and operating system, (b) the computational environment (CE)—the run-time system, (c) mobile object systems—the computations currently running on the CE, and (d) a network or communication subsystem that interconnects CEs located on different hosts.

To establish a parallel with Java[1] the architecture maps as follows: (a) is the native operating system, for instance UNIX, (b) is a web browser, perhaps Netscape, (c) applets, (d) the Internet. In the long run the distinction between OS and CE may well disappear.

In this architecture, the computational environment is the key to overall system security. The protection mechanisms incorporated in the implementation of the CE enforce the chosen security policy. These protection mechanisms must be flexible enough to accommodate the policies of different organizations as well as comprehensive enough to ensure that the policy can not be breached [10][20] [16][21].

Protection mechanisms may be placed at all component boundaries with the goal to control and regulate interaction between components. Figure 1 lists the five boundaries that require security: (1) communication between hosts and CEs (*i.e.* computation mobility) must be secured, this to prevent disclosure of the information contained in the data portion of computations and corruption of either data or code, (2) incoming computations must be authenticated and granted access rights, this to determine on which principal's behalf the computations will execute, who should be charged and what they are allowed to do, (3) access to the host's local resources must be controlled, this to protect the host, (4) the CE must be protected from potentially malicious computations (and vice versa), this to prevent computation from by-passing the security built-in the envi-

---

1. Java does not support mobile computations. The language was designed for code-on-demand (remote dynamic linking) applications. Yet, it shares many concerns with mobile objects environments and may be extended to support full-fledged mobile computations [32].

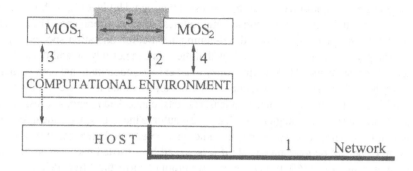

Figure 1 Security issues: (1) transfer security, (2) authentication and authorization, (3) host system security, (4) computational environment security, (5) mobile object system security.

ronment, (5) mobile object systems must be protected from each other, this to prevent a computation from disrupting another or gaining privileged information.

Transfer, Authentication and Authorization

Issues (1) and (2) are typical problems for distributed systems. It is natural to turn towards solutions developed in that field. Secure network communication and authentication require cryptographic techniques. Possible solutions include the Secure Socket Layer [14] for secure network communication, and Kerberos or some of its derivatives [31] for authentication.

Host protection

Issue (3) relates to access control mechanisms similar in purpose to those of operating systems. Yet, as Lepreau et al. [23] noted today's operating systems can not solve the problems raised by mobile code. They only provide flat protection domains while one of the implicit needs of mobile application are recursive protection domains. Recursion is needed to model the encapsulation of mobile computation within the CE and their restricted rights which must be limited to subset of the rights of the CE, *i.e.* the protection domain of the CE encapsulates the protection domains of the computations. An aspect, unrelated to OSs, which is a weak point in current environments is the *flexibility* of access control. Most Java implementation adopt an all-or-nothing approach that is not satisfactory [16][21] or even secure [9][10][22]. Flexible access control is the subject of on-going research [16][19][21][48]. As an aside, we emphasize once more the relationship between OSs and CEs: in most cases flexible access control requires the implementation of a superset of the OS access control mechanisms, outside of the OS. For instance, Goldberg *et al.* [16] propose to curtail all system calls using the `ptrace` functionality of Solaris.

Computational environment protection

Issue (4) may be approached from different angles. The bottom line is always to prevent computations to damage their CE. Operating systems face a similar problem as they have to protect themselves from the processes they run. Unlike OSs, mobile computation architectures usually are built as single address space environments. The associated reduction in space and improved CE-computation communication speeds improves overall performance. The down side is that the CEs can not rely on address space protection mechanisms[1]. The security policy of all existing computational environments is nevertheless to restrict computations to use a well-specified interface to interact with the CE. A policy that rules out, or at least restricts, unchecked memory accesses. These are common in unsafe language such as C. To enforce the policy, the code of computation must be safe, code which may be either in source form, bytecode, or native object form. Code can be guaranteed safe if it is signed by a trusted party (as in the MMM Caml web browser [34]), if it carries its own proof of correctness (*e.g.* PCC [30]), if the language is safe and the bytecode can be verified to adhere to the high level language semantics (*e.g.* Java), if the code executes in a highly restricted environment and is not allowed to emit illegal instructions (*e.g.* Agent Tcl [18]), or if the code is rewritten into a safe version (*e.g.* Omniware [47]). Malice need not be confined to mobile computations.There may be even more reasons for the CE to try to subvert its computations than the converse. For instance, CEs may extract payment for service not rendered or steal the secrets of visiting computations. This raises the question whether anything can be done to provide execution and secrecy guarantees? Very little research has addressed the issue. Published results on detection of malicious CEs are so restricted that they have little practical use[2].

Mobile object system protection

Issue (5)—security at the interface between mobile computations—implies control over communication channels between computations. All communication must be regulated by protection mechanisms. The goal is that the administrator of a computational environment should be able to choose a security policy that fits the organization's security requirements and be able to impose that policy on all computations running in the CE.

This chapter will focus on security of inter-computation communication. The chapter is organized as follows. Section 2 present security requirements for communication between mobile computations. Section 3 reviews existing communication mechanisms and points out their failings. Section 4 presents two new mechanisms that remedy the problems identified in the previous section. Section 5 present our conclusions. The appendix list some example attacks.

---

1. Portions of an address space may be protected via software fault isolation (SFI) [47]. SFI introduces an overhead as memory accesses need to be checked [47]. This overhead could be reduced if the code generator was trusted as is the case of run-time code generation and just-in-time compilers.

2. [28] detects malicious platforms by duplicating computations and executing them on different hosts. After each stage results are tallied and a voting algorithm is used to pick the correct result to use in the next stage. Unfortunately, computations must be deterministic, a requirement not often met in practice.

3 Protecting Mobile Object Systems

This work departs from the main research track in security of mobile programs by shifting the attention from host security to security of mobile computations. In effect, our emphasis is on trying to control interactions between mobile objects systems. Our thesis is that there can be no overall security if computations are not secured. Such security places requirements on the design of the language and environment. This section details threats related to communication channels.

Mobile object systems

Before discussing the threat model we present the relevant characteristics of mobile object systems. An *object* is a record with fields containing references to other objects, called instance variables, and fields containing operations, called instance methods. An object has an *interface* which describes which of its fields may be accessed by other objects. Every object is an instance of a *class*. We model classes by objects. Each object has a special instance variable that refers to its class object. The variable of the class object are thus shared variables for all of the instances. We shall assume that the language is run-time safe[1]. An *object graph* is the instantaneous representation of the state of a group of objects. Very briefly, an object graph consists of a set of vertices and a set of directed edges. There are two kinds of vertices: objects, classes. Edges represent references between objects (*e.g.* values of instance variables). We say that an object o' is *reachable* from o if there is a path from o to o' in the object graph g. An *object system* obj is the transitive closure of the object graph rooted at obj. This transitive closure represents the state of the system. A *computation* is a sequence of method invocations and variable accesses performed on the objects of a system obj. An object system is run in a *computational environment* which associates an authorization to every object system and controls the system's execution and its consumption of resources. *Mobile object systems* are object systems that may move between computational environments.

Protection domains

Any meaningful discussion of security requires a notion of protection domain. Security is relative to the entities that are to be protected. Protection domains group entities that must be protected together and are the level of granularity for protection mechanisms. In operating systems, for instance, the basic protection domain is the process. The default security policy is confinement, the OS draws a protective boundary around the set of memory pages accessible to each process. The protection mechanism is implemented in the address translation scheme that maps virtual addresses into physical ones. Most mobile environments present a single system image[2] and it is more difficult (or costly)

---

1. Run time safety ensures that arbitrary memory accesses are forbidden (*e.g.* no pointer arithmetic), type casts are checked, access to array and other variable length data structures is checked for overflow. These guarantees may be obtained by a combination of run-time checks, language restriction and type checking.

2. Single system image does not necessarily imply single address space. Distributed systems such as Emerald [3] and Obliq [2] provide a global address space. Java, Telescript [40] and Agent Tcl [18] have a single address space.

to define protection domains in terms of memory pages. In object systems, it is natural to describe protection domains in terms of object graphs. Domains may be populated implicitly or explicitly. Implicit protection domains are defined in terms of reachability in object graphs, Java leans in this direction. Explicit protection domains are defined by enumeration, Telescript falls in that category with its explicit 'owner' and 'sponsor' fields [40].

Threat model

We consider four kinds of threats in this chapter:

attack	description
Breach of secrecy	direct access to the state of another computation either due to a failure to enforce proper security or an insecure communication channel.
Breach of integrity	modification of the state of a computation by another computation by sending state-modifying messages to objects of the victim.
Masquerading	usurping the authority/identity of another computation for a series of actions, e.g. tricking the victim into executing some code fragment.
Denial of service	excessive consumption of a finite shared resource such as processing time, memory, or the communication subsystem.

Assuming that communication between protection domains is restricted to a set of CE-provided communication channels, preventing breaches of secrecy or integrity requires that channels be secure and never open up the objects of a protection domain to inspection or modification from another domain. In the following, we show that the strong typing and encapsulation of object-oriented languages fail to protect against such attacks as they do not preserve disjointedness of object graphs. Similarly for masquerading attacks, they can be set up by using polymorphism to inject code in other computations. Finally, denial of service attacks can be mounted by abusing the communication system[1].

Furthermore, *covert communication channels* must be prohibited. This is necessary if the security policy forbids information leaks between computations running at different levels of trust. For instance consider a scenario in which a computation requests the right to read a private file (but not to communicate over the net) and another the right to communicate over the net (but not to read private files). Both requests are acceptable from the stand point of security, as the program that has sensitive data is not able to communicate with remote machines and the program that can communicate with the outside world has no private data. The security problem is that if a covert channel can be established, the information gained by the first program may leak outside of the en-

---

1. Denial of service attacks can be mounted by using inordinate amounts of any finite resource [52]. For denial of service all that we wish to say is that use of the communication system must be accounted for. This is a failing of Telescript where it is possible to misuse the communication system [40].

vironment. We will give examples how to set up high-bandwidth covert channels in Java (see also [51]). Note that discovery of low bandwidth storage and especially timing channels is an active research topic [41].

Discussion

It has been argued that object-oriented principles can be used for security [1][40][49][17]. The claim hinges on the use of encapsulation and strong typing to restrict the way a client (the program that uses an object) can interact with the object. Another claim that has been often repeated is that objects can be used as capabilities [17]. Capabilities are kinds of permits for manipulating entities, they are mostly used in operating systems [4][6][37]. It is also common to see arguments to the effect that information hiding is a form of security mechanism [17]. Morrison *et al.* argued that although objects may be used to *implement* capabilities, they are not in themselves equivalent to capabilities [29]. On a more general note the object-oriented paradigm was conceived to foster good software engineering principles. Trying to contort its features into security mechanisms is bound to fail. Our claim is that object-oriented programs are *not* more secure than programs written in any other paradigm. Some language features, such as strong typing, may help. But others, such as pervasive reference semantics, polymorphism and subtyping, are hindrances. Finally, we will show that method invocation is not a secure communication mechanism for cross domain calls. The next section reviews existing communication mechanisms and discusses their advantages and disadvantages for inter-computation communication. The last section introduces two proposals for improving communication in mobile object systems.

4 Security and Communication

Inter-computation communication mechanisms may be classified into four categories: shared memory, generative communication, datagrams, and procedure calls or in object-oriented programs method invocations. The important characteristic of communication is that it encapsulates a crossing of protection domain boundaries. From the view point of security, values which traverse such boundaries must be controlled and sharing of values between protection domains must either be forbidden or, at least, regulated.

4.1 Shared memory

Sharing memory between object systems can be done at the level of physical pages in memory, or at a slightly higher level by shared variables. Sharing of memory pages requires operating system support while the sharing of variables is implemented by the CE.

Physical sharing is a low level communication mechanism, in object systems the natural granularity is that of objects not pages. Page sharing requires that all memory accesses be checked; to be efficient this must be implemented in the operating system. This is at odds with the basic portability requirement of mobile object systems. Furthermore the interaction of shared memory with allocation strategies and garbage collection is not well understood.

Shared variables represent a more disciplined way to share memory as they are type safe and can be implemented straightforwardly in a CE that provides a global address space for computations. Sharing implies that the objects graphs of computations are not disjoint. As a communication mechanism, shared variables allow data to be exchanged between computations at no cost. This advantage is mitigated as concurrent computations usually have to synchronize their reading and writing of shared data. For security, shared variables present several problems. It is necessary to decide which computations are allowed to share variables. Often sharing decisions are static and remain in effect for the entire program execution, whereas security needs to be more dynamic as permission may be granted and revoked depending on external factors. But the main problem associated with sharing is that it does not mix well with reference semantics of objects programs. Sharing a value that has references to other values in a protection domain means that a large part of the object graph may be compromised. In fact, the object graphs of different computations may become so thoroughly intertwined that it will not be possible to ascertain if a given method invocation has a target that is within the current protection domain or if the invocation is a cross domain call. Shared variables are thus more akin to a covert channel than to a disciplined communication mechanism. This is not all. Shared variables can be used to mount secrecy, integrity, masquerading and denial of service attacks as discussed below.

Shared variables are available in most Java implementations as the computational environment (the ClassLoader, to be exact) loads classes only once. Thus if two applets use the same class, they will refer to the same class object and thus share all of the variables of the class (static variables in Java terminology). Applets with common classes have intersecting object graphs. The examples 1 and 2 in appendix demonstrate how easily a class variable can be hijacked and turned into a security hole. Example 3 demonstrates the difficulty of discovering covert channels. The work on information flow analysis tries to address similar problems; this work is still far from complete and its integration in a language like Java would require sever restrictions of the language [11][41][43][44][45][46]. Examples 4 and 5 are attacks that can be mounted once a protection domain has become accessible. Example 6 shows how to use shared variable to kill all running user threads in a Java CE. Example 7 shows the Telescript approach to protection based on explicit ownership checks.

4.2 Generative communication

Generative communication is a model of communication introduced by Gelernter with LINDA [15]. The generative communication model was designed to coordinate cooperating parallel computations. Computations communicate by generating new data objects, called *tuples*, and writing them in a shared data structure, called the *tuple space*, which plays the role of an associative memory. This model has been adapted for use in object-oriented programs [27][8] without addressing security issues. Not only do all problems of shared variables apply to generative communication, but there are issues related to accounting. Existing designs do not allow any form of resource accounting over tuple space resource usage.

4.3 Datagrams

Datagrams are self-contained data packets. Communication by datagrams[1] involves the exchange of unformatted packets of raw data, *e.g.* through a socket interface. Thus, to send objects or other complex data structures it is necessary to serialize the data into a portable representation and then unserialize it at the receiving end. Such serialization guarantees that the disjointedness of object graphs is preserved by datagram communication. Recall that we assumed that the language is run-time safe. One of the key requirements for run-time safety is that pointers can not be forged. This has a desirable side effect: unserialized data can not contain pointers (only references between objects serialized together are allowed). Thus there is no way to establish bridges between object systems in the same address space via datagram communication. The only security risk is that of masquerading attacks shown in example 4. This kind of attack is made possible by subtyping which allows the caller to provide subtypes of requests objects. Thus datagrams are not fully secure, a remark that applies to Java remote method invocation [50]. But the main problem of datagram communication is efficiency. For simple built-in data types the cost of datagram is at least that of copying the data twice (once into a communication buffer, and once from the buffer), plus a system call. This is already much slower than a procedure call. The cost is even higher for objects which can contain recursive structures. Objects need to be flattened at the cost of potentially multiple method invocations per object, in addition the serialization process must take care of cyclic references. This cost is not acceptable for high frequency communication.

4.4 Method invocation

Direct method invocation is the normal method of communication between objects in the same protection domain, that is within the same object system. It does seem "natural" to extend it to cross-domain communication. The argument in favour of method invocation is that with strong typing and encapsulation it is possible to restrict what a client may be able to do with an object. The weaknesses of method invocation are tied to reference semantics and subtyping. Example 5 shows that an attacker may gain access to a large portion of the victim's object graph without breaking the interface. The problem is that the interface of an object says nothing about sharing between objects. Thus strong typing is not a sufficient protection.

Once object graphs cease to be disjoint, security is basically a lost battle. For instance, an object *o* may belong to a protection domain α but executes in response from an invocation coming from an object in protection domain β. Who's authority is to be invoked? Where should memory and time consumption be charged? Telescript tried to address these issues by advocating that each object must defend itself. Thus in Telescript objects have to check the origin of messages before answering. If a message originates from a 'friend' it should be answered otherwise it should be ignored. The predictable result is an inefficient mess as each software designer must try to code coherent and comprehensive security in the objects. Furthermore, (1) changing security or composing code originating from different organizations is near to impossible, (2) validat-

---

1. We use the term 'datagram' to avoid 'message' which is confusing in an object-oriented context.

ing security requires inspection of all classes, and (3) efficiency is degraded by the massive access checks, most of which unnecessary. Telescript [40] also provides 'read only' parameter, it is not clear from available documentation if this property is recursive and applies to objects reachable from the read only parameter. If it is not recursive, it is worse than useless, and if it is recursive it implies a staggering amount of run-time checking.

There is another kind of attack that uses method invocation against which strong typing fails to protect. This attack uses subtyping to pass arguments that conform to the expected types but contain dangerous implementations as shown by example 4. These kinds of masquerading attacks are not restricted to the type of the arguments. Each object obj given as argument to a method invocation is the root of an object graph defined by taking the transitive closure of all objects reachable from its instance variables. To prevent a masquerading attack it is necessary to guarantee that none of the objects in the graph rooted at obj is dangerous. This is not easy in polymorphic languages.

We would like to stress that the semantics of method invocation in languages such as Java and Telescript are fit for local communication but no to enforce security, strong typing and encapsulation notwithstanding. The problem is that method invocation knows nothing about protection domains.

4.5 Summary

We have discussed mechanisms for inter-computation communication among mobile object systems. Shared memory is too low-level and does not map well on high level abstractions. Shared variables are too undisciplined and open up systems to all kinds of threats. Generative communication has the same security weaknesses as shared variables. Datagrams are secure but inefficient as all data has to go through a costly serialization procedure. Method invocation fails to enforce security boundaries due to reference semantics of object-oriented languages and subtyping.

As a conclusion we shall compare the weaknesses of three approaches to communication. The first is the one of Java based on method invocation and shared variables. Java fails to provide any systematic security guarantees because there is no concept of program in the language. Programs, computations, or applets, are known at the level of the run-time or the operating system but not within the language. If there is no concept of computation in the language it is not surprising that there is no concept of protection domains either. Security is therefore pushed back into libraries and the run-time. This is a recipe for disaster as inconsistent policies and programming errors are bound to keep providing ways to break security [9][10]. Telescript takes a more explicit approach, there is a concept of computation and protection domain: the agent. But, all protection is dynamic and mostly in the hands of programmers. This is even worse than Java's approach to (in)security. The security code must be spread out over all classes and all applications. It is thus virtually impossible to say anything about the security of the overall system short of formally validating the code of all applications. A daunting task. As a general principle: *security of a programming system is inversely proportional to the ease of writing an insecure program.* Telescript, unlike Java, provides the means to check security but does not force these checks to be performed. Thus, we contend that Telescript security is fundamentally low. A last example is afforded by the Agent Tcl system. Although not an object-oriented language it does offer secure inter-computation communication messages based on datagrams. The basic data format is that of strings of text. The problem of this approach is speed, the overhead of communicating through strings will prevent this approach to be used in large applications that involve significant exchange of structured values.

5 Proposing Two Secure Communication Mechanisms

We now outline two communications mechanisms that are currently being implemented in the framework of the SEAL project at the University of Geneva. The goal of these mechanisms is to provide a finer control over security while remaining efficient. In particular, security should not depend on the programmer not forgetting to put checking code or on other good programming practice. We want a certain level of security to be mandatory in the system.

5.1 Sealed Method Invocation

As shown in Section 3.4, method invocation between mobile object systems fails to ensure security. Breaches of the four categories described in Section 2 may occur.

- Breach of secrecy and breach of integrity:

  These two security failures may occur for the same reason: an object system obj 1 could get a reference ref to data belonging to another object system obj 2 via method invocation (see appendix, example 5). If ref is used by obj 1 to read a value it could be a *secrecy* violation; if ref is used by obj 1 to write a new value, it could be an *integrity* violation.

- Masquerading and denial of service:

  Any unknown code fragment code executed by an object system obj may lead to security failures because, when executed, code belongs to obj, forming a part of obj. Consequently, code may access (read/write) any data of obj or may consume any system resources of obj. Unknown code execution is incompatible with security enforcement but unknown code execution is a paradigm advocated by object languages by the means of method invocations and subtyping. When an object invokes a method meth it may ignore the implementation of meth.

We propose an extension to the object programming paradigm that prevents attacks of the four categories. The goal of this proposal if to give programming language extensions where *un-secure programs cannot be expressed*. In that sense our approach is more ambitious that one defining a system where *secure programs can be expressed*.

Sealed object

Our proposal is based on the introduction of a special kind of object: *sealed objects*. A sealed object is an object that may use all the traditional features of the object-oriented paradigm. A sealed object may belong to a class (with the restriction that this class must not contain variable or refer to classes that do), it may have instance variables. It may point to other objects or sealed objects. It may allocate its own objects or sealed objects. Sealed objects differ from traditional objects only because they do not implement methods. Instead, they implement *sealed-methods* relying on *sealed method invocations*.

Sealed method invocations differ from traditional method invocations on the following points:

- Formal parameters and results of sealed invocations are passed by deep copy. This ensures that no breach of secrecy or integrity may occur because sealed method invocations prevent any reference sharing between two communicating sealed objects. As soon as a value is concerned by a sealed method invocation, a fresh deep copy is created and passed.

- Sealed method arguments are either monomorphic or use the sealed object hierarchy for their formal parameters and for their results. This ensures that no masquerading or denial of service may occur. Restricting sealed method arguments to be monomorphic means that dynamic dispatch is not used on those arguments and thus, the executed code is as known by the caller. The monomorphic restriction is recursive on the type structure of the argument. Allowing polymorphism for the sealed object hierarchy does not compromise security because sealed objects *are* secure. Let us suppose that each sealed object is allocated, by its enclosing sealed object, some system resources (such as disk file resources, memory resources or even cpu resources). If a sealed object obj1 received another sealed object obj2, obj1 does not need to know the code executed by obj2 because obj1 controls via its system resources allocation the consumption of obj2. Furthermore, whatever obj2 implements, it can not violate the secrecy or the integrity of obj1 because their communications are restricted to sealed invocations.

Sealed method invocations are fast because the extra-cost of an inter mobile object system communication is just the cost of the copies. Which is much less than the cost of serialization, for example. Moreover, some of these copies can be avoided in any of the following situations: a static analysis proves that the reference to a send object is never used in the sending sealed object, a static analysis determines that the receiving object will not attempt to modify the passed object or, lastly, if the passed value is an immutable value.

Sealed objects and sealed method invocations succeed in enforcing a strict general security policy but they cannot be used to implement several specific policies. For instance, two sealed object are not allowed to use specific, more flexible, sealed method invocations. The sealed method invocation is the same for all the sealed objects. Otherwise the efficiency of the approach would be compromised.

Capsules

The deep copies can sometimes be too large, up to the entire system, and may reveal sensitive information. There is a need for sending arbitrary subgraphs which need not be entirely consistent. For this we propose the mechanism of capsules, which is related to the Octopus model of Farkas and Dearle [12][13] to the substitutions of Mira da Silva [36] and to the work on adaptive parameter passing of Lopes [25]. A capsule captures a portion of the state of an object system with the guarantee that no reference exists between the capsule's contents and the rest of the system. Thus a capsule contains an object graph that is disconnected from the rest of the system. The role of capsules in communication is crucial, as they represent the only way to exchange partial data structures between protection domains. To create a capsule, it is necessary to identify, a portion of the object graph of the application, and to unlink it from the application so that no reference remains from inside the capsule to the outside and vice versa. A capsule is specified by a root object o and a list of fencepost objects *Fence*. The capsule is a subgraph containing only objects which can be reached from o without passing through any fencepost f ∈ *Fence*. Object in the set of fence posts *Fence* will be replaced by *placeholders*. Placeholders are abstract specifications of the object they replace. They are tuples: the first field is a type specification, the remaining are optional and encode additional information required to recreate the original object. Once a capsule has been constructed it is not possible to send message to the objects it contains as those objects are partially unlinked. In that sense, the contents of the capsule are passive. To use a capsule's contents, it is necessary to open the capsule and provide replacement objects for all placeholders. A capsule can be opened only once.

Capsule can capture as much state as needed, including the state of all threads of control and all the attached code, or as little as a single object. The usefulness of capsules for communication comes from the fact that they create disjoint subgraphs from the main object system. For the sake of mobility it is crucial to control very tightly the amount of data transferred. Placeholders are thus used to limit the size of the object graph to store in the capsule, and they also define the point where to reconnect the contents of the capsule to the environment.

5.2   Sealed Object Spaces

Sealed method invocation still has one minor drawback, it is a directed communication mechanism. Sometimes undirected communication or multicast communication may be desirable. Sealed method invocation is also synchronous, that is, the receiver must answer all requests in order. We propose to add generative communication as an alternative to method invocation when communication must be undirected or asynchronous. The generative communication model of LINDA was designed to coordinate cooperating parallel processes [15]. In LINDA, processes communicate by generating new data objects, called *tuples*, and writing them in a shared data structure, called the *tuple space*. This *tuple space* is an associative memory from which a process can retrieve tuples by pattern matching. We propose a new mechanism called *Sealed Object Spaces* which enhances the LINDA model with security and accounting features and shift the emphasis from coordination to communication between potentially hostile computations.

Sealed object spaces (SOSs) are purely local structures to a computational environment, in this respect they differ from the Jada proposal outlined in [8]. Multiple SOSs can coexist within a single environment. A computation may be connected to zero, one or more SOSs. It may retrieve values from an object space by pattern matching. Pattern matching relies on trying to match *tuples* with *anti-tuples*. An anti-tuple is a tuple with some "holes". An element is either a literal value or a formal. For an anti-tuple to match a tuple, all actuals of the anti-tuple must be equal to corresponding elements of the tuple. All formals must have a type which is a supertype of the corresponding element in the tuple. The process of querying a SOS proceeds as follows: (0) create an anti-tuple, (1) try to match the anti-tuple with values stored in the SOS, (2) if a match is found, bind the formals of the anti-tuple to the actuals of the tuple, (3) otherwise block, until a matching tuple is written to the object space. All SOS operations are atomic.

SOSs extend the LINDA model in two respects: keys and capsules. Keys are used to control who can retrieve a tuple and allow computations to set up fine-grain access control policies on portions of the shared space. Capsules are used to pass non-primitive objects safely.

Keys allow object spaces to be used for private communication. The principle is simple, every tuple with a field which contains a PublicKey can only be matched by an anti-tuple containing the corresponding PrivateKey. New public/private key pairs can be created and it is possible for agents to communicate private keys. These keys are objects managed by the object space. They can be viewed as capabilities in an operating system [37]. Using keys it is possible to have secret conversation, in fact a third party is not even able to determine that values were exchanged between two computations.

As SOSs use sealed method invocation, all values passed into a SOS are guaranteed to be reference free.

Accounting is under the care of the object space, which keeps track of memory consumption and time spent retrieving tuples on the behalf of a computation. Charging computations for processing time is straightforward as tuples are "passive" while in the object space. This means that unlike other proposals, matching is kept simple, in particular we do not invoke methods on the tuples or their components [27]. The memory used by each computation is equal to the size of all of its tuples still in the object space. The ownership of a tuple changes when it is input by another computation. Issues such as expiration policies for old tuples and tuple garbage collection are currently being investigated.

6 Conclusion

This chapter has investigated security in mobile object systems and focused on communication security between mobile object systems executing on the same computational environment. The conclusions that we have come to are that security measures based on strong typing and encapsulation fail to protect effectively mobile object systems from breach of integrity and secrecy, masquerading and denial of service attacks. In systems such as Telescript and Java, the choices for communicating between object systems are either to use mechanisms which are highly inefficient but secure (datagrams) or fast but insecure (shared variables, method invocation).

As a solution this chapter outlined two proposals to add security in mobile object systems. The first is to introduce sealed objects, which are objects that enforce strong security boundaries around their subobjects. The second proposal builds a secure generative communication paradigm based on sealed objects.

Acknowledgments
The authors wish to thank Christian Tschudin and Michael Zastre for their comments on a draft of this paper. This research has been carried out within the ASAP project (Swiss SPP-ICS program grant no 5003-45332).

References

[1] B. Bershad, S. Savage, P. Pardyak, E. G. Sirer, D. Becker, M. Fiuczynski, C. Chambers, and S. Eggers. Extensibility, Safety and Performance in the SPIN Operating System. In *Proceedings of the 15th ACM Symposiumon Operating Systems Principles (SOSP-15)*, pages 267–284, Coppper Mountain, CO, 1996.

[2] K. A. Bharat and L. Cardelli. Migratory applications. In *Proceedings of ACM Symposium on User Interface Software and Technology '95*, Pittsburgh, PA, Nov. 1995.

[3] A. Black, N. Hutchinson, E. Jul, H. Levy, and L. Carter. Distribution and abstract types in Emerald. *IEEE Trans. Softw. Eng.*, 13(1):65—76, Jan. 1987.

[4] A. C. Bomberger, A. P. Frantz, W. S. Frantz, A. C. Hardy, N. Hardy, C. R. Landau, and J. S. Shapiro. The KeyKos nanokernel architecture. In *Proceedings of the USENIX Workshop on Micro-Kernels and Other Kernel Architectures*, pages 95—112. USENIX Association, April 1992.

[5] L. Cardelli. Mobile computation. Position paper, Digital SRC, 1996.

[6] J. S. Chase, H. M. Levy, M. J. Feeley, and E. D. Lazowska. Sharing and protection in a single address space operating system. *ACM Transaction on Computer Systems*, May 1994.

[7] D. Chess, B. Grosof, and C. Harrison. Itinerant agents for mobile computing. *IEEE Personal Communications*, 2(4):34 — 49, Oct. 1995.

[8] P. Ciancarini and D. Rossi: Jada: coordination and communication for Java agents. In [42].

[9] D. Dean. The security of static typing with dynamic linking. In *Fourth ACM Conference on Computer and Communications Security*, Zurich, April 1997.

[10] D. Dean, E. W. Felten, and D. S. Wallach. Java security: From Hotjava to Netscape and beyond. In *1996 IEEE Symposium on Security and Privacy*, Oakland, CA, May 1996. IEEE, IEEE.

[11] D. Denning and P. Denning. Certification of programs for secure information flow. *Communications of the ACM*, 20(7):504 513, July 1977.

[12] A. Farkas and A. Dearle. Octopus: A reflective language mechanism for object manipulation. In *Proceedings of the Fourth International Workshop on Database Programming Languages*, Lecture Notes in Computer Science. Springer-Verlag, 1993.

[13] A. Farkas and A. Dearle. The Octopus model and its implementation. *Australian Computer Science Communications*, 16(1), 1994.

[14] A. O. Freier, P. Karlton, and P. C. Kocher. The SSL protocol (version 3.0). Technical report, Netscape Communication Corporation, Mar. 1996.

[15] D. Gelernter. Linda in context. *Commun. ACM*, 32(4), Apr. 1989.

[16] I. Goldberg, D. Wagner, R. Thomas, and E. A. Brewer. A secure environment for untrusted helper applications: Confining the wily hacker. In *The Sixth USENIX Security Symposium Proceedings*, pages 1—13, San Jose, California, July 1996. The Usenix Association.

[17] T. Goldstein. The gateway security model in the Java electronic commerce framework. White paper, Sun Microsystems Laboratories / Javasoft, Decemeber 1996.

[18] R. S. Gray. Agent tcl: A flexible and secure mobile-agent system. In *Proceedings of the Fourth Annual Tcl/Tk Workshop*, pages 9—23, 1996.

[19] D. Hagimont, S. Krakowiak, J. Mossière, and X. R. de Pina. A selective protection scheme for the java environment. Technical Report RT-Sirac-96-12, SIRAC, 1996.

[20] B. Hailpern and H. Ossher. Extending object to support multiple interface and access control. *IEEE Transaction on Software Engineering*, 16(11):1247—1257, November 1990.

[21] T. Jaeger, A. D. Rubin, and A. Prakash. Building systems that flexibly control downloaded executable content. In *The Sixth USENIX Security Symposium Proceedings*, pages 131 —148, San Jose, California, July 1996. The Usenix Association.

[22] M. D. LaDue. Hostile applets on the horizon. 1996.

[23] J. Lepreau, B. Ford, and M. Hibler. The persistent relevance of the local operating system to global applications. In *Proceedings of the 1996 SIGOPS European Workshop*, 1996.

[24] B. Liskov, A. Adya, M. Castro, M. Day, S. Ghemawat, R. Gruber, U. Maheshwari, A. Myers, and L. Shrira. Safe and efficient sharing of persistent objects in thor. In *Proceedings of SIGMOD '96*, Montreal, Canada, June 1996.

[25] C. V. Lopes. Adaptive parameter passing. In *Symposium on Object Technologies for Advanced Software (ISOTAS'96)*, volume 1049 of *Lecture Notes in Computer Science*, Konazawa, Japan, March 1996. Springer-Verlag.

[26] D. Maier, J. Stein, A. Otis, and A. Purdy. Development of an object-oriented DBMS. In *OOPSLA'86 Conference Proceedings*, pages 472—482, Portland, OR, September 1986. ACM.

[27] S. Matsuoka and S. Kawai. Using tuple space communication in distributed object-oriented languages. In *OOPSLA'88 Proceedings*, pages 276—284, Sept. 1988.

[28] Y. Minsky, R. van Renesse, F. B. Schneider, and S. D. Stoller. Cryptographic support for fault-tolerant distributed computing. In *Proceedings of the 1996 SIGOPS European Workshop*, July 1996.

[29] R. Morrison, A. Brown, R. Connor, Q. I. Cutts, G. Kirby, A. Dearle, J. Rosenberg, and D. Stemple. Protection in Persistent Object Systems, In *Security and Persistence*, pages 48—66. Springer-Verlag, 1990.

[30] George C. Necula. Proof-carrying code. In *24th ACM SIGPLAN-SIGACT Symposium on Principles of Programming Language (POPL'97)*, pages 106–119, Paris, France, January 1997.

[31] B. C. Neuman. Proxy-based authorization and accounting for distributed systems. In *Procceedings of the 13th International Conference on Distributed Systems*, Pittsburgh, PA, May 1993.

[32] M. Ranganathan, A. Acharya, S. Sharma, and J. Saltz. Network-aware mobile programs. Research report, University of Maryland, 1996.

[33] R. Riggs, A. Wolrath, J. Waldo, and K. Bharat. Pickling state in the java. In *The Second Conference on Object-Oriented Technologies and Systems (COOTS) Procedings*, pages 241—250, Toronto, Canada, June 1996. USENIX Press.

[34] F. Rouaix. A Web navigator with applets in Caml. In Fifth WWW Conference, Paris, France, May 1996.

[35] A. Rudloff, F. Matthes, and J. Schmidt. Security as an add-on quality in persistent object systems. In *Second International East/West Database Workshop*, Workshops in Computing, pages 90—108, Klagenfurt, Austria, 1995. Springer-Verlag.

[36] M. Mira da Silva: Mobility and Persistence. In [42].

[37] A. S. Tanenbaum, S. J. Mullender, and R. van Renesse. Using sparse cabilities in a distributed operating system. In *Proceedings Sixth International Conference on Distributed Computer Systems*. IEEE, 1986.

[38]   A.S. Tanenbaum, editor, Report of the Seventh ACM SIGOPS European Workshop, Con-
       nemara, Ireland, 9-11 Sepetember 1996.http://www.cs.vu.nl/~ast/

[39]   L. Tang and S. Low. Chrg-http: A tool for micropayments on the World Wide Web. In
       The Sixth USENIX Security Symposium Proceedings, pages 123 — 129. The Usenix As-
       sociation, July 1996.

[40]   J. Tardo and L. Valente. Mobile Agent Security. In *Proceedings of the 41th International
       Conference of the IEEE Computer Society (CompCon'96)*, February 1996.

[41]   C.-R. Tsai V. D. Gligor and C. S. Chandersekaran. On the identification of covert storage
       channels in secure systems. *IEEE Transactions on Software Engineering*, 16(6):569—
       580, June 1990.

[42]   J. Vitek, C. Tschudin, (eds): Mobile Object System: A first look at mobile object-oriented
       programs, Springer-Verlag, 1997.

[43]   D. Volpano. Provably-secure programming languages for remote evaluation. *ACM Com-
       puting Surveys*, 28A(2):electronic, December 1996.

[44]   D. Volpano and G. Smith. On the systematic design of web languages. *ACM Computing
       Surveys*, 28(2):315—317, June 1996.

[45]   D. Volpano and G. Smith. A type-based approach to program security. In *7th Int'l Joint
       Conference on the Theory and Practice of Software Development*, April 1997.

[46]   D. Volpano, G. Smith, and C. Irvine. A sound type system for secure flow analysis. *Jour-
       nal of Computer Security*, 28(2):1—21, 1996.

[47]   R. Wahbe, S. Lucco, T. E. Anderson, and S. L. Graham. Efficient software-based fault iso-
       lation. In *Proceedings of the Symposium on Operating Systems Principles*, 1993.

[48]   K. M. Walker, D. F. Stern, L. Badger, K. A. Oosendorp, M. J. Petkac, and D. L. Sherman.
       Confining root programs with domain and type enforcement (dte). In *The Sixth USENIX
       Security Symposium Proceedings*, pages 21 — 36. The Usenix Association, July 1996.

[49]   J. E. White. Telescript Technology: The foundation for the electronic marketplace. Gener-
       al Magic White Paper, General Magic, Inc. 1994.

[50]   A. Wolrath, R. Riggs, and J. Waldo A distributed object model for the Java system. In
       *The Second Conference on Object-Oriented Technologies and Systems (COOTS) Proced-
       ings*, pages 219—231, Toronto, Canada, June 1996. USENIX Press.

[51]   C. Yoshikawa, B. Chun, and D. Culler. Web graffiti & high bandwirth covert channels
       using java. January 1997.

[52]   C. F. Yu and V. D. Gligor. A specification and verification method for preventing denial
       of service. *IEEE Transactions on Software Engineering*, 16(6):581—595, June 1990.

Appendix: Security Weakness in Object-Oriented Programs

Example 1: Shared variable communication

Most current implementations of Java do not create multiple class objects. So, when a class is used in different computations, all computations use the same class and their object graphs are not disjoint. This may be considered a security hole as it creates covert communication channels between computations and permits to launch secrecy and integrity attacks. We give an example in Java.

<u>Victim</u>

The victim is an applet that includes a class with a protected class variable last.

```
class Victim extends Object {      // Victim is a subclass of object; class variable
      protected static Victim last; // last that points to the last obj created
      Victim createFromClone() {    // a creation method that takes the last victim,
         last = last.clone();       // clones it, and increases its idNum.
         last.idNum++;
      }
      private int idNum;            // idNum is an instance variable
      ...                           // there are other methods, e.g. new.
}
```

<u>Attacker</u>

The attacker must be aware of class Victim. This is straightforward as Java does not have the means to hide class definitions. An attack is mounted by subclassing the Victim class and adding methods for reading and writing instance variables.

```
class Attacker extends Victim {   // Attacker extends Victim with a method that
      static Victim getLast() {      // return the last Victim created.
         return last;
      }
      static void setLast(Victim l) {
         last = l;                  //A method to set the last
      }                             //Victim created.
}
```

The effect achieved by this attack is that the opponent may get at portions of the object graph of the victim, either for reading, or writing. A possible defence involves changing the declaration from protected to private. This is not always possible as the class Victim may originate from a library or other classes may require access to that attribute. In any case, such a solution distorts the design of the class. The code for this fix is thus:

```
class Victim extends Object {
      private static Victim last;
```

An alternative, is to forbid subclassing altogether. This may not always be appropriate.

```
final class Victim extends Object {
      protected static Victim last;
```

Example 2: Blocking synchronized methods attack

This example explores another breach of integrity arising from the use of synchronized class methods. In Java, class methods may be declared synchronized to regulate concurrent execution.

Victim

The victim defines a synchronized class method.

```
class Victim extends Object {
    protected synchronized void myMethod() {
        ...
    }
}
```

Attacker

The attacker need only to acquire (and not release) the synchronized method to block the victim.

```
class Attacker extends Victim {
    protected synchronized void myMethod() {
        while(true);
    }
}
```

When the attacker calls the synchronized method myMethod(), the method will block itself and all other instances of the class Victim that try to call the method. A possible defence is to make the method private or to forbid subclassing altogether. Note that in this example it is the synchronization lock that is shared between different computations.

Example 3: Shared variable covert channel

This last example with shared variables demonstrates the ease of setting up covert channels. To establish confinement it is needed to be able to prevent information from flowing in unauthorized ways between applications. The point, here, is that shared variables make it virtually impossible to determine if a method invocation is a cross domain call. Consider the following intentionally simple example:

```
myObj = WriteObject new();
Things[1] = myObj;
...
myObj.write(data);
```

Is the invocation of write a source of information leakage? On the face of it, this code seems secure. Yet, the call could be a covert channel if the array Things was a static variable:

Victim

```
class Bridge {
    static Object[] Things;
    void someMethod() {
        ...
      myObj = WriteObject new();
      Things[1] = myObj;
        ...
      myObj.write(data);
    }
}
```

Attacker

The attacker (or accomplice) needs only define a subclass and try to catch the assignment to the array.

```
class BridgeReader extends Bridge {
    void looping() {
        ...
      thisObj = Things[1];
      thatObj = Things[1];
      while (thisObj == thatObj)
         thisObj = Things[1];
      thisObj.read() .... // covert channel
        ...
```

The method `looping` tries to read the object assigned to the first position of the `Things` array. Its success depends on the scheduling, but the point of this example is that it is *possible* to establish covert channels so that communication needs not be restricted to the identified shared variables. Furthermore, this example shows that in some cases it may be difficult to prove that a code fragment is secure.

Example 4: Masquerading attacks

Masquerading attacks may occur when the opponent is allowed to invoke methods of the target. This kind of attack is also valid across address spaces if RMI is used [50].

Victim

The victim contains an innocuous looking class that merely checks whether the date passed as argument corresponds to the user's birthday.

```
class DateChecker
    private Date birthday;
    public today(Date d) {
        if (d.sameDay(birthday)) {
            ...
        }
    }
```

Attacker

The attacker needs to obtain a reference to the DateChecker object, and instead of passing it a date it passes an instance of class BadDate. This class overrides method sameDay to perform some malicious action with the authority of the victim.

```
class BadDate extends Date {
     public bool sameDay(Date d) {
        while(true) {
           ... do something nasty
        }
        ...
     }
}
```

The Java defence would be to define class Date as final. Final classes can not be subclassed, thus can not be used for masquerading attacks. Furthermore, all instance variables of Date must be final as well, and so on recursively. In effect forfeiting polymorphism. Of course, if Date or any of the classes it depends on is defined in a library this whole line of defence breaks down.

Example 5: Breaching secrecy and integrity

Breach of secrecy/integrity. This attack uses reference semantics of object applications running in the same address space to obtain a toehold in the object graph of the victim. The danger comes from that victim uses a value that belongs to another object graph to store its objects.

Victim

The victim needs only have a method that accepts some kind of container.

```
class Getter extends Object {
     private List listOfThings;
     public getList(List l) {
        listOfThings = l;
     }
}
```

Attacker

The attacker must obtain a reference to an object of type Getter for this kind of attack. Then by passing it a list the attacker is able to break security. This, because it is allowed to retain a reference on the object it gave.

```
class Badie
     private List watchList = new List();
     publicDoIt(Getter g) {
        g.getList(watchList);      // The attacker passes in the watchlist
        ...                        // then waits for the victim to fill it with
        watchList.doSomething();   // values and send watchlist some message
     }
}
```

Appropriate protection is to enforce strict disjointedness of object graphs.

Example 6: Breaching integrity

Breach of integrity. Another breach of integrity can be easily set with the Thread-Killer class [22] which kills user threads in the Java virtual machine. This attack works because Threads are objects which are not in protected domains and the ThreadKiller class is able to obtain references on them.

Attacker

The attacker must code a class that does the following operation. Note the original class discussed in [22] is slightly more elaborate and does not run the risk of killing itself.

```
class ThreadKiller {
    public static void killAllThreads() {
        ThreadGroup current, top, parent;

        top = current = Thread.currentThread().getThreadGroup();
        parent = top.getParent;
        while (parent!=nil) {
           top = parent; parent = parent.getParent();
        }
        find(top);
    }
    private static void find(ThreadGroup g) {
        if (g != null) {
           int numThread = g.activeCount();
           int numGroups = g.activeGroupCount();
           Thread[] threads = new Thread[numThreads];
           ThreadGroup[] groups = new ThreadGroup[numGroup];
           g.enumerate(threads, false);
           g.enumerate(groups,false);
           for (int i = 0; i <numThreads; i++) {
              Thread t = threads[i];
              if (t != null) t.stop();
           }
           for (int i = 0; i <numGroups; i++) {
              find(groups[i]);
           }
        }
    }
}
```

Appropriate protection is to forbid access to objects that belong to the object graph of another applet.

Example 7: Explicit protection domains

The Telescript protection model is more elaborate than that of Java. In short, each object and method has both an owner and a sponsor. The owner is the principal to whom the object belongs and the sponsor is the principal on whose authority the object executes. Telescript provides a way to access the owner and sponsor from outside of their environment.

The secure programming style advocated in [40] boils down to the following style (expressed in Java for simplicity). The class Protectee is the class that should be protected, the class Protector implements a security policy. All methods of Protectee are redefined in Protector to check source of the call.

```
class Protectee {
     public void method_1() { ... }
     ...
}
class Protector extends Protectee {
     public void safe_method_1() throws AccessViolation {
        Sponsor sponsor = sponsor.name.authority;
        Class class = client.class;

        if (friends.find(sponsor) || okClasses.find(class) ) {
        ...
     }
}
```

The problem with this is that in general aliasing makes it quite difficult to be sure which objects actually need to be protected. This means that if any serious degree of security is required, all non-trivial objects will have to be protected. This implies a level of inefficiency that makes a system built this way unusable and a burden on programmers that is not acceptable. Finally, security is spread all over the application and can not be easily verified without validating the entire code base.

Safe and Secure Execution Mechanisms for Mobile Objects

Kazuhiko Kato

1 Introduction

In most conventional distributed systems, distributed processes exchange *messages*. In mobile object systems, on the other hand, distributed processes exchange *objects* which might be executed within the process or the site in which the receiving process is located. Security issues are problematic in ordinary message-passing distributed systems [15], but the situation is more problematic in mobile object systems. The seriousness can be understood by considering a human analogy. The conventional message-passing distributed systems corresponds to a telephone system in our society. A message exchanged by telephone lines is simply a list of words in a natural language, and the interpretation of the words is the responsibility of the receiver. The message itself never accesses or damages directly the computing resources of the receiver sites. Passing objects in a mobile object system, on the other hand, corresponds to sending a human agent. Both the agent and the place being visited must be accessed by each other in an authorized way. To determine and enforce the authorized way, human society has devised laws, rules, and customs. In a mobile object computer system, the system must enforce these.

Generally, the security-related issues can be simplified if the system environment is *closed*, as in, say, a single-user or single-group environment. In such an environment, the system can assume that only well-tested, reliable and safe objects are processed. A very similar situation is observed in the social context; a person belonging to a community can access any resources of the community without checking, but a visitor from a foreign community can only access resources in a restricted way. Some mobile object systems in the 1980's such as Emerald [7] assumed a closed environment, and did not address security issues.

The mobile object systems currently attracting world-wide attention requires to be used in an *open* environment, for example, the Internet or a corporation-wide intranet. In an open system, differing from closed systems, the system can assume few things. This makes the implementation of the system considerably sophisticated. For example, consider the dynamic class (code) loading mechanism of the Java system. The functional of dynamic code loading is not new; several dynamic programming languages such as Lisp and Smalltalk-80 have been providing such a function. The Java system, however, provides a class verifier that verifies whether the class to be loaded causes unsecure things. Such a verifier is unnecessary in a closed environment. We discuss the mechanisms of the Java's class verifier in Section 2.1.

This paper surveys the techniques currently known as safe and secure execution mechanisms for mobile objects. In this paper we distinguish *safety* and *security* in the following way. Safety means that illegal resource access is inhibited and handled in a systematic way. For example, in some programming languages, safe data structures are provided (such as lists in Lisp) to permit only safe operations to be applied to the data, or an exception handling mechanism is provided for the programmers to explicitly describe fault-handling. Security means to provide protection and integrity in the presence of malicious users. Notice that security subsumes safety. Encoding of an electronic mail message is a typical means of assuring secure communication. Thus, security issues can be divided into two sets: issues covered and not covered by safety. The former in general can be dealt with by preparing only mechanisms, while the latter can be dealt with by preparing both mechanisms and policies [19]. Often, a program that attacks security is designed not to violate safety, because if it did, it would be easily detected by the system. Thus, security maintenance always requires a security policy that draws a clear line between unsecure and secure things. The security maintenance mechanism watches and verifies every operation performed by a questionable object according to the given security policy.

Interestingly, the techniques developed for safe mobile objects are useful even for nondistributed computing. We mention three areas for example. First, recent component software architecture such as Microsoft's OLE and Apple's OpenDoc provide function that dynamically combine several software modules developed by independent vendors. Second, recent programming language processors provide foreign function interfaces that permit us to dynamically or statically load and link into them user programs that may be written in another programming language. Safety mechanisms would be very useful in debugging foreign functions. Third, the operating system research community has recently devoted efforts to load safe user modules into operating system kernels [2, 14]. A safety mechanism would be necessary in developing the loaded modules. Even after the debugging process for the loaded modules is complete, a safety or security mechanism is indispensable in a multiuser environment.

In this paper, we categorize the proposed approaches for safe and secure execution mechanisms for mobile objects into three types: interpreter approaches, native code approaches, and the software-hardware hybrid approach. These are explained in Sections 2, 3, and 4, respectively.

Security issues of mobile object systems are vast, and this survey focuses on only the execution mechanism issues. Issues not discussed but related closely to the secure execution mechanisms are those involving language design (e.g., [6]) and communication (e.g., [20]).

2 Interpreter Approaches

One obvious way to implement a safe mobile object system is to adopt the interpreter-based approach, which interprets every code by using a software interpreter. The interpreted code can be an intermediate compiled-code, frequently called *bytecode*, or a non-compiled scripting code. Bytecodes are efficient since parsing and possible optimization are performed statically (i.e., before execution), but sometimes the compiling process is inconvenient when dynamic code generation is required. Non-compiled scripting code is suited for dynamic code generation or changing at the cost of reducing execution efficiency. In both cases, the interpreter is implemented by all software, and the interpretation of each bytecode or scripting code can be controllable by the software.

Another appealing advantage of the interpreter-based approach is that it is well suited for heterogeneous hardware environments or heterogeneous platform environments (e.g., Windows, MacOS, Unix).

2.1 Java: Static Verifier and Security Manager

Java is a language designed to be used in a multi-platform network environment and it supports the mobility of object classes. Java assumes that Java programs have been compiled into bytecodes of the Java Virtual Machine (Java VM) [11]. The designer of the Sun Microsystem's Java language processing system attempted to reduce the runtime overheads required for safety by performing code-verification just before code execution. The receiver of the mobile code (i.e., mobile class in Java) initiates the "class verifier" to perform the following verification just before execution by Java VM:

1. It ensures that the sent class is appropriately formatted in the predefined format of a Java class file. The method used is *ad hoc*; the first four bytes must contain the right magic number, all recognized attributes must be of the proper length, etc.
2. It ensures that linking with other classes succeeds and does the linking itself.
3. It performs data-flow analysis on each method in the class to ensure the method does not perform unsafe operations. The items tested include: (a) The usages of the operand stack are right. (b) Branches must be within the bounds of the code array for the method. (c) The targets of all control-flow instructions are each the start of an instruction. (d) No instruction can access or modify a local variable at an index greater than the number of local variables that its method indicates it uses. (e) The code does not end in the middle of an instruction. (f) Execution cannot fall off at the end of the code.

After these have been verified, the code in the class is executed by Java VM. Java VM performs runtime checking as it executes its defined instructions. Some runtime checks performed are the following. (a) The referenced method or field exits in the given class. (b) The referenced method or field has the indicated descriptor. (c) The method currently being executed has access to the referenced method or field.

The Java's code verifier is designed mostly to provide safety. To deal with security issues, Java provides a special class library called *security manager* [5, 4]. A security manager enforces security policies related to what a program is allowed to do. The policies include critical operations such as inspection of the execution stack, access to local files, access to system properties, and permission to execute system commands. The permission checking methods defined in a security manager work like a "hook" for critical operations. For example, `checkRead` is a method for a security manager to determine whether the file read operation is permitted. By overriding the `checkRead` method, the user (security policy programmer) can give a security policy for file reading. When a security manager is associated to a Java application, `checkRead` is called whenever the application tries to perform the file read operation.

2.2 Safe-Tcl: Master/Safe Interpreter

Tcl is an interpreted scripting language [17] and Safe-Tcl is a variant of the language [18] that deals with security. Safe-Tcl separates the distrusted codes from the trusted codes.

For this, A Safe-Tcl application uses two interpreters: a *master interpreter* and a (slave) *safe interpreter*. The master interpreter retains full functionality, and only trusted scripts may be executed there. The safe interpreter is used for executing distrusted codes. All unsafe commands (e.g., file access, subprocess execution, interprocess communication) are made inaccessible in the safe interpreter.

To perform functions critical with respect to security in a controlled way, Safe-Tcl provides an *alias* mechanism. An alias is an association between a command in the safe interpreter, called the source command, and a command in the master interpreter, called the target. Whenever the source command is invoked by a script in the safe interpreter, the target command is invoked instead. The target command is typically a Tcl procedure, which implements a security policy. It receives all of the arguments from the source command, performs its function in a controlled way, and then returns its result to the safe interpreter as a result of the source command.

3 Native Code Approaches

The interpreter-based approaches described in Section 2 can be considered a natural extension of previous bytecode-based programming language systems such as Smalltalk-80 or Lisp; the extensions are concerned with safe and secure execution in a network environment. Recently, quite novel approaches have been proposed to implement safe mobile objects that permit the implementation of mobile objects in CPU-native code. This section surveys such approaches.

3.1 Software Fault Isolation: Code Modification Approach

Wahbe et al. [21] proposed a novel technique called Software Fault Isolation (SFI). The novelty of their approach is that, after receiving distrusted native mobile code, the code is modified so that it is safe in a sense that it achieves fault isolation within a single address space.

Before explaining, we will define some of their terminologies. We divide an application's virtual address space into *segments*, aligned so that all virtual addresses within a segment share a unique pattern of upper bits, called the *segment identifier*. A fault domain consists of two segments, one for a distrusted module's code, the other for its static data, heap and stack. *Unsafe instructions* are any instructions that jump to or are stored at an address that can not be statically verified to be within the correct segment.

SFI has two approaches. One approach is to insert a checking code before every unsafe instruction. The checking code determines whether the unsafe instruction's target address has the correct segment identifier. If the check fails, the inserted code will trap to a system error routine outside the distrusted module's fault domain. This technique was called *segment matching*. Wahbe et al. stated that on typical RISC architectures, each checking code in the segment matching requires four instructions.

The segment matching technique has the advantage of pinpointing the offending instruction, but its execution overhead is considerable. The other approach, called *sandboxing*, is to reduce the overhead. Before each unsafe instruction we insert a code that sets the upper bits of the target address to the correct segment identifier. Sandboxing does not catch illegal addresses but it prevents them from affecting fault domains other than the one generating the address. Wahbe et al. stated that on typical RISC architectures, the address sandboxing requires the insertion of two arithmetic instructions.

According to the experimental results by Wahbe et al. [21], the sandboxing SFI overheads for DEC MIPS and DEC Alpha workstations are only 4.3–5.0% on average.

3.2 Proof-Carrying Code

In Section 2.1 we discussed Java's static verifier approach. In this approach, the transfered code was verified per transfer on the receiver side. This required data-flow analysis and considerable overheads were inevitable. Necula and Lee [14, 13] proposed a novel technique called *proof-carrying code* (PCC). This approach does not rely on the usual authentication or code-modification mechanisms. Instead, a code producer creates its binaries in a special form, which we call proof carrying code. A PCC binary contains the encoding of a formal proof whereby the enclosed native code respects the safety policy that is initially obtained from the code receiver. The proof is structured in such a way as to make it easy to verify its validity without using cryptographic techniques or consulting external trusted entities. The execution time overhead of PCC binaries are low because safety checks only need to be conducted once, after which the receiver knows that it can safely execute the binary without any further run-time checking.

Both the key and largest difficulty of this approach are in the creation of the proof included in PCC. In order to create a proof, the code producer must prove a predicate in first-order logic. In general, this problem is undecidable, and full-automatic proof generation is impossible. Thus, the practicality of the PCC approach greatly relies on the progress of theorem-proving technology.

4 Hardware-Software Hybrid Approach

The techniques described so far are based only on software techniques and do not benefit from hardware functions. Recently, an approach has been proposed by the designers of the PLANET mobile object system [8]. This system makes up a protection domain by means of a virtual memory manipulation technique using a general-purpose memory management unit (MMU). Yet, source programs do not need to know the existence of protection domain barriers and the programmers need to know only object-encapsulation barriers, following the object-oriented principle.

4.1 PLANET: Orthogonal Protection Domain Approach

We start the explanation by discussing the relationship between the two barriers: object encapsulation and protection domain. *Object encapsulation* is one of the most crucial concepts in object-oriented programming. It means to separate clearly the inside and outside of an object and to make well-determined entries to the inside accessible from the outside of the object. *Protection domain* is an object space in which multiple objects can coexist. Objects in one protection domain rely on each other with respect to execution safety. That is, the system assumes that the objects in one protection domain

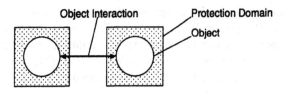

Fig. 1. One protection domain per object. Every object interaction requires cross-protection domain calls, i.e., remote method invocations.

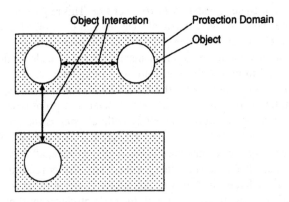

Fig. 2. Orthogonal protection domains. Object interactions are classified into two types: local (intra-protection domain) method invocations and remote (inter-protection domain) method invocations. If in a mobile object system the two object interactions can be specified in the same way, we say that the protection domain is orthogonal to object encapsulation.

do not violate or interfere with each other and the system performs no checking for safe execution. Thus, for fast object execution in one protection domain, the programmer or the language processing system may perform any optimization for mobile object codes, such as direct slot access.

One straightforward way to relate the object encapsulation concept to the protection domain concept is a one-to-one relationship; that is, to assign one protection domain per object, as shown in Fig. 1. This approach is used by many distributed object systems. Often a protection domain is implemented as a virtual address space, so one virtual address space is prepared for one object. In this sense, this approach yields only coarse-grained objects. In this approach, every object interaction requires interprocess communication, and thus requires considerable execution overheads.

The designers of PLANET propose that the protection domain concept for mobile object systems should be *orthogonal* to the object encapsulation concept [8]. That is, programmers observe only object encapsulation barriers but do not need to observe protection domain barriers at runtime. Therefore, object interactions are specified in the same way whether the interacting objects are in the same protection domain or not at runtime.

Supporting orthogonal protection domain is expected to contribute to both software productivity and execution efficiency. The same program code can be used regardless of protection domain setting at runtime. When objects are located in the same protection domain, the objects can interact with each other in a light-weight way by omitting safe execution checking or eliminating context switching overheads. When objects are located in different protection domains, execution speed is restricted but object interactions are rigorously checked.

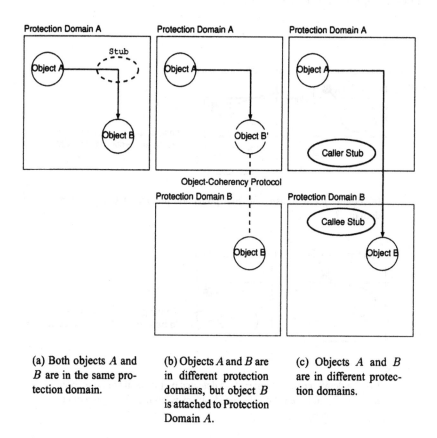

(a) Both objects *A* and *B* are in the same protection domain.

(b) Objects *A* and *B* are in different protection domains, but object *B* is attached to Protection Domain *A*.

(c) Objects *A* and *B* are in different protection domains.

Fig. 3. Three types of object interactions in PLANET.

PLANET takes an approach that implements one protection domain using one virtual address space, and enables dynamic load and unload of multiple mobile objects into a protection domain. For each protection domain, one protection policy is assigned; thus, the objects loaded to one protection domain share the policy. PLANET supports three types of object interactions:

- local (intra-protection domain) method-calls,
- method-calls for distributed shared objects,
- remote (inter-protection domain) method-calls.

The objects loaded to the same protection domain can use the first type of object interaction, and they can directly communicate with each other. In the second type of object interaction, method-calls are local the same as the first type, but the object-coherency protocols between the original object and attached image (objects B and B' in Fig. 3(b)) perform the necessary communication. The third type of object interaction requires inter-protection domain method-calls.

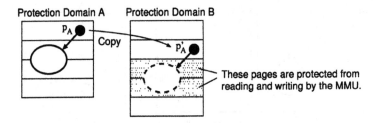

(a) Pointer p_A is transferred from protection domain A to protection domain B.

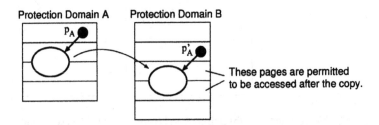

(b) The dereference of pointer p'_A is detected by the MMU in protection domain B, and then the referenced object is copied from protection domain A to B.

Fig. 4. VM-integrated RPC.

As mentioned above, PLANET supports orthogonal protection domains, and the above-mentioned three types of object interaction must be described by the application programmers in the same way. It is not difficult to achieve this with respect to the second type of object interaction, since the object-coherency protocols can work in a transparent manner for the programmers. It is problematic achieving orthogonality with respect to the third type, because the third type essentially requires the remote procedure call (RPC) mechanism [3]. The conventional RPC technique has crucial restrictions; address references (pointers) cannot be passed between different protection domains. This restriction prevents programmers from writing the same codes for both intra- and inter-protection-domain object interaction.

Recently, a technique has been proposed by Kono, Kato and Masuda [9, 10] to eliminate this restriction. PLANET employs this technique. By combining the MMU manipulation technique with an RPC stub-generation technique and a memory-coherency maintenance protocol technique, they developed a scheme that can treat remote pointers and local pointers in quite the same way.[1] We will briefly explain the technique, using Fig. 4. In the protection domain A, pointer p_A references the object O_A (Fig. 4(a)). When p_A is passed (as the argument of an RPC) to the protection domain B, we call the pointer p'_A. Then, the runtime system in A allocates a new memory area that is large enough to store O_A and sets the allocated address to p'_A. At this time, the runtime system in A sets MMU so that the allocated page area is protected from both reading and writing. By this setting, the use program in B can treat the local pointer p'_A as if it were remote in the following way. When a machine instruction of the user program in B tries to dereference the pointer p'_A, the MMU detects an access violation and the runtime system in B is called by the operating system (Fig. 4(b)). The runtime system in B asks the runtime system in A to send O_A and receive it. Then the runtime system in B sets the MMU so that the allocated page can be accessed by the user code. Reference [9] describes the technique in detail, including an eager sending scheme and a coherency maintenance scheme between the original and the sent copies. Reference [10] shows that the technique can be combined with another technique that can deal with higher-order functions in RPC [16].

Security policies are dealt with in PLANET in the following way. PLANET inhibits objects in an ordinary protection domain from directly initiating the system calls of the operating system; all the system services must be requested to system service objects located in a protection domain that is permitted to issue system calls. A user (security policy programmer) can define his security policy by overriding methods of the system service objects. Furthermore, a user can override "copy" methods, which are called in the object-coherency protocol routines (Fig. 4(b)) and in the RPC stubs (Fig. 4(c)), in order to describe a access control policy for the copied object.

5 Conclusion

Recent software trends such as Internet computing and intelligent software agents are accelerating the paradigm-shift of distributed programming from message passing to object passing. Mobile object technology may become a key technology in the computing systems of the next decade. The safe and secure execution of mobile objects is one of the most significant issues in implementing mobile object systems, and currently new techniques are being developed enthusiastically.

---

[1] The pointer translation technique integrated with virtual memory management was first proposed by Paul Wilson [22] to support a huge object space for persistent objects.

In this survey, we classified the previously proposed software-based approaches into two types: interpreter approaches and native code approaches. Researchers are currently working on hybridizing the two. One approach is to create just-in-time (JIT for short) compilers for bytecodes. In this approach, the executed portion of bytecodes are dynamically compiled into native codes. The hybridization is attractive in terms of the following aspects. First, a mobile object can be represented by one bytecode even in heterogeneous hardware and platform environments. Secondly, execution speed is comparable to native code. Thirdly, development of a JIT compiler requires considerable time as does that of an ordinary native compiler. Before a JIT compiler is developed, the user can use an interpreter that is much easier to develop and port. Last, the application codes do not need to be altered even when the language processor is changed from an interpreter to a JIT compiler. An interesting research issue for the JIT compiler approach is to maintain safety with low overhead even after compilation. Omniware [12, 1] solves this issue by using the SFI technique described in Section 3.1.

Acknowledgment

The author thanks Jan Vitek for his useful comments on the draft of the paper.

References

1. A. Adl-Tabatabai, G. Langdale, S. Lucco, and R. Wahbe. Efficient and language-independent mobile programs. In *Proc. of ACM Conf. on Programming Language Design and Implementation*, pages 127–136, May 1996.
2. B. Bershad, S. Savage, P. Pardyak, E. G. Sirer, D. Becker, M. Fiuczynski, C. Chambers, and S. Eggers. Extensibility, safety and performance in the SPIN operating system. In *Proc. of Symposium on Operating System Principles*, pages 267–284, Dec. 1995.
3. A. D. Birrell and B. J. Nelson. Implementing remote procedure calls. *ACM Trans. Computer Systems*, 2(1):39–59, Feb. 1984.
4. M. Campione and K. Walrath. *The Java Tutorial — Object-Oriented Programming for the Internet*. Addison-Wesley, 1996.
5. P. Chan and R. Lee. *The Java Class Libraries — An Annotated Reference*. Addison-Wesley, 1996.
6. General Magic Inc. An introduction to safety and security in Telescript, 1996.
7. E. Jul, H. Levy, N. Hutchinson, and A. Black. Fine-grained mobility in the Emerald system. *ACM Trans. Computer Systems*, 6(1):109–133, Feb. 1988.
8. K. Kato, K. Toumura, K. Matsubara, S. Aikawa, J. Yoshida, K. Kono, K. Taura, and T. Sekiguchi. Protected and secure mobile object computing in PLANET. In *Proc. of ECOOP Workshop on Mobile Object Systems*, 1996.
9. K. Kono, K. Kato, and T. Masuda. Smart remote procedure calls: Transparent treatment of remote pointers. In *Proc. 14th IEEE Int. Conf. on Distributed Computing Systems*, pages 142–151, Jun. 1994.
10. K. Kono, K. Kato, and T. Masuda. An implementation method of migratable distributed objects using an RPC technique integrated with virtual memory. In *Proc. 10th European Conference of Object-Oriented Programming*, pages 295–315, Jul. 1996.
11. T. Lindholm and F. Yellin. *The Java Virtual Machine Specification*. Addison-Wesley, 1997.

12. S. Lucco, O. Sharp, and R. Wahbe. Omniware: A universal substrate fro web programming. In *Proc. 4th Int. World Wide Web Conference*, Dec. 1995.

13. G. C. Necula. Proof-carrying code. In *Proc. ACM Symp. on Principles of Programming Languages*, Jan. 1997.

14. G. C. Necula and P. Lee. Safe kernel extensions without run-time checking. In *Proc. USENIX Association 2nd Symp. on Operating Systems Design and Implementation*, pages 229–243, Oct. 1996.

15. Object Management Group, Inc. CORBA security. Technical report, Object Management Group, Inc., 1995.

16. A. Ohori and K. Kato. Semantics for communication primitives in a polymorphic language. In *Proc. 20th ACM Symp. on Principles of Programming Languages*, pages 99–112, Jan. 1993.

17. J. K. Ousterhout. *Tcl and the Tk Toolkit*. Addison-Wesley, 1994. ISBN 0-201-63337-X.

18. J. K. Ousterhout, J. Y. Levy, and B. B. Welch. The safe-tcl security model. Technical report, Sun Microsystems Laboratories, Nov. 1996.

19. A. Silberschatz and P. B. Galvin. *Operating System Concepts*. Addison-Wesley, 1994.

20. J. Vitek. Secure object spaces. In *Proc. of 2nd Int. Workshop on Mobile Object Systems*, Linz, July 1996.

21. R. Wahbe, S. Lucco, T. E. Anderson, and S. L. Graham. Efficient software-based fault isolation. In *Proc. 14th ACM Symp. on Operating System Principles*, pages 203–216, 1993.

22. P. Wilson. Pointer swizzling at page fault time: efficiently supporting huge address spaces on standard hardware. *ACM Computer Architecture News*, pages 6–13, Jun. 1991.

Jada: Coordination and Communication for Java Agents

Paolo Ciancarini, Davide Rossi

Abstract. In this chapter we are going to analyze mobile code issues in the perspective of object oriented systems in which thread migration is not supported. This means that both object's code and data can be transmitted from a place to another but not the current execution state (if any) associated to the object. This is the case with the Java language which is often used in the Word Wide Web for developing *applets* which are little applications downloaded on the fly and executed in the client machine. While this mechanism is quite useful for enhancing HTML documents with sound and animation, we think that this technology can give its best in the field of distributed-cooperative work, both in the perspective of Internet and Intranet connectivity. Java is indeed a concurrent, multithreaded language, but it offers little help for distributed programming. Thus, we introduce Jada, a coordination toolkit for Java where coordination among either concurrent threads or distributed Java objects is achieved via shared object spaces. By exchanging objects through tuple spaces, Java programs and applets can exchange data or synchronize their actions over a single host, a LAN, or even the Internet.

The access to an object space is performed using a set of methods of the ObjectSpace class. Such operations are out (to put an object in the object space), in and read (to get or to read associatively an object from the object space), and others, mostly inspired by the Linda language.

Jada does not extends the syntax of Java because it is a set of classes. We show how it changes the way we design multiuser, distributed applications (such as the ones based on the WWW) allowing easy interactions between software components and agents.

Under this perspective we can outline a system of any scale which uses the dynamic linking capability of Java to distribute the code and the coordination facility of Jada to handle distributed entities inter-relations.

1 Introduction

Java is a new language and programming environment developed at Sun Microsystems and its main application field is in conjunction with the Word Wide Web (many WWW browsers can indeed download HTML documents which integrate Java code) so the natural Java environment is a distributed system.

Although Java is multithreaded and allows remote dynamic code loading, it is not a language for distributed programming. The only facility offered by the language for supporting distributed processing is a sockets library. However, programming distributed systems using sockets is notoriously boring, difficult and error-prone. An alternative strategy consists of adding to Java high-level coordination mechanisms: this is the theme of this chapter.

This document has the following structure: in Sect. 2 we discuss how dynamic linking can be exploited to allow code mobility in an object oriented environment; in Sect. 4 we shortly recall Java and we show how it handles mobile code; in Sect. 3 we give an small overview of coordination and coordination languages; in Sect. 5 we introduce Jada (Java+Linda); in Sect. 6 we discuss how we implemented Jada; in Sect. 7 we discuss how Jada can be used to solve well known coordination problems; in Sect. 8 we compare our system with other similar systems. Sect. 9 concludes the chapter.

2 Mobile Code

Stand-alone, centralized computers are rapidly replaced and integrated by networked, distributed computer systems. The most widespread computer model that takes advantage of these systems is client/server: on behalf of the user, the client computer requests services from a remote server; the server execute the requested computations and send a reply back to the client. The advantage of this model is that users with low cost machines can access complex services, and organizations can optimize companywide distribution of services to minimize cost and maximize efficiency. Now the networks are expanding to global, world-wide scale: each computer system is an access point to information from all over the world. People using the Internet are connecting from their sites (possibly their homes) to servers located anywhere in the network, crossing several types of physical networking (satellite, optical fiber, wireless, etc.), each with a very different type of bandwidth and latency. The overall performance and behavior are not that of local network or leased lines. In some cases people travel with their laptops or hand-held machines and connects them to the network just from time to time, which implies network connections can be geographically moved and turned on and off too (this kind of systems are usually referred to as *nomadic computing*). In this scenario the client/server model suffers some of its limitations: it is impossible, for example, to handle applications in which a client wants for the server to continue computations even though the client has been disconnected from the network (or even turned off), and get the results when it is back on-line. Is also difficult to deal with applications where the network bandwidth or latency make the application impossible to run with satisfactory response time. A solution to those problems is to use *mobile code*. In this model the code that have to be executed to satisfy a request is sent over the network to execute onto the remote place. This model easily overcomes client/server limitations about the client being off-line and latency and bandwidth issues. This is often the case with clients that need large amount of data from a server to compute some kind of operation that results in a small amount of data: we can ship the code to compute the operation to the server and get the reply later, without requiring any further network traffic.

2.1 Security issues

The use of mobile code introduces security issues: mechanism like authentication, authorization and privacy are required with this model in open distributed environments. To enforce security the underlying system must be safe: we need to be able to implement security mechanisms and precludes a program to defeat them. A system where pointer forging and arithmetics on pointers are allowed, or where filling a memory buffer with code data and jumping to it is possible will never be a safe system.

Thus the use of mobile code in open distributed environments requires a language and a environment that is safe; it will then be possible to introduce the various security mechanisms.

2.2 Dynamic Linking: code on the move

Once the mobile code has been sent over a network, the receiving host must run it. Different approaches are possible: the receiving host could wrap this code in its own address and data space and run it as a separate process; or it could use its entry point just like any other function's entry point of the running program and make a jump to it. In a object oriented environment we can think about a whole object to be received (with its transitive closure or part of it); a reference could be made to that object which could be then accessed just like any other object in the system. We can make this mechanism transparent with the use of dynamic linking: references to objects are solved at run-time, allowing dynamic system configuration/programming. New classes can be added to the running program allowing objects downloaded from a network to be integrated with the executing system. Thus dynamic linking can be exploited to elegantly implement mobile code systems, mostly in object oriented environments.

3 Coordination

We can think of a distributed program as an agent world in which agents are spatially dispersed and act autonomously (this image fits quite well the distributed objects model) [Tol94]. Processes (sequence of actions performed by an agent) are the executions of methods and communications are message sent to objects. Synchronization actions (starting, blocking and unblocking, terminating) cover the remaining mechanisms in object invocation. A service occurs when an object invokes methods of another object (the invoker is the service-user and the invoked object is the provider).

Coordination is about the actions for synchronization, communications and service usage and provision. *Computation* is about the actions of processes.

3.1 Coordination Languages

The coordination languages have their focus on separation between coordination and computation, not meaning that they are independent or dual concepts, but meaning that they are orthogonal: they are two dimensions under which an agent world can be examined [CG92]. Most of the coordination languages are based on shared data spaces, like Linda [Gel85] (where focus is given on communication issues) and Laura [Tol92] (where focus is given on services), and a set of operators to access the data in the spaces.

4 Java

Java is an object oriented language whose syntactical structure resembles C++. However, it inherits a better object-oriented semantics from SmallTalk and Objective C [AG96].

The language model is somehow limited but its strongest point is its great simplicity.

Java programs are made of *objects*. Java objects are instances of *classes*. A class can inherit from a base class (just one, multiple inheritance is not supported) to extend the behavior of that base class.

Java programs are compiled into a binary format [Gos95] that can be executed on many platforms without recompilation using a "bytecode interpreter", also known as *Java Virtual Machine* (JavaVM). The bytecode is linked on the fly when loaded to be run [Gos95]. All the dependencies in the byte-code are symbolic and are resolved only at load time. The loading of a class code happens only when it is required. Furthermore the user can extend the manner in which the Java Virtual Machine dynamically loads classes, creating, for example, a network class loader in order to load a class code from a remote server, implementing code mobility.

Thus, the JavaVM contains mechanisms to check the code it has to run, in order to avoid viruses and security violations.

Java is architecture neutral: every machine-dependent code is not part of the language itself but of its standard library. Java libraries are collections of classes called "packages". We can think of Java as an environment built by the language itself and its *standard packages*. Several aspects of the language depend indeed from the standard packages as defined by Java designers. For instance, multithreading is native in Java, but there is no way to create a thread other than using a method of the Thread class.

4.1 Java and the Internet

HotJava, a WWW browser, has been the first Internet application of Java. What made it different from other browsers is its ability to run Java code "embedded" within HTML documents. This way HTML documents become "active", namely it is easy to put animation in HTML pages. Moreover, the same mechanism can be used to extend a browser in a natural way, implementing, for example, editors, spreadsheet, and groupware applications made of distributed objects. The most important consequence of having Java-enabled browsers like HotJava is that a Java application can be "spread" around the network. The simplest way to take advantage of this feature is to think about a Java application just like a document. Watching a Java application means let it run in your host, possibly integrated within your browser. The Java way to obtain this is to build each piece of Java code to be run in a browser as an "applet". It results that, extended this way, the Word Wide Web can be seen as a geographically scaled, obiquitus, mobile objects environment.

An *applet* is the byte-code result of a compilation of a class that extends the class Applet contained in the java.applet package. This means that each applet inherits a standard behaviour from Applet and has to comply with a set of conventions which let them run within a Java-compatible browser.

4.2 Distributed Java applications

Besides the basic classes shown above, Java suffers the lack of mechanisms for distributed programming. The only way we have for two applets/applications to communicate is to use sockets to establish a bidirectional point-to-point link. Moreover, sockets require the client and server to engage in applications-level protocols to encode and decode messages for exchange, and the design of such protocols is cumbersome and can be error-prone, also: applets have security restrictions that limit the usability of sockets. Things get even worse when objects must cooperate in complex fashions.

In a first attempt to seriously overcome this kind of limitations a distributed object model for Java has been proposed: the *remote method invocation* (RMI). RMI uses the well known CORBA [BN95] approach which, while it allows easy distributed objects basic interactions, doesn't allows any kind of mobility.

Our approach is a step further: we want add to Java coordination capabilities in order to allow any kind of complex interactions between potentially remote objects.

5 A toolkit for programming distributed Java applications

We try to solve the coordination problem for Java using a well known approach, namely adding Java a minimal set of coordination primitives: in particular, we add operations to access Linda-like multiple object spaces [CG92, Cia94].

We designed Jada aiming for simplicity rather than performance. Jada, like Linda, is a minimalist coordination language. Differently from other Linda-like implementations, which usually include a preprocessor necessary because Linda slightly changes (i.e. it constrains) the host language syntax, Jada is based on a set of classes to be used to access an object space, allowing the users to keep their standard Java development tools.

In a mobile agents system, Jada allows to coordinate the interactions among system's entities using high level mechanisms (and not just message passing), allowing a complete and transparent decoupling among entities, as we will show later.

5.1 Object Spaces

An `ObjectSpace` is an objects container with a set of methods for accessing its contents. `out` is the method to put objects in the `ObjectSpace`, `in` and `read` are the methods to get objects from the `ObjectSpace` (Jada allows many kind of these basic operations).

To create an object space we write:

```
ObjectSpace my_object_space=new ObjectSpace();
```

To put an object in the object space we can write:

```
my_object_space.out(new String("foo"));
```

To access the `ObjectSpace` for getting objects we use an associative mechanism: when the user calls the `in` method he have to pass it an object which is used as a matching pattern. The object the `in` method will return (if any) is an object from the object space that matches the given matching pattern (the same applies to the `read` method; the difference between `read` and `in` is that `in` removes the returned object from the object space).

To allow enough flexibility to the matching operations we introduce the concepts of *formal* and *actual* objects: a formal object is an instance of the `Class` class (the meta-class used by Java). Any other object is an actual object.

The Jada matching rules are:

- **actual-actual**: two actual items are matching if
  - they implement the `JadaItem` interface: the method `matchesItem`, applied to the object in the object space, passing as parameter the other object, returns `true`.
  - they do not implement the `JadaItem` interface: the method `equals`, applied to the object in the object space, passing as parameter the other object, returns `true`.
- **actual-formal**: a formal item matches any object which is an instance of it.
- **formal-formal**: two formal items are matching if they represent the same class.

Please note: in the current version of Jada the matching mechanism is object based and not object oriented; this means that inheritance is not applied when checking for two objects to be of the same type: the matching is performed just on object which are directly instance of the same class; we are planning to extend this matching mechanism to inheritance in the future.

These matching rules are quite simple yet very powerful; but are sometimes not expressive enough to match the requests of the user. Thus we introduce the `Tuple` class, an object container class with an extended matching mechanism which is more expressive.

5.2 Tuples

In Jada a *tuple* is a set of objects (also referred as *items*) and it is represented by the `jada.Tuple` class.

This is an example of Jada tuple:

```
Tuple my_tuple=new Tuple(new Integer(10),"test");
```

Such a tuple includes two items (we say that its cardinality is two); the first item is an `Integer` object, the second one is a `String` object. We define actual and formal items within a tuple the same way we defined them for Jada.

To use associative object space access with tuples we can use the tuples' matching mechanism: two tuples a and b are matching if they have the same cardinality and each item of a matches the corresponding item of b. The usual Jada mechanism is used to check if the items are matching.

Thus, the tuple

```
Tuple a=new Tuple(new Integer(10),"test");
```

matches the tuple:

```
Tuple b=new Tuple(new Integer(10),new String().getClass());
```

Note that to exchange a tuple (and generally any kind of object) two threads do not need to perform a pair of `out` and `read` operations at the same time (Jada does not need rendez-vous communication). In fact, suppose the threads `ta` and `tb` want to exchange a message: `ta` will put a message inside the object space, `tb` will read the message from the object space. If ta performs the out operation before tb performs the read operation it does not have to wait for tb: it simply continues its execution, the tuple is now stored into the object space. When tb performs the read operation it will be able to read it.

Instead, if tb performs the read operation before ta performs the out operation, tb will be blocked until an object that satisfy the read request will become available (i.e. until ta performs the out operation).

The in and read methods are indeed blocking. If you want the thread not to be blocked when a matching object for the in and read operations is not available you can use the in_nb and read_nb methods: they access the object space the same way as in and read but if no matching object is available they simply return null (a more sophisticated flavor of in and read that aborts after a time-out is available too).

5.3 ObjectServer and ObjectClient

To allow remote access to an object space, the jada.net.ObjectServer and jada.net.ObjectClient classes are provided. We used a simple client/server architecture to manage the object spaces; in fact, each object space is a shared remote resource accessed through an object space server.

The object space server is addressed using the IP address of the host it runs on and with its own port number (as usual with socket connections). This way we can run (almost) as many object space servers as we like in a network, so that applications can independently operate on several, distributed object spaces. ObjectServer is a multithreaded server class which translates requests received from the ObjectClient class in calls to the methods of the ObjectSpace class.

In fact, both ObjectServer and ObjectClient are based on ObjectSpace. ObjectServer and ObjectClient communicate using sockets.

ObjectServer uses ObjectSpace to perform the requested operations.

The ObjectClient class extends ObjectSpace changing its internals but keeping its interface and behavior (apart from some new constructor and few new methods). Thus, a ObjectClient object is used just like a ObjectSpace one, except that it provides access to a remote object space which can run in any host of the network.

What ObjectClient does is to interface with a remote ObjectServer object (which holds the real object space) and requests it to perform the in, read and out operations and (eventually) to return the result.

5.4 Security concerns

As for the definition given above the Java run time system is safe. JavaSoft is working on a set of packages to ensure security, mainly using cryptography. Since we want to keep Jada as small as possible and we want to use in its development standard, widely spread tools, we are waiting for these tools to be available in order to add to Jada a set of mechanisms to allow user access control to the remote servers and for using cryptography on the data sent along the network.

6 Some details on the implementation

Jada is implemented as a set of classes that allow either Java threads or Java applications to access associatively a shared object space using a small set of Linda-like operations.

An object space can be either local to the application or applet (ObjectSpace, to be shared between threads) or remote (ObjectClient, to be shared between applications or applets) in order to build a distributed application.

In the latter case an object space server (ObjectServer) must be running in a host of the network.

In Fig. 1 we graphically outline how an application can access a remote tuple space.

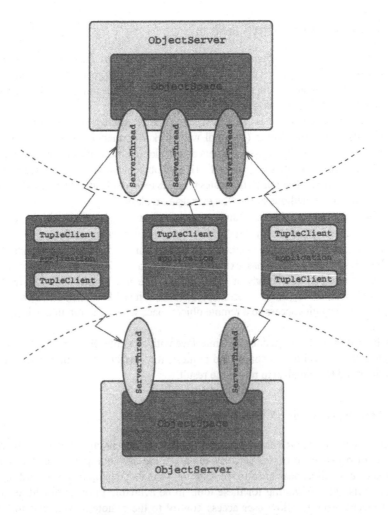

Fig. 1. Client/server relationships in Jada

6.1 Serialization

To handle object space access we need our classes to provide:

- a method to dump the object contents to a byte stream, in order to be able to send a tuple across a network or to save its state to a file. (dumpItem).
- a method to restore a tuple given a set of bytes read from a byte stream. (buildItem).

These two tasks are operations we usually need when dealing with distributed objects and they are often referred as *serialization* operations. Jada allows two serialization mechanism:

- serialization via JadaItem. If the object we want to serialize implements JadaItem he must have defined the code for the dumpItem and buildItem methods which are used respectively to dump the object to a stream and to build an object from a stream.
- serialization via JadaSerializer. If the object we want to serialize does not implement JadaItem there must be a JadaSerializer object defined for such object type that as been passed to the Jada runtime system using the addSerializer method of the JadaSystem class. This must be done on both client and server side. JadaSerializer is an interface that must be implemented by classes which are used to serialize objects. These classes must then have defined the code for the dump and restore methods, which are used to serialize the object. When the Jada system is initialized the default serializer for the Integer, Float and String classes are provided to the system.

When, in the future, some standard serialization operation will be provided as part of the Java environment we plan to add these operations as a third serialization mechanism (at the time of this writing serialization support for Java is expected for the new release of the language which is undergoing beta test phase).

Serialization must, of course, also be supported by tuples' items (we indeed need to know how to dump/restore them in order to dump/restore a tuple).

The Tuple class itself implements the JadaItem interface so we can use a Tuple object as a field of a tuple.

6.2 ObjectSpace

An ObjectSpace object in Jada is an object container which offers a set of thread-safe access methods. Thread-safe means that accessing an ObjectSpace from different threads at the same time is safe since monitors are used to handle requests avoiding problems with critical regions.

The methods are the usual in, read and out (along with their multiple, non-blocking and time out-aware variants). All these methods are actually just wrappers for the doInRead and doOut methods, which are the real "engines" for this class. All the synchronization and repository management code is part of these methods. This allows to easily redefine ObjectSpace behaviour by extending its class just like we did with ObjectClient. For example the doOut method of ObjectSpace takes care of putting the specified object in the object space or use it to reply pending in or read requests. The `ObjectClient`'s version of doOut, instead, sends the tuples to an object server and asks it to manage the storing/replying. The same applies for `ObjectClient`'s version of doInRead. We need indeed just to change these two methods to deal with a remote tuple manager (which is a `ObjectServer` object) and use socket connections to talk with it.

6.3 ObjectServer

As stated above an `ObjectServer` object is used by `ObjectClient` objects to access a (possibly remote) object space. An `ObjectServer` has an `ObjectSpace` object in it which is used to manage the object space. Each time an `ObjectClient` perform a request the `ObjectServer` spawns a new thread to perform the requested operation. From the architectural point of view we can think about `ObjectServer` /`ObjectClient` like a stub/proxy system.

If we analyze the behavior of a Jada program we can distinguish two main cases:

– the use of an `ObjectSpace` shared among concurrent threads belonging to the same application, a situation symbolically depicted in Fig. 2.

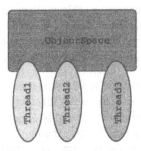

Fig. 2. Local threads accessing an object space

Each shape in such a picture represents a thread running within an application. Thread1, Thread2, and Thread3 are interacting with the object space (using `ObjectSpace` methods). The `ObjectSpace` object manages their access and takes care of handling critical regions managing. Note that some of the thread may have blocked calling a method to perform a blocking in or read operation.

– the use of an `ObjectSpace` shared among concurrent threads belonging to different applications. In this case we have to use an `ObjectServer`/`ObjectClient` architecture to access the shared space, as we shown in Fig. 3.
Thread1 and Thread2 are now part of an application while Thread3 is part of a different one. The former are using the same `ObjectClient` object to access the object space, while the latter uses a private one. When a thread performs a request calling a method of the `ObjectClient` object, the request if forwarded to the `ObjectServer` object, using a network connection, which runs a thread to handle

it. Each thread run by the object server then corresponds to a remote thread which performed a request (this is actually not always true because of the optimizations we did to the package, this general concept, however, is more easy to understand).

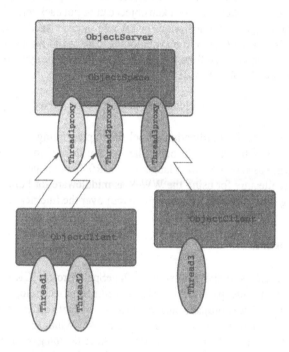

Fig. 3. Remote threads accessing an object space

We can see how the former situation is automatically replicated in the latter one inside the application which runs the ObjectServer, where the threads that are created to handle remote requests behave just like the threads in a local ObjectSpace, giving evidence to the implicit scalability of Jada's architecture.

7   Programming with Jada

Using Jada to allow threads to exchange data is quite an easy task but we can do even better. We can use Jada to coordinate threads, thus easily solving many well-known coordination problems:

- server/client model: a server read requests in form of objects from the object space. A client performs a request putting an object in the object space.
- master/worker model: the master put jobs in form of objects in the object space, then reads results from it. Workers read jobs from the object space, execute their task, and then put the result into the object space.

- producer/consumer model: we decouple a producer and a consumer using the object space as temporary repository for data to be exchanged.
- mutual exclusion: we can use an object as a "token" to enter a critical section: any thread need to get such a token to enter the section. Upon exiting the section the thread releases the token (i.e. the token object can be put back into the object space).
- message passing, either synchronous or asynchronous: a sender puts the message into the object space (and in the synchronous case waits for an ack object). The receiver reads the message from the object space (and in the synchronous case puts an ack object in the object space).

Many other concurrency problems can also be easily solved using shared object spaces [CG90].

We are using Jada as coordination kernel for implementing more complex Internet languages and architectures. In particular, we are developing on top of Jada the Shade/Java agent based coordination language [CCR96], and PageSpace [CKTV96], a coordination architecture for using the WWW as middleware for building cooperative applications (eg. groupware, electronic commerce) over the Internet.

8 Related work

Jada has been developed in the context of the PageSpace project [CKTV96]. The main idea at the basis of PageSpace is to exploit coordination technology to enhance the WWW middleware. Other projects pursue a similar goal with different approaches.

In fact, although it explicitly refers to Linda, the WWWinda approach [GNSP94] is quite different from what we have described here. Since the integration between WWW browsers and their helper applications is extremely rudimental (it is only possible to activate the external application and to deliver the data to be displayed), the WWWinda research team designed a flexible, modular WWW browser architecture based on the Linda programming language. Several independent tools, each implementing a different part of the whole WWW browser, are activated according to needs, sharing screen space, HTTP responses, and user interaction. This allows for a highly modular architecture, where new services and tools can be added without modifications in a homogeneous framework. In order to allow cooperation among helper modules, these all make use of a shared tuple space. Tuples allow to upgrade the simple "activate with these data" paradigm of browsers' helper applications to a more complete coordination protocol. For instance, WWWinda has been used to coordinate a distributed digital orchestra, in which several browsers simulating musical instruments (possibly running on different machines) extract from the shared tuple space the tune to be played note by note. No instrument is aware of how many other instruments are present, and new ones can be added on the fly, even in the middle of a performance.

All features of WWWinda, that we define a "client-side coordination toolkit" are easily implementable in Jada.

Instead, the WU Linda Toolkit [Sch95] is a simple interface between a WWW browser and a WWW server implementing a tuple space service. Access to the shared tuple space is provided to clients: users can fill in an HTML form with the appropriate

Linda command to interact with the tuple space. The main application on show is a disc-load viewer that allows a first glance check of current disk usage of the computers of a cluster of workstations. Each workstation hosts a WU Linda client which posts tuples in the shared tuple space describing the current load of the disks it controls. These tuples are then collected and rendered in a user-friendly way via HTMl to any browser querying the application.

Again, all features of WU Linda, that we define a "server-side coordination toolkit" are easily implementable in Jada.

Jada applets are very similar to Oblets, or "distributed active objects" [BN96]. An *oblet* is a program written in Obliq and executed on a browser. Each oblet can use high-level primitives to communicate with other oblets running on possibly remote browsers.

The Bauhaus "Turingware Web" designed in Yale (the homeland of Linda) is similar at least in spirit to the WU Linda toolkit [Hup96]. The main idea consists of using a standard browser to access a Bauhaus server. Bauhaus is a coordination language based on nested multiple tuple spaces (multisets) which can be used in this case for both controlling the hierarchical structure of the pages of a web site, and for associating agents and their activities to the pages themselves. For instance, one attribute of a page could be the list of users "acting" in such a page, who are displayed by a graphic icon and can interact using some ad-hoc cooperation services.

This application of coordination technology to the WWW is based on a language richer than Linda. We are also investigating similar extensions, based on multiple tuple spaces, in a coordination language called Shade, whose kernel is currently written in Jada [CCR96].

9 Conclusion

Jada provides:

- coordination inside the object oriented programming framework: no syntax extension for Java, just a set of classes. Each data type used by Jada is a Java object.
- dynamic tuple creation: being an object, a tuple can be created with new and many different constructors are provided in order to build a tuple from a string, an array of object or, simply, from a set of arguments.
- multithreading support: Jada is multithreading aware: different threads can access the same object space; blocking request are managed at thread-level.
- open systems support: at any time threads or applications can perform operation on an object space.
- multiple objects associative access: we provided modified flavors for the in and read requests in order to allow the use of multiple matching objects.

Acknowledgments. We thank Robert Tolksdorf for discussions and suggestions. We thank for support the EU Open LTR project Pagespace n. 20179. We have been partially supported also by Italian CNR - "Progetto Coordinato Programmazione Logica".

References

[AG96]   K. Arnold and J. Gosling. *The Java Programming Language*. Addison-Wesley, 1996.

[BN95]   R. Ben-Natan. *CORBA: A guide to CORBA*. McGraw-Hill, 1995.

[BN96]   M. Brown and M. Najork. Distributed Active Objects. *Computer Networks and ISDN Systems*, 28(7-11):1037–1052, 1996.

[CCR96]   S. Castellani, P. Ciancarini, and D. Rossi. The ShaPE of ShaDE: a coordination system. Technical Report UBLCS 96-5, Dipartimento di Scienze dell'Informazione, Università di Bologna, Italy, March 1996.

[CG90]   N. Carriero and D. Gelernter. *How to Write Parallel Programs: A First Course*. MIT Press, Cambridge, MA, 1990.

[CG92]   N. Carriero and D. Gelernter. Coordination Languages and Their Significance. *Communications of the ACM*, 35(2):97–107, February 1992.

[Cia94]   P. Ciancarini. Distributed Programming with Logic Tuple Spaces. *New Generation Computing*, 12(3):251–284, May 1994.

[CKTV96] P. Ciancarini, A. Knoche, R. Tolksdorf, and F. Vitali. PageSpace: An Architecture to Coordinate Distributed Applications on the Web. *Computer Networks and ISDN Systems*, 28(7-11):941–952, 1996.

[Gel85]   D. Gelernter. Generative Communication in Linda. *ACM Transactions on Programming Languages and Systems*, 7(1):80–112, 1985.

[GNSP94] Y. Gutfreund, J. Nicol, R. Sasnett, and V. Phuah. WWWinda: An Orchestration Service for WWW Browsers and Accessories. In *Proc. 2nd Int. World Wide Web Conference*, Chicago, IL, December 1994.

[Gos95]   J. Gosling. Java Intermediate Bytecodes. In *Proc. ACM SIGPLAN Workshop on Intermediate Representations*, volume 30:3 of *ACM Sigplan Notices*, pages 111–118, San Francisco, CA, January 1995.

[Hup96]   S. Hupfer. *Turingware: An Integrated Approach to Collaborative Computing*. PhD thesis, Dept. of Computer Science, Yale University, New Haven, CT, May 1996.

[Sch95]   W. Schoenfeldinger. WWW Meets Linda. In *Proc. 4th Int. World Wide Web Conference*, pages 259–276, Boston, MA, December 1995.

[Tol92]   R. Tolksdorf. Laura: A Coordination Language for Open Distributed Systems. Technical Report 1992/35, Technische Universität Berlin, Fachbereich 20 Informatik, 1992.

[Tol94]   R. Tolksdorf. *Coordination in Open Distributed Systems*. PhD thesis, Techniche Universitet, Berlin, Germany, December 1994.

Part III
Implementation

Performance-Oriented Implementation Strategies for a Mobile Agent Language

Frederick Knabe

Abstract. The use of larger and more complex mobile agents in distributed applications has created a need for agent programming systems that deliver better performance. The implementation of Extended Facile, a mobile agent language, uses several strategies to boost performance. We review four main techniques: allowing agents to use different transmissible representations, optimistically transmitting machine code with agents, stripping agents of data and code that can be found at their recipients before transmitting them, and performing agent compilation lazily. Quantitative measurements show that these methods can boost absolute and relative performance.

1 Introduction

Over the last two years interest in mobile agents has increased dramatically. Mobile agents, or more generally the ability to transmit code-containing objects between communicating participants, offer compelling advantages for constructing flexible and adaptable distributed systems. Uses of agents range from enriching client–server interfaces while reducing communication costs, to simplifying the temporary installation of applications retrieved over the network. Many innovative uses are just now beginning to emerge.

As mobile agents are used in more sophisticated applications, their performance becomes an important characteristic. There is an increasing need for performance-oriented implementations of the programming systems that provide the basic compile-time and run-time support for mobile agents.

An agent programming system can affect the costs of using agents at several points. First, it must prepare agents for transmission (*marshalling*) and then transmit them over the network. By reducing the size of agents, the agent system can make these steps faster. Second, it must prepare received agents for execution. This preparation might include verifying the agent or compiling it into a locally executable form, and it adds latency before the agent can start running. Finally, the agent system must execute the agent. Naturally the execution should be as fast as possible.

I have implemented an agent programming system that uses several implementation strategies and techniques to reduce these costs. The system is an extension of Facile [12, 20], a higher-order, mostly functional programming language that integrates support for concurrency and distribution. Extended Facile [16] defines agents simply as functions and thus takes advantage of the easy way in which functions can be manipulated in a functional language. The extension retains Facile's strong static typing and adds support for transmitting code between heterogeneous machine architectures, accessing resources on remote sites, and executing agents without implicit callbacks.

Extended Facile supports multiple transmissible representations, allowing agent programmers to trade off between agent size, latency before execution, and execution speed by selecting which representations should be transmitted for an agent. Optimistic transmission of machine code can dramatically reduce latency and execution time for a small overhead in agent size. *Closure trimming* and dynamic linking are used to decrease the size of agents by removing library functions and data before transmission. Finally, lazy compilation addresses the compilation latency before execution by amortizing it over a greater portion of the run of an agent.

Sections 2 through 4 address these implementation strategies in turn. We consider performance results in Section 5 followed by related work in Section 6. We present conclusions in Section 7.

2 Transmissible Representations

A basic difficulty in implementing support for mobile agents is handling the transmission of code between heterogeneous machine architectures. Because machine code is specific to a particular architecture, it cannot be executed on another architecture unless a simulator or translator for the first architecture is available, which is rarely the case. Thus agents must be transmitted in other representations that a recipient can use and understand.

Because a recipient can surely understand its own machine code format, one solution to the heterogeneity problem is to generate machine code for all possible destination architectures when an agent is initially compiled. The appropriate machine code for the recipient's architecture can be selected and transmitted at run time, an approach taken in Emerald [18], or all the machine code representations can be transmitted [11, 17], allowing later retransmission. However, in an open distributed system this solution suffers many disadvantages: there are likely to be many architectures for which each compiler must know how to generate code, the addition of new architectures to the system means all existing agents must be recompiled, storing multiple representations swells the size of agents, etc.

A better solution, and the one that is adopted in most agent programming systems, is to transmit agents in an architecture-independent representation. The representation might be source code or the result of several translation steps, and to execute it the recipient must either interpret it or compile it to local machine code. Because this compilation must be performed at run time, it should be as fast as possible. A lower-level representation is likely to compile faster than a higher-level one such as source, because fewer compilation steps must be performed. However, for a sender to generate a low-level representation that is still architecture independent it may have to make certain worst-case assumptions about the target, such as how many registers it has. Such assumptions may allow the low-level representation to be compiled faster, but at the cost that the resulting machine code executes more slowly than machine code generated from source. Thus there is a potential trade-off between the compilation time for a received agent and the agent's subsequent execution speed.

If an agent is interpreted rather than compiled, source is once again a possible representation for its code. However, byte-coded virtual machine code is likely to execute faster. A single representation may support both compilation or interpretation, in which case the recipient must decide which to use. Interpreted code is likely to run slower than compiled code, but it can be used immediately upon receipt: There is no delay while compilation is performed. The choice of whether to compile or to interpret is affected by the demands of the application (for example, an interactive application may need to execute the agent as soon as possible) along with the expected running time of the agent.

Extended Facile uses a hybrid strategy that combines the best elements of both sending machine code and sending an architecture-independent representation. There are two components to the strategy:

− More than one transmissible representation is supported.
− Several representations can be transmitted *together.*

The reason to support more than one representation is that it allows the programmer of an agent to pick the representation most suited for the execution characteristics of that agent. If the agent is a batch job being sent to a CPU server, for example, the programmer might pick a high-level representation. Such a representation could be compiled with as many optimizations as possible on the server; the cost of performing these optimizations would presumably be outweighed by the faster execution speed during the long run of the agent. In contrast, an interpreted representation or a lower-level compiled representation (i.e., with more worst-case assumptions) might be more suitable for an interactive agent that performs little or moderate computation. Representations may also vary on other dimensions that affect performance. One in particular is compactness of the representation: For a large agent sent over a slow link, transmission time may be a significant. A programmer targeting users with dial-up or wireless links would then need to consider which code representations are smallest.

The primary reason for allowing several representations to be transmitted together is to allow a machine-code representation to accompany an architecture-independent one. In this way we gain the benefits of each approach. If the recipient shares the architecture of the sender, the machine code can be used, eliminating the start-up delays of compilation and providing maximum performance. Otherwise, the architecture-independent representation can be used, either with interpretation or with compilation.

Transmitting machine code optimistically in this way has a cost: Transmission times will be higher. This strategy may therefore not be appropriate for slow links. On the other hand, an agent programmer may assume that users on slow links are probably using Intel x86-based computers. She may therefore decide that the potential improvement in execution speed by sending Intel machine code justifies the extra transmission costs.

Note that giving the recipient the choice of which architecture-independent representation to use is not a good reason to allow several representations to be transmitted together. A recipient is unlikely to know the execution characteristics of an agent, and therefore would not have the information to pick the best representation.

Extended Facile supports three architecture-independent representations, all of which are intermediate representations from the original Facile compiler. The highest-level representation, *lambda language,* is interpreted on receipt. It is a simple lambda calculus variant that consists of about twenty constructs. The other two representations are different forms of continuation-passing style, or CPS. *Middle CPS* is higher-level than *final CPS,* which includes more worst-case assumptions about the number of registers on the target architecture. More complete descriptions of CPS and lambda language may be found in [1].

3 Closure Trimming and Dynamic Linking

An agent in Extended Facile is simply a function, which in turn is implemented as a *closure.* A closure is a tuple that consists of the code for a function and the values it uses from its lexical environment. These values may be data or other functions. When a function is created at run time, it is not new code that is being created but rather a new closure with existing code and new values. The code of an agent is fixed at compile time, which permits operations such as the generation of the code's transmissible representations to take place then instead of at run time.

Representing agents as closures provides an easy way for the sender to associate data and other functions with an agent's code based on decisions made at run time. When the agent is transmitted, not only its code but the other elements of its closure are transmitted as well. The downside of this approach is that because closures can contain closures, the size of an agent can become very large when it is recursively marshalled at transmission time. The times to transmit the agent and to prepare it for execution both increase.

One way around this problem is not to transmit all the elements of an agent's closure at once. An initial subset is sent, and the remaining elements are only retrieved when they are needed by the executing agent. If they are not needed, they are never transmitted. The cost of this approach is that each retrieval incurs the network latency associated with the original agent transmission; these costs may outweigh any benefits from an initially smaller transmission. Moreover, if in the meantime the connection to the originating site has been lost, then the retrievals fail and the agent does as well.

A further disadvantage is that using a facility for automatic retrieval of closure elements implies the use of *implicit callbacks.* An implicit callback is one that is not directly obvious from the program code; it is inserted by the compiler or initiated by the run-time system. Implicit callbacks are normally used to hide the distributed nature of applications, the argument being that hiding distribution simplifies programming. The problem is that distributed dependencies and the costs of network access are also hidden, leaving programs fragile and prone to serious flaws [21]. In general, callbacks should only be programmed explicitly, leaving the programmer to evaluate their appropriateness.

Even without callbacks, we can still reduce the size of transmissions. Of the values that are in an agent's closure when we prepare it for transmission, some may be *ubiquitous.* These are values for which we assume that an "equivalent" implementation of the value also exists on all the sites to which the agent may be transmitted. An agent that refers to a ubiquitous value need not take the value with it; instead, the agent can be linked to the value's local implementation when it is received at other sites.

The most likely candidates for ubiquitous values are library functions and values that store system state. Defining these values as ubiquitous gives us two main advantages. First, they do need not be transmitted with agents, so transmissions are smaller and fewer values must be marshalled and unmarshalled. Library functions are used frequently in Facile programs, and the savings in not transmitting them are significant. For example, the function to print "hello, world" marshals to 790 kilobytes if the standard library containing the `print` function is pulled in but to just a few hundred bytes if it is not.

The second main advantage is that agents can access *nontransmissible values*. Although any value can be transmitted in Facile, some values incorporate system state or system-specific functionality and therefore are meaningless to transmit. An example is a file descriptor. The descriptor type is normally implemented as an integer in Facile, and integers can certainly be transmitted, but a descriptor is of no use outside of its home address space. We want agents to be able to access such system values both on their originating site and after transmission. If these values are defined as ubiquitous, agents will always use the locally available implementation.

Ubiquitous values need not come only from standard libraries. Consider a server that supports an interface to special image processing hardware on its host. There may also be a local software implementation of the values in the interface. Given a function that performs image processing through use of these ubiquitous values, we could either run the function locally or transmit it to the server, depending perhaps on the server's reported load.

3.1 Proxy and Ubiquitous Structures

The implementation of ubiquitous values in Extended Facile uses the same basic mechanisms as are used to implement *remote values*. Remote values are values that are not present on an agent's originating site but that are available on recipients. To program access to any special resources (machine-specific libraries, databases, etc.) that a recipient provides to agents but that are not available on the agent's originating site, a programmer uses remote values.

A remote or ubiquitous value is identified by its name, its type, and its membership in a set of other remote or ubiquitous values, i.e., a module (called a *structure* in Facile). How the module is named on one site to the next does not matter. Identifying a value by using its membership in a module with a particular signature helps to distinguish between values from different modules that coincidentally have the same name and type but different implementations or functionalities. This method is not foolproof, but in the absence of naming based on full specifications it is a compromise that works well in practice.

An agent writer who wants to program an access to a remote or ubiquitous value starts with the signature that specifies structures providing the resource. For a remote value, the programmer then creates a *proxy structure* that introduces a placeholder name for structures that match the signature. If it is a ubiquitous value, the programmer must supply a local implementation for the structure that matches the signature (in the case of system libraries, these implementations are already available). Access to the remote or ubiquitous value is then programmed just like access to members of a normal structure. Because the signature describes the type of the resource, the compiler can also type-check uses of the value in the agent program, preserving Facile's strong static typing.

3.2 Closure Trimming

An agent that uses ubiquitous values may be executed locally on the originating site or remotely on a recipient. However, when the agent is transmitted the local implementations of the ubiquitous values are left behind, decreasing transmission time. Implementing this step requires two operations. The first is active at compile time, and the second during marshalling at run time.

When an agent function is compiled, its body is scanned for references to ubiquitous values. The compiler then stores with the function a map recording which elements of the function's run-time closure are ubiquitous.

During marshalling, the map is retrieved and used to identify and remove ubiquitous values from the marshalled closure. As the closure is trimmed, placeholders are inserted for the removed ubiquitous values. The placeholders contain the identification information for each trimmed value.

When the agent's closure is reconstructed on the recipient, the placeholders are looked up in the recipient's list of exported structures and are replaced by appropriate pointers. This operation serves to link the agent dynamically with the resources on the recipient. Both ubiquitous values and remote values (which are represented from the start by a placeholder) are resolved in the same way.

4 Lazy Compilation

Before a received agent can be used, its code must be made locally executable. If native code or an interpretable representation is available, we skip the latter operation. For other representations, however, we must compile the code.

Compilation can be a time-consuming process, and because the recipient must perform it at run time, it plays an important role in the performance of function transmission. We can potentially improve performance in two ways by *deferring* compilation until a function is called for the first time:

- If the function is never called, we avoid the cost of compilation altogether. This case may occur if the function is in a part of a larger agent that does not always get used or if the recipient will simply forward the agent elsewhere.
- For an agent consisting of multiple functions, deferral can reduce the latency between when an agent is received and when it starts executing, an important factor in interactivity. Functions are only compiled as their part of the agent is activated. Through deferral, the compilation latency is amortized over a greater portion of the agent's execution.

When the compilation does occur, we must consider the trade-offs in performing optimizations. Optimizing increases compilation time but may produce code that runs faster, so it may be desirable for code that runs for a long time.

Lazy compilation can be done either explicitly or implicitly. If done explicitly, a function is received as a special object which the programmer must then pass to a compilation routine to produce an executable form. If done implicitly, a received function looks no different from a locally defined one and can be called normally.

The latter approach is used in Extended Facile because it produces a much cleaner programming model.

Lazy compilation is implemented in Extended Facile by creating a special *trigger closure* for each function in an agent when it is received. The trigger closure encapsulates the transmissible version of a function. When the trigger is called, it compiles the function and overwrites itself with the new closure. By overwriting the closure, rather than creating a new one in memory, we ensure that any existing pointers to the closure remain valid. The details are as follows:

1. When a function closure is marshalled, a record representing it is placed in the outgoing message. The new record is larger than the original closure record. All of its entries are null except for the last. The last entry points to a *transmission record* containing the function's code string, values extracted from its closure, placeholders for remote and ubiquitous values, and other information. The new closure record is large enough to contain later all the functions of the original closure record (normally only one, but more for mutually recursive functions) and all the values used by the functions, including ubiquitous and remote values, as well as the transmission record.

   Thus, a marshalled closure record looks like

   ```
   (null,null,...,null,<info>)
   ```

2. Closure records are detected on unmarshalling through a special tag. After copying the record out of the message, the unmarshaller replaces the null entries by pointers to the code string for the local trigger function. However, the last null pointer (the second-to-last entry in the record) is replaced by a pointer to the recipient's compilation function. The unmarshalled record looks like

   ```
   (<trigger>,<trigger>,...,<trigger>,<compiler>,<info>)
   ```

   Note that there will be more triggers than functions in the original closure. Pointers to trigger code are only needed at those locations in the original closure where there were function pointers. However, on unmarshalling it is convenient to fill in all but the last two slots with triggers; the extra triggers do no harm, and we are guaranteed that all function pointer locations have been properly filled.

   In Facile, a function value is really a pointer into a closure record. The location pointed to is itself a pointer to the function's code string. When the code is executed, it retrieves values it needs from the closure record using addressing relative to its own entry in the record.

   The trigger code is specially written so that it contains no free variables and thus requires no values from its closure. It is this property that allows pointers to the trigger code to be placed anywhere in the closure.

3. When the closure is applied to an argument and called, the trigger code scans forward in the closure record until it finds the beginning of the record and the run-time tag with the record's length. Using this information, it finds the second-to-last entry of the closure (the compilation function) and calls it. The trigger passes the argument it has been passed (which is intended for the target function) and the closure itself to the compilation function.

4. In Facile, multiple processes run within a single address space. Because more than one process could call an uncompiled function simultaneously, the compilation function first seizes a lock shared by all processes in the address space and checks if the target function has been compiled since the trigger was called. If not, the compilation function looks in the closure record passed to it and finds the transmission record in the last entry. It compiles the transmissible code string, producing a linkage function that is then applied to the values that should appear in the target function's closure. The result is a new closure that is then copied onto the initial trigger closure, which is large enough that the transmission record in the last field is left untouched (it will be used if the function is retransmitted).

The compilation function releases the lock, calls the new executable closure with the argument originally passed to the trigger, and finishes by returning the result. On further calls to the closure, the target function will be executed directly; the triggers have been overwritten.

Further subtleties are involved when compiling nested functions and are described fully in [16].

5 Performance Results

To quantify the effect of the preceding implementation strategies for Extended Facile, I measured the performance of the system on several micro-benchmarks and a suite of small agent applications using a Sparc Classic with 32 MB of memory. Although the results are specific to the Extended Facile implementation, they do provide an indication of the efficacy of the techniques in improving performance.

The first set of experiments examined the benefits of using different transmissible representations for different agent applications. Table 1 compares the performance of lambda language, which is interpreted on receipt, the two compiled representations, middle CPS and final CPS, and, as a baseline, native machine code. The upper part of the table shows figures for a set of CPU-intensive sorting agents that varied in size (*large* or *small*) and running time (*long* or *short*) by roughly an order of magnitude. The lower part shows figures for several interactive agent applications with low CPU demands. The values are the sum of the the marshalling, transmission, unmarshalling, compilation, and execution times for each representation and workload. Transmission was either over a LAN (with a bandwidth of approximately 550 KB/sec) or a transatlantic WAN (approximately 40 KB/sec). Each value is shown to the number of significant figures corresponding to its error range at the 95% confidence level.

Not surprisingly, the results in each column show that the choice of representation and whether compilation or interpretation is used can dramatically affect performance. In the small–long sorting agent, for example, compilation wins significantly because its overhead is small compared to the running time of the agent. In contrast, the interactive applications show better performance for interpretation. The two compiled representations also vary in performance between one another: Though final CPS takes less time to compile, the representation is twice as large as middle CPS (yielding longer transmission times) and runs slightly slower. These differences are reflected in generally better

Table 1. Aggregate performance (in seconds) of different transmissible representations.

	large–long		large–short		small–long		small–short	
	LAN	WAN	LAN	WAN	LAN	WAN	LAN	WAN
lambda$_{int}$	348.1	360.0	35.44	47.3	668.2	669.4	33.01	34.3
middle	24.11	29.0	17.33	22.2	9.36	9.87	1.665	2.17
final	17.05	30.0	10.77	23.8	12.11	13.5	1.400	2.8
native	7.05	9.2	0.91	3.0	7.65	7.82	0.379	0.551

	directory		browser		map		schedule	
	LAN	WAN	LAN	WAN	LAN	WAN	LAN	WAN
lambda$_{int}$	0.32	2.8	0.23	1.70	0.25	1.7	0.6	4.7
middle	3.75	5.15	2.42	3.28	2.35	3.22	6.67	9.0
final	2.30	5.9	1.53	3.65	1.48	3.6	4.08	10.5
native	0.17	0.85	0.16	0.66	0.19	0.68	0.26	1.5

Table 2. Performance (in seconds) for different workloads using multiple representations. Representations in boldface are used by the recipient.

	large–long		large–short		small–long		small–short	
	LAN	WAN	LAN	WAN	LAN	WAN	LAN	WAN
middle	24.11	29.0	17.33	22.2	9.36	9.87	1.665	2.17
middle+native	24.27	31.3	17.50	24.5	9.37	10.05	1.679	2.36
middle+**native**	7.44	14.4	1.29	8.3	7.69	8.36	0.418	1.10
final	17.05	30.0	10.77	23.8	12.11	13.5	1.400	2.8
final+native	17.21	32.4	10.93	26.1	12.12	13.7	1.413	3.0
final+**native**	8.04	23.2	1.90	17.0	7.74	9.3	0.474	2.1

	directory		browser		map		schedule	
	LAN	WAN	LAN	WAN	LAN	WAN	LAN	WAN
lambda$_{int}$	0.32	2.8	0.23	1.70	0.25	1.7	0.6	4.7
lambda$_{int}$+native	0.38	3.5	0.27	2.24	0.29	2.2	0.7	6.0
lambda$_{int}$+**native**	0.36	3.6	0.28	2.25	0.29	2.25	0.57	5.9

performance for final CPS on the LAN, where transmission time is less significant, except for very CPU-intensive agents (such as small–long).

Altogether the results show that supporting more than one general transmissible representation allows the agent programmer to change significantly the performance of an application. Nevertheless, the performance of these general representations is always poorer than native machine code. Our next step is to examine the benefits and costs of optimistically transmitting machine code along with a general representation.

Table 2 compares the performance of optimistically sending native code along with the fastest general representations for the different agents. For the CPU-intensive agents, these representations are middle CPS and final CPS, while for the interactive agents it is interpreted lambda. The columns show the cost of sending and using only the general

Table 3. Effect of closure trimming on the sizes (in bytes) of marshalled agents.

	directory	browser	map	schedule
trim all	60232	36744	35592	103300
trim libs	108456	80540	79492	151384
no trim	247100	200348	200264	274692

Table 4. Effect of closure trimming on transmission times (in seconds).

	directory	browser	map	schedule
trim all	0.110	0.069	0.068	0.18
trim libs	0.196	0.146	0.15	0.27
no trim	0.441	0.365	0.360	0.50

Table 5. Effect of closure trimming on compilation times (in seconds).

	directory	browser	map	schedule
trim all	3.54	2.16	2.15	6.38
trim libs	4.95	3.50	3.51	7.69
no trim	12.5	9.94	10.11	14.8

representation, sending native code optimistically but not being able to use it on the recipient, and sending native code optimistically and being able to use it.

The results are mixed. For the CPU-intensive agents, the performance penalty for sending native code that is not used is only 1% or less on the LAN, climbing to 7 to 10% on the WAN due to the greater contribution of transmission times to performance. However, in return for this overhead, when the native code can be used the speedups range from 1.2 to 13! In these applications using optimistic transmission is a clear win. On the other hand, the interactive applications show that optimistic transmission is always a loss. Here the running times are so short that sending native code only adds overhead that is not recouped through faster execution.

In general, the performance of optimistic transmission depends on many factors. In Extended Facile, for example, the general code representations are quite verbose compared to machine code (twice the size or more), which makes the relative overhead of sending machine code less. The speed of the network, the performance of native code versus that of the general representations in agents of different sizes and running times, and the probability of being able to use the machine code at the recipient all come into play. Nevertheless, the potential speedups are significant enough that this implementation strategy should be considered in agent programming systems.

Turning to the performance of closure trimming. there are two categories of ubiquitous values in Extended Facile whose performance we can assess. The first consists of system library values. These are ubiquitous by default and no action is required from the programmer to gain the benefits of trimming them. The second category consists of values from ubiquitous structures. These structures must be explicitly defined by the programmer.

Synthetic benchmarks are not a good choice for evaluating closure trimming because they are unlikely to reflect how ubiquitous values are used in real programs, so we restrict our analysis to the interactive agent applications. These applications use library values and include some programmer-defined ubiquitous structures.

The key metric for assessing the effect of closure trimming is the size of a marshalled agent. The more values from an agent's closure that are marshalled together with it, the larger the size. Transmission and compilation times are proportional to this size.

Table 3 shows the sizes for the four agents marshalled in the middle CPS representation. Three levels of closure trimming are represented: full trimming of programmer-defined ubiquitous values as well as the library values, trimming of just the library values, and no trimming at all. The results are for only one code representation because the sizes simply scale for the others; for example, the native code sizes are one-half the middle CPS ones. Tables 4 and 5 show how the sizes translate into transmission and compilation times. These times are for a LAN, so the contribution of transmission times is minor.

Overall, the results show that closure trimming substantially improves performance. In the interactive agent applications, trimming the library values alone reduces marshalled sizes by 45 to 60% and combined transmission and compilation times by 48 to 65% (compare the first and second entries in each column). Closure trimming therefore offers a benefit even if the programmer does not define any ubiquitous structures herself. The improvement is greatest for the browser and the map agents because the library values add about the same amount to each of them (between 120 and 139 kilobytes), and this amount is proportionately larger for these smaller agents.

Further benefits can be realized after the library values have been trimmed by explicitly using ubiquitous structures. The data show that the sizes of the agents drop by 32 to 55% and the associated times by 18 to 39% (the difference between the second and third entries in each column).

The times do not drop as much as the sizes do in these latter figures. The reason is that compilation times are affected by the complexity of code as well as its size, so we cannot expect the decreases to be identical. If the transmission times were a larger factor in the times, we would expect the changes in times to reflect the changes in sizes more closely.

Though closure trimming adds complexity to the language implementation and, outside of the library values, requires actions from the programmer, it is an important optimization. Moreover, it is worthwhile for programmers to define and use ubiquitous structures.

Finally, we consider lazy compilation. Table 6 shows how combined compilation and execution times are spread out over a series of interactions with a selection of the preceding agent applications. Compilation is a poor choice for these agents, as we discussed earlier, but nevertheless we can see how lazy compilation makes the best of a bad situation. Rather than concentrating all the compilation as pre-execution latency, the system spreads it over the run (note that the execution times, as shown by the row

Table 6. Times (in seconds) between a series of user interactions with several agents.

lambda$_{int}$	0.26	0.16	0.07	0.04	0.18	0.042	0.46
middle	4	2.24	1.0	0.52	1.678	1.21	3.95
final	2.5	1.20	0.5	0.29	1.02	0.76	1.98
native		0.13	0.12	0.049	0.0231	0.16	0.0315 0.18

for native code, are quite short in each interaction). More CPU-intensive agents than in this example would perform better with compilation than interpretation, and lazy compilation would continue to deliver the benefit of amortizing the latency.

6 Related Work

Performance has so far received relatively little attention in agent programming systems. This situation is partly due to the youth of the area; much work is still being devoted to higher-level issues such as language design. Performance studies for different implementation strategies generally do not exist.

Nevertheless, there are a number of implementations that use strategies and techniques related to the ones developed for Extended Facile. Almost every system addresses the problem of heterogeneous machine architectures. The more experimental of these simply transmit code in source form. Those systems based on Lisp or Scheme (e.g., Avalon/Common Lisp [7], Messenger Scheme [10]) use the `eval` primitive to compile or interpret code, while other systems (e.g., Safe-Tcl [3], Tps [15]) use directly interpreted source code.

More sophisticated systems usually use an interpreted intermediate representation. Obliq [5] and a derivative, Phantom [9], use abstract syntax trees for the transmissible representations. Compact byte-coded representations are used in Telescript [22] and Java [13].

Run-time compilation is relatively rare, in part due to the complexity of its implementation and the greater difficulty in making ports. Though it is not an agent programming system per se, Omniware [8] provides the necessary infrastructure to receive, compile, and execute code at run time. Omniware compiles a RISC-like virtual machine representation to native code; the generality of the virtual machine allows any language to be targeted to it. Run-time compilation of virtual machine code has also been investigated for heterogeneous process migration [2, 19].

Currently there is work on Java to support run-time compilation, which will allow it to use either compilation or interpretation. Otherwise, Extended Facile's capability to handle multiple transmissible representations via compilation and interpretation and its support for optimistic transmission are unique.

Lazy compilation for transmitted agents is another unique feature. However, the general technique of lazy program generation has been investigated in other contexts. Heering et al. [14] developed a syntax-oriented editor where the user is permitted to change the syntax interactively. Changes to the syntax require the generation of new parsers, but this operation takes too long for interactive performance. Parsers are therefore generated lazily; when part of the parser is needed that does not exist, the parser generator creates it. Another feature of their system is incremental generation: After a syntax change, as much of the previously generated parser is retained as possible.

Brown [4] developed a lazy compiler for BASIC to solve the problem of an entire program not fitting into memory. Statements are compiled as they are encountered, and when memory is filled, all object code generated so far is discarded. This approach required several innovative addressing methods.

Chambers and Ungar [6] introduced lazy compilation into SELF, a "pure" object-oriented language (i.e., every type, including primitive ones such as integers, is implemented as an object). SELF provides an interactive loop where programs can be compiled, executed, and then changed. However, compilation times were unacceptably long. The time was primarily spent generating code for uncommon actions, so by deferring compilation of these actions to the rare times they occurred at run time, interactive performance could be significantly improved.

In general, lazy compilation of programs has received little attention to date because there have been few reasons to defer compilation until run time. For mobile agents, compilation is possible only at run time, because the code is not available until then.

7 Conclusion

As mobile agents grow in size and complexity with the development of more sophisticated applications, the performance delivered by their underlying programming systems becomes more important. Extended Facile, though far from being a mature system, offers several implementation strategies that can improve this performance.

Agents vary significantly in their sizes and execution characteristics. An agent programming system can deliver better performance if it allows the programmer to specify (perhaps via a hint) whether an agent should be interpreted or compiled on receipt. By making a choice based on how CPU-intensive an agent is, the programmer can boost performance by an order of magnitude or more. Other, more complex strategies using multiple representations with different compilation characteristics can also be used, although these strategies risk overwhelming the programmer or application designer with too many options.

Optimistic transmission of machine code can also improve running times at a small cost in overhead. Again, the characteristics of the agent application (as well as the system overall) can help determine when to use this feature. Although the transmission of machine code violates the security model for some agent systems (such as Java), systems with security based on low-level analysis or code transformation or with security provided by the operating system can take advantage of it.

Closure trimming combined with ubiquitous values provides a means to shrink the size of agents. As presented, this technique is relatively specific to Extended Facile. However, the general principle is to allow the identification and removal of those values associated with an agent that should not be transmitted with it, and to replace those values with local ones when the agent is received. For a language such as Java, this technique is largely irrelevant, because run-time values cannot be associated with agent code (i.e., agents are not closures). But in more general agent systems where agents accumulate state and context as they traverse the network, it represents an important performance optimization.

Lazy compilation, though it is relatively complex to implement, offers a way to boost apparent performance by redistributing pre-execution latency to other parts of an agent's run. One important characteristic is that it does not necessarily require any effort from the agent programmer, so its addition to a system can be completely transparent.

Besides these methods for improving performance there are other possibilities. On a WAN, downloading latency can be more significant than compilation latency for interactive applications. In this case, methods are needed that allow an agent to begin execution even before it has been completely received. Another possibility is to combine interpretation and compilation for a received agent. An agent might begin executing via an interpreter, but during its execution compilation of its code proceeds in the background. As functions are compiled, they replace their interpreted versions. Such a scheme presents challenging implementation problems but once again offers potential performance benefits.

References

1. Andrew W. Appel. *Compiling with Continuations*. Cambridge University Press, 1992.
2. G. Attardi, A. Baldi, U. Boni, F. Carignani, G. Cozzi, A. Pelligrini, E. Durocher, I. Filotti, Wang Qing, M. Hunter, J. Marks, C. Richardson, and A. Watson. Techniques for dynamic software migration. In *ESPRIT '88: Proceedings of the 5th Annual ESPRIT Conference*, volume 1, pages 475–491, Brussels, November 1988.
3. Nathaniel S. Borenstein. Email with a mind of its own: The Safe-Tcl language for enabled mail. In *Proceedings of the 1994 IFIP WG6.5 Conference on Upper Layer Protocols, Architectures, and Applications*, Barcelona, May 1994. North-Holland.
4. P. J. Brown. Throw-away compiling. *Software—Practice and Experience*, 6(3):423–434, 1976.
5. Luca Cardelli. *Obliq: A Language with Distributed Scope*. DEC Systems Research Center, May 1994.
6. Craig Chambers and David Ungar. Making pure object-oriented languages practical. In *Conference on Object-Oriented Programming Systems, Languages, and Applications (OOPSLA)*, pages 1–15, Phoenix, Arizona, 1991. ACM.
7. Stewart M. Clamen, Linda D. Leibengood, Scott M. Nettles, and Jeannette M. Wing. Reliable distributed computing with Avalon/Common Lisp. In *International Conference on Computer Languages*, pages 169–179. IEEE, March 1990.
8. Omniware: A universal substrate for mobile code. Colusa Software white paper, 1995. Available at http://www.colusa.com/.
9. Antony Courtney. Phantom: An interpreted language for distributed programming. In *USENIX Conference on Object-Oriented Technologies (COOTS)*, Monterey, CA, June 1995.
10. Giovanna Di Marzo, Murhimanya Muhugusa, Christian Tschudin, and Jürgen Harms. The messenger paradigm and its implication on distributed systems. In *Workshop on Intelligent Computer Communication (ICC)*, 1995. Also available at http://cuiwww.unige.ch/tios/msgr/msgr.html.
11. F. Brent Dubach, Robert M. Rutherford, and Charles M. Shub. Process-originated migration in a heterogeneous environment. In *Seventeenth Annual ACM Computer Science Conference*, pages 98–102, Louisville, KY, USA, February 1989.

12. Alessandro Giacalone, Prateek Mishra, and Sanjiva Prasad. Facile: A symmetric integration of concurrent and functional programming. *International Journal of Parallel Programming*, 18(2):121–160, April 1989.

13. James Gosling and Henry McGilton. The Java language environment. White paper, May 1995. Sun Microsystems, 2550 Garcia Avenue, Mountain View, CA 94043, USA. Available at http://java.sun.com/.

14. J. Heering, P. Klint, and J. Rekers. Lazy and incremental program generation. *ACM Transactions on Programming Languages and Systems*, 16(3):1010–1023, May 1994.

15. Dennis Heimbigner. The Tps reference manual Version 2.1a. Arcadia Technical Report CU-ARCADIA-104-95, Department of Computer Science, University of Colorado, Boulder, Colorado 80309, USA, March 1995.

16. Frederick C. Knabe. *Language Support for Mobile Agents*. PhD thesis, School of Computer Science, Carnegie Mellon University, Pittsburgh, Pennsylvania 15213, December 1995. Technical report CMU-CS-95-223.

17. Charles M. Shub. Native code process-originated migration in a heterogeneous environment. In *1990 ACM Eighteenth Annual Computer Science Conference Proceedings*, pages 266–270, Washington, DC, USA, February 1990.

18. Bjarne Steensgaard and Eric Jul. Object and native code thread mobility among heterogeneous computers. In *15th ACM Symposium on Operating Systems Principles (SOSP)*, Copper Mountain Resort, Colorado, December 1995.

19. Marvin M. Theimer and Barry Hayes. Heterogeneous process migration by recompilation. In *11th International Conference on Distributed Computing Systems*, pages 18–25, Arlington, TX, USA, May 1991. IEEE.

20. Bent Thomsen, Lone Leth, Sanjiva Prasad, Tsung-Min Kuo, André Kramer, Fritz Knabe, and Alessandro Giacalone. Facile Antigua Release programming guide. Technical Report ECRC-93-20, European Computer-Industry Research Centre, Arabellastr. 17, 81925 Munich, Germany, December 1993. Available at http://www.ecrc.de/.

21. Jim Waldo, Geoff Wyant, Ann Wollrath, and Sam Kendall. A note on distributed computing. Technical Report SMLI TR-94-29, Sun Microsystems Laboratories, 2550 Garcia Avenue, Mountain View, California 94043, USA, November 1994.

22. James E. White. Telescript technology: The foundation for the electronic marketplace. General Magic white paper, 2465 Latham Street, Mountain View, CA 94040, 1994.

Dynamic Linking for Mobile Programs*

Anurag Acharya, Joel Saltz

Abstract. Dynamic linking provides functionality that is necessary for secure flexible use of mobile programs but it introduces a new class of runtime errors - unbound procedure names. In this chapter, we present a compiler-directed technique for safe dynamic linking for mobile programs. Our technique guarantees that linking failures can occur only when a program arrives at a new execution site and that this failure can be delivered to the program as an error code or an exception. We use interprocedural analysis to identify the set of names that must be linked at the different sites the program executes on. We use a combination of runtime and compile-time techniques to identify the calling context and to link only the names needed in that context. Our technique is able to handle recursive programs as well as separately compiled code that may itself be able to move. We discuss language constructs for controlling the behavior of dynamic linking and the implication of some of these constructs for application structure.

1 Introduction

Mobile programs can move from host to host during execution. At migration points, the execution stack and the heap of the program are transferred from original host to the target host; execution continues at the target host. Mobile programs have been proposed as a suitable model of computation for the Internet [6, 18, 23]. To access local resources or to use site-specific operations available at individual hosts, they need to be able to name them. The mapping between program names and local procedures/operations has to be established dynamically. There are three reasons for this. First, dynamic linking allows the host to retain fine-grain control over what mobile programs can do. If a program cannot refer to the operation that opens local files, it cannot open local files. Second, dynamic linking allows the program to use the same names for identical operations for different hosts. For example, the name open() can be used while executing on any host to refer to the procedure used to open local files. Third, the same program could visit different hosts every time it is run.

Dynamic linking provides functionality that is necessary for secure flexible use of mobile programs but it introduces a new class of runtime errors - unbound procedure names. Dynamically linked static programs can avoid this problem by making sure that all the procedures that a program might refer to are available; only the actual linking is delayed till runtime.[2] It is still possible to have access-control/authentication errors but

---

* This research was supported by ARPA under contract #F19628-94-C-0057, Syracuse subcontract #353-1427

[2] Unbound procedure names can occur even on a single host, if the environment has changed since the program was last processed by the linker. This can happen, for example, after a new version of a shared library has been installed.

that is not because the program can not name the procedure for an operation; it just does not have the right to perform the operation. Linkers for mobile programs do not know where the program might be executed and, therefore, are unable to provide a similar guarantee.

There are two approaches for dealing with this problem. The first is to make sure that the execution environment on every host is exactly identical. This restriction is stronger than requiring that every host provide a well-known interface (for example, the Java^{TM} [10] API or Telescript [23]). Instead it requires that every environment provide nothing else. This would eliminate an important reason for program mobility. For example, a program that searches distributed data repositories can improve its performance by migrating to the repositories, performing the search on-site using local repository-specific procedures that can efficiently process the data in its native form and returning the result to the requesting site.

The second, and a more flexible, approach is to accept these failures as yet another class of failures possible in a distributed system and to insert checks that localize them and allow the program to take corrective action. This can be achieved by requiring that dynamic linking operations be performed only as a part of a change-execution-site operation (which we refer to as go). The operation succeeds iff valid bindings can be found for all names that the program could possibly refer to while executing on the target host. Else the operation is aborted and the execution continues on the source host with either an error code or an exception (depending on the language). The program can take corrective action by seeking an alternative site or using an alternative way of accessing the site (e.g. using an remote interface with lesser functionality).

The second approach requires identification of the set of names that the program could possibly refer to while executing on the target host. This has to be done for every call to go in the program. There are three ways in which this could be done. The first and the simplest alternative is to require that a valid binding for every name in the program is available on each execution site. In general, this can succeed if and only if all environments are identical. But that defeats the purpose. The second alternative is to require the user to do the identification. For simple programs, this could work well but for more complicated programs, especially programs with deep call-graphs, it could be difficult. The third alternative is to use compiler analysis.

In this chapter, we present a compiler-directed technique. We use interprocedural analysis to identify the set of names that must be linked at each call to go (we refer to these as *linksets*). Calls to go embedded in procedures that are called from multiple sites pose a problem for a compile-time approach. It is not possible to distinguish between different call-sites of the enclosing procedure. This forces the analysis to be overly conservative and include names from paths corresponding to all call-sites. Since programs can contain calls to site-specific procedures, linking for fairly simple programs cannot be completed (see Figure 1 for an example). We use a combination of runtime and compile-time techniques to identify the calling context and to link only the names needed in that context. An explicit goal of our technique is to perform analyses that might be expensive only at compile-time and to defer only simple processing to run-time.

We first present a simple version of the technique that assumes all code that could contain a go is compiled together. That is, all the code that is to be linked in dynamically

```
proc execute_on_A()                    proc clean_and_go(string hostname)
   cleanup_and_go("A");                   finalize_local_state();
   execute_A_specific_fn();               go(hostname);
end                                       initialize_on_new_host();
                                       end
proc execute_on_B()
   cleanup_and_go("B");
   execute_B_specific_fn();
end
```

Fig. 1. A simple program that cannot be completely linked if calling context is ignored.

does not contain a call to go. We then relax this constraint and show how separately compiled mobile code can be dealt with. This also allows our technique to deal with *library sites* [22]. Library sites are an intriguing idea - these are sites that provide pre-compiled mobile code that can be picked up by mobile programs for execution on other sites. For example, an organization with multiple hosts could provide a library site which provides code needed to access data on all hosts belonging to the organization. We then discuss language constructs that can be used to control the behavior of dynamic linking and the implications of some of the constructs for application structure.

2   Linking Mobile Programs With Non-Mobile Code

The basic idea of our technique is quite simple. For every call to go, determine the set of calls to go that are *visible* from it. We say program point B is visible from program point A iff there exists at least one path from A to B in the control-flow graph that has no call to go; calls to go are said to *hide* the code that they dominate (in the sense of dominators in control-flow graphs [24]). We refer to the set of gos visible from a particular go as its *departure-set*. If the program arrives at a host by this go and it does not terminate on this host, it will depart from the host via one of the calls in the departure-set. For every go, we compute the set of names referred to on any path between itself and its departure-set. If the language does not allow procedure calls, we are done. This set of names is the linkset at the go in question. For realistic languages, this simple scheme runs into the problem of preserving the calling context. Calls to go embedded in procedures that are called from multiple sites are the primary problem as it is not possible to distinguish between different call-sites of the enclosing procedure. This forces the analysis to be overly conservative and include names from paths corresponding to all call-sites. Since programs can contain calls to site-specific procedures, linking for fairly simple programs cannot be complete (see Figure 1 for an example). To get around this problem, we use compiler analysis to generate the linksets for program fragments and simple runtime support that uses information from the execution-stack to quickly construct the complete linkset for any particular go.

In this section, we describe our proposed technique. We first describe the program representation used for the compiler analysis. We then present the analysis algorithm and the data structure that is generated based on the information collected. This data structure is used at runtime by the dynamic linker. Finally, we describe how the complete linkset for a go is constructed at runtime. We use a running example to illustrate the analysis as well as the dynamic linking procedure.

2.1 Program representation

For this section, we make three assumptions about the language: (1) programs can move only by using an explicit go, (2) programs are first-order and (3) all the code that might contain a go is compiled together; none of the code that is dynamically linked has an embedded go. We shall remove the third assumption in the next section. Extending our analysis to programs that use higher-order functions or to programs that can move without an explicit operation is beyond the scope of this chapter.

We use a modified version of the *full-program representation* (FPR) introduced by Agrawal et al [1, 2]. In our version, a program is represented by a directed multigraph; nodes correspond to program points and edges correspond to a control-flow path or paths between program points. There are five kinds of nodes: a pair of *entry* and *exit* nodes for every procedure; a pair of *call* and *resume* nodes for every call-site and a *go* node for every call to go. Dummy entry and exit nodes are inserted for functions that are to be linked dynamically. For every call-site, two edges are inserted: (1) an edge between the call node corresponding to the call-site and the entry node corresponding to the called procedure and (2) an edge between the exit node corresponding to the called procedure and the resume node corresponding to the call-site. For procedures that are to be linked dynamically, an edge is inserted between the corresponding entry node and the exit node. This encodes the assumption that there is no call to go within these procedures. In addition, an edge is inserted between a pair of nodes iff there exists at least one path in the control-flow graph which does not pass through any of the other nodes. More concretely, an edge is inserted between a pair of nodes iff there is at least one path between the two nodes that does not contain a procedure call or a call to go. For nodes i and j, the edge (i, j) represents the code corresponding to all paths in the control-flow graph between the corresponding program points.

We illustrate the program representation using an example. Figure 2 contains our running example. The corresponding program representation is shown in Figure 3. Note that each edge corresponds to the group of control-flow paths between the two nodes it connects. For example, the edge between *A_entry* and *call1* consists of the statement i = 0 and the edge between *res1* and *call2* consists of code in *frag1* as well as the loop header. Also note that each basic block can be part of more than one paths and, therefore, can be included in the code corresponding to more than one edge. For example, the header for the while loop appears in three edges: $(res1, call2)$, $(res3, call2)$, and $(res4, call2)$ corresponding to the initial entry, the loop-back from if branch and the loop-back from the else branch respectively.

In the next subsection, we present the analysis algorithm.

```
Proc A()                                    Proc B()
   i = 0;                                      ......    - - - - - - - - -  frag3
   B();          - - - - - - - - -  cs1       go(....); - - - - - - - - -  go1
                                              ......    - - - - - - - - -  frag4
   ........      - - - - - - - - - frag1      end
   while (i > 100)
      C();       - - - - - - - - -  cs2      Proc D()
                                                B();    - - - - - - - - -  cs6
      ........   - - - - - - - - -  frag2
      if (condition)                            ......  - - - - - - - - -  frag5
         D();    - - - - - - - - -  cs3       end
      else
         E();    - - - - - - - - -  cs4      Proc E()
      endif
      i++;                                      ......  - - - - - - - - -  frag6
   endwhile;                                  end
   D();          - - - - - - - - -  cs5
end
```

Fig. 2. Running example. The cs*i* annotations mark the call-sites, the frag*i* annotations mark code fragments that have no calls and no gos.

2.2 Analysis algorithm

The basic intent of the algorithm is clear enough - collect all names that occur on all paths between a go and its departure-set. The primary problem is preserving the calling context for calls to go embedded in multiply-called procedures. This problem is illustrated in Figure 4. If the calling context is not taken into consideration, the linkset for the top go consists of the names occurring in the blocks of code corresponding to edges 1, 2 and 3. Since the code corresponding to edges 2 and 3 may never be executed on the same host, it is possible that no host will provide the procedures referred to in both links.

To resolve this problem, we do not create complete linksets at compile-time. Instead, we partition the paths between a go and a member of its departure-set into a set of segments using resume nodes as separators. In Figure 4, this results in three segments, corresponding to edges 1, 2 and 3. Intuitively, each segment corresponds to the portion of the path that lies entirely within a single procedure.[3] The compiler analysis computes the linksets for individual segments. It also marks if the segment ends in a go node or a resume node. Intuitively, this indicates whether this is the final segment in a path. The complete linkset for a go is constructed at runtime by threading together the linksets for individual fragments. At runtime, the linker determines the calling context

---

[3] This intuition is *precise* only if there are no calls to procedures that do not have a go as the the first statement. In other cases, there is some merging of paths between procedures, but the intuition is nevertheless helpful.

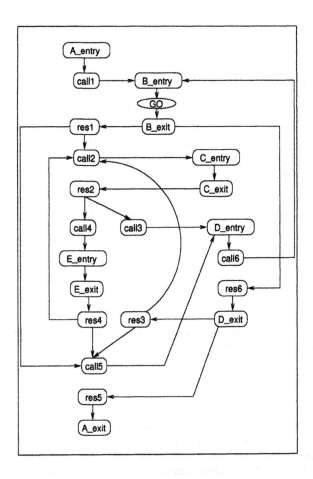

Fig. 3. Program representation for the running example.

either by inspecting the return addresses on the runtime-stack or by inspecting a call-stack maintained separately. It walks backward over the stack. For each call-site, the associated linkset is collected. The walk continues till either it reaches the final segment of a path or it reaches the bottom of the stack. In Figure 4, if the go occurs when called from the left-hand-side, the linksets for edges 1 and 2 are collected; if the go occurs when called from the right-hand-side, the linksets for edges 1 and 3 are collected.

The algorithm to construct the linksets for path segments is presented in Figure 5. We would like to draw attention to some aspects of the algorithm. This algorithm computes a set of names for every node in the program representation graph. Only the sets corresponding to go nodes and resume nodes and root_nodes are used to create the linksets. The sets corresponding to call and entry nodes are computed for algorithmic convenience and are propagated to parent nodes (if a parent exists). The sets corresponding to exit nodes are always empty. Root_nodes are entry nodes for procedures

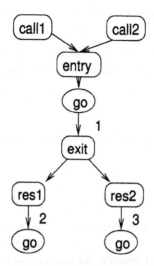

Fig. 4. Simplified example to illustrate the calling context problem.

that are not called in the code being compiled. Linksets for root_nodes are used for initial linking on the node that the program begins execution. They are also needed to handle separately compiled code. Note that the set of names corresponding to a go node are never propagated. However, the set of names corresponding to a resume node could be propagated to the corresponding *call* node. This is needed if it is possible that during the execution of the procedure called at that site, there might be no call to go and control might reach the resume point while the program is still at the current host. This condition is represented in the algorithm by the call to visible(entry(p), exit(p)) which determines if the exit node of the procedure is visible from its entry. Recall that we say program point B is visible from program point A iff there exists at least one path from A to B in the control-flow graph that has no call to go. If there exists no such a path, the set of names for the resume node is not propagated. The reason for this is simple: if there is no path through a called procedure P that does not contain a go, the program will migrate to another site before this call returns. In that case, there is no need for binding names that are visible from the resume point which implies there is no need to include the names in the linkset for this resume node in the linkset of any of the calls to go that precede the call under consideration.

   Another point to note is that procedures that are not available during the compilation (that is, the procedures that are to be dynamically linked) are assumed to be empty for the purpose of this algorithm. These procedures are compiled separately and their entry nodes contain the set of names that need to be linked for their execution.

   To illustrate the operation of the algorithm, we present the linksets for the running example (Figure 2) in Table 1. Note that two of the resume nodes, res2 and res4 do not need linksets as the procedures called at these sites, $C()$ and $E()$ respectively, are not mobile (their execution cannot encounter a go). The names in the code fragments frag4 and frag5 are dominated by either a call to go or a call to a procedure that calls go. This is the reason why they do not appear in the linkset for res1. All other

Program point	Linkset
go1	nm(frag4)
res1	nm(frag1) ∪ {C} ∪ nm(frag2) ∪ nm(frag3) ∪ nm(frag6)
res3	{C} ∪ nm(frag2) ∪ nm(frag3) ∪ nm(frag6)
res5	φ
res6	nm(frag5)

Table 1. Linksets for the running example. The *nm* function is used for illustrative convenience. It returns the list of names in a code fragment.

code is visible from res1.

It is easy to see that this algorithm terminates. The linksets for all nodes are initialized to φ. Each iteration of the propagation phase visits every node exactly once and each iteration (except the last one) increases the linkset of at least one node by at least one name. The number of iterations cannot be more than the product of the number of nodes and the number of names. This is an extremely loose bound. For non-recursive programs, the algorithm needs exactly two iterations. For recursive programs, it needs one iteration more than the maximum *syntactic* depth of recursion: programs that have only self-recursive procedures take two iterations, programs with at most pair-wise recursive procedures take three iterations and so on. Each iteration is a depth-first traversal of the directed acyclic graph corresponding to the program. The visited markers ensure that no node is visited twice in the same iteration.

In the next subsection, we present the algorithm used by the linker to construct complete linksets.

2.3 Constructing complete linksets at runtime

The compiler analysis described in the previous subsection generates two data structures for the linker: an array of structures corresponding to resume nodes and an array of structures corresponding to go nodes. Each structure contains two fields: the linkset containing the names that have to be linked and a boolean indicating whether this linkset is terminal. The boolean is extracted from the reaches_exit field of the corresponding node (see Figures 5 and 6 for a description of how this is computed). The algorithm for the linker is given in Figure 7. The do_link() procedure does the actual linking. For every new procedure linked, it extracts the linkset from the entry node and checks if valid bindings for all names in names can be found in the execution environment available on the current host. If this check fails for some reason, it returns an error_code (or an exception if the language supports exceptions).

To illustrate the operation of the algorithm, we consider the two calls to D() in the running example (Figure 2). For the go embedded in the call at cs3, the complete linkset consists of the union of the linksets for go1, res6 and res3; the linkset for the other call at cs5 is the union of the linksets for go1, res6 and res5.

```
function successors(node p)
  returns the set of nodes that are successors of p
function names(node p, node q)
  returns the set of names referred to in code
                         associated with (p,q)
function entry(node p)
  if p is a call node
    returns singleton set with corr. entry node
  else
    returns singleton set with entry node of enclosing proc
function exit(node p)
  if p is a call node
    returns singleton set with corr. exit node
  else
    returns singleton set with entry node of enclosing proc
function resume(node p)
  if p is a call node
    returns singleton set with corr. resume node
  else
    returns singleton set with entry node of enclosing proc
function proc(node p)
  if p is a call or resume node
    returns singleton set with name of the corr. proc.
  else
    returns singleton set with name of enclosing proc.
function visible(node p, node q)
  if q is visible from p
    returns true
  else
    returns false
```

Fig. 5. Algorithm to compute the linksets (part I).

3 Linking Mobile Programs With Mobile Code

In the previous section, we assumed that the procedures to be linked dynamically did not have a call to go. In this section, we relax that assumption. This allows us to deal with the possibility of *library* sites; sites that provide code to be picked up by programs for execution on other nodes. We first describe what new problem is introduced by allowing dynamically linked procedures to move. Next, we describe our solution and show that it works.

The main problem introduced by allowing dynamically linked code to move is that it is no longer possible to accurately compute the predicate $visible(p, q)$ which indicates whether there exists at least one path between nodes p and q that does not have a go. This problem does not arise for dynamically linked code that can not move – the analysis algorithm can safely and accurately model the missing code by a null statement (as mentioned in section 2.1). As a result, the compiler analysis is no longer able to

```
function linkset(node p)
  if (p->visited ≠ 0) return p->linkset;
  p->visited ← 1
  prev_val = p->linkset;
  if (p->nodetype ==  entry
         || p->nodetype ==  go
         || p->nodetype ==  resume)
       succset ← successors(p);
       foreach q in succset
           p->linkset ← p->linkset ∪ linkset(q) ∪ names(p,q)
  else if (p->nodetype ==  call)
       if (visible(entry(p),exit(p)))
           p->linkset ← p->linkset ∪ proc(p)
                        ∪ entry(p)->linkset ∪ resume(p)->linkset
       else
           p->linkset ← p->linkset ∪ proc(p)
                        ∪ entry(p)->linkset
  else /* p->nodetype ==  exit */
       p->linkset ← φ
  p->reaches_exit ← visible(p,exit(p))
  if (not_equal(prev_val,p->linkset))
       changed ← 1
  return p->linkset
end


procedure compute_linksets()
    foreach p in allnodes
       p->linkset ← φ
    changed ← 1
    while (changed == 1)
       changed ← 0
       foreach p in allnodes
           p->visited ← 0
       /* a root_node is the entry for a proc. that
        * is not called in the code being compiled */
       foreach node in root_nodes
           linkset(node)
    endwhile
end
```

Fig. 6. Algorithm to compute the linksets (part II).

```
structure {  nameset names; boolean terminal; } res_pts[numres];
structure {  nameset names; } go_pts[numgo];

/* res_seq contains the sequence of resume node identifiers.
 * the order corresponds to walking backward in the stack */
function dyn_link(sequence res_seq)
    item res;
    nameset names;

    if (res_seq == NULL) return SUCCESS
    res ← car(res_seq);  res_seq ← cdr(res_seq);
    names ← φ;
    while (res->terminal ≠ 0)
        names ← names ∪ res->names;
        if (res_seq == NULL) break;
        res ← car(res_seq);  res_seq ← cdr(res_seq);
    endwhile

    if (do_link(names) == SUCCESS)
        return SUCCESS
    else
        return error_code
end
```

Fig. 7. Algorithm used by the dynamic linker to construct complete linksets.

determine when the linkset for a resume node should propagated to the call node and beyond.

One possible solution is to delay linking code that may be mobile to just before it is invoked. But that would violate the guarantee we would like to offer: that linking failures can happen only at calls to go. Another possible solution is ignore the fact that the linked code can contain gos and to use the analysis described in the previous section. This would result in possibly more names being linked at a go than otherwise – since linksets are possibly being propagated further than they should be. This might appear to be a conservative approximation but it is not. Consider the example in Figure 8. Assume that $B()$ is the procedure to be linked dynamically. If we ignore the fact that $B()$ might contain a go, we will propagate magic_host_specific_code to the linkset corresponding to go(ordinary_host). When go(ordinary_host) is executed, the linker will fail trying to find magic_host_specific_code on ordinary_host. We propose a third alternative and show that it preserves the fail-only-at-go guarantee and avoids the problem mentioned above.

The basic idea is simple. We cannot safely and accurately propagate linksets at compile-time; we cannot delay linking till the linked procedure is invoked; all linking must happen at gos. Therefore, the only option left is to delay the propagation of linksets till one of the gos that they are visible from. This is similar in spirit to our scheme of reconstructing complete linksets at runtime.

Available at compile-time	**Unavailable at compile-time**

```
Proc A()
   go(ordinary_host);
   B();
   magic_host_specific_code()
end
```

```
Proc B()
   go(magic_host);
end
```

Fig. 8. Example to illustrate that moving names past gos is unsafe.

We modify the program representation described in section 2.1 such that *no* edge is inserted between the dummy entry and exit nodes that represent procedures not available at compile-time. By doing so, we encode the assumption that all control-flow paths in a procedure that is unavailable at compile-time have at least one call to go. As a result, linksets are never propagated past calls to unavailable procedures. We extend the compiler analysis to determine the resume nodes that are visible from each call-site of an unavailable procedure. In addition, each name in a linkset is annotated with the list of its call-sites that are visible from the corresponding program point. We extend the data structures generated by the analysis to include an array of structures corresponding to call-sites of unavailable procedures. Each structure contains the set mentioned above and a boolean that indicates whether this procedure contains at least one path from its entry to its exit that does not contain a call to go. The algorithm presented in Figure 5 already computes this predicate at each call-site; the only extension is to store the value for use at runtime. We extend the linking algorithm such that whenever a new procedure is linked in, the corresponding boolean value is checked. If it indicates that the exit of the procedure is not visible from the entry, our compile-time assumption is valid and the operations described in Figure 7 suffice. If this is not the case and there is at least one path between the entry and the exit of the procedure, the compile-time assumption is invalid and the linksets should have been propagated. To handle this case, the linker inspects the set of resume nodes associated with this call-site and adds the linksets corresponding to all of them to the set of names to be linked.

It is quite easy to see that this scheme preserves the *fail-only-at-go* guarantee and that at each go, the linkset constructed does not contain any name that it would not have contained if all mobile procedures were available at compile-time. The first part is obvious. To assure ourselves about the second part, we need to observe a couple of points about linksets and the visibility property. First, a name appears in a linkset iff a reference to the name is visible from the program point the linkset is associated with. Second, visibility is transitive. If a procedure P is to be linked at a go site G, then at least one call-site of P is visible from G. If the exit of P is visible from its entry, then all program points visible from the exit are also visible from the entry and transitively from G. Therefore, if the procedure was available during compile-time, all the names in the linksets corresponding to all resume nodes visible from the call-site would be included in the linkset for G and would be linked whenever control reaches G. This is exactly what happens with our scheme.

4 Language Constructs and Application Structure

In the previous sections, we have described algorithms to determine what needs to be linked at particular points in a mobile program. In this section, we discuss language constructs that allow the programmer to control the behavior of the linking procedure. Our desire is to discuss the alternatives for user-directed linking – how much control can be given to the user without forcing her to explicitly specify linking operations.

There are four flavors of dynamic linking that might be useful for mobile programs, two of which require no user directives and two that can be controlled by user directives. To illustrate the differences between these schemes, we present code, under each scheme, for searching multiple information repositories for data that satisfies some user-specified predicate.

Local-only: linking done at a site is valid only at that site. When a program departs from a site, all bindings created at that site are voided. This form of linking is used by Java, Telescript and Agent-TCL [11]. This guarantees that departing programs do not retain bindings to local operations. However, this works only if the code that is to be linked in does not contain a go. Also, library sites are not possible. Figure 9 presents the multi-site search program under a *local-only* linking regime. At each site, the search operation is rebound to a locally provided routine that understands the local data format. Note that the linking technique described in section 2 can be used for programs that use *local-only* linking. Local-only linking can be easily extended to remote code servers. In this case, code retrieved and linked at a site is used only while the program is at that site. Once the program leaves this site, the binding is voided and has to be re-established at the new site.

```
function search_multiple_sites(sitelist,predicate,home)
        results ← null;
        foreach site in sitelist
            go(site);
            tmp ← search(predicate);
            results ← combine(results,tmp);
        end
        go(home);
        return results;
    end
```

Fig. 9. Version of multi-site search using local-only linking.

code-with-a-reference-is-sticky: this scheme allows a program to retain bindings for procedure names that have at least one reference – either an activation record for the procedure is on the stack or a pointer to the procedure is stored in a data-structure on the heap. Bindings for all other names is voided when the program departs from a site. If at a subsequent migration, there are no references to the procedure in question (the activation record has been popped off the stack or the data-structure referring to the procedure can no longer be reached from by the program), the binding is eliminated and the code is garbage-collected. This form of linking permits library sites. Elimination of the binding when it is no longer in use allows programs to pick up different copies of the procedures by visiting different library sites. This would be useful, for example, if library sites were associated with specific organizations and provided the code needed to access data on all execution sites belonging to the organization. The program would pick up a local version of the procedure whenever it visits hosts belonging to a new organization. Figure 10 presents an extended version of the multi-site search program which uses a *code-with-a-reference-is-sticky* linking scheme. This program is aware of organizational boundaries and uses to pick up a new version of the `search` operation for each organization it visits. Note that with a small extension to keep track of references to procedure names, the linking technique described in section 3 can be used for programs that use *code-with-a-reference-is-sticky* linking. This form of linking can be easily extended to handle remote code servers. In this case, remotely linked code is used as long there is a reference to it. Once the last reference is lost, it is garbage collected like other code. As far as we know, no system currently provides this form of linking.

```
function search_multiple_orgs(orglist,predicate,home)
        results ← null;
        foreach org in orglist
                orghome ← get_org_home(org);
                go(orghome);
                tmp ← search_org(org,predicate);
                results ← combine(results,tmp);
        end
        go(home);
        return results;
end

function search_org(org,predicate)
        results ← null;
        sitelist ← getsitelist(org);
        foreach site in sitelist
                go(site);
                /* inlined search code */
                results ← combine(results,....);
        end
        return results;
end
```

Fig. 10. Version of multi-site search using code-with-reference-is-sticky linking. This program is aware of organizational boundaries and uses to pick up a new version of the `search` operation for each organization it visits.

user-specifies-sticky-links: the idea here is that the user can specify which names once bound should be bound forever. Programs that need to pick up similar procedures from multiple library sites would have to name them differently. The main difference between this linking scheme and a scheme in which the user completely controls the linking is that sticky links cannot be rebound, user-specified linking can rebind names. Figure 11 presents a version of the multi-site search program which searches two distributed repositories, each repository can be searched using the same code. Note that with a small extension to keep track of stickiness annotations, the linking technique described in section 3 can be used for programs that use *user-specifies-sticky-links* linking. As far as we know, no system currently provides this form of linking.

```
function search_two_repositories(rep1,rep2,predicate)
    sticky proc search1(), search2();
    results ← null;
    sitelist ← get_site_list(rep1);
    foreach site in sitelist
        go(site);
        tmp ← search1(predicate);
        results ← combine(results,tmp);
    end

    sitelist ← get_site_list(rep2);
    foreach site in sitelist
        go(site);
        tmp ← search2(predicate);
        results ← combine(results,tmp);
    end
    go(home);
    return results;
end
```

Fig. 11. Version of multi-site search using user-specifies-sticky-links linking. Each of search1() and search2() are bound on the first server visited in the corresponding repository.

user-specified linking: in this case, the user explicitly specifies which names are to be bound to which operations on which sites. An example of this would be the net_import() primitive provided by Obliq [4] (as well the NetObj.Import primitive provided by Network Objects [3] that has been used to implement it). While this provides the greatest flexibility of all schemes, a programmer can rebind names as and when needed, it requires her to manage all linking operations. Figure 12 presents a version of multi-site search program that uses one form of *user-specified linking* to rebind the search operation depending on the characteristics of the site.

```
function
search_multiple_sites(sitelist,predicate,home,codeserver)
        results ← null;
        foreach site in sitelist
                go(site);
                site_attr ← get_site_attr();
                bind(search,codeserver,site_attr);
                tmp ← search(predicate);
                results ← combine(results,tmp);
        end
        go(home);
        return results;
end
```

Fig. 12. Version of multi-site search using user-specified linking. This program uses the flexibility of user-specified linking to retrieve site-specific code from a central code server.

5 Related Work

Various forms and implementations of user-specified linking have been described in the literature. At the simplest level, the *eval(env,expr)* primitive that has long been available allows the user to control the bindings for the free variables in the expression *expr*. Obliq [4] and Network Objects [3] allow the programmer to query a name-server and obtain a reference which can then be bound to a name in the program. The fragmented-objects model [19, 20] proposed by Shapiro includes a detailed interface for binding and unbinding references in a distributed system. First-class environments [9] can also be used for various scenarios in whch user-specified linking might be useful. Miller&Rozas [14] propose to use first-class environments to remove the need for a distinguished top-level interaction environment for Scheme. Jagannathan [13] proposes a *reification* operator that returns the current environment as a first-class object and a *reflection* operator that merges a set of bindings from a named environment into the current environment. Queinnec&DeRoure [17] propose a chain-environment function which can compose environments. This can be used to share common environments between different programs/users. These schemes provide varying degrees of flexibility and convenience but all of them require the user to explicit manage the linking.

There has also been considerable work on efficient (and safe) implementation of dynamic linking, particularly in the context of shared libraries and kernel extensions [7, 12, 15, 16, 21]. These schemes focus on the linking procedure and the performance of the linked code. They do not address the issue of determining what needs to be linked.

Dynamic linking issues for mobile programs, in particular the need to be able to name procedures that access resources local to an execution site, have been previously considered by Cardelli [4] and Knabe [8]. Knabe [8] proposes that certain functions be specified to be *ubiquitous* - that is, they are available on all sites and that all remaining code should be carried by the mobile program. This does not allow for site-specific procedures. The Obliq language presented in [4] handles this problem by packaging the execution environment available at a site as an object and using its methods to access the procedures available at that site. The responsibility of determining whether the environment available on a host provides all names needed by the program resides with the user. An Obliq-like language with types would, however, be able to use runtime type-checking to ensure that the type of the object encapsulating the execution environment matches what the mobile program expects to find at the site [5]. This would ensure that link errors occured only during a change-execution-site operation. The environment expected by the mobile program can be computed as a part of compile-time type-checking.

6 Summary

In this chapter, we have presented a compiler-directed technique for safe dynamic linking for mobile programs. Our technique guarantees that linking failures can occur only when a program arrives at a new execution site and that this failure can be delivered to the program as an error code or an exception. We use interprocedural analysis to identify the set of names that must be linked at the different sites the program executes on. We use a combination of runtime and compile-time techniques to identify the calling context and to link only the names needed in that context. Our technique is able to handle recursive programs as well as separately compiled code that may itself be able to move. We discuss language constructs for controlling the behavior of dynamic linking and the implication of some of these constructs for application structure.

Acknowledgments

We would like to thank Shamik Sharma for providing a sorely needed sounding board for our ideas. We would also like to thank M. Ranganathan for several discussions. The algorithms presented in Figures 5, 6 and 7 were formatted using the code.sty style file written by Olin Shivers.

References

1. G. Agrawal, A. Acharya, and J. Saltz. An interprocedural framework for placement of asynchronous I/O operations. In *Proceedings of the 1996 International Conference on Supercomputing*, pages 358–65, May 1996.
2. G. Agrawal, J. Saltz, and R. Das. Interprocedural partial redundancy elimination and its application to distributed memory compilation. In *Proceedings of the ACM SIGPLAN'95 Conference on Programming Language Design and Implementation*, pages 258–69, Jun 1995.
3. A. Birrell, G. Nelson, S. Owicki, and E. Wobber. Network objects. In *Proceedings of the 14th ACM Symposium on Operating System Principles*, pages 217–30, Dec 1993.
4. L. Cardelli. A Language With Distributed Scope. In *Proceedings of the 22nd ACM Symposium on Principles of Programming Languages*, Jan. 1995.
5. L. Cardelli. Personal communication, Nov 1996.

6. L. Cardelli. *Mobile Computation*, chapter unknown. Springer Verlag, 1997.
7. C. Cowan, T. Autrey, C. Krasic, C. Pu, and J. Walpole. Fast concurrent dynamic linking for an adaptive operating system. In *Proceedings of the Third International Conference on Configurable Distributed Systems*, pages 108–15, May 1996.
8. F.C.Knabe. Language and compiler support for mobile agents. PhD Thesis, Carnegie Mellon University, Nov. 1995.
9. D. Gelernter and S. Jagannathan. Environments as first class objects. In *Proceedings of the 14th Annual ACM Symposium on Principles of Programming Languages*, pages 98–110, Jan 1987.
10. J. Gosling and H. McGilton. The Java Language Environment White Paper, 1995.
11. R. Gray. Agent TCL: A Flexible and Secure Mobile-agent System. In *Proceedings of the Fourth Annual Tcl/Tk Workshop (TCL 96)*, July 1996.
12. E. Ho, C. Wei-Chau, and L. Leung. Optimizing the performance of dynamically-linked programs. In *Proceedings of the 1995 USENIX Technical Conference*, pages 225–33, Jan 1995.
13. S. Jagannathan. Dynamic modules in higher-order languages. In *Proceedings of the 1994 International Conference on Computer Languages*, pages 74–87, May 1994.
14. J. Miller and G. Rozas. Free variables and first-class environments. *Lisp and Symbolic Computation*, 4(2):107–41, Apr 1991.
15. M. Nelson and G. Hamilton. High performance dynamic linking through caching. In *Proceedings of the Summer 1993 USENIX Conference*, pages 253–65, 1993.
16. D. Orr, J. Bonn, J. Lepreau, and R. Mecklenburg. Fast and flexible shared libraries. In *Proceedings of the Summer 1993 USENIX Conference*, pages 237–51, 1993.
17. C. Queinnec and D. D. Roure. Sharing code through first-class environments. In *Proceedings of the 1996 International Conference on Functional Programming*, May 1996.
18. M. Ranganathan, A. Acharya, S. Sharma, and J. Saltz. Network-aware Mobile Programs. In *Proceedings of the USENIX 1997 Annual Technical Conference*, pages 91–104, Jan 1997.
19. M. Shapiro. Flexible bindings for fine-grain distributed objects. Technical Report 2007, Institut National de Recherche et en Automatique, August 1993.
20. M. Shapiro. A binding protocol for distributed shared objects. In *Proceedings of the 14th International Conference on Distributed Systems*, Jun 1994.
21. E. Sirer, M. Fiucynski, P. Pardyak, and B. Bershad. Safe dynamic linking in an extensible operating system. In *The First Workshop on Compiler Support for System Software*, Feb 1996.
22. J. White. Talk at the DAGS'96 Workshop on Transportable Agents, Sep 1996.
23. J. White. Telescript Technology: Mobile Agents, 1996. *http://www.genmagic.com-/Telescript/Whitepapers*.
24. M. Wolfe. *High Performance Compilers for Parallel Computing*. Addison-Wesley, 1995.

Adaptive Compression of Syntax Trees and Iterative Dynamic Code Optimization: Two Basic Technologies for Mobile Object Systems

Michael Franz

Abstract. We are designing and implementing a flexible infrastructure for mobile-object systems. Two fundamental innovations distinguish our architecture from other proposed solutions. First, our representation of mobile code is based on adaptive compression of syntax trees. Not only is this representation more than twice as dense as Java byte-codes, but it also encodes semantic information on a much higher level than linear abstract-machine representations such as p-code or Java byte-codes. The extra structural information that is contained in our mobile-code format is directly beneficial for advanced code optimizations. Second, our architecture achieves superior run-time performance by integrating the activity of generating executable code into the operating system itself. Rather than being an auxiliary function performed off-line by a stand-alone compiler, code generation constitutes a central, indispensable service in our system. Our integral code generator has two distinct modes of operation: instantaneous load-time translation and continuous dynamic re-optimization. In contrast to just-in-time compilers that translate individual procedures on a call-by-call basis, our system's integral code-generator translates complete code-closures in a single burst during loading. This has the apparent disadvantage that it introduces a minor delay prior to the start of execution. As a consequence, to some extent we have to favor compilation speed over code quality at load time. But then, the second operation mode of our embedded code generator soon corrects this shortcoming. Central to our run-time architecture is a thread of activity that continually optimizes all of the already executing software in the background. Since this is strictly a re-compilation of already existing code, and since it occurs completely in the background, speed is not critical, so that aggressive, albeit slow, optimization techniques can be employed. Upon completion, the previously executing version of the same code is supplanted by the newly generated one and re-optimization starts over. By constructing globally optimized code-images from mobile software components, our architecture is able to reconcile dynamic composability with the run-time efficiency of monolithic applications.

1 Introduction

This chapter introduces two new basic technologies for mobile object systems: a highly compact representation for portable code and a run-time architecture that reconciles the traditionally conflicting goals of modularity and performance through the use of a dynamic code optimizer embedded within the operating system. The two technologies are complementary to each other: while the high semantic level of the machine-independent representation makes it particularly well suited for supporting code optimizations, its conciseness accelerates I/O operations, partially compensating for the effort of load-time code generation. The unusual compactness of object files also facilitates their retention in a memory cache, leading to more efficient optimization cycles later.

In the following, we give an overview of each of the two technologies, pointing to further publications and on-line documentation where appropriate. The *Slim Binary* mobile-code format [FK96] is the outgrowth of the author's doctoral dissertation work [Fra94a, Fra94b], while the system architecture incorporating dynamic optimization is ongoing research at UC Irvine. We also report on the current state of our implementation, specifically the availability of an integrated authoring and execution environment [Oberon] for mobile software components that is based on the Oberon System [WG89, WG92], and a family of plug-in extensions [Juice] for the *Netscape Navigator* and *Microsoft Internet Explorer* World Wide Web browsers that recreate this execution environment so that Oberon-based components can be used within these browsers.

2   Representing Mobile Code

In the course of the past six years, the author has designed and successfully implemented a portability scheme for modular software that is based on dynamic code generation at load time [FL91, Fra94a, Fra94b, FK96]. At the core of a suite of implementations is a machine-independent program representation called *slim binaries*[1]. This representation is based on adaptive compression of syntax trees and achieves exceptional information densities. For example, it is more than twice as dense as Java byte-codes. In fact, the author knows of no denser program representation; standard data compression algorithms such as LZW [Wel84] applied to either source code or object code (for any architecture, including the Java virtual machine) perform significantly worse than our dedicated syntax-tree-directed method (Figure 1).

Reducing the network-transfer time of mobile components (by a factor of more than two in comparison to Java byte-codes, for example) is an advantage that should not be underestimated, considering that many network connections in the near future will be wireless and consequently be restricted to small bandwidths. In such wireless networks, raw throughput rather than network latency again becomes the main bottleneck.

Taking the *Oberon System* developed by Niklaus Wirth and Jürg Gutknecht [WG89, WG92] as a starting point, the author and his graduate students have implemented a family of run-time extensible systems [Oberon] in which the slim binary format is used instead of native object code, yielding seamless cross-platform code portability. Currently, we support three different architectures: *MC68020* and *PowerPC*

---

1. The name "slim binary" was deliberately chosen to contrast "fat binary", which has been used to describe object files that contain multiple instruction sequences for different target architectures. Slim binaries provide a similar functionality as fat binaries, namely the ability to be executed on more than one hardware architecture, but they consume only a fraction of the storage space.

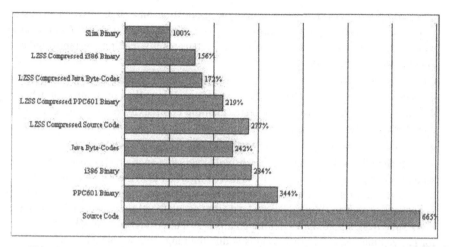

Figure 1 Relative Size of Representative Program Suite in Various Formats

under the Macintosh operating system, and *i386* under Microsoft Windows 95. In all three implementations, native object code is generated on-the-fly at load time from the slim binary representation, in a manner that is transparent to the user. From the user's perspective, "object files" simply become portable. The implemented systems support dynamic linking (with dynamic code generation) of extension code into running applications and the target-machine independent use of mobile code distributed as a slim binary across a network.

In the systems we have implemented, the time required for reading "object files" is reduced dramatically due to the compactness of the slim binary representation. This applies to code read from an external storage medium as well as to code received over a network. The time that has been saved due to reduced input overhead is then instead spent on dynamic code generation at load time, making the implemented scheme almost as fast as traditional program loading.

The interesting aspect of trading reduced input/output overhead for a greater amount of processing at load time is that hardware technology is currently evolving in its favor. Raw processor power is growing much more rapidly than the speed of input and output operations (Figure 2). Any computer application that reduces its input/output overhead at the expense of additional computations can benefit from this effect in the long run, even if the immediate performance gain doesn't seem to reward an increased algorithm complexity. Code generation happens to be a particularly good example, because processor instruction sets are not optimized for information density but have other constraints such as regularity and ease of decoding. Hence, object files are usually much larger than they need to be.

The process illustrated in Figure 2 has had the effect that dynamic code-generation at load-time has now become practical and will continue to increase its appeal. As Figure 3 illustrates, the additional cost of using slim binaries rather than native code has plunged dramatically over the last 6 years as the performance gap between processors and storage has widened. Figure 3 compares the times required for reading and dynamically compiling from slim binaries all of the applications in a large representative suite of Internet applications (a *WWW* browser, a *Telnet* application with *VT100* emulation, an electronic mail system, and further tools) versus simply reading pre-fabricated executables of the same applications.

Of course, as processors become more complex, the techniques required to generate good code for them tend to be more elaborate also. It is still an open question whether the speed of processors will grow faster than the complexity of generating adequate code for them. However, as described in the next section, the inclusion of dynamic re-optimization in our architecture makes this question largely irrelevant.

It should also be noted that the *absolute delay* that an interactive user experiences when code is generated dynamically is more important than the *relative speed* in comparison to traditional loading. On the fastest computers of our benchmarks, it takes about two seconds to simultaneously load all of the applications contained in the benchmark suite from slim binaries. Although this is still almost twice as much as is required for native binaries, the extra second is within the range that we have found users to be willing to tolerate. In return for a minimally increased application-startup time, they gain the benefit of cross-platform portability without sacrificing any run-time efficiency; all code generation occurs strictly before the execution commences.

Further, typical users of our system do *not* start all of the applications in the program suite at the same time. Quite the opposite: due to the extensible, modular structure

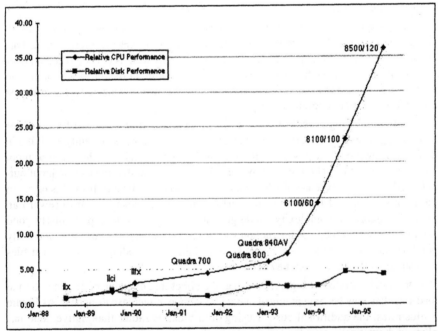

Figure 2 Different Growth Rates of Processor Power vs. I/O Speed for Different Models of the Apple Macintosh Computer Family (as Measured by the Tool Speedometer 4.02)

of our system, the incremental workload of on-the-fly code generation is usually quite small. Most of the applications are structured in such a manner that seldom-used functions are implemented separately and linked dynamically only when needed; moreover, there are many modules that are shared among different applications and need to be loaded only once. Hence, the effective throughput demanded of our on-the-fly code generator is much smaller than might be expected when extrapolating from systems based on statically-linked application programs.

2.1 The Slim Binary Representation: Some Technical Details

Unlike other program representations that have been proposed for achieving software portability, such as p-code [NAJ76] or Java byte-codes [LYJ96], the slim binary format is based on adaptive compression of syntax trees, and not on a virtual-machine representation. Every symbol in a slim-binary encoding describes a sub-tree of an abstract syntax tree in terms of all the sub-trees that precede it. During the encoding of a program, more and more such sub-trees are added to its slim-binary representation, steadily evolving the "vocabulary" that is used in the encoding of subsequent program sections.

The key idea behind this encoding is the observation that different parts of a program are often similar to each other. For example, in typical programs there are often procedures that get called over and over with practically identical parameter lists. We exploit these similarities by use of a *predictive compression algorithm* that allows to encode recurring sub-expressions in a program space-efficiently while facilitating also time-efficient decoding with simultaneous code-generation. Our compression scheme is based on adaptive methods such as LZW [Wel84] but has been tailored towards encoding abstract syntax trees rather than character streams. It also takes advantage of the *limited scope* of variables in programming languages, which allows to determinis-

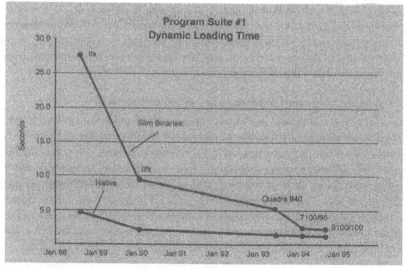

Figure 3 Time Required for Loading Representative Program Suite

tically prune entries from the compression dictionary, and uses *prediction heuristics* to achieve a denser encoding.

Adaptive compression schemes encode their input using an evolving vocabulary. In our encoding, the vocabulary initially consists of a small number of primitive operations (such as *assignment*, *addition* and *multiplication*), and of the data items appearing in the program being processed (such as *integer i* and *procedure P*). Translation of the source code into the portable intermediate representation is a two-step process (Figure 4). First, the source program is parsed and an *abstract syntax tree* and a *symbol table* are constructed. If the program contains syntax or type errors (including illegal uses of items imported from external libraries), they are discovered during this phase. After successful completion of the parsing phase, the symbol table is written to the slim binary file. It is required for placing the initial data-symbols into the vocabulary of the decoder, and for supplying type information to the code generator.

Then, the abstract syntax tree is traversed and encoded into a stream of symbols from the evolving vocabulary. The encoder processes whole sub-trees of the abstract syntax tree at a time; these roughly correspond to statements on the level of the source language. For each of the sub-trees, it searches the current vocabulary to find a sequence of symbols that expresses the same meaning. For example, the procedure call *P(i + 1)* can be represented by a combination of the operation-symbols *procedure call* and *addition*, and the data-symbols *procedure P*, *variable i*, and *constant 1*.

After encoding a sub-expression, the vocabulary is updated using adaptation and prediction heuristics. Further symbols describing variations of the expression just encoded are added to the vocabulary, and symbols referring to closed scopes are removed from it. For example, after encoding the expression *i + 1*, the special symbols *i-plus-something* and *something-plus-one* might be added. Suppose that further along in the encoding process the similar expression *i + j* were encountered, this could then be represented using only two symbols, namely *i-plus-something* and *j*. This is more space efficient, provided that the new symbol *i-plus-something* takes up less space than the two previous symbols *i* and *plus*. Using prediction heuristics, one might also add *i-minus-something* and *something-minus-one* to the vocabulary, speculating on symmetry in the program. This decision could also be made dependent on earlier observations about symmetry during the ongoing encoding session.

2.2 Advantages and Disadvantages of Slim Binaries

Using a tree-based, nonlinear representation as a software distribution format has the apparent disadvantage that the portable code cannot simply be interpreted byte-by-byte. The semantics of any particular symbol in a slim-binary-encoded instruction stream are revealed only after all symbols preceding it have been decoded. Conversely, the individual symbols in an abstract-machine representation are self-contained, permitting random access to the instruction stream as required for interpreted execution. However, in exchange for giving up the possibility of interpretation, which by its inherent lack of run-time performance is limited to low-end applications anyway, we gain several important advantages in addition to the extreme compactness already mentioned.

The tree-based nature of our distribution format constitutes a considerable advantage when the eventual target machine has a super-scalar architecture requiring

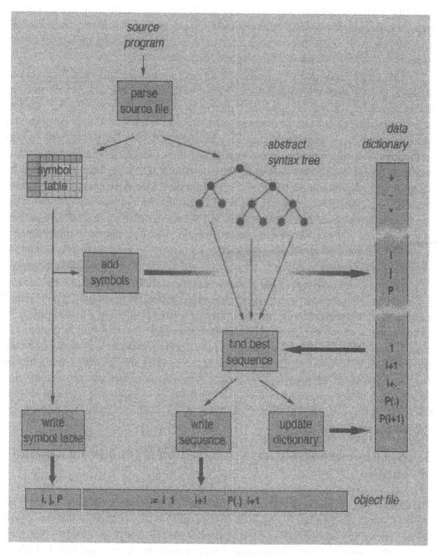

Figure 4 Translation from Source Code into a Slim Binary

advanced optimizations. Many modern code-optimizations rely on structural information that, although readily available at the syntax-tree level, is lost in the transition to linear intermediate representations such as Java byte-codes, and whose reconstruction is difficult. For example, the code for a processor that provides multiple functional units can often be improved by reordering the individual instructions so that the functional units are operating in parallel (instruction scheduling). Two instructions in the program can be exchanged if they are functionally independent of each other, and if no branch originates or terminates between them. The tree-based slim binary representation preserves the control-flow data required for this and related optimizations, giving it an edge over linear representations that require an additional time-consuming pre-processing step for extracting the needed structural information. In order to achieve the same efficiency with byte-codes, these would have to be instrumented with hints about block boundaries [Han74], which is inelegant and space-consuming.

One might argue that the presence of this extra semantic information also makes the *reverse engineering* of slim binaries easier, exposing the trade secrets of software developers. It is true that any intermediate format that preserves the abstract structure of programs can be reverse-engineered to produce a "shrouded" source program, i.e. one that contains no meaningful internal identifiers [Mac93]. However, with current technology, reverse-engineering to a similar degree is possible also from binary code and from linear byte-codes. Many of the algorithms that have been developed for object-level code-optimization [DF84, Dav86] are useful for these purposes. Moreover, the statement [DRA93] is probably correct that portable formats are such attractive targets to reverse-engineer that suitable tools will become available eventually, regardless of how difficult it is to produce such tools. It would, therefore, not make much sense to jeopardize the advantages of slim binaries in an attempt to make reverse-engineering more difficult.

As a further advantage of our mobile-code representation, unlike most linear representations, every node in a slim-binary encoded syntax tree is strongly typed, and all variable references are accompanied by symbolic scope information. This simplifies the task of *code verification*. The problem with mobile code is that it may turn out to be malicious or faulty and thereby compromise the integrity of the host system. For example, variables in private scopes must not be accessed from the "outside", but a mobile program may have been generated by a rogue compiler that explicitly allows these illegal accesses. Hence, incoming code must be analyzed for violation of type and scoping rules. For our tree-based representation, this analysis is almost trivial; for linear code, it is not.

3 A Run-Time Architecture based on Dynamic Re-Optimization

The *granularity of code generation* has a profound influence on the quality of the resulting object code. In general, large pieces of code provide more opportunities for optimizations than small ones. Traditional compilers limit their search for possible optimizations to the individual compilation unit: a recent study by Aigner and Hölzle [AH96] demonstrates how the execution times of several benchmark programs can be improved considerably simply by combining all of the source files into one large file prior to compilation. More sophisticated link-time optimization strategies, such as the Titan/Mahler system [Wal92], partially overcome this effect, as they are able to perform certain inter-module optimizations on already compiled code. However, even these advanced schemes still assume a context of static linking and are unable to optimize calls to dynamic link libraries.

As an illustration of the underlying problem, consider an application program A that calls a routine R. The compiler may want to inline R at a specific call site, replacing the call to R by an instance of R's body into which the actual parameters have been hard-coded. Since the body of R can then be optimized in the context of A, this might lead to significant further simplifications. However, none of this is possible if R is implemented in an external dynamic-link library, because the library may be changed independently of the application program.

Hence, the needs of optimizing compilers run counter to the principle of dynamic composability that fundamentally underlies mobile-object systems. These are usually made out of a large number of relatively small components. Consequently, they have to pay a performance penalty for their added flexibility, as optimizations such as procedure inlining and inter-procedural register allocation can usually not be performed across component boundaries at reasonable cost. Note that the technique of *just-in-time* compilation that is currently gaining in popularity is compounding the problem, as it compiles methods individually as they are called.

Our system is able to overcome these limitations. The key idea is to perform the translation from the slim binary distribution format into executable code not just once, but to do so continually. When a piece of mobile code is initially activated in our system, its slim-binary representation is translated into native code a single burst, putting compilation speed ahead of code quality so that execution can commence immediately. However, the resulting code will usually not be executed for long. Immediately after a component has become active, its code becomes a candidate for *re-optimization*.

In our architecture, code generation is provided as a *central system service*. A low-priority thread of control uses the idle time of the machine to perpetually *integrate*

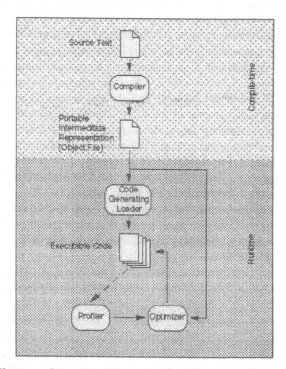

Figure 5 Schematic Overview of the Run-Time Architecture

all components loaded at that moment, recompiling the already executing code base again and again in the background into fully optimized, quasi-monolithic code images. Whenever such an image has been constructed, it supersedes the previously executing version of the same code and re-compilation commences again (Figure 5).

Since a single code image is being constructed out of a large number of individually-distributed parts, code optimizations that transcend the boundaries of these parts can be put to use without limitation. Furthermore, all of this occurs in the background while an alternate version of the same software is already executing in the foreground, so that the speed of re-compilation is not critical. This means that far more aggressive optimization strategies can be employed than would be possible in an interactive context. Run-time profiling data can also be exploited during re-compilation [Ing71, Han74, CMH91] so that successive iterations yield better and better code.

Hence, iterative dynamic re-compilation can provide the run-time efficiency of a globally optimized monolithic application in the context of mobile objects, or even surpass it due to the fine-tuning that profiling makes possible. It leads to a new execution model that combines the advantages of conventional application programs with those of dynamically configurable component-based systems. We call this model *quasi-monolithic*, since it exhibits most of the characteristics of a monolithic application. Unlike monolithic applications, however, a quasi-monolithic executable is extensible and can be augmented at any time by further components that are linked to the monolithic core. Eventually, the components "outside" of the monolithic core will get drawn inside it, as the run-time code generator integrates them on successive iteration cycles.

3.1 Quasi-Monolithic System Architectures: Further Considerations

Run-time re-optimization affords not only a profitable utilization of a processor's idle cycles, but is also an ideal task to be handled by a temporarily unused processor in a multi-processor system. Such a re-optimization cycle requires no synchronization with the rest of the system until it is completed. This applies even to memory accesses: a run-time code generator takes a series of (possibly cached) "portable object files" as its input and produces a completely new code image as its output; it need not have access to the currently executing object code and can make a copy of any profiling data prior to beginning its cycle. Hence, run-time code generation, if executed concurrently with application programs by a dedicated processor, could be implemented in such a way that it doesn't slow down the remaining processors (although we haven't done this yet). As processor costs decline, it may become perfectly viable to add a further processor to a computer system specifically for handling dynamic re-optimization. This may in fact be more cost-effective than attempting true multiprocessing when the problem set is not well suited for parallelization.

There is, however, still a price to be paid for the increased performance of quasi-monolithic code: inlining, loop unrolling and other optimizations such as *customization* [CU89] can lead to a much larger memory requirement for the whole system. This behavior is likely to be more pronounced for well-structured modular applications, in which all common functions have been "factored out", than for application programs that are not so well-structured, since dynamically compiling a collection of modules into a quasi-monolith has the effect of "multiplying out" many of the functions that were previously factored. Hence, while programs that make pervasive use of shared dynamically-linked libraries are expected to benefit most from dynamic re-optimization, they are also likely to demonstrate the downside of the technique most clearly. While we contest that the rapidly diminishing cost of memory is a small price to pay for the advantage of achieving high performance and modularity simultaneously, one of the goals of our research is to develop techniques for limiting the memory requirements of our method. It should be possible to eventually develop good heuristics for this purpose based on the dynamic history of recompilation effects and the available run-time profiling data.

We expect that integral run-time code-generation and re-optimization will become a common feature in component-based systems. Already today, operating-system manufacturers are beginning to support for software-portability solutions such as the Java Virtual Machine [LYJ96]. Initially, this support will come in the form of just-in-time compilers that translate portable program representations into the native code of a target machine. To attain further benefits, however, the operating system's code itself will need to be accessible to the run-time code generator, so that all-encompassing quasi-monolithic code images can be created. We trust that this additional step will eventually also be taken in mainstream operating systems, as it promises better performance for the small and rapidly diminishing price of greater memory consumption.

4 Current State of the Implementation

The work described in this chapter has originated and continues to evolve in the context of the *Oberon System* [WG89, WG92]. Oberon constitutes a highly dynamic software environment in which executing code can be extended by further functionality at run-time. The unit of extensibility in Oberon is the *module*; modules are composed, compiled and distributed separately of each other. Oberon is programmed in a language of the same name [Wir88] and has been ported to a wide variety of platforms [Fra93, BCF95].

For all practical purposes, Oberon's modules supply exactly the functionality that is required for modeling mobile objects. Modules provide encapsulation, their interfaces are type-checked at compilation time and again during linking, and they are an esthetically pleasing language construct. The only feature that we have recently added to the original language definition is a scheme for globally unique naming of qualified identifiers. Hence, when we have been talking about "components", or "objects" above, we were referring to Oberon modules.

We have already come quite far in deploying the ideas described here in a broader sense than merely implementing them in a research prototype. The current Oberon software distribution [Oberon] uses the architecture-neutral *slim binary* format to represent object code across a variety of processors. Our on-the-fly code generators have turned out to be so reliable that the provision of native binaries could be discontinued altogether, resulting in a significantly reduced maintenance overhead for the distribution package. Currently, our implementations for Apple Macintosh on both the *MC680x0* and the *PowerPC* platforms (native on each) and for the *i80x86* platform under Microsoft Windows 95 all share the identical object modules, except for a small machine-specific core that incorporates the respective dynamic code generators and a tiny amount of "glue" to interface with the respective host operating systems.

The latest release of this distribution also contains an authoring kit for creating mobile components that are based on a reduced system interface modeled after the Java-Applet-API. We have created *plug-in extensions* for the *Netscape Navigator* and *Microsoft Internet Explorer* families of WWW browsers, again both for the Macintosh (PowerPC) and Microsoft Windows (i80x86) platforms, that implement runtime environments providing this API in conjunction with on-the-fly code generation. Users are able to create components within the Oberon environment that can then be run not only within Oberon, but also from within the third-party browsers. We call our mobile-component architecture "Juice" [Juice], as it complements Java in many ways. The two kinds of mobile components can live on the same page and communicate with each other through the browsers API. Our implementations of Oberon and the Juice plug-in modules can be freely downloaded from our Internet site [Oberon, Juice].

5   Summary and Conclusion

We have presented two new technologies that we believe to be vital for future mobile-object systems:

- The *slim binary* machine-independent software distribution format is extremely dense, which will be an important benefit when wireless connectivity becomes pervasive. Already today, its tree structure presents advantages over linear byte-code solutions when advanced optimizations are required.

- The quasi-monolithic run-time model of code execution, made possible by iterative dynamic code optimization, may very well become a necessity as the average unit of distributed code gets smaller and smaller. Only by constructing all-encompassing fully cross-optimized code images at run-time will it be possible to exploit the full power of future superscalar processors for such software.

Hardware is currently developing in favor of these two techniques, as wireless communications are becoming a reality while processor power is increasing rapidly, making dynamic code generation practical. Cheaper processors also mean that eventually a dedicated additional processor could be employed to perform background re-optimization of code ultimately executed by a primary processor. This utilization of extra processors might in fact often be more cost-effective than attempting genuine multiprocessing.

Acknowledgment

The Oberon System has turned out to be a stable foundation for projects far beyond its original scope. The author gratefully acknowledges the original creators of Oberon, Niklaus Wirth and Jürg Gutknecht, and the co-author of the Oberon/Juice software distribution, Thomas Kistler. Thanks also go to Martin Burtscher and Markus Dätwyler for collaborating on the system's implementation.

References

[AH96]   G. Aigner and U. Hölzle; Eliminating Virtual Function Calls in C++ Programs; *ECOOP'96 Conference Proceedings*, published as *Springer Lecture Notes in Computer Science*, No.1098, 142-166; 1996.

[BCF95]   M. Brandis, R. Crelier, M. Franz, and J. Templ; The Oberon System Family; *SoftwarePractice and Experience*, 25:12, 1331-1366; 1995.

[CMH91]   P. P. Chang, S. A. Mahlke, and W. W. Hwu; Using Profile Information to Assist Classic Code Optimizations; *SoftwarePractice and Experience*, 21:12, 1301-1321; 1991.

[CU89]   C. Chambers and D. Ungar; Customization: Optimizing Compiler Technology for Self, a Dynamically-Typed Object-Oriented Programming Language; *Proceedings of the ACM Sigplan '89 Conference Programming Language Design and Implementation*, published as *Sigplan Notices*, 24:7, 146-160; 1989.

[Dav86]   J. W. Davidson; A Retargetable Instruction Reorganizer; *Proceedings of the ACM Sigplan '86 Symposium on Compiler Construction*, Palo Alto, California, 234-241; 1986.

[DF84]   J. W. Davidson and C. W. Fraser; Code Selection through Object Code Optimization; *ACM Transactions on Programming Languages and Systems*, 6:4, 505-526; 1984.

[DRA93]   United Kingdom Defence Research Agency; *Frequently Asked Questions about ANDF, Issue 1.1*; June 1993.

[FK96]   M. Franz and T. Kistler; Slim Binaries; *Communications of the ACM*, to appear; also available as Technical Report No. 96-24, Department of Information and Computer Science, University of California, Irvine; 1996.

[Juice]   M. Franz and T. Kistler; *Juice*; http://www.ics.uci.edu/~juice.

[FL91]   M. Franz and S. Ludwig; Portability Redefined; in *Proceedings of the Second International Modula-2 Conference*, Loughborough, England; September 1991.

[Fra93]   M. Franz; Emulating an Operating System on Top of Another; *SoftwarePractice and Experience*, 23:6, 677-692; 1993.

[Fra94a]   M. Franz; *Code-Generation On-the-Fly: A Key to Portable Software*; Doctoral Dissertation No. 10497, ETH Zürich, simultaneously published by Verlag der Fachvereine, Zürich, ISBN 3-7281-2115-0; 1994.

[Fra94b]   M. Franz; Technological Steps toward a Software Component Industry; in *Programming Languages and System Architectures*, Springer Lecture Notes in Computer Science, No. 782, 259-281; 1994.

[Han74]   G. J. Hansen; *Adaptive Systems for the Dynamic Run-Time Optimization of Programs* (Doctoral Dissertation); Department of Computer Science, Carnegie-Mellon University; 1974.

[Ing71]   D. Ingalls; The Execution Time Profile as a Programming Tool; *Design and Optimization of Compilers*, Prentice-Hall; 1971.

[Juice]   M. Franz and T. Kistler; *Juice*; http://www.ics.uci.edu/~juice.

[LYJ96]   T. Lindholm, F. Yellin, B. Joy, and K. Walrath; *The Java Virtual Machine Specification*; Addison-Wesley; 1996.

[Mac93]   S. Macrakis; *Protecting Source Code with ANDF*; Open Software Foundation Research Institute; June 1993.

[NAJ76]   K. V. Nori, U. Amman, K. Jensen, H. H. Nägeli and C. Jacobi; Pascal-P Implementation Notes; in D.W. Barron, editor; *Pascal: The Language and its Implementation*; Wiley, Chichester; 1981.

[Oberon] Institut für Computersysteme, ETH Zürich, and Department of Information and Computer Science, University of California at Irvine; *Oberon Software Distribution*; http://www-cs.inf.ethz.ch/Oberon.html or http://www.ics.uci.edu/~oberon.

[Wal92]   D. W. Wall; Experience with a Software-Defined Machine Architecture; *ACM Transactions on Programming Languages and Systems*, 14:3, 299-338; 1992.

[Wel84]   T. A. Welch; A Technique for High-Performance Data Compression; *IEEE Computer*, 17:6, 8-19; 1984.

[WG89]   N. Wirth and J. Gutknecht; The Oberon System; *SoftwarePractice and Experience*, 19:9, 857-893; 1989.

[WG92]   N. Wirth and J. Gutknecht; *Project Oberon: The Design of an Operating System and Compiler*; Addison-Wesley; 1992.

[Wir88]   N. Wirth; The Programming Language Oberon; *Software-Practice and Experience*, 18:7, 671-690; 1988.

A Type-Based Implementation
of a Language with Distributed Scope

Dominic Duggan

Abstract. Several languages have been designed and implemented for programming mobile computations. This chapter describes a mobile code language based on extending the popular ML language. The language design, and its implementation, are distinguished by the use of run-time type information for computation. This is intended to motivate the use of run-time types in implementations of languages intended for distributed programming and mobile computations, particularly languages such as ML that provide type polymorphism.

1 Introduction

Several languages have been proposed for programming mobile computations in distributed systems [6]. Several of these mobile code languages are described in this volume; Cugola et al [8] give an overview and comparison of many of these languages.

This chapter addresses the issue of how use can be made of type information at run-time in mobile code languages, and in particular in languages that provide *type polymorphism*. A popular and well-known example of a language with type (or parametric) polymorphism is the ML language [22]. ML is an interesting candidate for a language for mobile computations since it already incorporates full lexical closures. The Obliq language [7, 6] demonstrates how lexical closure can be used to encapsulate mobile computations. The Extended Facile language [17] extends the Standard ML language with several mechanisms for distribution and mobility, making use of the fact that closures are first-class in ML to provide code mobility. Although Extended Facile incorporates a type system with type polymorphism, no use is made of this information at run-time.

The Java language [12] makes some use of type information at load-time and at run-time. Class files in Java incorporate type information collected by the compiler, and a byte-code verifier in the Java computational environment uses this information to re-type-check the Java byte code at load time. Java also incorporates a form of typecase construct (using the instanceof operator), which allows a program to check the specific class of an object at run-time. Similar mechanisms are found in object-oriented languages such as Simula-67 and Modula-3 [5, 23]. Java does not currently provide type polymorphism, although this is being seriously investigated for the language. As argued in this chapter, extending Java's notion of dynamic typing to a language with type polymorphism requires a major change in the approach to using run-time type information.

In this chapter we describe an implementation of a distributed dialect of ML that makes use of type information for run-time computation. In Sect. 2 we describe some of the modifications we have made to the ML semantics as part of this work. In this dialect, type variables exist at run-time, rather than being stripped away as in Extended Facile.

Type variables in polymorphic procedure definitions are bound to types at run-time. The program may examine the bindings of these type variables, and branch based on these bindings. This facility is motivated by its use in marshalling support in the language.

In Sect. 3 we consider a type-based implementation of this ML dialect. We pay particular attention to the interaction between run-time type information and lexical closures, since the latter are a key aspect of code mobility in the language. Finally Sect. 4 provides our conclusions. App. A gives a brief overview of the ML language.

2 Language Changes

Our implementation is for a dialect of Standard ML incorporating some changes to the usual semantics. These semantics are intended to support distributed programming in ML, and in particular mobile distributed applications. The main point about these changes is the motivation they provide for our type-based implementation.

2.1 Dynamic Typing

Although static typing is clearly useful for reliable and efficient code, dynamic typing is also necessary for distributed programming. The need arises for several reasons, chiefly the fact that two programs may be compiled completely separately and only come in contact via network communication at run-time. Some use of type information must be used at that point to check the well-typedness of the communication. Following the experience with Modula-3 Network Objects [4], we take the position that the well-typedness of the communication should be determined using purely local information available to the two programs, and without the use of any kind of global protocols or "type servers." This approach appears crucial for scalability.

Dynamics constitute a mechanism for adding dynamic typing to statically typed programming languages [2]. Some evidence for the usefulness of dynamics in distributed programming is provided by Krumvieda's implementation of Distributed ML [18]:

> The lack of a dynamic type or some other method of implicitly attaching marshalling functions to SML types hampered much of DML's interface development and complicated its signature. Although DML was originally intended to support dynamic types, the necessary work never materialized and group type objects have proliferated and propogated through its implementation and coding examples.

The approach of dynamics essentially involves the addition of an operation, dynamic, for bundling a value with its type, and also the addition of a typecase construct, for examining a type bundled in a dynamic:

```
(if true then dynamic(3) else dynamic("hello")) : dynamic
fun print (x: dynamic) =
   typecase x of int(xi) ⇒ puts(makestring(xi))
```

Related mechanisms are found in many modern languages intended for distributed programming, for example in the `Pickle` module in Modula-3, and in the `any` type in the OMG CORBA.

However there is a problem with using dynamics in polymorphic languages, and that is its interaction with parameterized types. Consider for example extending the previous example to define a print server that can print lists (bundled as dynamics):

```
fun print (x: dynamic) = typecase x of
    (α list)(ys) ⇒ for each y in ys, do print(dynamic(y))
```

The problem is in how to recurse over the elements of the data structure. In the approach suggested by Leroy et al for adding dynamics to ML [21, 20], the elements of the data structure are rebundled as dynamics, as shown above. This is necessary because the print operation is defined for dynamics; nothing is known about a list element y except that it has some opaque type α, so the `dynamic` operation must be used to associate a type tag with such an opaque value.

There are several problems with this approach. For one thing, the failure point due to run-time type errors no longer occurs once, when a dynamic is unbundled, but is distributed over the code which recursively traverses the data structure. Because dynamics essentially associate type tags with individual data values, this approach also makes some fairly natural compiler optimizations impractical. Even worse, it is impossible to recurse over dynamic data structures with mutable components (as discussed in [9]). Finally if we think of the `dynamic` and `typecase` constructs as being the bundling and unbundling of pickled values (as made precise below), then there is a significant performance penalty associated with the repeated bundling and unbundling of the data structure.

Part of the distribution support in our ML dialect is a new construct for computing with dynamics which allows pickled data structures such as lists and trees to be unbundled once and then traversed,. In our approach, the above example is *intuitively* implemented as:

```
fun print (x: α) =
    typecase α of (β list)(ys) ⇒ for each y in ys, do print(y)
```

Here we have changed the semantics of `typecase`: rather than examining type tags associated with data items, type descriptions are now separated from data and passed as type parameters to polymorphic functions. There is still a need for a mechanism for bundling a value with its type description, and this is exactly what is provided by dynamics. However in computing with dynamics, we extract these two elements (the data item, and its type description), and recurse over the type description separately from recursing over the data value.

In the second example above, there is a single recursive loop where the print operation traverses the list. Since the print operation needs to examine the type tags of the list elements, it is necessary to rebundle each list element using the `dynamic` operation. In the third example above, there are now two recursive loops: one traverses the type description of the data items (starting with the type description of the initial data item which is a list), while the other recursive loop traverses the data item itself (the list in this example).

In computing with dynamics, we explicitly separate a value from its type description, and correspondingly we separate a loop over a dynamic data structure into two loops: one over the type description, and one over the bundled data structure. As a result, in the example just presented, the unbundling of the pickled list is done once, at the point where the print function is applied, rather than repeatedly on each recursive call to print. This overcomes all of the aforesaid problems with recursing over dynamic data structures using traditional approaches. The actual language constructs are described in [9]; the point of this example is to demonstrate the usefulness of run-time type information for distributed programming.

2.2 User-Definable Marshalling

We think of dynamic as the basis for marshalling primitives for a programming language, analogous to the use of the Pickle module in Modula-3 (which in turn is used quite heavily in the implementation of Network Objects [4]). Whereas Pickle relies on the ubiquitous use of run-time type tags in Modula-3, dynamic places no such restrictions on the language. Regarding the Pickle module, Birrell et al say [4]:

> It is difficult to provide fully general marshalling code in a satisfactory way. Existing systems fail in one or more of the following ways. Some apply restrictions to the types that can be marshalled, typically prohibiting linked, cyclic or graph-structured values. Some generate elaborate code for almost any data type, but the resulting stub modules are excessively large. Some handle a lot of data types, but the marshalling code is excessively inefficient.

Because of this, the Pickle module allows the programmer to register user-defined type-specific marshalling and unmarshalling operations (called *specials*). Specials are dispatched on the basis of run-time type tags associated with data structures.

An obvious question is, how can we provide a similar facility in a language with type polymorphism? Our language is designed to provide mechanisms for user-definable marshalling [9]. Essentially we treat the dynamic and typecase constructs as marshalling and unmarshalling operations, and then allow the programmer to define instances of these operations for particular types. With this approach, the dynamic operation has three parts:

1. A type function τ_{pkl} that maps from a type to a *pickle type*. Essentially a type must be mapped to some external representation type, that the underlying implementation knows how to marshall. It should be stressed here that τ_{pkl} is a function that maps from types to types, and indeed recurses over compound type descriptions.
2. A pickling function pickle, which is a polymorphic function of type $\alpha \rightarrow \tau_{pkl}(\alpha)$.
3. An extraction function extract, which again is a polymorphic function, this time of type $\tau_{pkl}(\alpha) \rightarrow \alpha$.

All three of these are functions that recurse over type description. User-defined marshalling operations are provided by extending each of these three functions with new cases for a particular type:

$$\texttt{defdynamic } \overline{\alpha} \texttt{ t}_1 = \overline{\alpha} \texttt{ t}_2 \texttt{ with } (e_1, e_2)$$

This extends the current definition of $\texttt{dynamic}$ with[1]:

1. A new case in the definition of τ_{pkl}:

$$\tau_{\text{pkl}}((\overline{\alpha}) \texttt{ t}_1) = (\overline{\tau_{\text{pkl}}(\alpha)}) \texttt{ t}_2$$

where τ_{pkl} is represented by a special type constructor $\texttt{IDynamic}$ within the $\texttt{defdynamic}$ definition.

2. $\texttt{pickle}: \alpha \to \tau_{\text{pkl}}(\alpha)$ is extended with an instance of type:

$$e_1 : (\overline{\alpha_n}) \texttt{ t}_1 \to (\overline{\tau_{\text{pkl}}(\alpha_n)}) \texttt{ t}_2$$

3. $\texttt{extract}: \tau_{\text{pkl}}(\alpha) \to \alpha$ is extended with an instance of type:

$$e_2 : (\overline{\tau_{\text{pkl}}(\alpha_n)}) \texttt{ t}_2 \to (\overline{\alpha_n}) \texttt{ t}_1$$

At a use of the $\texttt{dynamic}$ operation on a value e of type τ_{wit}, the definition of τ_{pkl} is closed up, and (implicitly defined) $\texttt{pickle}$ and $\texttt{extract}$ operations are specialized to the type of e. The specialized version of $\texttt{pickle}$ is then applied to e. Thus we obtain a pair of type:

$$\tau_{\text{pkl}}(\tau_{\text{wit}}) * (\tau_{\text{pkl}}(\tau_{\text{wit}}) \to \tau_{\text{wit}})$$

A dynamic is essentially a pair of this form, where existential type quantifiers are used to abstract over the original type of e and the corresponding pickle type:

$$\texttt{dynamic} = \exists \alpha \cdot \exists \beta \cdot \beta * (\beta \to \alpha)$$

We refer to these as *self-extracting dynamics*.

For example, a plausible pickle type for integers is as 32-bit big-endian words, while lists may be pickled as arrays. This is described by a pickle type function τ_{pkl} with the cases:

$$\tau_{\text{pkl}}(\texttt{int}) = \texttt{bigEndianWord32}$$

$$\tau_{\text{pkl}}(\alpha \texttt{ list}) = \tau_{\text{pkl}}(\alpha) \texttt{ array}$$

A programmer-defined marshalling operation for lists should specify a function of type $(\alpha \texttt{ list}) \to (\tau_{\text{pkl}}(\alpha) \texttt{ array})$, assuming the existence of a marshalling operation of type $\alpha \to \tau_{\text{pkl}}(\alpha)$. A programmer-defined unmarshalling operation should specify a corresponding inverse function.

---

[1] We use a vector notation for brevity: $\overline{\tau_n}$ denotes the vector $\tau_1, \ldots, \tau_n$, and n is sometimes omitted where it is not critical. We also employ the postfix concrete syntax used by ML for the application of type constructors.

A data item of type `int list list` is then marshalled as a value of type `bigEndianWord32 array array`. To accomplish this, the marshalling operations for integers and lists are treated as clauses in the definition of a global marshalling operation. The call to the hypothetical marshalling operation of type $\alpha \to \tau_{\mathrm{pkl}}(\alpha)$ corresponds to a recursive call to this global marshalling operation, which then dispatches to the appropriate clause for the list element type. In this way, the marshalling (and unmarshalling) operations make essential use again of recursion over a type description for computation.

Herlihy and Liskov [15] describe another approach to user-definable marshalling in polymorphic languages, in the CLU language. Their approach is based on *constrained genericity*: a marshalling operation for a bag ADT, for example, is parameterized by a marshalling operation for the element type of the bag. This is similar to type classes in Haskell [13]. However the implementors of the Glasgow Haskell compiler report [25]:

> The Haskell type-class system caused us an enormous amount of extra work
> (beyond simple Hindley-Milner types), and we are still far from satisfied with
> the efficiency of the resulting programs. The compiler technology required to
> recover an acceptably efficient implementation is very considerable.

The type system underlying our approach to user-definable marshalling takes a more conservative approach, avoiding the "open-world" assumption that is at the root of the implementation problems with type classes. Our approach admits an implementation of marshalling based on passing run-time type descriptions to the marshalling code.

The point of this description is to motivate the use of run-time type information in our implementation. To date, most ML implementations strip away type information at compile time [3], and a tagged run-time is used for garbage collection and marshalling/unmarshalling [24]. We briefly cite some other reasons for why run-time type information is desirable in a distributed ML implementation:

1. Run-time type information can be used as a basis for untagged garbage collection in polymorphic languages, and for example eliminates the need for tag bits to distinguish integers and pointers [29].
2. Run-time type information can also be used as the basis for specializing data representations and code in polymorphic languages. For example an array of floats can be represented as unboxed 64-bit entries, while a generic array uses 32-bit boxed pointer entries or 32-bit unboxed integer entries. A polymorphic function that operates on an array can dispatch based on the element type of the array to one of three implementations [14, 28].
3. Finally run-time type information can also be used to extend the Java idea of load-time bytecode verification to polymorphic languages. This cannot be done in Rouaix' MMM Web browser (based on Caml Light) because the bytecode is untyped; Rouaix instead relies on trusted compile servers for security [27].

All of this is motivation for run-time type information, and in particular for run-time type parameters to polymorphic functions, in our implementation. ML has the particular property (similarly to Ada and C++) that polymorphic functions are second-class. Therefore it might be assumed that run-time types are not necessary: instead polymorphic functions can be specialized at their use-sites to their monomorphic instances. This is what is done in Ada and C++ implementations. However there are some objections to this approach:

1. Experience with Ada for example suggests that this leads to a significant growth in code size. The size of the code is a point that must be considered for programs that are meant to fit inside telephones.
2. If polymorphic library functions are down-loaded across the network, it is unreasonable to expect the loader to be able to specialize the code to the types at its use sites. The approach of monomorphic specialization is not compatible with separate compilation of polymorphic functions.
3. Finally, monomorphic specialization is not possible with first-class polymorphism. Although first-class polymorphism leads to a undecidable type inference problem, our dialect combines first-class polymorphism and decidable type inference, through a novel form of primitive objects with polymorphic methods.

2.3 Objects

Our ML dialect includes built-in objects (rather than attempting to represent objects as closures, as is more commonly done). Our reason for doing this is to provide container objects with polymorphic methods. For example, it is possible in our type system to define objects with interfaces of the form:

```
α List = { car: α,
           cdr: α List,
           map: (α → β) → β List }
```

Suppose an object has type int List; then the map method must be a polymorphic function, where β at run-time is specialized in different ways at different invocation sites, for example:

```
val x = ... : int List
x.map makestring : string List (* makestring: int → string *)
x.map singleton : (int List) List (* singleton: α → α List *)
```

Our language is the only ML dialect that allows this form of definition of objects with polymorphic methods. No alternative type systems have been suggested that combine type inference and this facility. This facility is based on the provision of built-in objects in the language. For reasons of space, we omit further elaboration of how this is done and what form objects take in our language. Some further description is provided by Duggan [11, 10].

Since our ML dialect already contains built-in objects, it is natural to use them as an abstraction for network connections, location transparency and third-party transfer, as is done in distributed object systems. As with Obliq, we allow all objects to be potentially network objects. A true object is transmitted as a network reference, that is unmarshalled at the receiving node of a communication as a proxy calling back to the true object.

Our object system shares some common foundations with Obliq objects. The latter objects are object-based, with their foundations in the primitive object calculus of Abadi and Cardelli [1]. For reasons related to how we provide container objects, our objects are class-based: an object is composed of two components, a method suite and a state component (record of instance variables). Method suites are primitive and are essentially Abadi and Cardelli objects (with self types). Because of our interest in container object types, our object types are actually based on an extension of Abadi and Cardelli object types to parameterized object types. For example ListM, the type of the method suite for list objects, is defined as:

$$\tau \ \text{ListM} = \{ \ \text{car}: \forall \alpha.\alpha,$$
$$\text{cdr}: \forall \alpha.(\alpha \ \tau) \rightarrow (\exists \gamma.(\gamma \ \text{ListM}) * (\alpha \ \gamma))$$
$$\text{map}: \forall \alpha.\forall \beta.(\alpha \ \tau) \rightarrow (\alpha \rightarrow \beta) \rightarrow (\exists \gamma.(\gamma \ \text{ListM}) * (\beta \ \gamma)) \ \}$$

and this type is actually a (parameterized) Abadi and Cardelli object type. Our objects are obtained by combining a method suite and a state component, and using existential types to encapsulate the indexing type constructor of the state component:

$$\alpha \ \text{List} = \exists \gamma.(\gamma \ \text{ListM}) * (\alpha \ \gamma)$$

Because of this relationship to Abadi and Cardelli objects, it is possible to add some of the features of Obliq to our language. For example, object migration in Obliq is provided using object cloning with a network address, and method aliasing, and we believe these can be added straightforwardly to our system.

2.4 Type Equivalence

Datatypes play a particularly crucial rôle in transmitting values in a type-safe way between address spaces. Type tags are transmitted with values to facilitate unmarshalling and type-checking at the receiving site, as described in the next section. The complication with datatypes as defined in Standard ML is that datatypes are generative; however it appears unreasonable to expect the same datatype to have the same stamp in two different address spaces. Accordingly we no longer assume that datatypes are generative; equivalence of datatypes is based on structural equivalence. We do not resort to circular unification, but keep the normal unification algorithm by making the folding and unfolding of recursive datatypes explicit (in data constructor application and pattern-matching, respectively). Modula-3 also assumes structural equivalence of recursive types, but allows name equivalence with *branded types*. In distributed programming, branded types are required to be given the same user-defined brands in all address spaces. We obtain a simple form of user-defined brands by including the name of a datatype in the identity of that type. Type-checking hashes from a datatype definition into a *type table* to obtain an integer typecode for that datatype. These typecodes are the basis for run-time type information in programs, with the type table saved by the compiler and reloaded at run-time, and indexed by the typecodes in the code.

3 Implementation

Our implementation of our extended ML dialect comprises a compiler, written in SML/NJ, and a bytecode interpreter. The compiler comprises a new frontend and type-checker (a frontend with subtype inference is in development), and a backend based on the Moscow ML compiler. The backend is modified to provide code for run-time types, among other things. The interpreter is based on the bytecode interpreter for the CAML Light language [19], modified again to support run-time types.

3.1 Compiler

The type-checker for the compiler incorporates several novel features. Currently dynamics and user-definable marshalling are not fully implemented. However the frontend does gather all of the information necessary to generate code for run-time types. In particular every `let`-defined variable records the type variables abstracted over in that polymorphic definition, and every use site for such a variable records the instantiations for those parameters. In the translation from the abstract syntax of the frontend to the Lambda language of the backend (adapted from Moscow ML, adapted in turn from CAML Light), both ordinary variables and type variables are translated to de Bruijn numbers, indexing into environment slots at run-time.

The compiler also supports objects with polymorphic methods and object cloning, as well as some other features (e.g. higher-order polymorphism).

Our treatment of datatypes deserves some mention, since they are at the core of our treatment of run-time types. As already noted, equivalence of datatypes is based on structural type equivalence. When a datatype is defined in the program, the compiler hashes into a table of type descriptions, the *type table*. Once an entry has been located for a datatype, the datatype is referenced by a *typecode*, essentially the index of that datatype declaration in the type table.

A similar approach is used for records and primitive types. An ML record (without subtyping) is represented as a record type constructor applied to the tuple of the field types. Finally a type table entry may be the global signature for a method. First-class polymorphism is achieved in our language by requiring that method types be declared globally [11, 10]. As a simple example, consider the declarations[2]:

```
methodtype get : α Object{get,set} → α
methodtype set : α Object{get,set} → β → β Object{get,set}
```

Then a cell object with type int Object{get,set} encapsulates an integer value and two methods. The second method, set, is a polymorphic function which may be treated as a first-class value (passed as an argument, returned as a result, inserted in a data structure), as long as it is bound to an object. Each global declaration for a method signature adds a corresponding entry for the method type to the type table. So an object type can be represented as a sequence of (method name, typecode) pairs[3].

Datatype and record entries in the type table also contain a *fingerprint*, a 64-bit checksum that with high probability is unique for that datatype or record. Fingerprints are

---

[2] This is a gross oversimplification of our object model. For example, method signatures may contain self types that do not constrain the object types in which they appear. Furthermore ML-style "polymorphic records" are obtainable by parameterizing global method signatures by type variables [11, 10].

[3] This is something of an oversimplification, since method types have much more structure than we have described here.

constructed as part of the process of hashing into the type table. Their real usefulness is at run-time, in transmitting typecodes between address spaces. A typecode is transmitted across the network by sending its fingerprint. On receipt of a fingerprint at the receiving site, this is used to hash into the type table for the corresponding typecode.

This is essentially the approach taken to transmitting types in Modula-3 Network Objects [4]. A complication with a polymorphic language such as ML is that it is not sufficient to transmit a single fingerprint for a type. For example we may transmit a closure with an internal value of type int list list. Although the receiving site type table has entries for int and list, it would be unacceptable to expect it to have entries for every possible combination of these type constructors. Types in ML are finite trees, with nodes labelled by type constructors (typecodes) and type variables. A type is transmitted by linearizing it as a sequence of fingerprints (and indexes for type variables). The tree is reconstructed at the receiving end by mapping from fingerprints to typecodes, using the type table.

The type table, built by the compiler, therefore has several applications at run-time. Beyond mapping between typecodes and fingerprints, it also provides information about the structure of datatypes. The compiler saves that information in the type table required at run-time, into the bytecode file produced by compilation.

A major change to the Moscow ML backend was to allow transmission of code segments as parts of closures. The CAML Light interpreter (for which Moscow ML is intended) keeps all bytecode together in a single memory block, which is clearly unacceptable for transmitting code. Our backend compiles each code segment into a separate string constant, saved as part of the global data in the output of a compilation. Whereas CAML Light addresses code using 16-bit offsets into the code area, in our implementation there are two 16-bit indexes: first, the global table address of the code string, and second the offset within that string.

3.2 Interpreter

For a given source file, the compiler produces a binary file containing structured literals (including code strings), references to C primitive functions, and the type table information useful at run-time. Each such binary file is loaded in by the interpreter at run-time, and dynamically linked in. Among other things, this means adjusting references to C primitive functions to point to the corresponding entries in a table of C function pointers. A header at the beginning of a bytecode file identifies the code string for the initialization code.

The CAML Light interpreter [19], on which this is based, maintains several data structures for execution. Arguments are passed to functions on an argument stack, and results are left in an accumulator register. Besides a table for global values, there is also an environment for the currently executing closure. A return stack is used to save return points on non-tail recursive function calls.

A function begins executing with an APPLY instruction. This expects a closure in the accumulator, and at least one argument on the argument stack. The environment of the closure is installed as the new environment, the first argument is popped off the argument stack and added to the environment, and control jumps to the first instruction of the closure's code. The latter is typically a sequence of GRAB instructions, which pop further arguments off the argument stack and add them to the environment. If at any point a GRAB instruction finds that the argument stack is empty, it builds a new closure in the accumulator, and returns (using the last return point saved on the return stack).

To avoid some copying, part of the environment is saved in an environment cache on top of the return stack. Values moved from the argument stack to the environment are initially moved to the environment cache. If for example a GRAB instruction finds an empty argument stack, it reallocates the environment with space for the values in the environment cache, as part of building a new closure.

The main complications that we dealt with in adapting this interpreter, were extending it to support transmissible closures, and to support run-time type information. For run-time type information, the greatest complication comes with closures. In order to marshall the closure, the environment slots must be marshalled. But the type of a closure tells us nothing about the types of the environment slots. So closures must be "self-describing" [29]: every slot in a closure is a pair, of a value and its type. Every instruction which extends the environment needs to be modified to add this type information also. In the example described above of an application, the APPLY instruction adds the type of the first argument to the environment cache, as it moves the first argument from the argument stack to the environment cache. Each GRAB instruction adds the type of its argument to the environment cache similarly. The type description for each formal parameter is constructed at compile-time, and saved in the bytecode file as a structured literal. These type descriptions are then installed in the global data table as part of loading the bytecode file. The APPLY and GRAB instructions refer to the types of their arguments by indexing into the global data table for the corresponding structured literal.

It is of course possible that a type description for a formal parameter may contain free type variables. Consider for example the type of the formal parameter in a polymorphic identity function. Type variables are treated at run-time just as ordinary variables, therefore the environment contains bindings both for ordinary variables and for type variables. Type variables in environment type entries are indexes into the corresponding slot in the same environment where the binding for that type variable is stored.

Free type variables may also appear in the types that are passed at run-time as actual arguments to polymorphic functions. These type variables refer to slots in the environment at the call site. There are essentially two alternative approaches to treating the bindings for these type variables: delay lookup of the type variables until necessary, by transmitting all type arguments as suspensions [29]; or replace all type variables in type arguments at the point where the polymorphic function is called. We have chosen the latter approach, since it appears much simpler than the former "lazier" approach. For example, the bindings for type variables in the environment are always ground with the latter approach, avoiding a lot of space inefficiency with type suspensions. This approach is also taken by the TIL compiler [28].

To understand this, consider the following example[26]:

```
fun f x y = let fun g z () = z
                in dynamic (g y)
             end ;
f 5 "hello";
```

After adding type arguments to the code, this becomes:

```
fun f α β x y =
    let fun g γ z () = z
    in dynamic (g β y)
    end ;
f int string 5 "hello";
```

Variable	Binding	Type
α	int	TYPE
β	string	TYPE
x	5	α
y	"hello"	β
γ	string	TYPE
z	"hello"	γ

The table on the right contains the bindings in the environment at the point where the dynamic operation is called. This is the environment that must be marshalled with the closure argument to dynamic. The types of x, y and z contain free type variables, and these type variables in turn are bound in the environment. In particular, γ is bound to the binding for β at the point where g is called. Performing this lookup "eagerly" at the point where g is called avoids the need to dereference a chain of type variable aliases at run-time.

As another example, consider:

```
fun f x y = let fun g z () = (#1 z , #2 z + 1)
            in dynamic (g ((true , y), x))
            end ;
f 5 "hello";
```

After adding type arguments to the code, this becomes:

```
fun f α β x y = let fun g γ z () = (#1 z , #2 z + 1)
                in dynamic (g (bool * β) ((true , y), x))
                end ;
f int string 5 "hello";
```

The environment at the point where the closure is marshalled is then:

Variable	Binding	Type
α	int	TYPE
β	string	TYPE
x	5	α
y	"hello"	β
γ	(bool * string)	TYPE
z	((true,"hello"),int)	(γ * int)

The argument type of g is γ * int; at the call site for g, the type parameter γ is instantiated with bool * string. This latter type comes from evaluating the type bool * β in the environment where β is bound to string. This example demonstrates that types may need to be computed at run-time in our implementation.

A complication with all of this is how to represent the types of polymorphic functions in environments, since these types bind type variables. In the end, we finessed the issue by assuming that function types are represented at run-time by a single type CLOSURE. Since polymorphic functions take type arguments at run-time, all polymorphic types are represented simply as the type CLOSURE. Since closures are self-describing, marshalling does not need to know the domain and range types of a closure type.

Marshalling a value is based on its type, rather than any run-time tags associated with values. If the type is an object type, then an object reference is transmitted, and is unmarshalled at the receiving site as a proxy object. Similarly to Obliq, this is also how mutable reference cells and arrays are transmitted. If the type is a primitive type, then the built-in marshalling support for that type is used. If the type is a record type, then it is marshalled as a vector in the obvious way. Finally if the type is a datatype, then the type table is used for marshalling. Assuming the value has type $(\tau_1, \ldots, \tau_n)$ t, where t is a datatype defined with type parameters $\alpha_1, \ldots, \alpha_n$, then the value is a tagged memory block, and is marshalled as follows. Since the value is a datatype value, the typecode for t indexes into the corresponding type table entry, and the memory block tag associated with the value indexes into a table of data constructor types. The types of the fields in the memory block are obtained by substituting τ_i for α_i in the corresponding data constructor type, for $i = 1, \ldots, n$. After this substitution, any remaining free type variables correspond to variables bound in the current environment; these variables are looked up in the environment as they are found.

Not surprisingly, marshalling of closures introduces the greatest complications. Essentially the marshalling algorithm must recurse over the closure, marshalling each value in the environment using the associated type information. However the complication is with global values that are referenced in the code. Clearly an index into a global table slot in one address space, carries no meaning if the code with that reference is transmitted to another address space. Therefore the marshaller scans the code string as it marshals a closure; for each reference to a global value that it finds in the code string, it adds a copy of that value to the environment of local values in the closure. Marshalling of the code string then requires that some instructions that access global values (including APPLY and GRAB, that expect type descriptions in the global table) be replaced with local equivalents, where the 16-bit offset is now an index into the closure environment.

There are other reasons for modifying the code string during marshalling. Operations on references and arrays must be replaced by calls back to the originating site. Also calls to C primitives (which index a table of C function pointers) must be replaced by references to the names of the C primitives, for relocation during unmarshalling.

3.3 Implementing Distribution

The Obliq extension language uses Modula-3 Network Objects as its transport mechanism. We use a comparable approach, except that we use the ILU multi-language remote object system for transportation [16]. When a mutable reference cell or array is transmitted as an object, we create an ILU object with Get and Set methods, and the network address for this object is transmitted. The ILU objects we use are extremely uninteresting. All marshalling and unmarshalling, and dynamic interface checking, is (for now) done in our implementation.

We provide export and import operations for establishing network connections and performing third-party transfer, and these are implemented using the analogous ILU operations. When the export operation is performed for an ML true object, an ILU true object is generated. This latter has two methods, a GetType method and a Send method, and information about the ML true object (its memory address, and its type descriptor). The ILU export ("publish") operation is used to register the ILU object with the ILU name server. Another program obtains the network reference by performing the import operation. This uses the ILU import ("lookup") operation to retrieve the network address of the ILU true object from the name server. The ML import operation then executes the GetType method to retrieve the type descriptor for the object, and check that the import operation is well-typed. If this run-time type check succeeds, then an ILU proxy object and an ML proxy object are generated. The ML proxy object uses the ILU proxy object to delegate any method calls to the true ML object at the sending site.

4 Conclusions

We have described the design and implementation of a dialect of ML intended for mobile distributed application programming. A distinguishing characteristic of this implementation is the use of run-time type information, motivated by several constructs in the language. This is intended to motivate the use of run-time types in implementations of polymorphic languages intended for distributed programming.

There are still some interesting issues to be worked out. We have not considered abstract data types in this account. Although it is easy to extend the abstype construct of Standard ML to support the defdynamic construct, the abstype construct is now considered obsolete. How should defdynamic be combined with ADTs defined using the module system? This issue is important, because it determines how the visibility of the representation type for an ADT is controlled as values are bundled as dynamics and then unbundled [9].

Although our implementation supports run-time types, and these are used in various ways, we have not yet implemented all of the language constructs described in Sect. 2. The problem here is how to relate the semantics of type-safe user-definable marshalling, to a real implementation. For example, we do not seriously expect to transmit an unmarshaller with every pickle. More realistically we would expect to transmit the type pickle function, τ_{pickle}, as a vector of pairs of fingerprints, and ensure that the unmarshalling code at the receiving site uses the same representation types for pickles. Our current marshaller is similar to the algorithm used in the Modula-3 Pickle module, and for example preserves sharing and does not require a seekable output stream. A naive implementation of the semantics of user-definable marshalling would require an excessive amount of copying and buffering. A more realistic incorporation of this semantics into our marshaller is under development. Finally, the marshalling of closures appears expensive; to what extent can some of this work be done at compile time instead of at run-time, as is done in Extended Facile [17].

References

1. Martin Abadi and Luca Cardelli. *A Theory of Objects*. Springer-Verlag, July 1996.
2. Martin Abadi, Luca Cardelli, Benjamin Pierce, and Gordon Plotkin. Dynamic typing in a statically typed language. *ACM Transactions on Programming Languages and Systems*, 13(2):237–268, 1991.
3. Andrew Appel. Run-time tags aren't necessary. *Lisp and Symbolic Computation*, 19(7):703–705, July 1989.
4. Andrew Birrell, Greg Nelson, Susan Owicki, and Edward Wobber. Network objects. In *Symposium on Operating Systems Principles*, pages 217–230. ACM Press, 1993.
5. Graham M. Birtwistle, Ole-Johan Dahl, Bjorn Myhrhaug, and Kristen Nygaard. *Simula Begin*. Studentlitteratur (Lund, Sweden), Bratt Institute Fuer Neues Lerned (Goch, FRG), Chartwell-Bratt Ltd (Kent, England, 1979.
6. L. Cardelli. Mobile computations. In J. Vitek and C. Tschudin, editors, *Mobile Object Systems*, Lecture Notes in Computer Science, chapter 1. Springer-Verlag, 1997.
7. Luca Cardelli. A language with distributed scope. In *Proceedings of ACM Symposium on Principles of Programming Languages*, pages 286–297, San Francisco, California, January 1995. ACM Press.
8. G. Cugola, C. Ghezzi, G. P. Picco, and G. Vigna. Analyzing mobile code languages. In J. Vitek and C. Tschudin, editors, *Mobile Object Systems*, Lecture Notes in Computer Science, chapter 8. Springer-Verlag, 1997.
9. Dominic Duggan. Dynamic typing for distributed programming in polymorphic languages. Submitted for publication, December 1994.
10. Dominic Duggan. Container objects with polymorphic methods and self types. Submitted for publication, March 1996.
11. Dominic Duggan. Object type constructors. In *Workshop on Foundations of Object-Oriented Languages*, New Brunswick, New Jersey, July 1996.
12. James Gosling and Henry McGilton. The Java language environment. Technical report, Sun Microsystems White Paper, May 1995.
13. Cordelia Hall, Kevin Hammond, Simon Peyton-Jones, and Philip Wadler. Type classes in Haskell. *ACM Transactions on Programming Languages and Systems*, 18(2):109–138, March 1996.
14. Robert Harper and Gregory Morrisett. Compiling polymorphism using intensional type analysis. In *Proceedings of ACM Symposium on Principles of Programming Languages*, San Francisco, California, January 1995. ACM Press.
15. Maurice Herlihy and Barbara Liskov. A value transmission method for abstract data types. *ACM Transactions on Programming Languages and Systems*, 4(4):527–551, 1982.
16. Bill Janssen and Mike Spreitzer. ILU: Inter-language unification via object modules. Position paper for Workshop at Proceedings of ACM Symposium on Object-Oriented Programming: Systems, Languages and Applications, October 1995.
17. F. Knabe. Performance-oriented implementation strategies for a mobile agent language. In J. Vitek and C. Tschudin, editors, *Mobile Object Systems*, Lecture Notes in Computer Science, chapter 13. Springer-Verlag, 1997.
18. Clifford Krumvieda. *Distributed ML: Abstraction for Efficient and Fault-Tolerant Programming*. PhD thesis, Cornell University, Ithaca, New York, August 1993.
19. Xavier Leroy. The ZINC experiment: an economical implementation of the ML language. Technical Report 117, INRIA, 1990.
20. Xavier Leroy and Michel Mauny. Dynamics in ML. *Journal of Functional Programming*, 3(4):431–463, 1993.

21. Xavier Leroy and Pierre Weiss. Dynamics in ML. In *Proceedings of ACM Symposium on Functional Programming and Computer Architecture*, 1991.
22. Robin Milner, Mads Tofte, and Robert Harper. *The Definition of Standard ML*. The MIT Press, 1990.
23. Greg Nelson. *Systems Programming in Modula-3*. Prentice-Hall Series in Innovative Technology. Prentice-Hall, 1991.
24. Atsushi Ohori and Kazuhiko Kato. Semantics for communication primitives in a polymorphic language. In *Proceedings of ACM Symposium on Principles of Programming Languages*, pages 99–112. ACM Press, 1993.
25. Simon Peyton-Jones, Cordy Hall, Kevin Hammond, WIll Partain, and Philip Wadler. The Glasgow Haskell compiler: a technical overview. In *Proceedings of the UK Joint Framework for Information Technology (JFIT) Technical Conference*, Keele, England, 1993.
26. Piotr Przybylski. A type based implementation for a language with distributed scope. Master's thesis, University of Waterloo, 1996.
27. Francois Rouaix. A Web navigator with applets in CAML. In *Fifth International World Wide Web Conference*, Paris, France, May 1996.
28. David Tarditi, Greg Morrissett, Perry Cheng, Christopher Stone, Robert Harper, and Peter Lee. TIL: A type-directed optimizing compiler for ML. In *Proceedings of ACM SIGPLAN Conference on Programming Language Design and Implementation*, Philadelphia, Pennsylvania, May 1996. ACM Press.
29. Andrew Tolmach. Tag-free garbage collection using explicit type parameters. In *Proceedings of ACM Symposium on Lisp and Functional Programming*, pages 1–11, Orlando, Florida, 1994. ACM Press.

A   Overview of ML

Although generally regarded as a "functional language," ML should perhaps be more properly regarded as a "higher-order procedural language." This emphasizes one of the most important aspects of the ML semantics, its support for first-class closures. This comes without any philosophical commitment to "purity;" ML contains mutable variables, assignment and while loops, so it can be considered as an algorithmic language just as Algol, Pascal, etc. Our dialect also contains objects, for various reasons [10].

As noted, one of the attractive aspects of ML, for application programming, is its support for type inference. For example, we may define a function as follows:

```
fun f (x,y,z) = (y ∧ "hello", (hd z) + x + 1)
```

and the compiler is sophisticated enough to deduce that f has type:

```
int * string * int list → string * int
```

Functions with underconstrained types give rise to type variables in types. This in turn is the basis for type polymorphism:

```
fun f (x,y) = x
f : α * β → α
```

Types (such as int and real) are generalized to *type constructors*, such as for example list. The latter index families of types with a certain structural similarity. For example the type constructor `list` indexes a family of types all of the form $(\tau \ \text{list})$, such as `int list`, `(int * string) list`, `(int list) list`, etc. Type variables place structural constraints on the possible use types of polymorphic functions; for example, the polymorphic append function has type:

$$(\alpha \ \text{list}) * (\alpha \ \text{list}) \rightarrow (\alpha \ \text{list})$$

Data structures are built using *datatypes*, which are essentially the types of immutable acyclic directed graphs. For example, the list datatype may be defined as:

```
datatype α list = nil | cons of α * (α list)
```

This introduces `nil` as a list of type $(\tau \ \text{list})$, for any τ, and `cons(x,xs)` as a list of type $(\tau \ \text{list})$, for any x of type τ and xs of type $(\tau \ \text{list})$. The language includes a `case` construct for accessing a value of a datatype:

```
fun append (xs,ys) =
    case xs
      of nil ⇒ ys
       | cons(x',xs') ⇒ cons(x',append(xs',ys))
```

While in general ML uses structural type equivalence, name equivalence is used for datatypes. Each datatype definition is uniquely identified by a compile-time stamp. So, in type checking, equality of datatypes reduces to equality of integer stamps. So the following fails to type-check:

```
datatype foo = foo of int
fun bar x = case x of foo(y) ⇒ y (* bar: foo → int *)
datatype foo = foo of int
val it = bar(foo(3))
```

Mutable values are distinguished in the type system, using the `ref` primitive type constructor. Operations are provided for creating a mutable reference cell (`val x = ref 3`), assignment (`x := 5`), and explicit dereferencing (`!x`).

Interaction of Java and Telescript Agents

Peter Dömel

Abstract. This chapter gives an introduction into the two object-oriented programming environments *Telescript* and *Java* which both allow to write *mobile code*. It illustrates some of the more interesting features of these languages as platforms for *mobile object systems*. Further emphasis lies on the cooperation of agents in these two object-oriented worlds. Moreover, several descriptions of some higher-level agents scenarios are given.

1 Introduction

What is a *software agent*? When you pose this question to ten qualified people independently from each other, it's likely that you will get ten different explanations. Because of this situation it seems to be useful to briefly reflect again about the concept of agents and mobile agents in the context of this chapter, in order to avoid probable misunderstandings. A discussion of the advantages and disadvantages of mobile software agents has already been given in part I of this volume (especially the chapter by Chess et.al.).

One use of the word *agent* is to denote a program which has a certain knowlegde and a certain skill in a certain area and it supports users with these abilities. Generally speaking, software agents may be viewed as offering personalized value added services. Ideally, you may think of a software agent as a computer program acting on behalf of its user, like human agents already do for many years.

Let's look for example at a travel agency: The travel agents have a certain knowledge about airlines, hotels and car rental companies. They also have a certain skill: They know who to call and how to use the booking systems. And they act on behalf of their customers by making all the reservations and purchases for them. Another example for an agent may be a stock broker.

From chapter by Jim White we know that the computational environment *Telescript* was designed to allow the development of mobile objects systems. With its introduction, Telescript established the notion of *mobile agents* as a synonym for mobile computations, i.e., running programs which may autonomously migrate themselves from host to host in a computer network. When agents may autonomously decide what to do in exceptional situations, they are called *intelligent agents*.

While agents do not necessarily need to be mobile[1], there may be several advantages resulting from the mobility of the programs, depending on their purpose.

A stationary agent uses a network service by remotely invoking its operations. The results are transmitted back over the network to the agent which processes them. Depending on the results, further operations are invoked and the results are sent back to the agent (see figure 1).

---

[1] In fact, there are big discussions among computers scientists going on, whether agents should be mobile or not.

Remote Procedure Calls (RPC)

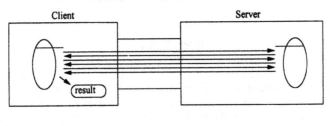

Remote Programming (RP)

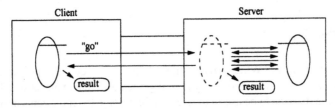

Fig. 1. Mobile agents allow for remote programming instead of RPC.

When the agent is mobile, the only difference is that it may leave its computer to 'go' directly to the machine offering the service. There it invokes all the operations locally and also processes the results locally, avoiding all the network traffic. Only when its job is finished does it return to its "home machine". The advantages of this kind of "remote programming" are:

− If the agent needs to invoke many operations to produce the desired result, it has a much better performance when there is no network involved.
− If the results of the invoked operations consist of large amounts of data, the performance may be improved when this data doesn't have to be sent over the network. This helps to reduce communication costs, bandwidth requirements and exonerates the network.[2]
− The agent may produce its results undisturbed by any network failures or breakdowns. No intermediate results will be lost and no operation has to be invoked again (sometimes, it wouldn't be possible at all[3] and the result would be completely lost in the RPC-case or the RPC-agent would at least have to completely start over again).
− Applications can implement their own protocols and APIs on server machines by simply sending mobile agents to the service providers (agents as middleware).

---

[2] Which may be particularly important in the fast growing Internet.
[3] When some internal server state had already been changed by the previous invocation.

- Mobile agents make it easier to implement value added and user-customized services.
- With the use of mobile code, automatic software upgrade processes become possible: Service providers can update the user's access software by simply sending new modules or completely new software packages to the user's client machine.

Some disadvantages of using mobile code are:

- The service and client platform have to provide an infrastructure to support mobile agents. The agents need an environment where they can 'live' inside the target machine. Network hosts or client machines have to receive the agents, reproduce their state and start them as processes or threads.
- Many new security issues arise, when mobile code is envolved:
  - The system has to be protected from malicious agents (e.g., viruses) which could steal data or system resources (see [1]).
  - Also the user's agents have to be protected from malicious providers of services and other user's agents.
  - A sophisticated accounting system is necessary for billing the agent owners. This includes mechanisms for secure identification of agents and the responsible real life person or organization as well as a fine granular capability granting mechanism to restrict what agents can do and see on the target system.
- Because sending agents may also be a 'costly' thing (in respect of using computing and network resources as well as time), a decision has to be made whether its better to send the complete agent or simply have it invoke a remote operation.

2 Telescript

As already mentioned, Telescript is a computer language which was designed to program the network[4] by enabling programs to autonomously move themselves from host to host in order to do their job.

The language was designed by Jim White, Doug Steedman, Chris Helgeson and others at General Magic, where it was developed to support so called PICs[5]—small handheld PDA[6]-like devices with little memory and slow network connections (either wireless by radio mail or cellular phones or wired to the phone network). The mobile Telescript agents enable users to initiate offline activities in networked servers, thus extending the capability of the communicators while reducing the bandwidth requirements and communication costs.

2.1 AT&T's PersonaLink

For about two years the telecommunications company AT&T offered a Telescript service called *PersonaLink* as the network to be used by PICs like Sony's *MagicLink* or

---

[4] Like Postscript was designed to program printers.
[5] PIC: *Personal Intelligent Communicator*
[6] PDA: *Personal Digital Assistant*

Motorola's *Envoy* running the operation system *MagicCap*[7] (also developed by General Magic). MagicCap offers a very intuitive user interface reflecting a real world environment with an office, a hallway with several rooms and a downtown area with different buildings representing different network services. It was designed to be used via a touch screen in order to keep the PIC devices small.

Users simply wrote *postcards* to communicate to each other. These postcards were a kind of active emails which to a certain extend may be compared to SafeTcl MIME messages (see [2]). They were carried by Telescript agents, which were sent into the PersonaLink Telescript server for delivery. Before sending a postcard, the user could 'tell' the agent different delivery options by attaching 'stamps' (graphical icons) to the card. Inside the network, the agent could, e.g., wait for a certain time before delivering its mail to a special PIC. When not successful up to a certain time, it could (depending on its options) convert it to a fax (dropping possible audio annotations, taking the starting pictures of contained animations and so on) and send it to a user's fax machine or an Internet mailbox instead of the PIC.

Receiving a postcard was receiving a Telescript agent which was delivering the postcard to MagicCap before it died. MagicCap integrated postcards into the runtime environment, so a postcard could contain active userinterface components (e.g., a button to automatically confirm a proposed meeting by sending another agent).

Despite it's interesting features, AT&T shut down PersonaLink in 1996. One reason might have been, that not enough users owned PICs running MagicCap compared to the millions of users of the evolving World-Wide Web. However, the support of PICs is only one field where mobile agents can be useful. This chapter will show, how users also may benefit from Telescript agents when using the WWW. MagicCap is interesting in its own right and became available as an application for Microsoft's Windows. This situation shows once again how difficult it is for new technology to survive without supporting widely used existing platforms.

Telescript was the first language where processes implicitly possess the ability to migrate themselves during runtime. Meanwhile, there are extensions and libraries which also allow computations in other languages (like, e.g., Java [3], Tcl [4]) to be mobile to a certain extend. This shows that the ideas and concepts behind Telescript are still of interest.

2.2   Language Characteristics of Telescript

Telescript is an interpreted programming language which is strongly typed and purely object-oriented. There are two levels of the language: *High Telescript*, the language used to write programs, is compiled into *Low Telescript*, a postscript like language which can be interpreted more efficiently by the runtime environment (the so-called *engine*). Low Telescript code still contains all the class information, so that an agent can carry the class definitions it needs to other hosts. Telescript provides inherent multi-threading support, several process synchronization mechanisms and a fine grained resource consumption control. Everything in Telescript is an object—all agents, e.g., are subclassed of the

---

[7] Cap: *communicating applications platform*

`Process` class, which implements active objects (threads). The engine provides object-persistence and automatic memory management: Whenever the system crashes, it can be restarted and the agents resume execution from a consistent state.

The language only supports single inheritance, but adds a new type of class. These so-called *mix-in classes* are classes, that can—like a baseclass—be 'mixed-in' to a new class definition which then inherits the interface and the implementation from the mix-in class. However, mix-in classes are not part of the normal derivation hierarchy and can be used whenever necessary.

For agent-agent and agent-service interaction, Telescript provides several high-level concepts. Among them are:

- *Agents* (mobile processes) which are able to migrate themselves to other *places* on the same or a different machine. They move themselves by executing a single inherited command: `go`. This command stops the agent's thread, collects all the objects owned by the agent as well as the execution stack, serializes, encrypts and encodes the agent, creates a communication channel and instantiates the agent on the other machine. There the agent's execution continues with the program statement following the `go`-statement which moved the agent.
- *Places* are stationary processes, which are usually used to implement services. Places are inhabited by agents.
- *Authorities* are objects tied to agents and places which unforgeable identify the real world institution (person or organization) which is responsible for the actions of the agent or place.
- *Tickets* are objects which describe an agents journey. They are usually used as argument to `go` and `clone` instructions and contain the source and destination addresses, as well as a description of the `way` (communication protocol) the agent should take.
- *Permits* are objects which define the capabilities of an agent or constrain its resource consumption. Agents receive a permit when they are created and when the permit is consumed, the agent dies. A place, e.g., may impose further restrictions upon entering agents, based on their identity. Table 1 lists the attributes of a permit. Its first section lists the capabilities and the attributes in the second section control the resource usage.
- *Meetings* are the way agents communicate with each other. To initiate a meeting, an agent has to present a valid *Petition*. Through the `meet` operation an agent receives a reference to the other agent and may call this agent's methods.
- *Object Ownership* makes sure that each agent can decide who gets access to its objects. Whenever an agent goes somewhere else, the system automatically collects its objects and voids any remaining references to these objects (maintained by other agents). The ownership of objects can be transferred between agents and/or places.

3 Telescript Web Tools (Tabriz)

The Internet became a huge source of information and offers already many different services. Because it can be very time consuming for people to cope with this overwhelming

canCharge	to consume teleclicks
canCreate	to create other processes
canDeny	to decrease capabilities of other processes
canGrant	to increase capabilities of other processes
canGo	to migrate to other places/machines
canRestart	to allow restart after crash
age	lifetime in seconds
charges	teleclicks (resource money)
hline extend	memory size in octets
authenticity	maximum authenticity
priority	maximum priority

Table 1. Attributes of a Telescript Permit object.

amount of data, agents—and especially mobile agents—could be an ideal tool to help users in this quickly changing environment. In fact, many of the already existing search indices, shopping agents, portofolio trackers and meta services (which combine other services to a new service) represent agents.

To make it possible to use the Telescript infrastructure in the Internet environment, a set of tools (called *Telescript Active Web Tools* or *Tabriz*)

- allow users to create and control mobile Telescript agents via ordinary web browsers, and
- also enable Telescript agents to access the WWW like users would do it, so that they can act on behalf of them.

3.1 Accessing Agents from the Web

Users talk to their agents by simply selecting special hyperlinks or filling out special forms with their web browsers. The forms and pages in turn are custom generated by their agents.

Figure 2 shows how a Telescript agent is created by the WebToTSPlace and sent to the UserHomePlace. Both these places are permanent and have been created during the startup of the system. The UserHomePlace is a special place where personalized pages of different users will be stored based on the users' profile and their activity during previous sessions. While the user is offline, agents will store the results of their work in this place. They may add sections to the user's home page as well as new hyperlinks to pages they have found or generated themselves. These pages could be stored directly in the UserHomePlace or in different places on other machines. The UserHomePlace might also offer pages for the management of still active agents and pending service requests like, e.g., monitoring a certain HTML page for modifications.

A Telescript engine serves as a backend to an ordinary HTTP-server accessed through the normal CGI mechanism. The HTTP-server provides a normal HTML page which contains the URLs to let users access Telescript services, e.g., a URL like

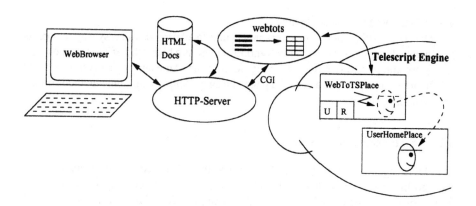

Fig. 2. Create and control mobile agents with a web browser

```
http://spock:3000/login/telescript/UserHome/getHomePage
```

This will cause the browser to establish a HTTP connection on TCP/IP-port 3000 with the HTTP-server running on host `spock`. That server processes the URL as follows: The part `login` will require the user to log in first. The part `telescript` will cause the creation of the CGI-process `webtots` which is creating the C++ representation[8] of a Telescript `dictionary` (an associative array) from all the data provided by the HTTP-server and the user (e.g. input to an HTML form). Finally, it establishes a connection to the Telescript engine. Because the above example URL does not contain any information which requests to reconnect to an already existing agent belonging to that user, the default will cause the `WebToTSPlace` to create a new agent and direct it to the `UserHomePlace`. There it will call the `getHomePage` method of this place to fetch the Telescript objects representing the user's home page and generate the page from these objects which finally will be returned to the user's browser.

The `webtots` place contains two mix-in's (see explanation of mix-in classes in section 2.2 on page 5) containing the service registry and the user account profiles (represented by the boxes 'U' and 'R' in figure 2). These are necessary to assign agents to identified users ('U' for user profiles) and route them to the appropriate services ('R' for service registry).

There are two types of agents: interactive and non-interactive agents. The interactive agents represent a web user's long-lived session. They have their own TCP/IP port[9] and maintain the state information of the session. These agents put the data which is necessary for browsers to reconnect into the pages they generate. Non-interactive agents on the other hand are used to implement offline activities of their users. They usually cooperate

---

[8] To communicate with external processes implemented in C++, Telescript agents can use the so-called *external methods framework* which provides the automatic translation of Telescript-objects into equivalent C++ objects and vice versa.

[9] This port is protected by a magic cookie in order to prevent the agent to be 'stolen' by another web user.

with interactive agents at some time.

An HTML API (application programmers interface) provides an easy way for agents to generate documents. They simply compose a page as a hierarchy of Telescript objects which are automatically rendered during output time. An example is given in section 4.2. In order to manipulate a part of a page, the agent simply calls some methods on the corresponding object.

3.2 Agents accessing the Web

In order for agents to act on behalf of their users, they also need the capability to access the web like users would do it with their browsers. This capability is provided by the WebAccessing mix-in ('W' in figure 3) which provides a high-level Telescript API and connects to the external process tstoweb to access the web. This process makes use of the libwww client library [5].

The web tools provide an HTML parsing mechanism, which transforms a page fetched from the web into the corresponding Telescript object hierarchy of the HTML API representation for further analysis by the agents.

However, Telescript agents may not only use the web as a data source. They may also make use of common databases with the help of special database access mixins ('D' in figure 3) which are used by information access agents. These hide the details of the data source and its API from other agents. This way, the database system can be replaced without affecting existing applications. In figure 3, the service provider agents (the ones 'looking' to the left) may provide excatly the same method interface, although they use different types of data sources (web/database system). This is another example for "agents as middleware".

3.3 A Distributed Marketplace Scenario

The example of figure 3 also serves to show several alternatives of how interactive and non-interactive agents may work together in a distributed environment to provide a flexible service.

There are two services made available through the FleamarketPlace and ClassAdsPlace which allow people to buy and sell things. It is assumed, that the two are located in two different cities close to each other: one could, e.g., be operated by a fleamarket organizer and the other by a newspaper which has a classified adverisments section. The service agents, however, are derived from the same superclass, which gives them the same method interface. Even if the ClassAdsPlace service agent should provide some additional methods, the client agents can interact with it because they know the interface of its superclass.

Services, like shops of an electronic marketplace, register with a service directory in the engine (the service registry 'R' in figure 3). Agents in search of a certain service can consult this registry.

Let's assume a user named Doro wants to buy a used pink parachute. Since this is something which is not usually offered every day in the newspaper, she hopes to find it with the support of software agents.

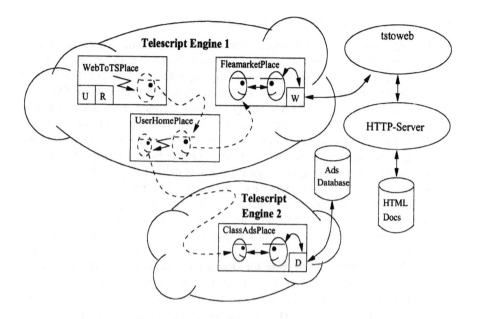

Fig. 3. Agents interacting and accessing the web.

She creates an interactive agent[10] and gives it a description of the pink parachute. This agent looks in the service registry of the WebToTSPlace for shops which sell used goods, finds the FleamarketPlace and the ClassAdsPlace and receives the necessary ticket objects to go there.

First it goes to the UserHomePlace adding itself to the list of Doro's uncomplete activities and making a remark on her main entry page. Then it creates a non-interactive agent (the little one in figure 3), gives it the order and the ticket for the ClassAdsPlace of the newspaper company's Telescript engine and goes to the FleamarketPlace. There it meets the service agent and asks it for the pink parachute. Unfortunately, there is currently nobody offering such a thing. So the service agent adds the request to a list of things to look for[11] and Doro's request agent puts itself to sleep. Whenever somebody is offering a pink parachute, the service agent will awake Doro's agent and tell it who the seller is. Then Doro's agent will go back to the UserHomePlace, add the description of the offer to Doro's private pages and send a message to her pager.

Meanwhile Doro's non-interactive agent went to the engine of the newspaper in the other city after it made a note about it in Doro's private pages. There are now several possibilities, how non-interactive agents can operate in such a distributed environment, depending on what the service providers think is appropriate for a special task. Let's assume that somebody named Sandy actually offered a pink parachute in the newspaper

---

[10] An agent derived from the webtools' InteractiveRequestAgent class.

[11] The service agent acts as a so-called *watcher-agent*.

and Doro's non-interactive agent got her address.

- It could simply go back to the `UserHomePlace` and add Sandy's address to Doro's pages together with some other updates and send Doro an email before it dies.
- It could have added a special URL to Doro's entry page before it left the `UserHomePlace` so that she can look for the non-interactive agent's results on the engine of the newspaper company. After it received Sandy's address, it would create a page for Doro and store it for her in the `UserHomePlace` of the newspaper company's engine. Then it would send her an email before it dies. Doro could follow the URL which the non-interactive agent has stored on her entry page to read the page stored in the newspaper company's engine. Then Doro would delete this page from the newspaper company's engine (otherwise a cleaning agent of the newspaper's company would remove it later depending on the page's expiration date).
- It could also be a policy, that non-interactive agents have no rights to store objects anywhere. In this case Doro's non-interactive agent would have gone back to the `UserHomePlace` of the first engine and simply sent Doro an email but it would also have waited there for Doro's interactive agent to return from the `FleamarketPlace`. Then this agent would take the non-interactive agent's results (Sandy's address), make a little report about the completed tasks and send Doro a note. It would add the report to Doro's private pages and remove the note it made in the "uncomplete activities" page. Then both the interactive and the non-interactive agent would die.

4   Linking Telescript and Java

Java is also an object-oriented language, modeled after C and C++. It was developed by James Gosling and others at Sun. Java is being positioned as an *Internet programming language*. Its runtime environment is provided by several web browsers (like Netscape and Microsoft-Explorer) which contain their own Java interpreter. This allows the automated downloading and execution of so-called *Java applets*: Java programs which usually possess a graphical output area inside an HTML document and can take user input from the common input devices like keyboard and mouse.

Similar to images, Java applets are embedded into web documents with a special HTML tag (see the example in section 4.2). The HTTP based downloading process is also very similar to the automated downloading of images. In case an applet needs to use classes which are not already installed in the runtime environment, a `Classloader` allows them to automatically download the missing Java class definitions.

This automated downloading and execution process gives Java programs a kind of *passive mobility*. The language itself doesn't allow programs to migrate themselves autonomously, but an *Object Serialization Package* [6] allows to exchange Java objects between networked computers which enables programmers to not only send Java code to other machines but also state information. Currently, a lot of work is going on to extend the Java runtime environment in different ways to allow the development of mobile Java agents (see, e.g., [7, 8]).

Compared to C++, some of the more 'complicated' features like multiple inheritance and templates have been removed. Java also has multithreading support and automatic memory management, and for security reasons there are no explicit pointers (like Telescript).

Java programs are usually pre-compiled into Java bytecode which can be interpreted more efficiently than most other interpreted languages. Another reason for this is that before the execution begins, a *bytecode verifier* makes sure that

- there are no stack over- and underflows,
- that parameter types are always correct,
- and there are no illegal type conversions
- as well as no object attribute access violations.

These a-priori verifications reduce the need for verifications during runtime.

Because mobile code in general brings up many new security issues in order to prevent systems and agents from malicious activities—think, e.g., of viruses which now could sneak into your system much more easily or people stealing credit card numbers from your agents while they are "in transit"—the developers of languages like Java and Telescript had to consider the experience gained from many "hacker attacks" in the Internet. In Java, e.g., the renounciation of pointers and the bytecode verifier help to provide more security, but there are also other mechanisms or simply restrictions of the capabilities of programs executing in remote systems. Applets, e.g., may currently not access the local file system of a client machine, nor may they usually open other network connections than to the server they came from.

More information about Java can be obtained from online resources like [9, 10] or from books like, e.g., [11] or [12].

4.1 Java-Telescript Cooperation

As we saw, Telescript allows remote programming of servers via mobile agents and Java can be used to remotely program network clients and already provides a large installed base of runtime environments in the form of web browsers on client machines. So Java and Telescript can perfectly complement each other:

- Java gives Telescript agents a face (a nice client-side user interface)
- Java allows Telescript agents to initiate computations on client machines
- Telescript provides the high level concepts for mobile agent programming
- Telescript allows Java to create and control server-side agents

In this section Java programs (applets and applications) are treated as *user interface agents* (or *GUI-agents*). They act as client-side agents which are sent by network services to the user's client machine to provide an optimized graphical user interface for online user-interaction. This may be better adapted to the service than HTML form based interfaces. The response time of such GUI-agents can be much shorter, because they can maintain multiple permanent communication connections to Telescript agents in the network and they can also process continous data streams.

However, they don't necessarily need to maintain these open connections which is why they can be called agents. Telescript agents can provide GUI-agents with data, which they may then process offline. E.g., a Telescript agent can search for 3D models of a special type of house. Then it would send the 3D description in form of points, polygons, colors and patterns to its corresponding GUI-agent, which then would be able to calculate 3D views of the houses directly on the client machine. This reduces the load of the server machine as well as the network and the users can have much faster simulations.

In general, the server agents can filter some data (obtained by querying databases or other web sources) and the GUI-agents can do the final processing of the data. Both types of agents can do their work 'offline'. They only connect to exchange some data.

But GUI-agents can do more:

- They can keep profiles of the user's preferences on the client machine.[12]
- In cooperation with service agents, they can provide a personalized view of the server environment, e.g., the user does not see the full range of services offered by a provider, but only the ones he or she is interested in.
- They can provide various kinds of cache functionality.
- They can collect statistical information about the user's activity, which can be used to optimize the user interface and the network service.

One early example of such a GUI-agent can be seen in a tool called WebMap [13], which analyzes a user's "journey through hyperspace" and maintains an always up-to-date two-dimensional graphical map of the web as far as the user has already seen it. This map is to help users not to "get lost in hyperspace" and to directly navigate in the user's "personal web" by remote-controlling the browser. WebMaps can be stored on the client machine and re-used in future sessions. When WebMap was developed, Java was not available, yet. That's why WebMap was written in [incr Tcl] [14], another object-oriented interpreted language based on Tcl which is also well suited for the development of mobile agents.

When a user is looking for services of a special type (e.g. CD stores), Telescript agents could be of assistance in different ways:

- They could simply try to find services of this type, and provide their user with a list of these services (similar to the widely used search engines like e.g. the *WebCrawler* [15]). When the user selects one of these services, the service provider could send a specialized GUI-agent to the client machine, which represents the user from the service provider's perspective.
- There could be a value added Telescript service, where the agents play the role of brokers. They would directly interact with all the stores and offer a homogenous user interface to all of them (a value added service).

4.2   Indirect Interaction of Java GUI-Agents and Telescript Agents

There are two types of applet/agent interaction: indirect via HTML and HTTP and direct using raw TCP/IP sockets. This section describes the indirect interaction.

---

[12] The current security restrictions make this impossible for Java applets. So in these cases Java applications have to be used.

In section 3.1 we saw, that Telescript agents can be controlled using HTTP requests. Java applets in turn are able to interact in a limited way with their hosting browser and submit URL requests. A natural solution is to have Telescript agents send Java GUI-agents to browsers by simply embedding HTML <APPLET> tags into the generated documents. The applets can indirectly be controlled by parametrizing their behaviour inside the <APPLET> tag.

The following example shows how this can be done using the Telescript HTML API. Several Telescript objects together describe the document which will be generated later at output time. This example also shows, how a complete definition[13] of a simple interactive mobile Telescript agent looks like:

```
MyAgent: class (InteractiveRequestAgent) = (
  public
    initialize: op(...) = {
      ^;
      *.myCGI.setValue("PATH_INFO", "indexPage");
      *.rewind("indexPage",*.myCGI);
    };

    createPage: op() HTMLParent|Nil = {
      // This will be the default page returned by this agent.
      page := HTMLPage("Hello World");
      HTMLString(page,nil,"Hello World",HTML_TITLE,1,HTML_CENTER,true);
      HTMLRule(page);
      HTMLString(page,nil,"This page was created by a Telescript agent.");

      // Send and parametrize a java applet
      applet := HTMLApplet(page,nil,"JavaSocketExample.class",
        HTML_CODEBASE,"/",HTML_HEIGHT,200,HTML_WIDTH,400,HTML_CENTER,true);
      HTMLParam(applet,"telescriptHost",*.myCGI.getValue("SERVER_NAME"));
      HTMLParam(applet,"telescriptPort",*.myCGI.getValue("SERVER_PORT"));
      HTMLParam(applet,"agentClass", "MyAgent");

      return page;
    };
); // MyAgent
```

The initialize method is the constructor which will be invoked, whenever an object of class MyAgent is created, but before the control is given to the agent's thread which will implicitly be created because of the derivation from the base class InteractiveRequestAgent. This base class also provides all the web connectivity. The '^' operator is a shortcut notation for invoking the superclass constructor with all the arguments given to the MyAgent constructor. The next two lines are a little "base class magic" which cause that the default page returned by the agent will be the one created by the createPage method. The '*' operator is a shortcut for the this reference to invoke base class methods.

The createPage method constructs a HTML page by building a hierarchy of HTML objects. The root is the page object which has four child objects: The centered title string "Hello World", a horizontal rule, the String "This page was created by a Telescript agent." and a centered <APPLET> tag defining an applet with a window size of 200 times 400 pixels. The applet object itself has three child objects which are the parameters for the applet: The name of the host running the

---

[13] The inclusion of header files was omitted here.

Telescript engine, the port to connect to the engine and the class name of an agent to be created by the applet (which here for simplicity will be another `MyAgent`). The attribute `myCGI` is an associative array containing all the CGI variables supplied by the HTTP server. The generated HTML code looks like this:

```
<HTML><!DOCTYPE HTML PUBLIC "-//W3O//DTD W3 HTML 3.2//EN">
<HEAD><TITLE>Hello World</TITLE></HEAD>
<BODY ><CENTER>
<H1>Hello World</H1></CENTER>
<HR>This page was created by a Telescript agent.
<CENTER><APPLET CODE="CreateMyAgent.class" CODEBASE="/"
  WIDTH=400 HEIGHT=200>
  <PARAM  NAME="telescriptHost"  VALUE="spock">
  <PARAM  NAME="telescriptPort"  VALUE="3000">
  <PARAM  NAME="agentClass"  VALUE="MyAgent">
</APPLET></CENTER>
<CENTER><FONT SIZE=3>Everything above this line was provided by your agent
  </FONT></CENTER>
<HR>
<CENTER><FONT SIZE=3>Everything below this line was provided by the place
  </FONT></CENTER>
<TABLE><TR><TD><FORM ACTION="/cgi-bin/telescript/endSession"  METHOD=GET
  ENCTYPE="x-www-form-encoded" >
  <INPUT  TYPE=HIDDEN NAME="PORT"  VALUE="10000">
  <INPUT  TYPE=HIDDEN NAME="HOST"  VALUE="spock">
  <INPUT  TYPE=HIDDEN NAME="MAGIC_COOKIE"  VALUE=",U8kEVZ.w,..F,">
  <B>Session Controls: </B><INPUT  TYPE=SUBMIT  VALUE="Kill Agent" >
</FORM></TD></TR></TABLE>
</BODY>
</HTML>
```

This output page does not only contain the HTML code generated through the `createPage` method of a `MyAgent`, but also a default header and trailer. In addition, the place which currently is inhabited by the agent has added some output to the generated page (the line "`... provided by the place`").

The page also contains some information in the hidden fields `PORT`, `HOST` and `MAGIC_COOKIE` to directly connect back to this agent via its personal port 10000. The form interface of this Telescript agent consists only of a submit button to kill the agent which will end the user's session.

The Java code for creating a simple Telescript agent of class `MyAgent` might look like this:

```
public class CreateMyAgent extends Applet {
  String telescriptURL, agentClass;

  public void init() {
    String telescriptHost = getParameter("telescriptHost");
    String telescriptPort = getParameter("telescriptPort");
    agentClass = getParameter("agentClass");
    telescriptURL = "http://"+telescriptHost+":"+telescriptPort+"/cgi-bin/telescript";
  }
  // ... (other code here)

  public void createAgentCallback() throws MalformedURLException {
    URL createAgent = new URL(null, telescriptURL+"?CLASS="+agentClass);
    this.getAppletContext().showDocument(createAgent);
  }
}
```

The constructor of the Applet reads the parameters for the Telescript hostname and accessport as well as the class of the agent to be created from the web page. The user may finally invoke the method `createAgentCallback` to create a Telescript agent of the desired class (which may have been replaced by the user interactively). This method creates a URL object to connect to the Telescript engine and appends some arguments to it (here the `CLASS` of the agent to be created). Finally it tells the browser to submit the necessary HTTP request by invoking the method `showDocument`.

4.3 Direct Interaction of Java GUI-Agents and Telescript Agents

The indirect HTTP based interaction described in the previous section is easy to use and very flexible. Because of the many translation stages, however, this method is not very efficient. In some cases, direct communication channels between Java GUI-agents and Telescript agent may be the preferred choice.

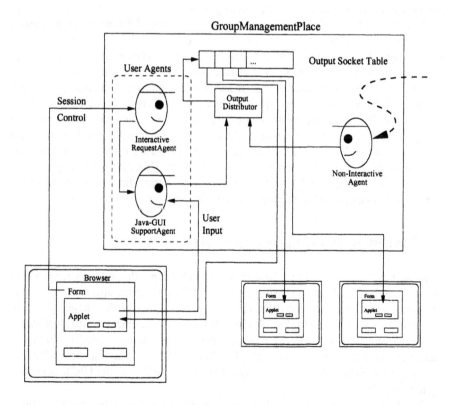

Fig. 4. Telescript– and Java GUI-Agents implementing groupware.

Both agent types may handle TCP/IP sockets in both client and server roles. Usually the agent which creates the other agent it wants to interact with plays the server role (mostly Telescript agents which send applets to the client machines). However, when Telescript agents go to another machine, they may be forced to use different TCP/IP ports after their arrival. In this case the Java GUI-agent will wait for the agent to reconnect after its migration is complete.

The example in figure 4 shows how direct communication channels can be used to provide a simple groupware framework (e.g. for collaborative drawing, game playing or a chat application). Telescript agents are used to manage a collaborating group of users. The question might arise "why is there a need for *mobile* agents?", and in fact such a groupware application can be done without mobile agents using other multicast mechanisms. However, the Telescript agents which provide the user interaction functionality can easily interact with and often benefit from *mobile* Telescript agents whenever the need should arise.

E.g., an automated scheduling system might send a non-interactive agent to the `GroupManagementPlace` to remind all the group members of an important date by simply giving it to the `OutputDistributor` object. Or a user who cannot join the group at the time of the 'online meeting' could send an agent from a PIC while travelling. This agent's job would be to capture a protocol of the messages exchanged by the group members.

The multithreading capability of Telescript and Java makes it easy to process input from several channels: for each input channel simply a new thread is created. In the example of figure 4 each user has his or her personal *InteractiveRequestAgent*. This agent generates an HTML form which contains the GUI elements for controlling the session as well as an embedded Java applet[14] for the interaction with other users of the group. Because there now are two input channels—session control input from the form and input from the Java applet—the InteractiveRequestAgent creates another Telescript agent responsible for the output socket of the applet. This *Java-GUI-SupportAgent* processes the user input and forwards the result to an output distribution object of the place which then distributes the information to the Java applets of connected users.

5   Conclusion and Acknowledgements

Many things are going on in the field of research about mobile agents. A few starting pointers can be found here: [16] (for Germany: [17]). Agents are also starting to raise more and more interest in the commercial area. New types of distributed operating systems like, e.g., *Inferno* [18] (which allows to integrate consumer electronics products with computer networks) already contain many of the features needed for an agent infrastructure. Inferno was developed at Bell Labs by a team including Dennis Ritchie who played a major role in the development of the C language, the UNIX operating system and *plan 9*.

The M0 messenger language [19] is also very interesting regarding communications and operating systems. The ARA research project [20], tries to give agents in different languages a real 'go'-capability like Telescript does and the ffMAIN infrastucture [21, 22] uses HTTP to send agents of arbitrary languages between special agent servers.

---

[14] See example in section 4.2.

Many of the security issues regarding agents are still not completely solved, and when there finally is a commonly accepted security paradigm and world-wide authentication mechanism, it will have to prove its worth in the unpredictable environment of the Internet. Probably the evolving electronic payment solutions will help with this problem.

What also is missing is a good infrastructure for routing agents to the right destinations, for helping them to find what they are looking for in network areas "where no agent has ever been before". The concepts developed with KQML (the Knowledge Query and Manipulation Language; see also [23]) may play an important role. Also the research about trading mechanisms seems to be useful here.

More and more people are becoming excited about *agents* these days and research in the field of *intelligent agents* has been going on for many years. However, until now there is no "killer application" for agents (like the Mosaic and Netscape browsers were for the development of the WWW), yet. The reason for this might be, that the web is based on rather simple mechanisms, but agent development has to deal with much more complex problems. So there is the danger, that people may become disappointed as quickly as they became excited. But regardless whatever the current mobile agent *image* looks like, the concept of mobile code nevertheless allows to create a new breed of distributed applications.

The *Telescript Active Web Tools* [24] (pre-release of the current *TabrizWare* [25]) were developed by General Magic's Internet group: Adam Hertz, Chris Bloom, Hamilton Hitchings, Jody Reed, Don Woods, Kate Greer and the author. Many thanks goes to Rita Burke and Gerd Döben-Henisch from the *Institute for New Media* (http://www.inm.de/) who helped to prepare this chapter ...

References

1. **Tardo, Joseph; Valente, Luis [1996]:** *Mobile Agent Security and Telescript*; Proceedings of COMPCON'96, IEEE 1063-6390/96, San Jose, Feb 1996, pp 58–63.
2. **Borenstein, Nathaniel S.; Rose, Marshall T. [1994]:** *EMail With A Mind of Its Own: The Safe-Tcl Language for Enabled Mail*; ULPAA'94, Barcelona; ftp://ftp.fv.com//pub/code/other/safe-tcl.tar.gz
3. **Gosling, James; McGilton, Henry [1996]:** *The Java Language Environment*; http://www.javasoft.com/doc/language_environment/
4. **Ousterhout, John [1994]:** *Tcl and the Tk Toolkit*; Addison-Wesley Publishing Company (ISBN 0-201-63337-X); http://www.sunlabs.com/research/tcl/, http://www.NeoSoft.com/tcl/
5. **Frystyk Nielsen, Henrik; Berners-Lee, Tim; Lie, Hakon; Baird-Smith, Anselm; Kahan, Jose; Groff, Jean-Francois [1996]:** *Libwww - The W3C Reference Library*; http://www.w3.org/pub/WWW/Library/
6. **Java Distributed Systems:** *Object Serialization*; http://chatsubo.javasoft.com/current/serial/index.html
7. **Hohl, Fritz; Baumann, Joachim; Strasser, Markus; Rothermel [1996]:** *Project Mole*; http://www.informatik.uni-stuttgart.de/ipvr/vs/projekte/mole.html
8. **Albayrak, Sahin; Ballmann, Siegfried; Harijono, Indra Gunawan; Többen Hermann [1996]:** *InAMoS: Intelligent Agents for Mobile Services, InAVAS: Intelligent Agents for Value Added Services*; http://dai.cs.tu-berlin.de/e/projekte/
9. **JavaSoft:** *Documentation Index*; http://www.javasoft.com/nav/read/docindex.html

10. **Gamelan:** http://www.gamelan.com/index.shtml
11. **Flanagan, David [1996]:** *Java in a Nutshell*; O'Reilly & Associates, Inc. (ISBN 1-56592-183-6); http://http://www.ora.com/catalog/books/javanut/, http://http://www.ora.com/info/java/
12. **Lemay, Laura; Perkins, Charles L. [1996]:** *Teach Yourself Java in 21 Days*; Sams.net Publishing (ISBN 1-575521-030-4)
13. **Dömel, Peter [1995]:** *WebMap - A Graphical Hypertext Navigation Tool*; WWW Fall'94; Computer Networks and ISDN Systems, Vol. 28: 85-97, Elsevier Science B.V., Netherlands; http://www.ncsa.uiuc.edu/SDG/IT94/Proceedings/Searching/doemel/www-fall94.html
14. **McLennan, Michael J. (michael.mclennan@att.com) [1994]:** *[incr Tcl]*; http://www.tcltk.com/itcl/
15. **Pinkerton, Brian [1994]:** *Finding What People Want: Experiences with the WebCrawler*; WWW Fall'94, Chicago; http://www.ncsa.uiuc.edu/SDG/IT94/Proceedings/Searching/pinkerton/WebCrawler.html
16. **Agent Research Pointers:** http://www.sics.se/ps/abc/survey.html/, http://www.agent.org/, http://www.doc.mmu.ac.uk/STAFF/mike/links.html
17. **Fünfrocken, Stefan [1996]:** *German Agent Page*; http://www.informatik.th-darmstadt.de/fuenf/work/agenten/agenten.html
18. **Lucent Technologies:** *Inferno*; http://www.lucent.com/inferno/
19. **Tschudin, Christian Frédéric [1995]:** *Protokollimplementierung mit Kommunikationsboten (in German)* KiVS'95 Conference, Chemnitz Germany; http://www.tu-chemnitz.de/fri/kivs/kivs95.html, file://cui.unige.ch/pub/msgr/papers/kivs95.ps.Z
20. **Peine Holger; Stolpmann, Torsten; Nehmer, Jürgen [1996]:** *Ara: Agents for Remote Actions*; http://www.uni-kl.de/AG-Nehmer/Ara/
21. **Lingnau, Anselm; Drobnik, Oswald; Dömel, Peter [1995]:** *An HTTP-based Infrastructure for Mobile Agents*; WWW Fall'95, Boston; O'Reilly & Associates, Inc., The World-Wide Web Journal, Forth International World-Wide Web Conference Proceedings (ISBN 1-56592-169-0), pp 461–471; http://www.w3.org/pub/Conferences/WWW4/Papers/150/
22. **Lingnau, Anselm; Drobnik, Oswald [1996]:** *Making Mobile Agents Communicate: A Flexible Approach*; The First Annual Confernce on Emerging Technologies and Applications in Communications, Portland, Oregon, pp 180–183;
23. **Finin, Tim; Thirunavukkarasu, Chelliah; Potluri, Anupama; McKay, Donald; McEntire, Robin [1995]:** *On Agent Domains, Agent Names and Proxy Agents*; Proceedings of the ACM CIKM Intelligent Information Agents Workshop, Baltimore; http://www.cs.umbc.edu/ cikm/iia/submitted/viewing/finin/
24. **Dömel, Peter [1996]:** *Mobile Telescript Agents and the Web*; Proceedings of COMPCON'96, IEEE 1063-6390/96, San Jose, Feb 1996, pp 52–57.
25. **General Magic:** *Tabriz*; http://www.genmagic.com/Tabriz/

Part IV
Appendix

Glossary

This glossary was prepared from material and comments contributed by Luca Cardelli, Gianpaolo Cugola, Carlo Ghezzi, Gian Pietro Picco, Christian Tschudin, Giovanni Vigna and Jan Vitek.

Anchored resource A resource which may not be moved to another host, these usually include the like of devices, user interface elements, or files.

Checkpointing Checkpointing, in this context refers to the operation of saving the execution state of a running computation.

Code closure A code closure is the collection of code fragments required for the successful execution a routine, thread or computation. A code closure is exact if it includes only the code fragments that will be executed. It is approximate if it includes code fragments that will not be executed.

Code fragment — A code fragment is a syntactically valid sequence of instructions.

Code Mobility — In the context of *mobile code languages*, the term mobility refers to mechanisms to move code among different *computational environments*.

Code On Demand paradigm (COD) — It is a paradigm to develop *mobile code applications*. MCAs developed using this paradigm can download and link on-the-fly part of their code from a different (remote) component that acts as a code server.

Component — Components are *resources* or *computations*.

Computation — A computation denotes an executing program composed of one or more active *threads*. Each computation consists of a *code closure* which specifies its behaviour, an *execution state* which stores all control information related to the execution the computation and a *data space* that includes all the *resources* accessible by the computation.

Computational Environment (CE) — The computational environment is a container for *components*. It provides some low level services and controls access to underlying resources of the host. The CE's implementation may be a run-time system on top of a standard operating system or an operating system in its own right.

Data space — The data space of an *computation* is composed of all the *resources* accessible from all the active routines of that computation.

Data closure — The data closure of an *execution unit* is the set of all local and non-local *resources* that are accessible by the currently executing routine. This *data space* constituent allows the computation to proceed, possibly calling other routines, but does not necessarily include the resources of the routine's caller.

Execution state — The execution state holds all the control information related to a computation. For example, the instruction pointer is part of the execution state.

External resources — Resources that are outside of the *computational environment*, e.g. a window in the host's windowing system.

Location — A location is a named *computational environment*. Locations names may be globally unique or relative to the current computational environment.

Mobile Agent — The term *Mobile Agent* lacks a widely recognized definition. In this context, we assume that a mobile agent is a synonym of *mobile computation*.

Mobile Code Applications (MCA) — Mobile Code Applications are software systems that exploit some form of *code mobility*.

Mobile Code Language (MCL) — A programming language supporting *code mobility*.

Mobile Object System — A mobile object system is an *object system* which can move autonomously from a CE to another CE in order carry out a computation.

Mobile Computation — It is a computation which is able to migrate autonomously to a different *computational environment*. Mobile computations imply code mobility.

Mobile Software Agent — see *Mobile Agent*.

Object System — An object system is a computation whose data space is composed of objects and whose code closure contains the code that specifies the behaviour of the objects.

Remote Evaluation paradigm (REV) — It is a paradigm to develop *mobile code applications*. Any *component* of an MCA developed using this paradigm can invoke services provided by other components (located on different *computational environments* by providing not only the input data needed to perform the service (like in a remote procedure call scheme) but also providing the code that describes how to perform the service.

Remote reference — A network reference allows a *computation* to access *components* that are located on a *computational environment* other than the one where the computation is being executed.

Resource — Resources are passive entities representing data.

State distribution — The use of network references enables an *execution unit* to own a *data space* that is composed of components spread on different *computational environments*. We refer to this situation with the term "state distribution", because a relevant portion of the state of a computation (the *data space*) is actually distributed on different CEs.

Thread — A sequential flow of control.

Ubiquitous resources — *Resources* guaranteed to be present in all the *computational environments*.

List of Authors (Feb 1997)

Anurag Acharya, M. Ranganathan, Joel Saltz

```
Department of Computer Science
University of Maryland, College Park 20742
{acha, ranga, saltz}@cs.umd.edu
```

Luca Cardelli, Krishna Bharat

```
Digital SRC
130 Lytton Ave
Palo Alto, CA 94301, USA
{luca, bharat}@pa.dec.com
http://www.research.digital.com/SRC/personal/Luca_Cardelli/home.html
```

David Chess, Colin Harrison, Aaron Kershenbaum

```
IBM Thomas J. Watson Research Center
Post Office Box 704
Yorktown Heights, New York, USA 10598
{chess, cgh}@watson.ibm.com
http://www.research.ibm.com/massdist/
```

```
Dept. of Computer Science
Polytechnic University
333 Jay Street
Brooklyn, NY 11201
akershen@poly.edu
```

Paolo Ciancarini, Davide Rossi

```
Dipartimento di Scienze dell'Informazione
University of Bologna - Italy
{cianca, rossi}@cs.unibo.it
```

Gianpaolo Cugola, Carlo Ghezzi, Gian Pietro Picco, Giovanni Vigna

```
Dip. Elettronica e Informazione, Politecnico di Milano
P.za L. Da Vinci 23, 20100 Milano, Italy
{cugola, ghezzi, vigna}@elet.polimi.it
```

```
Dip. Automatica e Informatica, Politecnico di Torino
C.so Duca degli Abruzzi 24, 10129 Torino, Italy
picco@polito.it
```

Peter Dömel

Gesellschaft fuer Finanzmarketing mbG (GEFM)
Duesseldorfer Str. 13
D-65760 Eschborn, Germany
Peter.Doemel@gefm.deuba.com

Dominic Duggan

Department of Computer Engineering and Science
Case Western Reserve University
Cleveland OH 44106, USA
dominic@alpha.ces.cwru.edu
http://k2.scl.cwru.edu/~dominic/

Michael Franz

Department of Information and Computer Science
University of California at Irvine
Irvine, CA 92697-3425, USA
franz@uci.edu
http://www.ics.uci.edu/~franz

Kazuhiko Kato

Institute of Information Sciences and Electronics
University of Tsukuba
Tenoudai 1-1-1, Tsukuba, Ibaraki 305, Japan
kato@is.tsukuba.ac.jp
http://www.softlab.is.tsukuba.ac.jp/~kato/

Sam Kendall

Ab Initio Software Corporation
kendall@init.com

Frederick Knabe

P. Universidad Catolica de Chile
Casilla 306
Santiago 22, Chile
knabe@acm.org

Miguel Mira da Silva

Universidade de Evora, Departamento de Matematica
Rua Romao Ramalho 59
7000 Evora, Portugal
mms@dmat.uevora.pt
http://khapital.ce.uevora.pt/~mms/

Christian Tschudin

Computer Science Department, University of Zurich, Switzerland
International Computer Science Institute, Berkeley, USA
tschudin@ifi.unizh.ch

Jan Vitek, Manuel Serrano, Dimitri Thanos

Object System Group
Centre Universitaire d'Informatique
University of Geneva
1211 Geneva 4, Switzerland
{jvitek, serrano, thanos}@cui.unige.ch
http://cuiwww.unige.ch/OSG/

Jim Waldo, Ann Wolrath

JavaSoft, a Sun Mircosystems Business.
{jim.waldo, ann.wolrath}@sun.com

Springer
and the
environment

At Springer we firmly believe that an
international science publisher has a
special obligation to the environment,
and our corporate policies consistently
reflect this conviction.
We also expect our business partners –
paper mills, printers, packaging
manufacturers, etc. – to commit
themselves to using materials and
production processes that do not harm
the environment. The paper in this
book is made from low- or no-chlorine
pulp and is acid free, in conformance
with international standards for paper
permanency.

Springer

Lecture Notes in Computer Science

For information about Vols. 1–1143

please contact your bookseller or Springer-Verlag